Albrecht's Hidden Lessons

The Albrecht Papers, Volume III

by William A. Albrecht, Ph.D.
Edited by Charles Walters

Albrecht's Hidden Lessons

The Albrecht Papers, Volume III

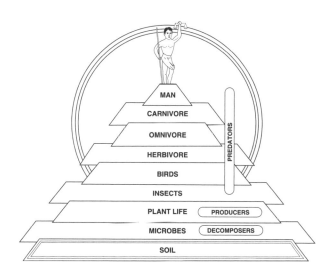

by William A. Albrecht, Ph.D.
Edited by Charles Walters

Acres U.S.A.
Austin, Texas

Albrecht's
Hidden Lessons

Copyright © 1989, 2013 by Acres U.S.A.

Acres U.S.A.
P.O. Box 301209
Austin, Texas 78703 U.S.A.
(512) 892-4400 • fax (512) 892-4448
info@acresusa.com • www.acresusa.com

Printed in the United States of America

Publisher's Cataloging-in-Publication

Albrecht, William A., 1888-1974; and Charles Walters, editor, 1926-2009
Albrecht's hidden lessons / William A. Albrecht. — 2 ed., Austin, TX, ACRES U.S.A., 2013
    x, 401 pp., 23 cm.
    First published as The Albrecht Papers, Volume III,
       Hidden Lessons in Unopened Books
    Includes Index
    Includes Bibliography
    ISBN 978-1-60173-037-4 (trade)

1. Soil fertility.　2. Soils and nutrition.　3. Soil science.
4. Agriculture — crops and soils.　5. Soil-plant relationships.
I. Albrecht, William A., 1888-1974 and Charles Walters, 1926-2009
II. Title.

SF96.7 A42 2013　　　　　631.4

Dedicated to
the memory of Eugene M. Poirot

Contents

About the Author

Dr. William A. Albrecht, the author of these papers, was chairman of the Department of Soils at the University of Missouri College of Agriculture, where he had been a member of the staff for 43 years. He held four degrees, A.B., B.S. in Agriculture, M.S. and Ph.D., from the University of Illinois. During a vivid and crowded career, he traveled widely and studied soils in the United States, Great Britain, on the European continent, and in Australia.

Born on a farm in central Illinois in an area of highly fertile soil typical of the cornbelt and educated in his native state, Dr. Albrecht grew up with an intense interest in the soil and all things agricultural. These were approached, however, through the avenues of the basic sciences and liberal arts and not primarily through applied practices and their economics.

Teaching experience after completing the liberal arts course, with some thought of the medical profession, as well as an assistantship in botany, gave an early vision of the interrelationships that enrich the facts acquired in various fields when viewed as part of a master design.

These experiences led him into additional undergraduate and graduate work, encouraged by scholarships and fellowships, until he received his doctor's degree in 1919. In the meantime, he joined the research and teaching staff at the University of Missouri.

Both as a writer and speaker, Dr. Albrecht served tirelessly as an interpreter of scientific truth to inquiring minds and persistently stressed the basic importance of understanding and working with nature by applying the natural method to all farming, crop production, livestock raising and soil improvement. He always had a specific focus on the effect of soil characteristics upon the mineral composition of plants and the effect of the mineral composition of plants on animal nutrition and subsequent human health.

Dr. Albrecht strove not to be an ivory tower pontificator trying to master and defeat nature, but to be a leader of true science and understand the wondrous ways of nature so we could harness them for the lasting benefit of all. A man of the soil, William A. Albrecht summed up his philosophy as such, "When wildlife demonstrates the soil as the foundation of its health and numbers, is man, the apex of the biotic pyramid, too far removed from the soil to recognize it as the foundation of his health via nutrition?"

Dr. Albrecht was a true student of the characteristics of soil and wasn't timid about his views — be they to a farmer in the field, an industry group or to a congressional subcommittee.

Respected and recognized by scientists and agricultural leaders from around the world, Dr. Albrecht retired in 1959 and passed from the scene in May 1974 as his 86th birthday approached.

About the Editor

Charles Walters was the founder and executive editor of *Acres U.S.A*, a magazine he started in 1971 to spread the word of eco-agriculture. A recognized leader in the field of raw materials-based economic research and sustainable food and farming systems, this confirmed maverick saw one of his missions as to rescue lost knowledge. Perhaps the most important were the papers of Dr. William A. Albrecht, whose low profile obscured decades of brilliant work in soil science. Albrecht's papers, which Walters rescued from the historical dustbin and published in an initial four volumes, continue to provide a rock-solid foundation for the scientific approach to organic farming. Additional volumes of Albrecht's papers were organized and edited by Walters for later publication. During his life, Walters penned thousands of articles on the technologies of organic and sustainable agriculture and is the author of more than two dozen books (and co-author of several more), including *Eco-Farm: An Acres U.S.A. Primer, Weeds, Control Without Poisons, A Farmer's Guide to the Bottom Line, Dung Beetles, Mainline Farming for Century 21* and many more. Charles Walters generously shared his vision, energy and passion through his writing and public speaking for more than 35 years and made it his lifelong mission to save the family farm and give farmers an operating manual that they couldn't live without. *The Albrecht Papers* are an important part of this message. Charles Walters passed on in January 2009 at the age of 83.

Foreword

This third volume of *The Albrecht Papers* deals with short papers written for popular consumption. Dr. William A. Albrecht was more than a friend of the farmer. He was chief counsel to farm practitioners first, and an adviser to fellow members of academia second.

Telling the Albrecht story — rather, the story Albrecht told — became workaday stuff at *Acres U.S.A.* almost from the first day of publication. For here was first-rate scholarship explaining soil fertility, microbes, organics and life in the soil in understandable terms, starting with the Creator's plan and ending with minds capable of thought and reason. Some of Albrecht's earlier papers had to do with legume inoculation. This was not a simple task. For one thing, farmers had a belief "that all you had to do was introduce the bacteria into the soil and the bacteria would compel the plant to fix nitrogen with their help," Albrecht said. "As a young man I had learned on the farm that you could not just get a fancy bull and he would make the cow have a calf, because the cow had something to do with her part."

Albrecht was more than a background scientist. As these papers suggest, he was a forceful spokesman for scientific sense and a voice for reason. By the early 1930s, soil mining techniques in the United States had reached a climax point. In the West this meant a hot-dry cycle and a Dust Bowl. In the East it meant faltering production in terms of protein. The first government lime program surfaced under the Agriculture Adjustment Act. Possibly half the soils in the United States were helped by liming. Lime and lime some more became a catch-phrase. You can't overdo it. As with most programs, this one was continued to comply with political strategy, not science, and Albrecht came up fighting from his chair.

There was more to reclaiming the soil than fighting acidity. Speaking into an *Acres U.S.A.* tape recorder, Albrecht put it this way. "Professor M.F. Miller [then head of the department] thought I should grow bacteria that would make the cow have a calf whether she wanted to or not. And I had to politely show the points I wanted to make." As usual, Albrecht had his "vision" to lean on — that is, his informed conceptualization. He liked to tap foreign scholars, and so he knew about Russia's Sergei N. Winograd-sky and Holland's M. W. Beijerinck, who had proved that nitrogen fixation took place in the soil without any legumes whatsoever. The essentials of rapid fixation were found to be absence of readily available nitrogen and the presence of carbohydrates, phosphate and lime. He pondered the findings of Thomas Way of England. It was Way who in 1852 discovered that when soil absorbed ammonia a corresponding amount of calcium was released to the drainage water. The exchange mechanism, he found, was seated in the clay. Continued study revealed that such an exchange did exist, and that it involved all cation (positively charged) elements. Moreover, it had been developed that the total exchange capacity of soil depended on both the colloidal clay and the organic matter. With these few points in mind, Albrecht continued observing as nature revealed herself.

He did more. He saw to it that his findings were communicated in the farm magazines, in the daily and weekly rural prints, and later on in health magazines, the journal of Natural Foods Associates and *Let's Live* magazine. Albrecht had certain sayings he repeated over and over again. He liked to emphasize things by putting them in quotation marks, some of which rest uneasily on the printed page with our more modern graphics. We have allowed these things to stand as written. Sources are listed in the back of the book. Albrecht's own footnotes, in those few cases where he used footnotes, appear under each pertinent source.

Withal, there is a wealth of information in this book. It has been styled after a column he wrote at times, "Hidden Ideas in Unopened Books." Once, during a day-long session with Albrecht, I asked the great scientist if "Hidden Lessons in Unopened Books" might not be a better title. He replied, "Yes — and when you get around to recycling some of these papers, why don't you do it that way?" So we have. Farmers will enjoy his "points well made." Others will find papers and sources that have evaporated from the scene. All will be carried back to foundation science as they read his lines.

At the end of each lesson, Albrecht would summarize. For this volume we have selected from his works a single paragraph that summarizes this third volume of *The Albrecht Papers*: "The plants will build the fertility up in the soil and starve to death themselves. If you put chemicals into the soil you've ruined that root. These laws of physiology hold. It doesn't make much difference whether it is a person or a plant. I'm convinced that the Creator knew his business, and man still hasn't learned."

— *Charles Walters*
Founder. Acres U.S.A.

1

FUNDAMENTAL ALBRECHTISMS

A BIOLOGICAL PROCEDURE

This country of apparent agricultural abundance is actually in a critical position so far as the production of quality, protein-rich foods is concerned. We are producing bulk, not quality, and we are paying for it in our own health as well as in the health of our plants and animals. We have succumbed to the idea that agriculture can be made an industrial procedure. But the truth is, it is a biological procedure.

MOTHER NATURE—FARMER SUPREME

All of man's knowledge concerning agricultural practices must be considered infinitesimal when compared to the absolute intelligence manifested by Mother Nature throughout her natural domain. Since time began, she has carpeted the earth's surface with greenery consisting of trees, shrubs, flowers and grass that perform in compliance with her universal laws. In each self-created habitat she has created and supported myriads of life forms ranging from the tiniest submicroscopic forms to the largest of animals. She has also filled the seas with fish and other aquatic life, both plant and animal. For untold centuries she has achieved her countless and perfect performances without the aid of man. From the richest prairie lands to the rugged mountain sides, in swamps and in jungles and even in our deserts Mother Nature has created conditions for the support of life that are without interruption from year to year and from century to century.

Into this perfectly conceived and established domain man has entered as a would-be farmer. His first attempt was with the grazing of herds of cattle and flocks of sheep. Next he began to turn the soil and to cultivate certain desired crops. But whatever man has done, and whatever success he may have attained has resulted from his intrusion into the natural domain and taking for himself the best arable land that nature, through the centuries, had built to the highest peak of perfection and productivity. If all of the land area on this planet that is farmed by man, whether ranches, farms or gardens in all of the Americas, Europe, Asia, Africa and all of the islands of the sea were totaled together, the sum would be less than one-third of the natural domain operated by nature without the assistance of man. Wherein, then, lies the greater wisdom and performance—in the universal intelligence of nature or the collective intellect of man?

Today's modern farmer requires great investment to conduct his enterprise. He requires several tractors, plows, discs, harrows, planters, cultivators, sprayers and many kinds of harvesting machinery. He needs to provide gasoline and oil, seeds, fertilizers, various sprays to control insects and weeds and usually he must avail himself of supplemental labor. If he raises livestock, he must provide special housing and water supply. He must plant, harvest and store crops to feed them. All of these artifices are required by man to farm his land—but not so with Mother Nature. She requires no investment, no fertilizer or sprays, and no outside laborers. Whereas man's method of farming tends toward depletion of soils, nature's methods tend toward constant maintenance and improvement of soils. How then does nature operate its vast domain? To answer this question, one must first understand that any and every kind of feed that exists originates from a living soil nurtured by sunshine and rain, or from the life-promoting and life-sustaining properties of the sea, both operating under the immutable laws of nature's domain. Man's technology has not yet produced a single ounce of edible protein, sugar or fat from any inert chemical or mineral substance.

The principle of life depends upon a continuous succession of its manifold life forms from generation to generation, whether the period be for one hour or a hundred years. All life forms are created by and sustained from the life that preceded it. It is from the soil that life has its beginning and it is back to the soil that life has its ending. It is in this area, between the dissolution and final decomposition of expired life and the renewal, maintenance and sustenance of renewed life that the soil's microorganisms perform their preordained task according to the perfect regimen demanded by the absolute laws of nature. A soil that is rich with the debris of farmer life may in turn be expected to support a vigorous population of thousands of different microbial life forms. A good mineral soil indicating 3% organic matter (60,000 pounds humus) per acre may be expected to support more than 1,000,000,000 microorganisms per pound of soil. One acre of such soil may be expected to support 6,000 pounds of such living microorganisms by actual weight.

This microbial life in soil includes both plant and animal forms and is generally referred to as the soil's microflora and fauna. These organisms include myriad species of bacteria, fungi, algae and others. They vary in size from submicroscopic viruses to larger algae forms. Their purposes are so manifold that to describe them all would more than fill all of the library shelves in the world. In such a manner, and no other, does nature perform her so-called farming practices. She depends solely upon the work and activity of billions upon billions of these microscopically small organisms who are willing and friendly workers and whose only wages are the food supply available to them and which they in turn convert into the world's most valuable product—humus—without which life would be exterminated from the earth. The illustration below denotes nature's plan of regeneration and maintenance of every life form she has created.

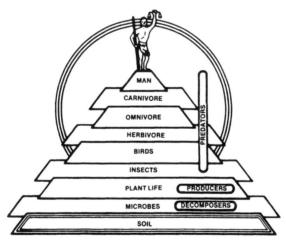

The lower three strata—soil, microbes, and plants—provide the integrated performances that promote the basic food supply upon which all the other succeeding strata of life depend as predators or consumers.

We must comprehend that the activity of microbial life in soil, along with the process of photosynthesis in plants, is solely responsible for directly or indirectly supplying the world's food supply. Eradicate this microbial life in the soil and you will have destroyed nature's method of farming and there will be no food for any of nature's creations. Its vigorous maintenance provides the crucial link for man's survival. Let every consultant and every member approach his farming problems with knowledgeable observation of nature's processes and serve them as a humble steward in full consonance with nature's ageless law. Let no man approach it as a mechanic to repair, alter or convert any of nature's compelling forces which operate in absolute accord with the Supreme Intelligence that directs them. Let no human intellect challenge or contend with this supreme governing intelligence, for in the end he will be found wanting and his fruits will be worthless.

SOIL IS THE KEY TO GOOD FOOD, GOOD HEALTH

It is an age-old saying that "to be well-fed is to be healthy." But as yet, health in its positive aspects has not been clearly defined. In its negative aspects, we have professional practitioners in great numbers. Deficiencies in health are, then, well recognized. Why should we not think of them as failures to be well fed, and to be faced through the question as to what constitutes good nutrition or good food as a guarantee of good health?

The question of good food, and plenty of it, goes back to the soil, by means of which food is produced. Unfortunately, there is danger in losing sight of the fact that agricultural production is food production, rather than production of only salable mass or bulk.

Bushels and tons are no longer sufficient criteria for what the soil is growing. When meat, milk and eggs are the great foods for health recovery and for its maintenance; and when these are the proteins rather than the carbohydrates, it might be well for us to think about food deficiencies—and thereby health deficiencies—as deficiencies in protein and all that comes along with them when we produce them on more fertile soils.

Unfortunately, animals do not create proteins. They only assemble them, provided the vegetation or foods they consume supplies the necessary amino acids, and other essentials required by the animals to carry out the assembling process.

When the cow went ahead of the plow, she was assaying the vegetation for its protein service to her in growing her body and reproducing it. But, when we sent the plow ahead of the cow, we moved both her and ourselves onto the vegetation and onto the soil that was not necessarily providing her with all the essentials for protein.

Animal health deficiencies then, are a reflection of feed deficiencies and soil deficiencies. Underneath the plants, the animals and ourselves, is the soil, the fertility of which makes possible the creation of proteins, carbohydrates, vitamins and all foods.

It is the soil fertility then, in its variable pattern that gives pattern to the possibilities of either being well fed or poorly fed. Its pattern can be the pattern of health deficiencies, too.

The soil fertility pattern is the result of climatic forces, namely rainfall and temperature. While food production is too commonly premised directly on the weather, it now can be more accurately premised on the soil and its fertility that are the resulting and accumulated effects of that variable weather.

The soil fertility deficiencies in our national soil pattern have given patterns to crops, as these are mainly carbohydrate foods and fattening foods, or as they are also proteins, minerals, vitamins and foods that grow the bodies and reproduce them. Soil treatments to make up soil deficiencies for better health are telling us that health deficiencies may come with those soil deficiencies.

Legumes that make more protein and thereby serve to feed young animals better cannot do this performance on deficient soils. Our crop pattern, as it is creating proteins or failing to do so, is both citing the soil deficiencies and also suggesting their connection with our national health pattern. Soil deficiencies include a long list of nutrient elements. Plant nutrition for good food production is a matter of providing in the soil the balanced ration which those plants need to put out proteins and high feed values, much as animal nutrition is a matter of supplying properly balanced rations to put out milk or meat, or just as good food and plenty of it is a matter of human health of high order. Nitrogen, phosphorus and potassium in fertilizers are a part of the picture. So are calcium and magnesium. Then, too there is a growing list of trace elements whose functions seem to connect them with protein production. The many proteins are the means by which bodies grow, multiply and protect themselves against disease.

Attention may well go to the growing amount of research in soil fertility, as this is nutritional foundation for the microbes, the plants, the animals and man, or the entire pyramid of life for which the soil is the foundation and the starting point of nutrition. Deficiencies in the soil so readily remedied by soil treatment with fertilizers, may well be given more consideration as reasons for deficiencies in our national health and the means of preventing them by growing more food of better quality in health than for just more bulk for sale.

SOIL FERTILITY IN ITS BROADER IMPLICATIONS

Food is fabricated soil fertility. It is food that must win the war and write the peace. Consequently, the question as to who will win the war and how indelibly the peace will be written will be answered by the reserves of soil fertility and the efficiency with which they can be mobilized for both the present and the post-conflict eras.

What is soil fertility? In simplest words, it is some dozen chemical elements in mineral and rock combinations in the earth's crust that are being slowly broken out of these and hustled off to the sea. Enjoying a temporary rest stop en route, they are a part of the soil and serve their essential roles in nourishing all the different life forms. They are the soil's contribution—from a large mass of nonessentials—to the germinating seeds that empower the growing plants to use sunshine energy in the synthesis of atmospheric elements and rainfall into the many crops for our support. The atmospheric and rainfall elements are carbon, hydrogen, oxygen, and nitrogen, so common everywhere.

Realization is now dawning that a global war is premised on a global struggle for soil fertility as food. Historic events in connection with the war have been too readily interpreted in terms of armies and politics and not premised on mobilized soil fertility. Gafsa, merely a city in North Africa, was rejuvenation for phosphorus starved German soils. Nauru, a little island speck in the Pacific, is a similar nutrition savior to the Japanese. Hitler's move eastward was a hope looking to the Russian fertility reserves. The hoverings of his battleship, Graf Spee, around Montevideo, and its persistance in Argentina were designs on that last of the world's rich store of less exploited soil fertility to be had in the form of corn, wheat, and beef much more than they were maneuverings for political or naval advantage.

Some of these historic martial events serve to remind us that "an empty stomach knows no laws" and that man is in no unreal sense an animal that becomes a social and political being only after he has consumed some of the products of the soil.

WE TAKE OUR SOIL FOR GRANTED

Because soil seems to be everywhere and because plants with their roots in the earth are all about us, we take both too much for granted. But now that there is no more "new land" available, we are beginning to see that we cannot continue to do so. We are even concerned about soil conservation.

Man, at the top of the pyramid of all the different life forms, has the help of many in reaching out over extensive areas of soil to collect his essential food elements and food compounds. There are some dozen different chemical elements coming directly from the soil. Man himself travels far to eat the fruits of these many different soils. Then, too, he is omnivorous, for he eats almost everything including vegetable, animal and even mineral. Thus he increases the possibilities of giving his body each of the dozen essential elements found in soil. Plants send their roots searching through the soil in collecting and fabricating man's food. Animals search through the plants to collect and construct still further for him. Man selects from all these foods—both plant and animal—the bulk and concentrates what he needs for energy, for growth, reproduction and other complicated body performances.

We have seemingly been far too removed from the soil. Nevertheless, the changing conditions in economics, in agricultural production, in the capacity of our soils to provide essentials, and in the nutritive quality of our foods—all are bringing us to think more about the soil. Because we have been taking our soils for granted, there are many instances to demonstrate that they have been going down in their fertility while we thought they are as good as when our fathers or grandfathers farmed them. A distinguished Hereford breeder accumulated a wealth of knowledge and sales experience with his choice breed during 50 years on the prairie soils of northeast Missouri. But to his disappointment in his later years he discovered that he had been oblivious to the fact that the soil of his extensive pastures had been going downward. His calf crops were too low because the females were not reproducing regularly. Some with the best pedigrees were calving only in alternate years, and calves were coming at most any time instead of as one crop in the spring season as nature has most young animals arrive.

On this farm the humus of the soil is no longer what it was 50 years ago. Today's soil has weakened the foundation on which both the breed and the breeder originally rose. It has grown old faster than the owner because it has given much of itself to the business but gotten none of the limestone, phosphate, green manures and other fertilizer it should have had in return. Fortunately, this question has been answered by another and younger Hereford breeder who is succeeding today on the same soil type and using foundation stock purchased from the older breeder. Their continued progress beyond the half century is assured because here is a breeder-farmer who does not take his soil for granted. He is rejuvenating the soil fertility by means of phosphates, limestone and any possible fertilizers that will help to make sod crops. "No," this younger farmer says, "we cannot take our soils for granted when they and their fertility are so basic to a type of agriculture that depends in a large measure on livestock."

Our human foods, too, have been taken for granted. We have measured them in terms of bulk, rather than in terms of quality grown into them by the soil. Processing foods has taken out much that the soil and nature's fabrication processes have put into them. Milk is measured by the volume or by the fat content—the former a measure of bulk and the latter mainly of fuel value. Its measure in terms of growth quality for the young cannot be recorded by these criteria. Correspondingly we accept bad teeth as though they were natural. Since bad teeth are but an exposed part of a bad skeleton, we need to take seriously this demonstration that we also have been taking our bone troubles for granted. We have failed to give attention to the soils from which must come the calcium and the phosphorus needed to construct sound bones and good teeth. Likewise, we forget it is by means of soil fertility that nature must construct the vitamins and other catalytic agencies that facilitate body growth processes from the food substances we consume. Human health too, depends on the soil which, common as it is everywhere, is seemingly still too far removed to be connected in our thinking.

Fertile virgin soils, plenty of land, and an abundance of humus and other fertility compounds in them were naturally an inducement to our mental lassitude, our indifference to erosion of the body of the soil, and to exploitation of its stores of humus and fertility. Soil conservation is now taking a national inventory of the disappearing hidden qualities in soil which sustains domestic animal life at profitable economic levels, and human life in good health and therefore of efficient citizenry. Our own future—but more particularly our place in the international future—points out forcefully that when our national health as well as our national wealth lie in our hands, we cannot long continue to take our soil for granted!

LIVE SOIL AND PASS-ALONG HUNGERS

The roaming of wild animals and their ravaging of farm crops usually connotes an effort to satisfy hidden hungers. In leaving the forest to graze on fertilized land, the deer signals his recognition of better nutritive values in the feed growing there. When they break through the fence dividing the fertility depleted pasture from the virgin soil of the highway or railroad right-of-way, domestic animals likewise reveal their intuitive recognition of the dependence of the feed for nutritive quality upon the fertility of the soil. They are driven by particular hungers to risk their lives against the barbed wire just as the wild animals risk their lives in coming into the open for feeds grown on better soil.

In pointing out the animal's ability to detect differences in the grazing according to differences in soil fertility—almost beyond the capacity of chemical means of detection—we are apt to think of differences only in the ash constituents. We forget that the animal is not looking to the plants for services as haulers of minerals but rather as synthesizers of the many organic and organo-mineral complexes that build the animal body and supply energy to keep it in action. Some of these complexes have been catalogued as we consider them in making up a ration or a diet. Can we doubt that many yet remain to be listed? Their complete chemical nature and the many kinds of services they perform are still unknown facts. It is the remaining unlisted complexes that may be the main provokers of the hidden hungers.

Fortunately, we are more able to combat these hungers at the point of origin—in the soil—than at any later stage in the agricultural assembly line. At that point, the problem is no more complex than supplying one or more of a few simple inorganic elements. A little effort here cures the deficiencies that cause hidden hunger in soil microbes and plants. Properly fed plants prevent deficiencies in their synthetic products that serve as animal and human foods. Here are solved the problems of providing the hosts of essential chemical compounds, the required amino acids, the necessary vitamins and the specific fatty acids.

These problems of provision in the diet are more nearly insurmountable than those of getting some dozen elements—major and minor—applicable as fertilizers on the soil. At any later stage, the problem is more complex, and the situation is more prone to induce the micro-hungers. It can truthfully be said that rapid progress is being made in recognizing hidden hungers. Many of them are now being prevented, because they are being diagnosed as originating in our declining soil fertility.

Soil treatments are no longer appreciated only because they encourage production of greater bulk per acre. They are being made on increasing acreages because they add nutritional qualities to relieve the long chain of hidden hungers coming up from the soil through the entire biotic pyramid to torment man at the top. For better reproduction of farm animals, for their better health and for ourselves as well, we are becoming increasingly concerned to know more about the fertility of the soil.

The disturbing and perplexing microhungers are hidden mainly from our thought, our recognition, and our full appreciation of their origin. But they are not hidden from our body physiology nor from our mental processes, when a little iodine, for example, as a fraction of a grain coming from the soil up through the plants to us is all that "stands between us and imbecility." It is a good sign for the future that we are coming to realize that our hidden hungers are provoking deficiencies in mind as well as body. We are coming to think about keeping up the soil in order to keep us mentally able, and to realize that our hidden hungers are pointing to soil fertility as a ready means for perfect health.

FERTILE SOILS MAKE BIG PLANTS

Crop yields have long been measured by the magnitude of the plant mass. If crops are grown for the simple purpose of selling them, and if we measure the returns by the greater monetary income from more pounds or bushels sold, then bigger plants may be the reason for making soils more fertile. In a broader sense, it is the fertile soils that make the plants grow bigger. Though there may be big plants of some kind that grow big on soils that are not very fertile for other plants, one cannot conclude, therefore, that any big vegetative mass proves the soil to be fertile. One can reason the converse of this quite safely and say "small, spindly, sick plants are indicators of an infertile soil."

Certain big plants are more apt to be indicators of fertile soils than others, if one knows something about what the plant is creating or making while it is growing. Crops, like the legumes, which are said to be hard to grow, are usually indicators of fertile soils when they are making big plants and especially a big output of seed. It is this reproductive aspect, the activity of making new cells, of creating proteins—through which alone life keeps flowing—and of multiplying its parts and its species, that really reports the fertile soils. Plants in nature are big and numerous because they have been multiplying themselves via production of more protein. The production of protein by plants is the real index of the fertility of the soil under the plants.

Perhaps you have never thought that what we consider plant growth is not necessarily multiplication of cells, for which more protein must be created by the biosynthetic, or life, processes of the plant. Instead, it may be only a case of blowing up to larger volume the cells laid down in embryonic age. It may be making bigger those cells by putting in more water or more sugar and other carbohydrates of photosynthetic origin. In the watermelon, and other cucurbits, this is the case. So the so-called growth reflects mainly the air, water and sunshine going into the resulting products of sugar equivalent, and not the fertility coming up from the soil to convert those carbohydrates into proteins, as we expect it to be done by legumes.

But when the embryo is the place where the cells are all laid down, even in very miniature, then the growth process there calls for much soil fertility and in balanced proportions of the different nutrient elements. Even a watermelon requires a fertile soil in a certain sense, but we are apt to be misled in believing that increasing size of plants or increasing amounts of plants products are necessarily proof of fertile soils. That has been readily demonstrated for soybean plants by shifting the fertility ratio or the balance between calcium and potassium. The function of the latter we associate with the plant's production of vegetative mass; the former with the output of protein by the biosynthetic conversion of the photosynthetic products or carbohydrates. Thus, by unbalanced soil fertility, we may be misled to believe that big plants mean big soil. But, with balanced fertility, we are correct and fertile soils mean big plants.

There is no fallacious reasoning in saying that less fertile soils give us the small, sick plants when, on other soils along side them, the plants are large. In the same field one can demonstrate this fact easily. Applications of the elements deficient in the soil soon show their effects in terms of bigger plants. Nitrogen on grasses in the pasture as a result of urine droppings are well known examples in the spots of tall-growing plants. Lime on legumes like the sweet clover and alfalfa, magnesium on soybeans, zinc on fruit trees, copper on clovers in Australia and numerous other soil treatments draw their lines of differences clearly out in the field. The sickly conditions of the plants give various signs and symptoms, as celery with its dark areas in the stalks when boron is insufficient; white colored soybean leaves except for green veins when magnesium is deficient in the soil; reddening leaves of cotton under potassium deficiency; clustered small leaves in rosette-like forms of fruit trees needing more zinc from the soil or from spray applications. All are telling us that infertile soils make not only small but also sick plants.

We are gradually coming to realize that plant growth is a creative activity by a life form demanding proper nourishment, if that growth is to go forward effectively. Bigger plants generally testify to a fertile soil, especially if bigger yields of seed and more extensive cell reproduction rather than cell enlargement is the reason for bigness. Conversely, small sickly plants are true indicators of poor nutrition given them by the soil. Closer observation of our plants, and more knowledge of the symptoms of plant hunger are bringing us around to feed our plants via the soil rather than turn them out to rustle for themselves. Only on fertile soils alone can our crops be truly big in the services we expect of them.

CORRECTING BORDERLINE SOIL CONDITIONS

It has often been said that "Most discoveries are the result of accidents, but only for the minds prepared to make them." The truth of that statement was experienced by one of the consultants of the Brookside Research Laboratories, New Knoxville, Ohio. He was called to observe a case of "core rot" of a field of onions just going into storage. Then right soon he had a similar request where nematode attacks had destroyed a field of carrots.

In both cases, the use of soil tests and the prescription of balanced fertility, as plant nutrition applied accordingly, restored the same successive crops to healthy production on the same fields. The fungus rot and the nematodes were thereby prevented. No cures were used. Instead, healthy and not "sick" crops were marketed thereafter. Prevention, at no special cost for such, but by an investment in creative powers, was a profitable discovery for the mind prepared for it. But that mind did not emphasize the fact of discovery. Rather it went to work, in practice, to deliver the next onion crop as a healthy one, and the next carrot crop pest-free. The consultant replaced the previous crop disasters by restored earnings for the commercial gardeners, by pay for arduous labor, by the costs of business maintenance, and by taxes paid on the land. The gardeners were not put out of their business of growing health-giving foods via fertile soils, rather than carrying sickly ones of poor food values on to the harvests by means of sprays and other dangerous chemicals.

Both these discoveries that "an ounce of prevention" in the form of a balanced plant nutrition from fertile soils "is better than a pound of cure" in the form of dangerous poisons, were made on sandy soils. Those were "fringe soils" for any crops to be high in self-protection by proteins of their own make. Fringe soils cannot readily produce (a) growth, (b) self preservation, and (c) fecund reproduction, as is the case for soils (a) with more clay holding larger supplies of available nutrient elements, and (b) more organic matter to carry into the plants, both the ash elements and larger organic nutrient molecules, whose nutritional services we do not yet comprehend fully. When most virgin soils in the mid-continent were well stocked with humus in their deep surface layers, and given annual dust deposits of windblown, less-weathered, nutrient-rich, rock mineral fertility, like loess, we have been slow to see failing or sickly crops as evidence of their troubles on "fringe" soils. Soil depletion is putting more and more acres of them under that classification.

It is such observations by keen-eyed consultants that are discovering that once-fertile soils are reclassifying themselves into the "fringe" group. Early discovery means prompt remedies. Those can come by prevention which always surpasses cures. Simultaneously, prevention of diseases and pests by improved plant nutrition means healthy crops giving better health to their consumers, whether those be beast or man. It was nature's habit of using prevention rather than cure, which gave us the healthy crops and animals which we took over in our agricultural production. We cannot continue in that industry by making more "fringe" soils. Nature still offers opportunities for making discoveries in prevention. The big question is, "Are we preparing our minds to make them through use of better soils?"

QUALITY VS. QUANTITY CROPS

Crop quality in its relation to soil fertility may have different properties and values in our minds. There is, however, no confusion about crop quantity. For the farmer the volume of output is important, but his volume is a quantitative matter of bushels of wheat per acre. Even though there may be some premium for harder wheat, this extra earning per acre by higher quality is small in contrast to the greater monetary gain he can make from more bushels per acre.

It is quality that is wanted by the baker, who uses the flour, as he looks to the market offering him his necessary goods. It is quantity that is wanted by the farmer as he looks to the same place to purchase from him the goods he has for sale.

Unfortunately, the consumer and the producer in this case do not meet each other. Nor do their separate desires meet through the common market. Both are content to serve the market rather than each other. Consequently, when lowered fertility in the surface soil layer makes many bushels of soft wheat with its low protein, the farmer sees his desires well satisfied by the market. He is then blind to, and unconcerned about, the desires of the miller and the baker on the other side of the market. They, too, do not see the declining quality of the soil—especially its declining nitrogen supply—as the reason for the increasing quantity of soft wheat in place of hard wheat of the high quality they desire. They may accuse the farmer of growing a poor variety, selected for quantity production when in fact he had been compelled by declining soil fertility to use it, in consequence of which his quality declined while quantity increased.

The quality of corn, like that of wheat, is also premised on soil fertility. Livestock feeders have been clamoring for help in providing more protein supplements. Corn producers and consumers have been oblivious to the fact that while there had been a tremendous increase in quantity there has been a serious decrease in quality amounting as protein to almost one-tenth of the total production.

It has been reported that during the last ten years the protein content of corn has fallen from an average of near 9.5 to 8.5%. Fattening power in the form of the starch of the grain has increased. Growth power in the form of protein has decreased. Consequently, while steers feeding on the corn may do well in laying on fat, they may not be building a muscular and bony structure strong enough to carry the extra weight to the market.

Starch production with its fattening and fuel values calls for little soil fertility. It calls more for air, water, and sunshine to fabricate this energy-providing food substance. Protein production, however, calls for nitrogen, calcium, and many other items from the soil in addition to the carbohydrates within the plant before it consumes much of its own supply of this photosynthetic product while it converts a part of it into the different amino acids of which the life-carrying and body-growing compound of protein consists. Soil fertility is in reality the foundation of quality in the cereal crops. But unfortunately, while watching the bushels of wheat and of corn increase to our economic satisfaction, we have been slow to see the decrease in quality or in protein that determines life itself.

Quality in agricultural products is calling for more soil fertility by which to make proteins rather than bulk.

Good nutrition and fecund reproduction and what we call good health in any form of life do not depend on quantity, but rather on the quality of the products consumed.

QUALITY GARDEN CROPS

It is a familiar advertising slogan that says, "Quality will be remembered long after price is forgotten." Implied in this are the simple facts that price is only an arithmetical number: it fixes itself in our minds readily; it is quantitatively cataloged; and its relations and implications are clearly understood. Quality, however, is not so simply measured, not so instantly recognized, and not so completely cataloged.

The appreciation of quality is more often a matter of time and experience with the goods. The importance of quality grows on us slowly and thereby gives us time to forget the price while the conviction grows that quality is, after all, the real value. Concerning the quality of our garden products in relation to the fertility of the soil, a much stronger conviction is yet to be expected.

In dealing with the soil as the basis of production, yields in bushels have long been the orthodox yardstick. This is quickly ascertained, easily tabulated and readily subjected to mathematical manipulations. However, when the productivity of the soil pushes itself into making those bushels more directly our own human food, then quality takes its place as the foremost criterion by which soil should be evaluated. In garden production we are slowly coming to consider the higher quality in our foods grown on fertile soils as more important than our transitory reactions to questions of price only.

We are beginning to see declining soil fertility causing declining quality in our garden products, despite our struggles to maintain their quality and price. Quality as a criterion for garden (food) production is taking on increasing importance.

Land as an economic asset is measured in acres. Soil as the foundation of the agricultural industry also is measured too commonly in the same two dimensions—length and breadth. Soil as the agricultural creative capacity must include a third dimension, namely depth. Now that erosion, by removing surface soil in the humid areas, has exposed much of the infertile subsoil there, we have gained rather forcibly a new appreciation of the productive quality of the upper horizon of the soil profile.

Yield varies both as quantity and also as quality, according to the depth of the surface soil. Shallow surface soils are considered "droughty." We are prone to believe that a shortage of water is responsible for the lowered yields of corn on thin soils even when the roots are taking water from the moist subsoil. The real trouble is that the roots are not finding their required fertility. Bushels per acre are reduced. So is the feeding value per bushel.

Quality of the crop does not vary directly with the quantity. Quality drops lower and faster more often than does the quantity. It may also improve faster than quantity increases. An increase in the depth of the surface soil does not necessarily represent merely a corresponding increase in capacity for quantity production; while doubling the depth of surface soil may double the yield, it may improve quality even more.

The mass of the soil is not an indication of the fertility absorbed on the clay, or of that held as nutrient reserves in the mineral other than quartz making up the skeleton of the soil. Nor is the soil mass an index of the active organic matter with its dynamic values rising and falling, as the cycle temperature of the season controls its behavior to make it correspond more closely with the demands of the growing crop.

Quality of the soil, that is its well-balanced supply of fertility, is beginning to stand out in our minds more prominently than do land dimensions, either as acres or as depth of the soil. Soil conservation is also coming to be recognized as something more than keeping the body of the soil at home on the farm. It involves, also, the development of a deeper, more fertile and therefore, a stronger soil body.

THE VALUE OF ORGANIC MATTER

The declining numbers of acres left for growing crops, and the dwindling supply of soil fertility, are bringing home to us the necessity of properly fertilizing our soils. The tonnage of available barnyard manure has long been insignificant as a source of fertilizer supply. Gradually we are coming to realize the basic fact that our soils are being rapidly worn out, because of our old concept of using them as a source for cash crops rather than as means of growing crops completely to nourish our animals and ourselves.

Organic matter, such as animal and plant manures and accumulated virgin soil, has always been the most desired form of fertility for growing our crops, and thereby in turn to feed well our farm animals and ourselves. Now that we have mined most of the original organic matter supply, to say nothing of the inorganic, we are debating the question among ourselves as to whether we can produce good foods and feeds from our crops when they are grown without organic manures to help fertilize them.

Soil itself originated from the rock minerals. In trying to learn what the soil feeds to the plant, we made a list of the inorganic elements found in the plants after reducing them to ashes. Inventories of the inorganic elements in the plants were then matched against inventories of the soil's similar contents. Such knowledge built up the inorganic concept. This knowledge also is serving well for our testing of the soil's needed supplies as against the growing plant's contents; for we have learned that a growing plant contains 13 or more essential inorganic elements which move into the crop from the soil. By the help of such tests, we make our decision when buying needed chemical fertilizers to act as supplements to the incomplete plant and animal matter of the soil.

Success to date in improving the yields of our crops, by means of commercial fertilizers, has naturally emphasized the crops' need of inorganic nutrients from the soil. Unfortunately, such success in some instances has made us prone to discredit the value of both plant and animal manures. It has encouraged us to believe that manure is worth no more than the total of nitrogen and inorganic elements it contains. Yet tests have shown otherwise when plants are grown by hydroponics, or water culture. The growing of plants in pure water, to which has been added the chemical equivalents of the manure's ash components, is not the equivalent of growing them in rotted manure itself.

Organic processes in general, however, and most biochemical reactions, do not give such speedy comparative performances. Even some inorganic reactions, particularly those including the element silicon, making up such large molecules as the clay, are slow and sluggish. Only lately have we become able to build up organic compounds like the synthetic fibers (rayon, vicara, orlon and others of industrial output) to substitute for those created naturally. Something of this sort may later become applicable for soil use.

Plants will grow when fed on strictly inorganic elements in water, but that fact is no refutation of the possibility that such a seemingly good diet for plants might not be a better one if supplemented by some organic compounds. The limitations of hydroponics indicate how much such plant growth procedure differs from that of plants growing in the soil.

Hydroponics may grow the plant, but that is not a process necessarily duplicating those activities involved in growing plants in the soil, even insofar as inorganic nutrients are concerned. Consequently the fact that plants can be grown with reasonably good yields, on wholly inorganic materials, does not prove that plants, if grown by different dynamics within the soil, may not take from the soil some organic compounds serving best for plant nutrition.

The pioneer farmer looked much to the organic matter of the soil to produce the crops for feeding his young animals. Early sales of commercial fertilizer, particularly in the South, met with resistance, due to the farmers' just contention that bird guano from South America helped their crops more than they were helped by Chile saltpeter.

Now we find that the antibiotics are doing wonders for us. Water extracts of the organic matter in soils serve as growth hormones in the laboratory for test plants. Hogs have long had the habit of rooting. They have been grown more rapidly under experiment if allowed on pasture, or if fed some sod soil or its equivalent in antibiotics, as compared to strictly dry lot feeding. Isn't it then time that we open our minds to the possibility that organic compounds, as well as inorganic, may be needed for better plant and animal nutrition, and for superior reproduction of their respective kinds?

Mushrooms are a food crop that grows by feeding wholly on organic matter. They grow in the dark; consequently they do not use energy directly from the sunlight. For energy, they must absorb organic compounds. They create living organic matter by using dead and decaying matter.

Some field tests have been conducted at the Missouri Station on the use of various kinds of combinations of organic and inorganic fertilizers for growing field corn. In these tests corn was grown on three plots treated as follows: (1) limestone, (2) limestone and phosphorus, and (3) limestone, phosphorus and potassium. On these three experimental plots sweet clover was grown as a green manure crop, then plowed under ahead of the corn. As a control, corn was also grown on three comparable plots which received exactly the same inorganic fertilized applications (1, 2, and 3), but in this case the sweet clover was allowed to occupy the plots for the entire season. The sweet clover plants grew to maturity and produced seed; the seed was harvested and the remaining plant residues were then plowed under in the fall to be followed the next season with a corn crop.

As a result of these treatments and applications, higher yields were obtained when larger and more complete combinations of inorganic fertilizers were used as in plot number 3. However, there was no significant difference in corn yield between using the sweet clover planting, earlier in the season as a green manure crop, as compared with letting it mature. The grain grown on each of these plots was harvested and later put in separate compartments of self-feeders, and made available to hogs. The hogs voted, as manifested by their appetite, in favor of organic matter in the form of mature sweet clover residues (plus the fertilizers used in plot number 3), as compared to the clover as an immature green manure crop.

Research by the late Dr. Francis M. Pottenger, Jr., of Monrovia, California, points out that differences in the way the feed was handled or processed for the animal making manure from it, may be reflected as corresponding differences in the character and manner of growth by the plants and their seeds on soil fertilized with such manure. For example, some dwarf bean plants were grown on the sand of various pens into which cats had buried their dung for the two preceding years. The pens included cats fed alike in all respects except for differences in their milk, which included: (a) condensed, (b) evaporated, (c) pasteurized, and (d) natural (raw) milk.

At the end of the tests, it was clear that the four different kinds of milk, fed to the cats, produced different growth effects on the bean plants which had been fertilized by these various cat dungs in the sand pens. Dung from all the cats that were fed heated milk produced only sparse plant growth. On the other hand, dung from cats fed the natural (raw) milk produced such fertile soil that a dense, healthy plant growth resulted.

The first weed growth later was removed, and the pens were then seeded to the ordinary white bean or dwarf growth habits. It was most surprising to note that in all six pens, in which the buried dung was from cats fed the heated milks (condensed, evaporated and pasteurized), the bean plants grew only as dwarf plants. But in the two pens in which the buried dung was from cats fed unheated milk, the bean plants grew, not as dwarf plants, but as pole beans with their vines going to the top of the screened sides of the pens. Here is an illustration that organic compounds, as well as the inorganic elements, may be traveling in cycles. First, from the soil into the plant, for their build-up into more complexity there, then into the animal, for possible digestive simplification there and later, through the excretions back to the soil, for another cycle nutritional service. It is particularly significant that the illustration cited relates to the amino acid tryptophan, which is the major deficiency protein of the corn grain.

When the effects from fertilizers on soils are measured only by yield variations in vegetative bulk, recorded as tons and bushels, there is little chance that we shall recognize crop differences demonstrating the varying effects between the use of inorganic and organic fertilizers. Our animals, however, tell us that the crop's nutritional quality reflects the different organic and inorganic compounds feeding the plants. When we learn to measure the crop's responses to soil fertility by more than bulk values and ash differences, then the contributions of the soil, both organic and inorganic, to plant nutrition will be more correctly realized.

SOIL FERTILITY PATTERN

In dealing with the subject of soil fertility and its implications for our teeth, or for any other part of our anatomy, it is essential that one establish certain facts and principles at the outset and then follow through.

The process of synthesizing proteins is a biosynthetic process; that is, one by the life processes of the plant. It seems to be a case in which some of the carbohydrates serve as the raw materials out of which the proteins are made. This is brought about by combining with these carbohydrates some nitrogen, some phosphorus, and some sulfur, all coming from the soil. At the same time, some calcium, and possibly several other soil-borne nutrient elements are required, while more of the carbohydrates are consumed as energy material for this conversion process.

If the Creator himself was making only such carbonaceous products as forests on those soils, shall we not believe that such products must represent about the limits of our possibilities when we take over and grow crops on them without adding fertility to the soil?

By modifying the relative amounts of calcium and potassium in the soil, much as they are modified under increasing weathering of the soil, the physiology of the plant is shifted to the production of less protein and to the production of more carbohydrates. Higher soil development and more rainfall and temperature then bring less protein production by any crop and therefore less proteins and minerals in our feeds and our foods.

The significant truth that brings the soil fertility into control of the composition of our food, and therefore of our health, comes out of the facts that in soils under construction by the limited climatic forces, or those with a wide calcium-potassium ratio, proteinaceous and mineral-rich crops and foods as well as carbonaceous ones are possible, and that in soils under destruction by excessive climatic forces, or those with a narrow calcium-potassium ratio, protein production is not so common while production mainly of carbohydrates by the crops is almost universal.

Out of these climatic, pedologic, and physiological facts there comes the major principle of concern to the dentists; namely, we have in the regions of higher rainfall the excessive carbohydrates in nature and therefore may expect them in the human diet. Where rainfall is high enough to encourage vegetation in abundance there we have a hindrance to sound teeth from nature herself, because of too much carbohydrate, or conversely, insufficient proteins and minerals, a fact—all too familiar to those in the dental profession—that militates against sound teeth. We need then to realize these facts and consider them by remembering our geographic location and in our management of the soil with human nutrition in mind.

That these shortages of minerals and proteins vary according to the pattern of soil fertility is demonstrated very clearly by the soils of the United States. The lower rainfalls of the western half of our country (the area of sparse population) have not removed the calcium and the other nutrient cations from the surface soil. These lime-laden, mineral-rich areas have been the prairie soils. It is on these that the legumes as protein-rich, mineral-providing forages flourish widely and profusely. It is these soils that were feeding buffaloes in the early days by their grass without purchased protein supplements. It is these soils that are giving us protein products in beef and lamb today.

When one looks at the eastern half of the United States (the area of dense population) this part of our country with its higher rainfall has soils leached so highly that most of the calcium has gone from these to the sea. In fact, that loss of calcium has made us classify them as acid soils, as though the acidity rather than the shortage of fertility were responsible for their failure to grow protein-rich legumes. They were originally growing only wood as forests. When cleared of these they have been growing starchy crops. It is on these eastern soils that we fatten the cattle that are born and grown on the soils farther west. These eastern soils can still grow hogs whose carcasses are mainly fat. Such soils if given fertility treatments can produce proteins by reproducing and growing the animals themselves but usually only with much help by attending veterinarians.

From all this there is the suggestion that more of our so-called diseases may well be statistically mapped for the United States and compared with the map of the soil fertility. If all other body irregularities as well as those of the teeth were so viewed, it is highly probable that many of our diseases would be interpreted as degenerative troubles originating in nutritional deficiencies going back to insufficient fertility of the soil.

Surely the millions of health records of our G.I. s will not be left lying idle in federal archives when they can be sorted out as specific diseases plotted as densities over the soil fertility pattern, and possibly give suggestions for combating the failing health that rests on the great fact that degeneration of the human body goes with the exploitation of the soil. If the decay of teeth is linked with the declining fertility of the soil, this concept of tooth troubles may well be a pattern to guide our thinking about other health troubles, not as calls for drugs and medicines, but for conservation in terms of a new motive, namely, better health via better nutrition from the ground up.

SOIL AND HUMAN HEALTH

It has long been an adage that "to be well fed is to be healthy." One can readily reason, then, that since the soil contributes the food, we are healthy accordingly as the soil makes that contribution properly. The soil is therefore in control of human health. The recognition of the fact that "we are as we eat" has not, however, so readily connected any particular soil area or certain level of soil fertility with our health condition, our stature, or our mental attitudes. We have been too nomadic in our living; our foods have come from such far flung sources; and we have so readily supplemented them with drugs and chemicals that we have not realized the true significance of the soil's contribution to our body mass as the basis of human health.

The simple mention of food, or nutrition, connotes carbohydrates, fats, proteins, minerals, and vitamins, much more quickly than it does the more fertile or less fertile soils, or soils in one climatic setting in contrast to those in another. This very word "carbohydrates" should suggest their meteorological origin in carbon dioxide and water as these components of this food portion come from the atmosphere and the rainfall. When carbohydrates, as we know them in sugars and starches of our diet, are considered so commonly as fattening foods and sources of energy, it is no wide step chemically from them to the food fats which also go to the air, water and sunshine as their source. These two energy providers, namely carbohydrates and fats, do not come, then, from the soil. Made up as they are of three simple chemical elements, namely carbon, hydrogen and oxygen, they constitute over 90% of our body weight. Because our bodies are made up of so little that comes from soil and of so much that is truly meteorological, this may be ample basis for the fallacious belief that our health depends on the weather. Though we cannot establish our complete separation from effects on our bodies by the weather, no one is ready to give weather as much as 90% control, represented in the carbon, hydrogen, and oxygen that are of origin above the soil and in no unreal sense from the weather.

The recent wide and general interest in minerals and vitamins, and the past emphasis by nutritionists on the importance of the proteins, are leading our attention to the soil as the basis of health. The mineral content of our bodies—according to simple chemical analysis—amounts to but 5%. Yet this small portion is made up of some dozen elements so important that absence or deficiency of any one of them brings disturbance or disaster to human health and growth. Then, too, quite different from the carbon dioxide and water of atmospheric origin that as gas and liquid readily distribute themselves universally, the dozen soil-borne elements are fixed. The plant roots must search them out and go to them. They do not go to the plant.

These dozen soil-borne elements as a majority in terms of numbers, more than in terms of bulk, take over the controls. It is by means of the soil fertility elements that the plan constructs its proteins to be passed in turn to the animals for construction by them of the protein tissue of their bodies. Then, too, it is among these dozen soil-given elements that we find the calcium and phosphorus that constitute bones. Also, in that list are sulfur, magnesium, potassium, iron, iodine, copper and others that enter into body growth as construction materials. They may also function in giving the catalytic services so commonly conceded to the vitamins. By these dozen elements the soil comes into control of our growth. It is these in the soil that enable it to provide what might be called the "mending" foods. It is the atmosphere that gives us the "rending" foods.

Weakness in human health and frailty in human body are readily connected with an excessive use of carbonaceous and fatty foods, such as the white breads, the pastries, the sweets and others. Dentists on examining the defective teeth often say "too much sugar, or too much carbohydrates." We have come to know that the "sweet tooth" is too often the decayed tooth at an early age. Poor bone growth in the rest of the skeleton can readily be associated with poor teeth when they are merely an exposed part of it. Excessive use of energy foods, or "rending" foods seems to be a trouble that aggravates itself when we enjoy sweets to their excess and to the danger of our health.

That this inclination to excessive eating through unsatisfied appetites may be traced to the soil is suggested when the pioneer man thinks first of wood and water as his necessities and locates himself finally as large concentrations of populations on the leached soils of the humid regions where forests are or were the dominant vegetation. We have just come to realize that forests are a crop dominantly carbonaceous itself in chemical composition. Trees suggest themselves as an expression of a soil fertility condition that can produce a little more than carbohydrate products in its crops when the soil is put into cultivation. May we not picture such soil regions with mainly carbonaceous foods, as energy or rending foods only, and therefore foods deficient and non-satisfying in a physiological sense? Are not these the areas to encourage excessive consumption of their carbohydrates and therefore poorer health? Can there not be a soil region of a certain fertility level as the basis for the sweet tooth?

We have also come to appreciate the fact that our food crops that are more proteinaceous and mineral-rich are grown on soils in lower rainfalls originally as prairie grass crops. Such areas represent soils that have not been leached of their mineral fertility. They still contain the essential elements that enable them to synthesize its proteins, its mineral compounds and other complexes which originate distinctly in plant fabrication and which contribute growth more than energy only to higher life forms subsisting on it.

The soils of the United States exemplify clearly their roles in production of mainly energy foods in the regions of higher rainfall in the South and East. Cotton and sugar cane as crops consisting of cellulose and sucrose, respectively, are readily connected with low health levels, indifferent mental attitudes and to many other deficiencies rather than the infertile soil basically responsible. Regions of high rainfalls, lower temperatures and forest vegetation also suggest less healthful conditions. These are prompted through food crops whose bulk is more carbonaceous and therefore more deficient in the mineral elements than come from the soil for more efficient food fabrication within the plants, and therefore better contribution to the growth of vigorous and healthy bodies.

As a contrast to the more humid regions, the drier regions may seemingly have been the frontier against which man has always struggled in his move from those more humid. Nevertheless, it has always been along that drier frontier that man has lived most healthily to carry on the struggle. The prairies with their drier summers, and periodic droughts have been considered by some as soils too dry to grow trees. But by virtue of the low rainfalls that have not leached their soils, those areas have retained within their soils at depths not beyond plant reach the essential mineral elements, or soil fertility, that make proteinaceous and mineral-rich rather than woody vegetation.

It is the prairie soils that have been the mainstay of our increasing populations. It is the fertility in these particular soils that has contributed to the prosperity of the United States while we followed through our subscription to the advice of Mr. Horace Greeley not so many years ago. It is the fertility equivalent in prairie soils in the different parts of the world as a whole that has determined the places where human population centers of greater densities have established themselves. Better health—the basis of better life—as it is dependent on the better soils has located the people of the world in greater concentrations in certain areas as we now find them. Unfortunately, the present great international conflict [WWII] is viewed mainly in terms of military, political and economic strategies. But in the final analyses it is little more than a struggle between men for possession of the soil resources by which they and their peoples can live as healthy folks and therefore as happy and prosperous human beings. The soil, in the ultimate consideration, will determine the outcome of the conflict and the stability of the future peace.

Food plants and their chemical composition as better contribution of health on prairie soils, and their proper contribution on forest soils, are well illustrated by hard, mineral-rich, and high-protein wheat in drier areas and soft wheat is mainly starch content in wetter areas. As cause for this difference in chemical composition, we must not look to the weather. Instead, we must look to the soil. When soils are more fertile and higher in mineral fertility, their crops are those normally richer in the nutrient elements like calcium, phosphorus, and other minerals. In fact any crop has a greater concentration of minerals if grown on the less weathered soils, and a lower concentration if grown on highly weathered soils of the humid region. Food values accordingly then in the vegetables, cereals and other food crops, for example, are higher when grown in prairie soils and lower when grown on soil originally in forests.

The patterns of animal distribution in numbers and health, and of human health reflect the differences in the soils. Cattle and sheep are associated with the ranges of the midlands and the West. It is there that they grow and reproduce for shipment to the more eastern cornbelt states for fattening on the carbonaceous crops. Animal diseases stand out prominently in the sheltered flocks and herds in the eastern states, while animals literally raise themselves in the large range areas of the West. Here it is the soil as it provides the mineral essentials to plants and they in turn fabricate them into feed that is at the basis of the cattle business on such a large scale with so little care in the West. It is the soil deficiencies in the originally forested soils of the East that bring on the animal troubles, and the problems of animal health in the milksheds of many eastern cities.

Human health, too, can be tabulated to give us a picture that will superimpose itself on the soil differences. When seven out of ten selectees are accepted in Colorado, but only three out of ten are taken in one of the southern states, there is a bold suggestion that human health depends on the soil. One need scarcely mention the prevalence of deficient teeth in some parts in contrast to that of healthy ones in other parts of the world—notably the "town without a toothache" in Texas—as presented in the studies by Dr. Weston A. Price. The advent of sterility into the American family at a startling early age in some parts of the country, and numerous other health manifestations also suggest that much that has too long been considered a disease in a sense of attack from the exterior is distinctly a case of malnutrition and one of weakening and breakdown from within.

Neglect of the soil in terms of its fertility content has been at the basis of this pessimistic view of human health as provoked by deficient soils. That there is hope ahead is readily recognized when the soil contributes only 5% of the plant, and only 5% to the human body. When there are only one dozen chemical elements within this small contribution by the soil, it is no great task to replace within the soil this list and this small amount. A ton of fresh vegetable growth would call for but 40 pounds of chemical elements to be put into the soil. By placing this complete list of elements into the soil as fertilizers, we can do the equivalent of pushing the soils out of their unfavorable and into favorable climatic conditions that control the soil in relation to human health. Then, too, by putting these essential minerals into nature's hands she will put them into plants and fabricate them into organic complexes much more serviceable in the guarantee of human health than if we consume them as drugs or pills.

Soil conservation has started as a growing national philosophy. It must become an action program for each of us. Barrenness and erosion of the surface soil have come because the humus and mineral fertility reserves originally within the soil have been cropped out or leached out. It is because nature no longer covers herself quickly. There has been the exit of these mineral nutrients and with them have passed out the nutrients common in better foods, and the basis of better health and sounder bodies. With the depletion of the soils come sterility and other reproductive troubles; the plagues in some areas of the older countries for some time past.

We are about to enter on a new age in which our efforts in soil conservation will be not only a struggle to retain the mass or body of the soil, but also to restore the chemical fertility and active organic matter content of the soil. We shall set in motion thereby the natural forces for better food and through it for better health. Soil conservation will then be a responsibility and privilege for each of us to share in better national health by prevention of disease through better foods, and thus in better health by way of more fertile soils.

2

BIOLOGICAL PROCESSES

BIOLOGY VS. TECHNOLOGY IN GROWING THINGS

Because our daily experiences of our living are so extensively and intimately geared to technology, and because so many of us are too far removed from what is truly biology, the growth of our agricultural crops is viewed as if it were a technological matter which we could readily manage. In the argument for that there is often cited the hydroponic tank with no more than water and a collection of salts of the inorganic or the ash constituents of the crops to be grown. But we have not demonstrated the hydroponics as means of growing very many kinds of crops, save for those which are mainly a vegetative, cellulosic mass carrying much water, sugar and starch.

Tomatoes, potatoes, spinach, flowers and similar crops whose reproductive potential has not been tested for a series of generations of growth under hydroponics have been demonstrators of this procedure. As a challenge to the hydroponic technology using the flowing, very dilute, often replenished, inorganic solutions, let us ask the proponents of this method (who are probably opponents of the highly organic soil as a necessity for crops) to grow one crop of mushrooms in their hydroponic tank as a substitute for the rotted manure of the mushroom bed. The crop growth by hydroponics, claimed to be rapid, is no match for the speed with which the mushroom mycelia literally run through the bed and grow the mushroom crop. But, as a beginning, and for a good start in our understanding of what makes things grow, the hydroponic idea is a very helpful demonstration. It uses water as a means to dilute the inorganic salts. It obviates the danger of too much salt. It permits renewal of the salt supply, since only by an enormous amount of water under such required dilution could enough salts be delivered to mature the crop. Water, however, is the medium for ionization of the salts to make their elements active for root entrance. Soil areas of crop production must contain both water and fertility compounds. Dry soils with salts in excess are the saline and alkaline areas with no crops. Hydroponic technology uses solutions so dilute that it duplicates the laws of gaseous behaviors and does not duplicate the soil where within root-reach the nutrient supply dare not be in highly concentrated salt form, but yet must be large enough in quantity, and in active form, to mature a significant crop.

Soil, as the assembly line, is then far different from hydroponics. So is the mushroom bed with its rotted manure. Decaying organic matter in the soil, similar to the clay there, is a colloid on which adsorbed nutrient elements are held, and from which they are exchanged to the plant roots. Also for the nutrient release, by the decay of the organic matter in the soil, the increasing rate of this process is timed to be highest when the seasonal conditions suit the speediest growth of the crop.

Nature has synchronized these two performances—that is, the decay of the residues of past crops and the growth of a new crop, by making the increase rate of decay of the organic matter within the living soil provide the means of increased nutrition of the crop above the soil. Hence, the cause of the crop growth in a living soil under nature's management. Crop growth is not the result so much, then, of a technology under man's manipulation. Rather it is an exhibition of the biology of Mother Nature.

Organic decay is an agency for the increased weathering of the disintegrated rock. By it the living soil makes the dead rock elements become active to support more life. Our thinking has not pushed forward our understanding of what makes things grow. Our comprehension of those processes has not gone much beyond the solution idea of hydroponics. We have not yet seen the soil as the handful of dust into which the moist breath is blown by the weather, nor comprehended how that can mean the creation of life. There is reason, then, why—for so many folks—there is as yet no concept of the living soil. Hence, there can be no living soil in their vision when so commonly "we are down on what we are up on."

AGRICULTURE IS BIOLOGY FIRST AND FOREMOST

In our research in the Department of Soils of the Missouri Experiment Station, we have labored for a number of years to work a combination so that we can get soil fertility and plant nutrition linked together in a language which we all understand. Those of us who are dealing with research projects in the Experiment Station are now thinking and planning for ten years ahead about problems on which we ought to spend Station money in the future, assuming that we shall get some. We are trying to make sure that we give just rewards for the money invested in the materials and for our time in the work.

In opening this broader subject of soil fertility and plant nutrition we may well be reminded that it is much broader than what is commonly included under that title. It will eventually encompass more than any of the rest of us might now include.

Much that is said about our scientific progress, in which we are about to believe that we have reached the pinnacle, deserves some rather critical examination. It seems that we are allowing ourselves to be so easily decieved by our success. There is a terrific danger in over-confidence. Even though we can fertilize the soil we are not quite yet controlling nature at that point of her activities. The burden of the thought is in those few words, namely, we do not yet create crops.

We are delighted in the technical progress which we have built up and which raises our standard of living when you consider technologies. Technologies apply only, however, when we consider our control of dead matter. As for me, I am not quite ready to put agriculture in the class of the science under control, like a technology is, for example, when you look at the assembly line of an airplane or an automobile. It is more nearly correct to talk about agriculture as an art, plus some science. It is not yet a case in which the science is in complete control. Agriculture is still an art, which we study by deduction, that is, we look at it as a natural behavior. We take a fragment out of it and put a little science into that portion. But when we take complete control we must have the science so well organized that we can put all the parts together and run the whole process from creation to death. Nobody as yet has been able to do that with agriculture.

Agriculture is biology first and foremost. It is technology and management second. We need only to remind ourselves of the last two seasons to be reminded how readily we use the weather as a scapegoat, when the crops didn't behave as we thought we would like to control them.

It is fitting, therefore, to provoke your thinking about the sciences applied to agriculture in a technological viewpoint only as a possible or even serious danger. Some of the agricultural troubles for which we are apologizing came about because we used technologies to upset the biology of agriculture. Much that is apt to be called agricultural science has upset the biology and we are coming now to reap the bad harvest. We are beginning to realize that the matter of agricultural production has been largely nature's performance. Very often we have not had very much to do with it. We have been copying and memorizing agricultural practices, but have not been comprehending the basic principles that operate under nature.

THE UPSET BIOLOGICAL PROCESSES

We may well list several cases in which we have upset agricultural biology rather than helped it. We have been taught that crop rotations build up soil fertility. Yet, nature uses continuous cropping and doesn't rotate the crops when she builds up soil fertility. We have upset the biology in that case very decidedly.

We are now trying to put a grass agriculture over much of the country where nature had tree culture. Then we are going to let the cow make up the difference between our ignorance of quality grass and the cow's knowledge of it. We put the plow ahead of the cow. The cow is about to be extinguished if, as a matter of legal procedure, we follow the philosophy of killing cows to get rid of diseases like brucellosis, hoof-and-mouth disease and others. How we ever got such a belief to prevail is strange, namely, that we can have cows when we keep killing them because we make them sick.

Primitive man lived on the dry lands. More recently in human history we began to farm those lands which have high rainfalls. Then, when rainfall goes back on us, we run to the federal treasury, as though that were the place where one gets any biological help. As another upset of biology, instead of leaving plant residues on top of the soil, as nature does, we bury them as deeply as we can.

Nature used different soils to make grasses on the prairies than she uses in making trees in the forest. Yet here are some folks who believe that the prairie grasses make prairie soils and the forest trees make forest soils.

Nature uses plant roots to make soils acid in order to get fertility into the plants. We want to put a carbonate in the soil so that the root cannot put its acid out any farther than barely off of itself. Yet plants nourish themselves by making soils acid. We fight the soil acidity by means of carbonate instead of feeding the plant with calcium and magnesium in the limestone.

Nature washes soluble fertility out of the soil into the sea. We make fertilizers soluble before we put them on the soil. If they remained there in that form they would soon be in the sea, too. Or, we mine the sea salts as soluble fertilizers, like potash salts, and put them through another round of going from the soil and into the sea.

We put cattle and grass into the plains where there are areas of ever-threatening drought and succeed, because that is where nature had successfully put a similar beast, the bison. But we put them on the grass amongst the forest tree soils under high rainfall and then wonder why their reproduction is failing.

Nature doesn't have animals live to get fat. Experiments point out that our animals are searching for anything else but fattening feeds. They are searching for those which help them protect themselves against disease and encourage them in their reproduction. But, when we feed animals, we cut the amount of protein in their ration down to the limit, because we want to make cheap gains rather than to give the animals the help they need to be healthy and to multiply. Instead of letting the animal live long, we cut their life spans down to the most early maturity we possibly can, and then call it "cheap gains."

Some significant economic aspects might well be considered critically when manipulated economics have manipulated machinery, money and technologies into agriculture, but have almost manipulated biology out. Bankers are about to believe that we can substitute capital for land. Certainly all the capital in all the banks cannot substitute for the soil of the land. We know of no bank with all its money that could by means of that wealth have a litter of pigs, lay an egg, or give birth to a calf. And yet we have folks believing that one can manipulate biology by means of economics. You can't do that any more with money alone than you can with machinery and technology.

We have not yet understood, nor appreciated, agriculture as a collection of complex, but well-integrated, biological processes. We have not seen the soil as plant nutrition and thereby as animal and human nutrition, or the soil as the very foundation of all agriculture.

SOME SOILS ANALYZED

The problem of relating soil fertility to a plant's nutrition, as well as to its drink, we put under study here at the Missouri Experiment Station many years ago.

It seems fitting to review the history of the mental procedures by which we attacked this problem of adequate soil fertility and its services in the growth of plants—at least in terms of this soil aspect when others were adequate to the best of our knowledge.

Many years ago we made a kind of problem analysis. Division of the prob-

REVIEWS: THE ECOLOGY OF MAN AND HIS EARTH

This book may be classified as an agri-ecological volume. It is one of the several recent ones in the growing science of ecology, which deals with "life forms in relation to their environment and to each other." Dr. Scarseth emphasizes man and his agriculture in their broader scope of some natural facts, considered as present problems but which are results of his modification of environment for the more economical living supports of himself through other forms struggling naturally for their own.

As a careful scientist, a closely observing naturalist, a sympathetic teacher and a broad-minded philosopher whose professional life was the study of soils, plants, animals and humans, Dr. Scarseth brought together what he considered significant under the subject, *Man and His Earth.*

The last word of that title includes the soils in their climatic settings as differing creative forces and varied biochemical potentials—all in scientific and technical details of a few of the major fertility elements, like nitrogen, phosphorus, potassium, organic matter and carbon dioxide (separate chapters) about some of which we boast in wise soil management. But very politely the author reminds us of our deficient comprehension of nature's laws remaining as secrets. He uses the singular, masculine, possessive pronoun very advisedly as a modifier of the term "earth."

Apropos of that subtlety, he employs the simile of the development of man to a mature one duplicating the maturation of the soil to its creative powers for climax crops of healthy plants and animals in man's absence. The thought then moves to emphasize the life of "The Mature Man" in the author's own Christian philosophy. "The mature man," he says, "is well adjusted to his environment. He lives within the factors and resources of his existence without destroying them . . . He is in balance with nature, and because of him his neighborhood is as good or better than before he came."

Very diplomatically he chides sharply when he says "One of man's difficulties appears to be his tendency to reproduce himself with very little restraint."

"Man's great power over his environment is not always tempered with self-restraint and unselfishness. The result of his greed and short-sightedness has in many cases resulted in bad ecology. There are many instances wherein man's relationship to his environment can only be called a temporary relationship and one wherein he can anticipate future difficulty that deserves some rather critical examination. It seems that we are allowing ourselves to be so easily deceived by our success. There is a terrific danger in over-confidence. Even though we can fertilize the soil, we are not quite yet controlling nature at that point of her activities. The burden of the thought is in those few words, namely, we do not yet create crops."

lem into its parts divided it according to the soil texture—namely, the sand, the silt and the clay. We decided on clay as the part of the soil to study first. That choice was predictable because in Missouri we have almost four million acres of claypan soils.

About those it was commonly said, "Oh, they will make only about 20-30 bushels to the acre. Your crops drown out in the spring and you dry out in the summer. The Putnam claypan soil is a nice silt loam. It has a level topography and it would be fine but it just doesn't deliver by production. Farmers on it have some silly ideas and ways about handling it. They bar off the corn in the spring, as they say, and then they hill it up in the summer. It is a terribly acid or sour soil. You can't grow legumes on it. You can't build up its nitrogen."

As an outcome we picked first on this Putnam silt loam and worked on its clay until now that clay is known all over the world by its technical name, Putnam clay. This basic research in the laboratory, in the greenhouse, and later in the field, has moved this soil into the corn growers' contests for the winning high yields per acre.

Let us follow with the next and inquire, "What is in sand as fertility for plant nutrition?" You may well reply, "It is largely quartz, it contains only silicon and oxygen. Those mineral grains do not weather down."

That is the reason the quartz crystals are still big grains. It never has weathered. It is a kind of soil skeleton. "Consequently, for the time being," we said, "let's throw that soil out of our mind and concentrate on the silt."

It also can be quartz. But then, too, it can be other than quartz. Its composition depends on the place where it is. The farther east one goes in the United States, and to the higher rainfalls, the more quartz there is in the silt of the soil. Silt doesn't have much capacity to hold fertilizer—neither does sand.

Because of their large particle size, these two have little capacity to absorb and to exchange nutrients to plants. But yet there is much silt blown in here from the floodplains of the Missouri River and from the west. It piles up along the river bluffs to give what is fairly good soil.

Thus the soils were catalogued for their order of importance for research attention. The silt fraction was set aside for later study when the initial study took to the clay soil.

We began with the claypan soil and its high content of clay since almost everybody wanted to enlist himself in what might be a fight with that tight clay. The early researchers bought and used much dynamite on it. They dug ditches of various kinds in it. They pushed it around with powerful machines. About the time they would have the treatment complete, the soil was behaving just about the way it was before.

Whether fortunately or unfortunately this clay has little or nothing inside of its crystal form of significant fertility contribution.

In some of the early work we did with it in the laboratory, we tried bubbling carbon dioxide through it only to discover that if you really treated it long and hard with carbonic acid, you could break out of it no more than about the iron that would be required to grow a crop. You might get a little magnesium out of it, too. But as a contributor of fertility we might credit it with iron, and one would be generous in doing that. From those early studies and the light they shed on the importance of the clay, there developed the research studies at this station leading to our better understanding of soil fertility and plant nutrition.

ROOT BIO-CHEMISTRY AND CLAY CHEMISTRY

We need to remind ourselves that the plant is carrying on a bio-chemical operation. It is not merely standing outdoors without being very definitely influenced by the soil. We discovered that when the same amount of fertility was adsorbed on less clay or the clay given a higher degree of saturation, the plant root in contact with that clay experienced an increasing efficiency with which that fertility moved into it and into the crop.

In that simple fact there is the basis for the practice of banding the fertilizer application in the soil in place of mixing it throughout a large soil volume. In limited soil volumes saturated with fertility rather than having it distributed all through the soils, to have the clay as a competitor colloid against your plant root is the basis for the efficiency in applying fertilizer in bands. The plant root finds the soil areas where it feeds itself to advantage. Clay has always been serving to remove a good deal of the fertilizer hastily from solution by absorbing it and thus getting rid of the dangerous salt effects, which the plants always suffered when we drilled fertilizer, with the exception of superphosphate, along with the seeding.

But as long as we used ordinary superphosphate or others containing a large amount of calcium, we could drill much more fertilizer with the seeding than one could without it. If potassium salts, or sodium salts were used with the seed, its germination and emergence were quickly disturbed. However, when plenty of calcium salts were mixed with them, then there was safety. Gypsum was that safety factor, often without our recognition of that saving service, to the plant's biochemical activities in the soil.

There is another interesting and significant fact we learned in our experiments. We could study one ion and vary it on the clay to get a certain behavior—with increasing saturation of the clay by that ion, provided the accompanying ions adsorbed on the clay behave differently even when the amounts exchangeable are constant; that they are held with different forces; that they move off variable into the atmosphere of their colloid; and that they exhibit different effects and different energies.

While using fertilizers and trying to explain the effects, the organic matter in the soil has been the saving grace for the plants in many cases. A low degree of saturation of the clay by the inorganic ions in the less fertile soils may be improved decidedly when we get more organic matter into those soils. When we put organic matter back into the soil we upset this more commonly considered set of inorganic chemo-dynamics of the soil, which must have initially dominated there. With less organic matter in the soil, we have a different rate of fertility deliveries and a rearrangement of the suite of ions on the clay. Organic matter, then, shifts the ration of the crop about very decidedly.

Considering the plant root as a factor in modifying soil fertility in plant nutrition, we have found that if the root was a protein rich one, it exhausted the inorganic fertility of the soil to a higher degree than any non-protein root. In other words, a legume is the quickest way we can take the inorganic fertility off the clay and deplete its fertility to a lower level than we can by any other crop. One might well raise the point whether legumes have been soil improvers. It suggests that we never really knew (we just had a kind of blind faith) that the growing of legumes improved the soil.

We know now from laboratory research and from field records that legumes can take the fertility out of the soil faster than the non-legumes. The question may well be asked: "Shall we go back to that plot and try to build up its fertility by seeding legumes, or shall we study the sciences of the soil and plant nutrition to work with the biology the best we can by applied nitrogen and other fertilizers?" With present high costs of production and high taxes, what solution have we for some of these problems except higher yields per acre via fertilizers for economy of production?

THE ROLE OF CLAY IN PLANT NUTRITION

"But what about the organic matter as a colloid similar to clay?" you might well ask. We found in our experiments some organic matter in the clay. About 1½% carbon and about 15 hundredths of a percent of nitrogen are found in our Missouri clay. They are still very tightly linked into the clay molecule even after you have oxidized the clay with hydrogen peroxide, and after electrodialysis to take out everything that you possibly can. These clay studies brought carbon and nitrogen in a ratio of 10:1 right in the collodial clay itself. That is the carbon-nitrogen ratio commonly given for well weathered soils. These organic elements seem to be a highly fixed part of the clay.

Because of these discoveries the clay had much later research consideration. We dispersed it in water. The larger particles were settled out, the coarsest clay was thrown out of the supernatant water by centrifuging. The remaining opalescent suspension was then electrodialized and the intense study of this clay began. It was on the basis of that attack and our increasing knowledge resulting therefrom that we are bold enough to talk about soil fertility and plant nutrition.

Because we have studied clay chemistry now for a long time we have moved to study plant chemistry in combination with that clay. In his first experience of bringing collodial clay chemistry into combination with the biochemistry of the plant, Dr. Hans Jenny met with disappointment in the plants so often that he was about to give up. But when near complete disgust with our theories, he finally caught the vision that the clay might be the dynamic center of the soil. He had thrown out two or three sets of plants before we rescued the situation. He had demonstrated the fact that it is a hard task to load the clay with enough fertility to feed a crop for its good health and growth. Subsequent trials demonstrated very clearly that the clay was the major center of the chemical dynamics in the soil which deal with the speedy process we might envision when we talk about growing a plant.

It was also discovered that the clay holds nearly the season's supply of plant nutrients, ready and exchangeable, for the root when it comes along. We have in the silt of the soil some of the reserve fertility that can be broken out when we consider that the soil is *resting*. Research found that the clay within the plant root zone must hold approximately a season's supply of fertility. That supply can be increased by adsorbing more nutrients on the clay or by adding more clay. It is this factor that determines different fertilizer use on soils of different textures. One can put a tremendous amount of fertilizer on a heavy clay soil and not see much difference, but yet the plants will register it pronouncedly. And that fact holds true whether you are considering fertilizers of nitrogen, phosphorus and potassium, or in the form of magnesium and calcium as limestone.

The fertility held within the root zone is not leachable by water. It is not in the free water of the soil, and is, therefore, not in the water-soluble condition when it moves to nourish the plant. We make fertilizers soluble so they will be speedily adsorbed on the clay, rather than held in water and be sucked in with the water by the plant. We have learned from these clay studies that calcium is the major nutrient for most any crop we grow. Our agricultural soils in general have less calcium when they are more acid (that is, they have more hydrogen); and as they have more calcium they have less hydrogen.

This simple nutritional situation of the importance of calcium—and the way the soil behaves under acidity as mainly a calcium deficiency—has kept us in ignorance about what soil acidity really is: namely, a fertility deficiency rather than a bad environment. The roots make the clay more acid when the plants grow, because the hydrogen from the root and the calcium from the clay are exchanging places. The legumes are taking tremendous amounts of calcium off the clay.

It was discovered that the degree of the calcium saturation on the clay determined whether the nutrients moved from the soil into the plant root, or vice versa.

The clay, then, is the seat of all these activities. First, there is the absorption of the nutrients from any solution. That activity is involved in our use of soluble fertilizers. Acceptance of hydrogen from the plant root by the clay, and the exchange from the clay to the plant root are the major clay activities. The clay also is the seat of the breakdown of the reserve silt minerals, as this decomposition serves to restock the clay, especially noticeable while the soils are commonly said to be *resting*. These are some of the basic facts about the soil's clay factor as it plays a significant role in plant nutrition.

THE SUSTAINING FERTILITY OF THE SOIL

If the soil fertility is to function efficiently in plant nutrition, we must give attention to the physiological requirements of the crop we expect to grow.

Do we know the proper ratios of the inorganic nutrients that ought to be moving off that clay into the plant root? As yet we do not, but researchers are giving suggestions. By means of colloidal clay we are trying to work out a concept of a balanced ration of calcium, magnesium, potassium, etc., on that clay, possibly for each different crop—because different crops are synthesizing different organic compounds.

We know that the legumes require more of the different elements than are required by the non-legumes. Legume tops and roots are running a bigger factory. They are creating collections of different proteins about which we don't know much. What do we know about the plant's nutrient needs during the different phases of the growing season? While all of the different phases of this problem are confronting us, our declining fertility is slipping down faster and the problem is becoming much larger.

The research on the clay at the Missouri Experiment Station suggests that restocking the clay, after exhaustion of its fertility supply by cropping, resulted from mineral breakdown in the silt fraction.

After we have studied the clay so much we are now studying the silt as a mineral reserve for crop nourishment. This separation is of more service in areas of low rainfall and less of soil development in the West than it is in the high rainfalls of the East. Probably the silt breakdown in many of the Midwestern soils and in others on coming east farther, has been the major supply of fertility. Therefore, our crop production is a weathering agent for soil minerals.

Dr. E.R. Graham has done some very clever work to show that we can use these reserve minerals in contact with the dynamic clay, and thus restock the clay. That is what limestone has been doing when we use it on the soil. That is what rock phosphate does, too. When we have the Missouri River hauling lots of unweathered silt in from the west. With rather dry winters, and with the wind blowing that unweathered silt out of the river bottom and depositing about 1,000 pounds per acre of Missouri soil every year, it would seem to be good agricultural foresight to think about this reserve material as a fertilizer which nature is giving us very generously each year.

This silt fraction, composed as it is of minerals other than quartz, should bring all of us to consider more seriously the *sustaining fertility* in the soil. While we have learned much about soils, we scarcely have knowledge enough to maintain production by starter fertilizer only, particularly when we put them at the top of the soil—where that is dried out during most of the time—and then blame the drought for the failure of the fertilizers in doing what some folks commonly expect of them.

The most neglected and most important chemo-dynamic factor of the soil is the organic matter. Organic matter may be said to be the *constitution* of the soil. As for a definition of the word *constitution* in that usage, we take its meaning when the doctor consoles the friends of a patient in serious illness by reminding them that the patient has a good constitution. According to its meaning as used in medical practice, a good constitution is the capacity of the individual to survive in spite of the doctors rather than because of them. The organic matter in the soil has been the capacity for our soils and our crops to survive in spite of the soil doctors rather than because of them.

There is the tremendous significance of the organic matter as a season's release of plant nutrition. This release is timed to increase during the growing season, or become larger as the temperature goes higher. The microbial activities follow vant Hoff's law and double their rate of decay of the organic residues with every 10 degrees rise in Centigrade temperature.

Nature has always been fertilizing with the organic matter which is dropped back to the soil from the previous plant generations which have died in place. Organic matter is still the most reliable fertilizer in terms of the nutrient ratios and of the time when maximums must be delivered.

THE IMPORTANCE OF SOIL

An age-old saying declares that "to be well-fed is to be healthy." But as yet, health in its positive aspects has not been clearly defined. In the negative aspects, we have professional practitioners in great numbers. Deficiencies in health are, then, well recognized.

The question of good food, and plenty of it, goes back to the soil, by means of which food is produced. Unfortunately, there is danger in losing sight of the fact that agricultural production is food production, rather than production of only salable mass or bulk.

Bushels and tons are no longer sufficient criteria for what the soil is growing. When meat, milk and eggs are the great foods for health recovery and for its maintenance; and when these are the proteins rather than the carbohydrates it might be well for us to think about food deficiencies—and thereby health deficiencies—as deficiencies in protein and all that comes along with them when we produce them on more fertile soils.

Unfortunately, animals do not create proteins—they only assemble them. When the cow went ahead of the plow, she was assaying the vegetation for its protein service to her in growing her body and reproducing it. But, when we sent the plow ahead of the cow, we moved both her and ourselves onto the vegetation and onto the soil that was not necessarily providing her with all the essentials for protein.

It is the soil fertility then in its variable pattern that gives pattern to the possibilities of either being well fed or poorly fed. Its pattern can be the pattern of health deficiencies, too. The soil fertility deficiencies in our national soil pattern have given patterns to crops, as these are mainly carbohydrate foods and fattening foods, or as they are also proteins, minerals, vitamins and foods that grow the bodies and reproduce them. Soil treatments to make up soil deficiencies for better health are telling us that health deficiencies may come with those soil deficiencies.

Our crop pattern, as it is creating proteins or failing to do so, is both citing the soil deficiencies and also suggesting their connection with our national health pattern.

Soil deficiencies include a long list of nutrient elements. Plant nutrition for good food production is a matter of providing in the soil the balanced ration which those plants need to put out proteins and high feed values, much as animal nutrition is a matter of supplying properly balanced rations to put out milk or meat, or just as good food and plenty of it is a matter of human health of high order.

Nitrogen, phosphorous and potassium in fertilizers are a part of the picture. So are calcium and magnesium. Then, too, there is a growing list of trace elements whose functions seem to connect them with protein production.

Attention may well go to the growing amount of research in soil fertility, as this is nutritional foundation for the microbes, the plants, the animals, and man, or the entire pyramid of life for which the soil is the foundation and the starting point of nutrition.

Deficiencies in the soil, so readily remedied by soil treatment with fertilizers, may well be given more consideration as reasons for deficiencies in our national health and the means of preventing them by growing more food of better quality in health than for just more bulk for sale.

SOIL ECONOMICS

Another aspect of organic matter about which we probably haven't thought much is the value of some organic compounds in cycle. That is, they may be dropped back as crop residues and the next crop's roots may be taking them up, using them and dropping them back again.

Plants need the various ring compounds in very small amounts to make some of the essential amino acids. They need the phenol ring in phenylalanine, one of the essential amino acids, essential for plant growth as well as for animals and ourselves. They need the indole ring, which is a phenol ring plus a side ring. It is the compound which gives the odor to feces when the digestion acts on the tryptophane of which that ring is a part. Tryptophane is the most commonly deficient amino acid, and is one of marked complexity.

Then there are also the sulfur compounds and the sulfur-containing amino acids. We might well wonder whether man and his flocks have not been geared together so closely in their past history because some of those excreted organic compounds were put back into the soil, and were going through the cycle over and over again as a help in the survival of both man and beast. Now we are trying to divorce ourselves from animals, but perhaps we haven't found the basis of safety for it.

Organic matter must find a new and more important place in our minds as the neglected half of plant nutrition and soil fertility. In terms of the inorganic half of that responsiblity we have partly understood about one-half of that phase, namely, the major cations. We don't know much yet about the cations of the trace elements. When it comes to those major inorganic ions—which are cations—we have a good concept of their chemodynamics for plant nutrition.

As for the anions like sulfates, nitrates, carbonates, and others, we do not yet know how they are handled by the microbes and the plant roots in the soil. We have much yet to learn when we have scarcely one-fourth of the field of soil fertility interpreted in terms of the basic principles of absorption, exchange, solubility, and what have you, when it comes to the problem of soil fertility and plant nutrition.

There is enormous opportunity for a big research program ahead. However, we have charted our course now and believe we have analyzed the problems, though by no means outlined the solutions for all of them. We need help from observing and thinking minds to take these concepts about soil fertility and plant nutrition out into the fields for test, whether our concepts are on the right or the wrong track.

Those who supply fertilizers have not discharged their responsibility completely when a carload of fertilizer has been delivered on the farm. They have the responsibility of making those goods serve properly in crop nutrition. Fertilizers must serve not just for increasing the crop bulk, but in terms of the necessary chemo-dynamics of soil fertility and plant nutrition which mean better nutrition for animals and man as well.

Our concern about soil fertility and plant nutrition naturally emphasizes their biological aspects. But even under demand for more food and need for a national agricultural policy, one dare not disregard some of the economics involved.

Unfortunately, agriculture uses soil fertility as its biological capital. To date such capital is still an unknown in the money marts, the bankers' vaults, and the political areas. According to present economics applied to agriculture, soil fertility capital is thrown into the bargain when we make a sale of agricultural products. Such values are not interpreted in dollars. The depletion of soil fertility, that is, the foundation for real food values, is not yet considered. Consequently the agricultural business does not have an accounting system for taxes on income, on lands, etc., set up to include fertility depletion allowances, allowed labor income, guarantees of perpetuity of capital assets, etc., to make agriculture, and the soil under it, self-perpetuating. Soil exploitation and land ruin with time are therefore inevitable.

In spite of this lop-sided kind of economics for agriculture, when economics look toward guaranteeing self perpetuation for most other forms of making one's livelihood—even for the laborer by means of strikes—we expect increasing food delivery from the soil. There is no economic alternative except that the soil must be mined.

That must be the result if food production by agriculture is to continue and to increase under the present economic disregard of fertility as the factor giving real value to the acres of land. No national agricultural policy for survival under high standards of living can come forth unless we finally realize that our national strength lies in the fertility of the soil and our future survival in the wise management and utmost conservation of it.

SOIL CONSERVATION

More fertility in the soil is the means by which plants do more than make energy feed values in their carbohydrates. It is this means, contributed by the soil rather than the weather, that makes protein synthesis possible. Growing our own protein means less attention to the weather and more concern about treating the soil with manures.

Better soils for better feeds to give better bearing of young, better milk production, and better health have not been in our thoughts in agriculture as much as the idea of more feeds for increasing the body weight through laying on of fat. Likewise in thinking about fertilizers and other soil treatment for crops, our measure of their efficiencies has been the increase in plant bulk.

Agriculture originally was primarily a food producing effort. Fundamentally it is still the sustainer of life. In the recent past, however, it has attempted to swing itself into the industrial class. But shortages of foods push one back quickly to agriculture for the production and consumption of them rather than for their sale. Conservation of soil may well measure its own efficiency, not by reporting how little soil is eroding, but how much protein per acre we are producing by use of the land without the loss of it.

Such is the philosophy of some of the trials carried out on the Missouri Soil Conservation Service Research and the Missouri Experiment Station.

Three pasture areas were under test as separate areas fenced out of a large, uniform bluegrass pasture. One was given no treatment. One was given furrows on the contour for water conservation. The third was renovated by some surface tillage and fertilizer applications. During the four years of the records, the pounds of beef produced per acre were: (a) 115, with no soil treatment; (b) 103, with contour furrows; and (c) 151, with renovation through fertilizers. These results point out clearly that merely holding back water was of no help as more feed value. Rather it was even detrimental. The tests point out positively that the soil treatments with extra fertility made more protein per acre.

When the plant is building protein it, too, does this in varying degree but according to the nutrients it gets. Quite contrary to expectations, more bulk of forage per acre is not necessarily proof of higher concentration of protein in the forage or hay.

Experimental studies have shown that it is not necessarily the large tonnage per acre that make the most protein per acre. Rather, it is the combination of nutrient mineral elements in the soil—or the fertility ration we feed the plant—that encourages its internal activity in protein production, rather than mere storage of carbohydrates.

These nutrient ratios for plants are suggested by the different degrees of soil development, for example, in the United States. On the highly developed or leached soils of northeastern, eastern and southern United States, which originally grew only forests and where the ratio of calcium to potassium is low or narrow, we may well expect carbonaceous or woody crops today.

In the midlands of the United States which originally grew grass with many natural legumes on less leached, calcareous soil—and also grew buffalo without purchased protein supplements—the crops were originally proteinaceous. Here the soil fertility suggests a high or wide ratio of calcium to potassium.

Plants making mainly carbohydrates build much bulk readily through sunshine power. But when plants build proteins, they burn much of these carbohydrates in converting them into proteins. As a consequence, this gives less bulk per acre. We can, therefore, not be certain that much crop means much protein, nor that even the crop, whose pedigree says it is a legume, is rich in protein.

Protein cannot be made by our crops drawing on only air and sunshine. They must draw on plenty of lime, phosphorus, potassium, nitrogen and other fertility elements in the soil. By supplying more fertility to the soil more of this essential that carries life—namely protein—can be provided, while at the same time we are making a more conservative use of that natural resource, the soil, by which all of us must be fed.

THE SOIL FERTILITY PATTERN

It is an old adage which tells us that "to be well fed is to be healthy." Besides the truth of that statement, there is additional value in considering the converse of it, namely, when we have failing health we ought to be thinking about it as caused by being poorly fed during some period of time in the near past—or even in the distant past. Being well fed is a matter that deals with behaviors over rather extensive lengths of time.

As an illustration, we may remind ourselves that the laying down of the permanent teeth begins in the seventeeth week of pregnancy. It is not a performance after birth, nor after the eruption of the wisdom tooth. Poor feeding is poor health. Poor nutrition during the seventeeth week and thereafter in pregnancy ought to make us expect and anticipate some trouble in permanent teeth that were initiated at that early time. The diagnosis of ill health isn't as simple as having a doctor tell you, "It must be something you ate."

Using the approach by means of the converse above or by the negative, we ought to say, "It is something you didn't eat." We know that such is true for vitamins when they tell us, by definition, "The vitamin is something that will kill you if you don't eat it." That is a negative approach, of course, but we would like to remind you that many times something we didn't eat in our early life registers as troubles in health late in life. This matter of being well-fed is a real problem when we know so little about the physiology of the body and what it needs to keep its physiology functioning proficiently.

In a preceding discussion, we pointed out that the animal still maintains its instincts with reference to food selection. It seems to be wise in that selection for the purpose of that animal's growth, reproduction and then death. Man has lost his instincts which warn him about his health. He has not yet developed judgment by which to guarantee his good health. So we ought to look to the animal and study it. Perhaps from suggestions coming even at that low level, we might have something. If we had the sense of mimicing the animal in some of these respects, we might profit by it.

When we put a fence around the cow to keep her in the pasture, she is limited to what happens inside of that fence. Her nutrition is limited to the creative powers of just that much soil. She is under stress and strain of possible deficiencies particularly as to her reproductive processes.

She demonstrates some acts which we ought to observe and some behaviors which we ought to interpret. If you see a cow going through the mixed herbage and selecting some more readily than the others, is that merely an idiosyncrasy of the appetite as we believe it is for a man who takes excessively of whiskey? Quite the contrary, it is a definite pattern of that animal's choice according to her better nutrition than we would choose it for her. The animal knows enough to balance the highly proteinaceous vegetation against the carbonaceous to give it a more balanced nutritive ratio. The animal modified that choice at certain times of the year in relation to the nutritional value of the crop. In the fall of the year, the plants are more carbonaceous and are woody. This encourages the animal's laying on of fat. In the spring of the year, the plants are more proteinaceous. It is that season when the animal is growing a body more than hanging fat on it.

Somehow or other in the great evolutionary scheme the births of the majority of our wild and domestic animals come in the spring. Some say it is because of favorable temperature. Perhaps we should say it is because of the nutritional values of the growing plants in serving the capacity of the animals to grow well and to make milk well at that season more than any time else.

The next time you look into the eyes of the cow, we hope you see some evidence of her wisdom as a nutritionist for herself. She is one who has sense enough to select the blue grass or the white clover or to take some plants chosen from others in a field, or to eat what we call weeds if they happen to be well-fertilized and grown on fertile soil. It is not a bit of contrariness on her part when she breaks through the fence for something on the other side. The animal is guiding her choice according to the nutritional values. Her selection of certain plants is not according to plant species; she doesn't know soybeans as an import from Manchuria, she doesn't know lespedeza as an import from Korea. But she does know the nutritional value to her of that plant in terms of the soil that grew it. She knows whether the plant offers her nutrition or whether it merely offers packing for her paunch.

LIME'S NUTRITIONAL SERVICE TO PLANT GROWTH

Putting lime on the soils of the humid region has been practiced under the belief that removal of the acidity of the soil was the benefit from such treatment. We now know that liming an acid soil is helpful because of the nutritional value of the calcium or lime to the crops, and because it helps to mobilize other nutrient elements early into the plant's growth.

Experiments, with a crop like soybeans, demonstrated clearly the need by the young seedlings for calcium early in their life, if they were to survive. Any forms of calcium salts showed their benefits. It was the same whether these salts reduced the soil acidity or whether they increased it.

If the soybean seedlings were planted in a lime-bearing sand for no longer time than ten days and were then taken up, washed, and transplanted into soil, the plants were taller, grew better and gathered more nitrogen from both the soil and the air ever after, than when the first ten days of their growth were in a lime-free sand.

Additional trials with other seeds have demonstrated the earlier emergence and better stands of the crop when the seeds were coated with lime or when this plant nutrient was dusted into the soil along with the planting of the seeds. All of these demonstrations indicate that the calcium of the lime is beneficial by the entrance of the calcium early into the seedling stage of plant growth.

More refined experiments were required to demonstrate the fact that lime as calcium and not as carbonate serves to mobilize or move other nutrients into the crop. Korean lespedeza, originally imported and claimed as an *acid soil crop*, showed clearly its higher concentrations of nutrients other than calcium, when the soil was given this element by the soil treatment of liming.

By growing test plants in a colloidal clay-sand mixture, it was shown that calcium was required to a relatively high degree of saturation on the clay, if the plants were to grow. As this degree of saturation was increased, or as the amount of clay with any degree of calcium saturation put into the sand was larger—to give the plants more calcium—there was more potassium, more nitrogen, and more phosphorus taken into the plants. Lime was the leader, apparently, of the nutrients and was bringing them into the plants.

Quite unexpectedly, it was discovered that when the calcium supply going from the colloidal clay into the plant was very meager, the nitrogen, the phosphorus, or the potassium might even be going in the reverse direction. This was taking place when plants like the soybeans seemed to be growing fairly well. In no case were any plants grown unless they were increasing in their calcium content by its migration from the soil into the plants.

Growth was impossible except as calcium was mobilizing itself into the crop early. Soybean plants that would look like a possible hay crop but not a seed crop had less nitrogen, or less phosphorus, or less potassium than the seed that was planted, because the soil did not offer enough calcium to mobilize these essential elements from the soil into the crop.

Here was ample reason for one to become lawyer for the defense of the un-suspecting cow that would be asked to consume a soybean hay crop grown on a lime deficient soil. This would be the case on soils for which the early pro-pagandists for this imported legume said,"this is a hay crop if not able to be a seed crop."

Fed on hay from this crop grown on such soils, the cow would gain less nitrogen, and less phosphorus, for example, on eating the hay crop than if she had eaten the seed that was originally planted. That a plant may be grow-ing and making vegetative bulk while it is losing nitrogen, or potassium, from the planted seed back to the soil may still be doubted. But when some of our animals demonstrate their health disasters on much that is called feed because it is plant growth, we ought to suspect that something like nutrients going in reverse direction might be taking place.

Lime as a soil treatment is quickly indicated by animal selection of the vegetation growing on it. All of this may be telling more than just more calcium recognized by the dumb beasts. It may be an indication of the better nutritional values created or synthesized within the crop because calcium has mobilized other fertility elements, as well as itself, into the crop more effec-tively.

Plants create nutritional values by means of calcium's nutritional service, and not by its removal of soil acidity.

SOIL . . . TO FEED US OR TO FAIL US

To the pioneer the climates were considered *good* or *bad* in relation to health. He often considered a change in climate as a remedy for bad health. Warm climates were the cure for tuberculosis at one time. But such temperatures with less rainfall and the foods on those less weathered, mineral rich soils were much better for health than was the case in the warm, moist climate and its mineral poor, protein deficient foods grown there.

The food, in terms of the fertile soil that is the result of the climate acting on the rocks, is what makes or breaks the body more than the comforts of the climate in terms of how wet or how dry, and how cold or how warm. The differences in the climate make differences in the fertility of the soil. The soil differences make the differences in the foods that either feed us or fail us. That failure is much in line with the proteins the soils produce or fail to produce.

Our own country is a good case for study of differences in climate. If one starts from the east side of the coast range with its desert and excludes the narrow Pacific area, to go eastward, there is a gradual increase in rainfall. There is a gradual increase in natural vegetation and in crop production. One is apt to emphasize the increase in water as responsible, rather than point out that the rocks are weathered more to make more soil and more nutrition from that source. Starting with the rock, this increase in rainfall is increase in weathering of it to make more soil with more clay in it. More rainfall is more soil *construction* in terms of its having enough clay to hold the essential nutrients, and to have enough of all of these to stock the clay for plant growth of the high protein nature, like legumes. This is our west. It is dry too often to support trees widely. It can grow grass since this crop can stop growing in a dry spell and then take off again. So our west is the plains country with its grass.

More significant is the soil construction in terms of its being well stocked with fertility. It has mineral rich, lime rich soils. Our west, beyond about the 97th meridian of longitude, has the calcareous soils. This nutrient is in the surface soil, often in the subsoil as a layer of *caliche*. Other nutrients too are still there, if the lime remains. Rainfalls are enough to give *soil construction*, but not *soil destruction* to wash out the lime and make the soil acid. Rainfall isn't enough to make massive grass growth. That very fact has left fertile soils that make every little bit of grass protein rich, mineral rich, and highly nutritious for protein production in the grass, in the wheat grain and in the bone and brawn of every little buffalo that soon became a big one and was able then, in turn, to make many more little ones.

In our East, that is east of the 97th meridian that divides our lime rich, protein producing soils from our acid soils, the increasing rainfall represents soil destruction, even though the clay content is high. Unfortunately the soil is weathered so highly that the carbonic acid from decay of vegetation had already taken most of the nutrients out and put acid, or the hydrogen ion, in its place. Plants putting their roots into that soil and offering to exchange

FEED THE SOIL TO FEED YOURSELF

Because animals play a large part in the final accounting of farm production, we are beginning to see the need of feeding animals better by adding fertility to the soil. And animals tell us, unfortunately, that they are not as certain of meat and dairy products as they used to be.

Much of this uncertainty may be traced right back to declining fertility in the soil. When we get only a 70% calf crop, we are inclined to blame the bull, since he is "half the herd." When only one animal needs to be sacrificed to correct a 30% trouble, we are likely to sell the bull and pin our faith anew on another one that may not give us even a 70% calf crop.

Reproduction is a delicate physiological performance. The fecundity of both female and male is influenced more by the soil than by the pedigree. Soils with depleted fertility produce forages that are consequently deficient in the plant compounds fabricated from the soil minerals. This means that shy breeders and aborters will be more numerous.

During wintertime, fuel value feeds are not of great help in fetus production, which demands calcium and phosphorus liberally. When a cow calves and goes into milk production, the demand on her body for daily delivery of calcium and phosphorus increase. Some soils are too deficient in these nutrients to enable the cow to go through pregnancy without developing acetonemia in late stages. Should she carry on her fetus building under strain, by sacrificing much of her own skeletal calcium and phosphorus for the offspring, she may break down in milk fever.

"Pregnancy disease," especially among ewes carrying twin fetuses, offers similar testimony. Rickets in calves, in spite of sunshine for vitamin D and of ample volume of milk, occur on soils highly exhausted of fertility.

Thus, animal deficiencies point the finger of responsiblity back to the soil and not to the drugstore. Fortunately, for better feeding values in grains and forages, and in the vegetable and animal products for human consumption, we see the need of putting the essential nutrient elements, calcium and phosphorus, back into the soil through a soil improvement program.

their root acid or hydrogen for calcium, magnesium, potassium, ammonia and other nutrients get little but their own acid back in the exchange. As a consequence they can make carbohydrates—woody, starchy growth—but they do little to convert those into proteins. Protein-producing crops like the legumes starve unless we fertilize the soil.

The pilgrim fathers found our East covered with forest trees. This woody crop was all the creator himself was making on those washed-out, so-called acid soils. More washed-out as they were in New England, the forests were conifers, not even hard woods giving a little protein crop in their seeds. And those still more washed-out by the higher temperatures on going south, again made only a coniferous forest crop possible even in nature, dropping all the leaves and their fertility reserves back annually to decay and rotate through succeeding crops.

Much rain to grow much vegetation may mean soils so washed out, or so low in fertility, that more bulk means less protein. It means less of the foods that really build the body by making muscle and other proteins. Big yields of vegetation may therefore be deceptive in terms of building the body and guaranteeing the reproduction. Higher temperature added to much rain aggravates the situation all the more, even though we may point with pride to big yields of tons or bushels per acre.

The pattern of woody growth of forests in the East, and of nutritious grass in the West, is an expression of the soil as fertility for protein production, more than an expression of more rainfall for bigger yields in the former and less in the latter. That pattern puts our preferred, high protein meat animals for beef in the West. It puts our short-lived, fat producer, the pig, in the East. *Grow* foods in the West, and only *go* foods in the East is an expression of differences in climate, yes; but more because these differences make differences in the soils representing either construction or destruction, in terms of their growing crops that feed us (protein) or fail us (fat).

Soil for creation of new life, more than for the fattening of an old one, is a challenge of managing the soil fertility. Nature suggests that grass to be nutritious cannot be moved about and will not feed us merely because it grows. It will fail us if we merely move it from the West to the East. If we move the grass that once made the buffalo, and makes the beef today, we must duplicate the soil fertility to feed the grass as well as it was fed in the West. Plants, like seals, will not perform well unless we feed them well. As the soils feed or fail the crops we grow, so will those crops feed or fail us in good nutrition.

FRINGE SOILS

It has often been said that most discoveries are the result of accidents, but only for the minds prepared to make them."

The truth of that statement was experienced recently by one of the consultants of the Brookside Research Laboratories, New Knoxville, Ohio. He was called to observe a case of core rot of a field of onions just going into storage. Very soon he had a similar request where nematode attacks had destroyed a field of carrots.

In both cases, the use of soil tests and the prescription of balanced fertility, as plant nutrition applied accordingly, restored the same successive crops to healthy production on the same fields. The fungus rot and the nematodes were thereby prevented. No cures were used. Instead, healthy and not sick crops were marketed thereafter. Prevention, at no special cost for such but by an investment in creative powers, was a profitable discovery for the mind prepared for it.

But that mind did not emphasize the fact of discovery. Rather it went to work, in practice, to deliver the next onion crop as a healthy one, and the next carrot crop pest-free. The consultant replaced the previous crop disasters by restored earnings for the commercial gardeners, by pay for arduous labor, by the costs of business maintenance, and by taxes paid on the land. The gardeners were not put out of their business of growing health-giving foods via fertile soils, rather than carrying sickly ones of poor food values on to the harvests by means of sprays and other dangerous chemicals.

Both these discoveries that "an ounce of prevention" in the form of balanced plant nutrition from fertile soils "is better than a pound of cure" in the form of dangerous poisons, were made on sandy soils. Those were "fringe soils" for any crops to be high in self-protection by proteins of their own make. Fringe soils cannot readily produce (a) growth, (b) self-preservation, and (c) fecund reproduction, as is the case for soils (a) with more clay holding larger supplies of available nutrient elements, and (b) more organic matter to carry into the plants, both the ash elements and larger organic nutrient molecules, whose nutritional services we do not yet comprehend fully.

When most virgin soils in the mid-continent were (a) well stocked with humus in their deep surface layers, and (b) given annual dust deposits of windblown, less weathered, nutrient-rich, rock mineral fertility, like loess; we have been slow to see failing or sickly crops as evidence of their troubles on "fringe" soils. Soil depletion is putting more and more acres of them under that classification.

It is such observations by keen-eyed consultants that are discovering that once fertile soils are reclassifying themselves into the fringe group. Early discovery means prompt remedies. Those can come by prevention which always surpasses cures. Simultaneously, prevention of diseass only silicon and oxygen. Those mineral grains do not weather down."

That is the reason the quartz crystals are still big grains. It never has weathered. It is a kind of soil skeleton. "Consequently, for the time being," we said, "let's throw that soil out of our mind and concentrate on the silt."

It also can be quartz. But then, too, it can be other than quartz. Its composition depends on the place where it is. The farther east one goes in the United States, and to the higher rainfalls, the more quartz there is in the silt of the soil. Silt doesn't have much capacity to hold fertilizer—neither does sand.

Because of their large particle size, these two have little capacity to absorb and to exchange nutrients to plants. But yet there is much silt blown in here from the floodplains of the Missouri River and from the west. It piles up along the river bluffs to give what is fairly good soil.

Thus the soils were catalogued for their order of importance for research attention. The silt fraction was set aside for later study when the initial study took to the clay soil.

We began with the claypan soil and its high content of clay since almost everybody wanted to enlist himself in what might be a fight with that tight clay. The early researchers bought and used much dynamite on it. They dug ditches of various kinds in it. They pushed it around with powerful machines. About the time they would have the treatment complete, the soil was behaving just about the way it was before.

FEED YOUR PLANTS WELL

There are increasing cases of evidence that good nutrition means good health. This is not an unfounded belief built on or propagated by mere fancy. It was that belief of many years ago that gave us the age-old saying that "To be well-fed is to be healthy."

That such is true also for plants was demonstrated in some of the first research using the finest portion, or the colloidal clay fraction of the soil, for nutritional experiments with soybeans as the best crop.

This finest fraction was separated out of the soil and washed in the electrolytic treatment to remove all the positively charged nutrient elements from the clay, and to replace them with the hydrogen, or the acid, ion. Such a clay, completely saturated with hydrogen, was an acid strong enough to represent a pH value of 3.6. One could then replace the hydrogen to any desired degree by correspondingly charged nutrient ions, thereby varying the soil acidity to any degree desired. More or less, clay could be put into quartz sand as means of varying the total of the nutrient ion or ions considered for plant nourishment.

Plants were put out according to this scheme to study nodule production and nitrogen use from the atmosphere by soybeans at different degrees of soil acidity—or degrees of calcium saturation of the clay—and at different amounts of total calcium offered per plant.

This same scheme served to demonstrate different degrees of susceptibility to fungus attack, varying from severe to absence . . . according as the increasing amounts of very acid clay, pH 4.4, put into the sand, offered increasing quantities of calcium or lime to each soybean plant. Quite unexpectedly, the diseased condition appeared in some of the pots while the plants in others were perfectly healthy. On careful observations of the quadruplicate plantings, it was evident that as there was more clay put into the sand (left to right in photo), there was less fungus attack.

It was not the high degree of soil acidity that was responsible for attack by the fungus on the plants, even though the clay was so acid that over three-fourths of its entire capacity for adsorption and exchange was taken up by the hydrogen or acid ion. Diseased and healthy plants were all on the same acid soil or exposed to the same degree of acidity. But with more of the calcium carrying (though acid) clay for more root contact in the sand-clay mixture, more calcium was taken up by the plants. It was this increasing amount of calcium, or lime, offered on more of the clay, even if it was a very acid one, that made healthy plants.

Here was an irrefutable demonstration that our plants, as well as our people, are telling us a basic fact of nature: that to be well-fed is to be healthy.

SOIL FERTILITY AND NUTRITIVE FOOD VALUES

We are gradually coming to believe that the soil, in terms of the food it grows, is a controlling factor in agricultural creation. The pattern of the soil fertility has only recently been worked out. That this fertility pattern maps out the nutritional quality of feeds and foods is not yet widely recognized or appreciated. We have been measuring our agricultural output in terms of only bulk and weight increase, rather than in terms of nutrition, reproduction, and better survival of the species. By subscribing to the production criteria of more tons and more bushels, we have watched the crops but have forgotten the soils that grow them.

When the dwindling fertility makes protein producing and mineral producing crops hard to grow, we fail to undergird them with soil treatment for their higher nutritional values in growing young animals. The life of the soil is not attractive. The death of it is no recognized disaster. The provision of proteins is our major food problem. Carbohydrates are easily grown.

Our reluctance to credit the soil with some relation to the nutritive quality of our feeds and foods, is well illustrated by the belief, persistent during the last quarter of a century, that the acidity of the soil is injurious, and that the benefit from liming lies in fighting this acidity. In truth, it lies in its nourishment of the plants with calcium and its activities in their synthesis of proteins and other food essentials. As yet we do not appreciate the pattern of soil fertility in the United States.

When a crop begins to fail, we search far and accept others if they make bulk where the predecessor didn't. We credit the newcomer with being "a hay crop but not a seed crop." If it cannot guarantee its own reproduction via seed, we call it feed for the cow.

The grazing animals have been selecting areas according to better soils. They have been going through fences to the virgin right-of-way. They have been grazing the very edges of the highway shoulders, next to the concrete, to their own destruction on the Coastal Plains soils. All these are animal demonstrations that the nutritive quality of feeds is related to the soil that grows it. But, to date, the animals rather than their masters, have appreciated this fact most.

Shall we keep our eyes closed to the soil's creative power via proteins, organo-inorganic compounds, and all the complexes of constructive and catalytic services in nutrition?

When the health and functions of our plants, our animals, and ourselves indicate the need, isn't it a call for agricultural research to gear production into delivery of nutritional values related to the fertility of the soil, rather than only those premised on bulk and the ability to fill?

By directing attention to the soil for its help in making better food, we may possibly realize the wisdom in the old adage that "to be well fed is to be healthy" and that good nutrition must be built from the ground up.

MINERAL HUNGER

Fortunately, we are better able to combat hungers at the point of origin, namely in the soil, than at any later stage in the agricultural assembly line. At that point, the problem is no more complex, probably, than supplying one or more of a few simple inorganic elements. A little effort there cures the deficiencies that cause the hidden hungers of the soil microbes and the plants. Properly fed plants prevent deficiencies in their synthetic products that serve as animal feeds and human foods. Here are solved the problems of providing the hosts of essential chemical compounds, the required amino acids, the necessary vitamins and the specific fatty acids. These problems of provision in the diet are more nearly insurmountable than those of getting some dozen elements—both major and minor—applicable as fertilizers on the soil. At any later stage the problem is more complex and the situation more prone to induce the micro-hungers.

Lespedeza hay grown after phosphate application and fed to sheep caused them to grow fleeces that were low in fat or yolk that scoured out too poorly to be carded except as broken fibers. Yet the same plant species grown on soil given both lime and phosphate helped to grow fleeces of heavy yolk and wool that scoured well and carded out as fibers of good quality for spinning and weaving.

Treating the soil to grow good quality wool was as simple as giving the soil some extra fertility in the form of calcium. Just what should have been chosen as the particular supplement to make this deficient lespedeza hay better sheep feed, so as to make better wool, is a problem not so simply and easily solved. It is clearly a case of hidden hunger, the *cure* of which is extremely perplexing but the *prevention* of which is as simple as the practice of liming the soil.

In our thinking about diseases, both empirical and scientific knowledge are influencing us to think less about cure and more about prevention by ministrations to sick soil. Once the mind thinks soil fertility, observations come rapidly.

Calves eating plaster, not the exposed first coat but the hidden last coat, in a fine barn prompted a farmer to ferret out a magnesium deficiency in his soils. Prompted by curiosity and intelligence to use some magnesium as a fertilizer he started a train of apparent miracles, including the curing of scours in calves, and some reduced mortality, less mastitis in the cows, better alfalfa, better corn, and other blessings in his farming program. When other major and minor elements given the cattle make them negative to the blood test for brucellosis, and when medical research is pointing to similar good suggestions of improvement of undulant fever patients, these are no longer hidden troubles. Attention to the soil fertility, the point of their origin as deficiencies rather than as diseases, is making them major hungers for major attention by more of us than those in the curative professions alone.

It can truthfully be said that rapid progress is being made in recognizing hidden hungers. Many of them are now being prevented because they are being diagnosed as originating in our declining soil fertility. Foremost among the gross nutrient factors of serious decline are those connected with the synthesis of proteins by plants. Soil treatments are no longer appreciated only because they encourage production of greater bulk per acre. They are being made on increasing acreages because they add nutritional qualities to relieve the long chain of hidden hungers coming up from the soil through the entire biotic pyramid to torment man at the top.

For better reproduction of farm animals, and for the better health for them and for ourselves as well, we are becoming increasingly concerned to know more about the fertility of the soil as the means by which such good fortune can be guaranteed. The disturbing and perplexing micro-hungers are hidden mainly from our thought, our recognition, and our full appreciation of their origin. They are not hidden from our body physiology nor from our mental processes when as little iodine, for example, as a fraction of a grain coming from the soil up through the plants to us is all that stands between us and imbecility.

It is a good sign for the future that we are coming to realize that our hidden hungers are provoking deficiencies in mind as well as body. We are coming to think about keeping up the soil in order to keep us mentally able to realize that our hidden hungers are pointing to the soil fertility as ready means for their prevention.

AMINO ACIDS IN LEGUMES ACCORDING TO SOIL FERTILITY

Agriculture and gardening are concerned with the synthesis of food. Our ultimate goal in this has always been the increase of production, *i.e.* greater numbers and more pounds per acre. Too often only such physical attributes of the products—even of people—are of prime consideration when some other criteria are of more fundamental importance. We neglect the quality of our food products and continue to measure our output only in bushels and tons per acre.

When the soil fertility declines, our attempts to adapt crops to a lower level of plant nutrition becomes a fallacy, that is, in terms of the demands of the human or animal diet. Of the many requirements of any diet, protein presents itself for first consideration. In the growth of any healthy animal, the major problem is this one of obtaining sufficient protein of the quality commensurate with good nutritional demands. Just as the furnace must be constructed prior to its service in consuming fuel, so must ill animals use proteins to build their bodies, prior to any consideration of their expenditure of energy.

In the animal the mere hanging on of fat is much of a luxury performance to which we have all wantonly subscribed. In agriculture we must become concerned with the biosynthesis of the building stones of the body; namely, the amino acids making up the proteins, and not be content to adopt as our criterion the photosynthesis of the carbohydrates composing the plant bulk.

While this plant bulk may reflect other factors of the environment, we have been able to trace many of our nutritional problems to the effects of the ash constituents coming via the plant. These soil-borne nutrients control plant metabolism more than we yet appreciate.

Biosynthesis requires these inorganic elements, not only to catalyze various reactions within the plant, but also to fashion and to build its structure. In turn, animals depend on the plants to synthesize the protein constituents for them. Herein lies the vital function of the soil. According as the different soils deliver divergent quantities of the inorganic elements, so we experience the pattern in the ecological array of the plant species. Each species represents a different organic composition according to the differences in the soil fertility.

In order to determine what fertility elements might be the cause of the diversities, alfalfa was grown on a single soil given treatments of the separate trace elements, manganese and boron, and a mixture of these with some others, as supplements to the common fertilizer elements calcium, phosphorus and potassium. Wide diversity in the amino acid array in the protein could scarcely be expected when relatively small amounts of these trace elements are applied on the surface of the soil. Yet the quality of the alfalfa protein in terms of its constituent amino acids was modified by these soil treatments, as shown in the accompanying table.

While a marked diversity manifested itself in the case of each amino acid, the methionine content varied most widely of all the amino acids measured in this study. Seemingly these results substantiate the hypothesis that these two trace elements, manganese and boron, function in the conversion of the carbohydrate into protein.

AMINO ACID CONTENT OF ALFALFA HAY ACCORDING TO SOIL
TREATMENTS WITH TRACE ELEMENTS

(Percentage of Dry Leaves)

Plot No.	Treatment	Valine	Leucine	Arginine	Histidine
1	Calcium	2.19	4.37	0.380	0.654
2	Calcium and manganese	2.40	4.89	0.434	0.807
3	Calcium and boron	2.13	5.55	0.418	0.726
4	Calcium and mixture*	2.59	5.24	0.415	0.835

Mixture of cobalt, copper, zinc, manganese, and boron.

Threonine	Tryptophane	Lycine	Isoleucine	Methionine
0.862	0.546	1.57	2.64	0.100
0.954	0.640	2.12	3.63	0.242
1.071	0.856	2.13	4.09	0.173
1.014	0.670	1.87	3.44	0.229

TOO MUCH NITROGEN?

That plants may go on a nitrogen jag has long been pointed out by the grazing cow. She lets the rich green spots of grass grow taller, while she grazes the short grass.

She can balance the protein and carbohydrate in her diet as she grazes selectively in her pasture. That is why she leaves more white clover but less bluegrass. That is why, by June, the pasture is mainly white clover.

Those deep green grass spots, fertilized by much nitrogen, do not appeal to her as providing a balanced diet perhaps, and so she by-passes them. At any rate, her body physiology directs her appetite to balance her ration. The excess of nitrogen represents an unbalance to her, and she says so by refusal.

"Too much is too much" only in relation to something else. If too much nitrogen is used in relation to the supply of phosphate, potash, calcium, or other growth factors, the unbalanced situation causes trouble.

We do know that when the right amount of nitrogen is available, and other necessary factors are adequate, then growth and yield can be truly spectacular. That animals instinctively select food which provides a balanced ration was suggested by some work by Dr. George E. Smith. In his test, rabbits were fed grasses grown on soil that had been treated only with nitrogen. (This work was part of studies leading to the bioassay of soil fertility, by using the animal to measure the value of soil treatment rather than a mere increase of yield in bulk.)

Nitrogen fertilizer on the grass, it was true, made a large and luscious green growth, if only the human eye judged it. But the rabbits, when fed the grasses from areas with different soil treatments, had their own criteria for judging the resulting food values.

The seemingly beautiful green, nicely cured grass hay was consumed only as a partial defense against starvation. And it did not keep the rabbits from getting dangerously close to that before their death was prevented by shifting the ration. Other rabbits, given grass hay from plots that had no soil treatment, maintained themselves by consuming the ration more completely.

In dealing with a ration of fertility elements for plants, we too commonly consider the plant ration as merely the sum of the separate items: of calcium, plus nitrogen, plus phosphorus, plus each of all the others necessary. These are taken into the plant and eventually delivered through it to the manger and thereby to the animal for its use. Through chemical analysis of plants, we believe that soil fertility is a collection of some ten or more elements taken from the soil for the use of animal and human bodies.

This concept suggests that, if that is all we need to do, we might just as well use a shovel and truck to haul calcium as limestone from the crusher to the mineral box. As a curative help to an animal already in disaster this may have some value. It illustrates the widespread failure to appreciate that plant nutrition is not as simple as limestone, plus phosphate, plus potash, plus any other thing in any amount merely dumped on the soil to produce crops to haul to the feeding rack.

An important matter in plant nutrition is the fact that plants must eat where they are. Unlike the cow, they can't pass up the place where there is too much nitrogen. Consequently, they run their own manufacturing business—or synthesizing the fertility of the soil into organic combinations by means of air and water—the best they can.

If there is much nitrogen, the plants weave this into chemical combinations with carbon, hydrogen, etc., that builds a lot of green vegetable bulk that may not keep the plant from lodging and may not result in seed to keep the species multiplying.

Root growth suggests that plants do make some selective searches through the soil. This is indicated when we find more roots around decaying organic matter, a piece of limestone, a granule of phosphate, or see the high concentration of roots in a fertilized portion or band in the soil. It is by such cafeteria-like browsing through the soil by the roots that the plant top is the final blending of fertility elements into the compounds that are built in a major way by photosynthesis. It is this soil fertility that enables the plant to determine the places where a certain kind of life is found in dominance. It is essential to point out that food which maintains the species registers its significance quickly and forcefully.

In considering the term *food,* one would scarcely give major emphasis to the caloric value of carbohydrates and fats as the commonly limiting factor. The delivery of calories is a function of most any carbon containing compound. The shortage of calories is not the first or most prevalent food deficiency. To date there has been no experimental suggestion that carbohydrates of specific chemical structure are required. We propose to consider proteins, and all that is associated with them, in their synthesis and transformation for nutritional services, as the major means of connecting soils and nutrition.

Since animals do not synthesize their proteins—or amino acids—from the elements, but are dependent for this creative activity and this nutritional support on the plants and the microbes (some of the latter living in the animal's alimentary tract), we must first undergird the plant's production of complete proteins, if our animals and we are to be well-fed in respect to this complex food constituent.

For an appreciation of the plant's struggle to elaborate the complete proteins for us generously, we must look to the many soil factors concerned. Different soil fertility factors represent differences in the array of amino acids, and in the amounts of each coming from the plants, as they are different species or as there are differences in chemical composition within the same plant species.

By such reasoning, then, human nutrition as a struggle for complete proteins goes back—not to agriculture as it represents industry or econonmics concerned with prices to be rolled back—but to fertile soils alone on which plants can create proteins in all completeness.

PROTEIN DEFICIENCIES . . . THROUGH SOIL DEFICIENCIES

Proteins alone are the substance through which life flows. This intensively concentrated study of the proteins bids fair to make the last half of the twentieth century the era of real nutrition. Unfortunately, it is the deficiencies of proteins—under failing nutrition and failing health—that are crowding this output of knowledge about them into such a limited time period.

Since proteins are the carriers of life, we may well learn of their nutritional services from biochemical investigations of them in the plants and animals as well as in man. Accordingly, it would be well to study what Dr. Fairfield Osborn, of Massachusetts Institute of Technology, would call comparative biochemistry, much as we study comparative anatomy.

That the microbe may be coming into its own in biochemistry is no flight of fancy. As a synthesizer of unusual compounds, its antibiotic products have attained prominence not only as protection but also as nutrition. We have been moving away from nutrition as a matter of merely dumping into the gastrointestinal hopper, the carbohydrates, fats, proteins, vitamins, minerals and water, as items measured and studied mainly as requirements in bulk for fuel. We have moved our thinking toward the delicately integrated functions of the chemical compounds for their services through their transformations.

This progress of integrating the comparative biochemistry of the entire biotic pyramid is particularly gratifying to a soil microbiologist and a student of soil fertility. It is gratifying to learn that not only the medical profession is using antibiotics for protection of man against invasion of himself by various microbes—even to the dangerous extent of sterilizing the entire intestinal tract—but also that nutritionists are turning from *fighting* to *courting* microbes, from the products of which we get highly improved nutritional values in all the food components when these are ingested together. But this movement of our thinking through comparative biochemistry from man down through animals and plants to the microbe should not stop there. Instead, it should lead our thought on down to the foundation of all life, to the base of the entire biotic pyramid, which is the soil fertility, the essential elements of the soil. It is from there that the synthetic performances, building all life forms, must take off.

The nutritional approach to so-called diseases has been showing much promise for better health. Students of the soil and its microbial flora see still greater promise for it, when the fertility of the soil under the vegetables and the forages rather than the species of the plant, name of variety, breed, or pedigree is recognized as the determiner of the nutritional values of those foods and feeds. That the invasions of the body by microbes should often be only symptoms of, and not responsible for, diseases, and that decadent health should be ascribed to malnutrition bringing on degeneration of tissues and functions are growing concepts of the facts. These concepts are being demonstrated in the mounting numbers of deaths from heart failure, cancer, diabetes, arthritis, anemias, leukemias, and arteriosclerosis.

The high value of proteins in nutrition for body regeneration is coming into prominence. It is now acknowledged by the profession itself that the "medical practice is highly dependent on nutrition." The use of protein hydrolysates for intravenous feeding during coma, ante- and post-surgery periods has already demonstrated nutrition, at high protein levels, as basic for recovery from disease regardless of whether this originates from degeneration or other causes. If these desperate situations of threatening death can be removed, or its grasping hand stayed off for a longer time—by the more complete list of amino acids suddenly thrown into the bloodstream—is it illogical to consider that the body's degeneration was possibly brought on by a long period of poor nutrition under protein deficiency?

Perhaps by looking at nutrition and the soil together, on a larger geographic scale or in a wider array, there will stand out more clearly the indications from the ecology of various life forms that protein deficiencies are provoked by deficiencies in soil fertility. By the term *ecology* we mean the particular order in the distribution of living species over the earth. Naturally, many factors come in to determine the places where a certain kind of life is found in dominance. It is essential to point out that food to maintain the species registers its significance quickly and forcefully.

In considering the term, *food,* one would scarcely give major emphasis to the caloric value of carbohydrates and fats as the commonly limiting factor. The delivery of calories is a function of most any carbon-containing compound. The shortages in calories is not the first or most prevalent food deficiency. To date there has been no experimental suggestion that carbohydrates of specific chemical structure are required. We propose to consider proteins, and all that is associated with them, in their synthesis and transformation for nutritional services, as the major means of connecting soils and nutrition.

Since animals do not synthesize their proteins—or amino acids—from the elements, but are dependent for this creative activity and this nutritional support on the plants and the microbes (some of the latter living in the animal's alimentary tract), we must first undergird the plant's production of complete proteins, if our animals and we are to be well-fed in respect to this complex food constituent. For an appreciation of the plant's struggle to elaborate the complete proteins for us generously, we must look to the many soil factors concerned. Different soil fertility factors represent differences in the array of amino acids, and in the amounts of each coming from the plants, as they are different species or as there are differences in chemical composition within the same plant species.

By such reasoning, then, human nutrition as a struggle for complete proteins goes back—not to agriculture as it represents industry or economics concerned with prices to be rolled back—but to fertile soils alone on which plants can create proteins in all completeness.

SUPPLEMENTARY REMARKS

When we speak of food and ask ourselves what's in it chemically to serve us fully, we come to the realization of how little we now know about the creation of ourselves in which the mind full of dust exercises the control. To the present discussion, let me add, if I may, the following supplementary remarks.

The soil contributes inorganic elements and some organic compounds, no doubt, for the nourishment of plants. Unfortunately, since our chemist has long been mainly an inorganic one, and recently an organic one, and since the former is so much simpler in concept and so much speedier in demonstration than to measure this contribution and thereby the soil's service for the nutrition of the plant and ourselves when we measure the concentrations of these as ash in the plant mass.

Such simple ash analyses fail to emphasize how important these inorganic contributions are in determining what the plant has synthesized for our dietary list of food compounds. On that list are those like the ten essential amongst the 20 old amino acids composing the proteins; like the between or more indispensible vitamins; or like the three required unsaturated fatty acids. Ash analyses fail to emphasize the differences in food output by plant activities because of different ratios of the inorganic elements in the ashy soot of them. Shifts in their relative amounts are not yet understood fully, much less appreciated, for the resulting shifts in carbohydrate, protein, vitamin, inorganics: etc., ratios. In speaking, then, of the variations in the minerals from the soil and within the plants, we are speaking symbolically. We are referring to those variations that may be very wide in both quantity and quality of nutrient output mainly as organics when we remind ourselves that these inorganics must be considered as doing much more than merely hitch-hiking from the soils to ourselves.

Plants contain very little of inorganic that is not of organic combination. They contain little that can be washed out by water. Our dietary essential "minerals" are taken, then, as organo-inorganic compounds. We are not actually mineral eaters. Neither are the animals. When any of them take to the mineral box isn't it an act of desperation? Cows eat soil or chew bones when ill with acetonemia, pregnancy troubles, or deficiency ailments. Hogs root only in the immediate post winter period after confinement to our provision for them and their behavior suggests past deficiencies to be quickly remedied in desperate digging of the earth. Observations of the wildlife and of our domestic animals in their choices prompt some powerful empiricism behind our ideas. Then, too, when the administering of the inorganics directly requires extremely large doses for effects in contrast to small amounts taken in food normally, shall we consider, then, that putting minerals on the tongue is a more wise health practice than putting them on the soil?

At first thought we all admit that the fertilization of all the tilled soils with all the fertility elements, major and minor, is a big order. However, is it an immediate necessity? Cannot a small pasture area so treated supply sufficient trace elements for the herds and flocks for a time? Would not a part of the garden treated likewise serve for the family? Very small dosages of the essential major or minor elements are required from the soil via plants, but when those of knockout magnitudes required as therapeutics are used to judge the amounts required for the soil treatments, our vision of the amounts required as fertilizers is decidedly distorted.

3

ASPECTS OF SOIL FERTILITY

Over a century ago the federal Congress pointed out the serious need for soil conservation. In view of this and also of the fact that conservation spells sound economics for those who manage and use the soil, it is disturbing that soil maintenance is still neglected.

In the printed report, *Executive Document Number 20, to the First Session of the 31st Congress by the Commissioner of Patents, the Honorable Thomas Ewbank, for the year 1849,* it is significant to note that this volume of assembled writings of capable authorities begins with emphasis on agriculture through the maintenance of the soil, which, they said, "should be carefully studied by everyone who desires to enjoy sound health and a long and happy life."

At that early date it was announced that the health of each of us is our own individual responsiblity, rather than the responsiblity of what is now confused as "public health" by administration (via medicated water supplies, for example). "Most of the ills that flesh is heir to, as well as maladies of plants," according to that document by the printers to the House of Representatives, "have their origin in the violation of nature's laws." Already the dependence of us all upon the fertility of the soil that is nutrition and health was recognized.

The initial paper of the annual report is by one Daniel Lee, M.D. He deplored the scant attention given to agricultural education. Even he began his remarks with emphasis on the soil. "It is indeed wonderful," he said (on the seventh page of the report of the Commissioner of Patents, under whom agriculture was listed at that early date), "how long those enlightened, reasoning farmers who, like Washington, cherish a due respect for their high calling, have had to beg and beg in vain of state legislatures, and of congress, for a little assistance to prevent the universal impoverishment of American soils. Whatever has been done to arrest the exhaustion of aerated lands has been effected not only without due aid from government, but in spite of a mistaken policy, which encourages the removal of all the elements of bread and meat from cultivated fields, and their speedy transportation beyond the possibility of restitution."

After six pages of citing the need for more agricultural statistics, Dr. Lee gives *A Few Facts About Soils* which deserve repetition, for they bear the same significance they did in 1849:

"Soils contain, as a general thing, not more than one part in a thousand of the atoms, in an available condition, which nature consumes in forming a crop of any kind. This statement expresses a fact of great practical importance; since the husbanding of these fertilizing atoms is the first step toward arresting the impoverishment of the earth. It is the matter in the soil which makes crops in one arrangement of its atoms, and forms manure in another condition of the same atoms, that the farmer should learn to preserve from waste and loss."[1]

"Soils of different degrees of productiveness, where their mechanical texture and physical properties are alike, always contain unlike quantities of the food of crops. It seems to make little difference how small is the amount of the lacking ingredient of the composition of cultivated plants. Its absence is fatal to the farther growth of the crop after its appropriate ailment fails in the soil. It is easy to discover the wisdom of this universal law."[2]

"Suppose nature should organize grass, grain and other plants, which serve as daily food of all the higher order of animals, as well without bone-earth (phosphate of lime) as with that mineral—would it be possible for such grass and grain to yield to the blood of domestic animals, and of man himself, that solid earthy matter which imparts strength to human bones and to those of oxen, horses, sheep and swine? Certainly not. Although *iron* is always present in the food and blood of animals, no farmer ever killed a calf, a pig, or an ox which had iron for the frame of its system. No anatomist ever saw a bone in a body of a person formed of other than the earthy atoms such as Providence has fitted for that peculiar function in the animal economy."

"The brains and muscles of all animals contain both sulphur and phosphorus, as constituent elements. If their daily food, derived as it is from the soil, lacked either sulphur or phosphorus, must not this radical defect in their nourishment soon induce weakness and disease, and finally result in premature death? To prevent consequences so disastrous and so obvious, nature refuses to organize plants without the presence in the soil, *in an available form,* of those peculiar atoms adapted alike to the wants of vegetable and animal vitality. This wise provision should be carefully studied by everyone who desires to enjoy sound health and a long, happy life."

"There are only some fifteen kinds of elementary bodies used by nature in forming every vegetable and animal substance produced on the farm, in the orchard, or in the garden . . . Every product of agricultural labor is either a vegetable or an animal substance; and in its production, not an atom of new matter is called into existence; nor is it possible to annihilate an atom when it decays."[3]

"In the language of science, all matter which is neither vegetable nor animal, including air and water, is *mineral.* All minerals are either solids, like sand, clay and lime; or liquids like water; or gases like common air. The farmer deals largely with atoms in each of these forms . . . He should know that plants alone subsist on mineral or disorganized food—that if it were not for plants in the ocean or on the land, neither marine nor land animals could have a being. In the absence of all vegetables it is obvious that all animals must be carnivorous or cease to consume the organized aliment. Being wholly dependent on mutual destruction for the means of subsistence, every day would diminish the aggregate supply of food, and the last animal would soon die of starvation."

It is helpful to reread some of these basic facts today, when the contention has been common that the soil has no effect on the nutritional or health values of the food products we consume. Also, when we and our food are so far removed from the soils that create both of us, the remarks by this doctor of medicine over a century ago are most significant. They verify the truth in the age-old statements, "We are what we are because of where we are," and "We are what we eat." There are many hidden helps for health in unopened books about nature's immutable laws exhibited by agriculture.

THE LIVING SOIL

When 85% of the population of the United States is urban and only 15% is rural,[1] it is quite evident that our high standards of living are expectedly associated with business, with economics, and with industrial activities of which the assembly line of technological manipulations may well be highly symbolic. By means of power, complicated machinery, numerous appliances, gadgets, etc., we have reduced the human labors connected with technology to the pushbutton dimension. It is in this technological sphere that we find our major progress. It is that progress which has put our people into a gradual population shift from one mainly nature made and rural about ten decades ago to one now so highly urban and man-made that the ratio of the latter to the former is more than five to one.

Nevertheless, when one sees the golf links near every city, and the parks within it, they suggest that the human being still yearns for the rural scene with its growing grass and all that the open country and its biological exhibitions of living, growing things can offer. Whether it be the backyard flower-gardening wife or the golf playing husband of the city dwelling couple, each is merely giving vent to the universal atavistic inclination to get back to the living soil. They exhibit their desires for contact with nature's assembly line out of doors by which the creation of growing things in the open country is so commonly brought about. That is an assembly line which starts and stops itself with the turn of the seasons but without concern or control by man.

Careful observation of any industrial assembly line, however, points out that it doesn't run itself. It has someone at each of the depots along its line feeding it with the respective parts in correct order and amount, if the production is maintained. Even there where the materials are inert, dead, fixed in quality, and not perishable; and where the final product is only a machine, or gadget; yet the living human mind is in direction of it.

The agricultural assembly line within the soil under Mother Nature's direction is no exception as to the many depots of it. The sand and the silt are the mineral reserve sections or depots. From them, by the weathering processes, the inactive nutrient elements of crystal structure are broken out to become ionicly active. Other elements, put into new combinations of different secondary minerals, form the clay. This is another and important depot along nature's assembly line within the soil. This is the major, seasonally active one in that its store of adsorbed nutrient elements must supply quickly the high demands for these by invading, growing plant roots. When once highly depleted, and in turn stocked with the non-nutrient hydrogen, or acidity, which is taken in exchange from the carbonic acid of the respiring root for what nutrients were passed on to it, the acid clay becomes an active weathering agent. It breaks the silt and sand reserve minerals down and restocks itself while we commonly believe that "The soil is resting."

The clay is the assembly line's major section or depot holding the exchangeable stock of calcium, magnesium, potassium and other cations, or those ions with positive electrical charges. It may also be holding some anions, or those with negative charges, like the phosphate, sulfate, nitrate, bicarbonate, and others. These latter, however, are more often held and passed on to the assembly line of agricultural production from the organic matter depots within the soil.

Thus within the soil there is a flow of fertility elements under their own activities from rock to the clay and from there to the root, all in the presence of ample moisture by which as a medium these ionic activities are possible. This fertility is the control by the soil of creation to which the sunshine supplies the power; the soil contributes the stored water; and the air gives the carbon dioxide originating mainly in root and microbial respiration in the soil; and in which the carbon and the water are fabricated by plants into the carbohydrates, i.e. sugars, starches, cellulose etc., or the energy foods for the plants, the animals, and man. Thus the green chlorophyll of the leaves really creates what is truly food for the plants. It is from the digestion of these that the plant gets its biochemical energy when it burns within its cells the sugars, or the fats made from these sugars, just as we do in burning carbohydrates and fats in our bodies. It is from the burning of parts of these compounds in the plant tissue that energy is provided to make the nitrogen combine into some of the changed carbohydrates and thus to synthesize the life carrying proteins.

Plants so growing and dying with their decaying roots left in, and tops returned to the soil are the organic matter from the digestion of which the microbial life within the soil must get its energy. It is thus that there results a living soil. Under virgin conditions then, or starting from the beginning of the mineral earth, the soil is first a rock that is making a temporary rest stop on its way to solution and to the sea. But soon it is no longer dead, inert, wholly inorganic, or of no more than plant ash equivalent. It is changed from the inorganic and the dead mineral material to become the organic and the living soil. It contains carbon. It supports a microbial flora. It contains a micro and macro flora. It has a micro and macro fauna. It is combustible. It takes in oxygen. It gives out respired carbon dioxide. It is truly living.

Soil is not a technological assembly line where only collections of the non-living are built together, or merely assembled and managed by man. Instead, it starts with the inorganic determiners of the course of creation. When a microbial spore, a dormant seed, a rootlet, a cutting, all living parts from other life, give the opportunity, these determiners at the various depots integrate—not only add—their contributions. The inorganic materials in a limited or less limited list of elements set the degree of complexity of the creation. The organic matter adds its many items as elements in cycle, and in the form of compounds not fully recognized as yet or understood in plant nutrition for their hindrance or their help. It is then the living soil that truly creates, since the organic matter under decay contributes compounds actually taken by plants roots as we know sugars, vitamins, and other compounds are. Thus it is a living soil with its assembly line integrating its many items which in summation mean growth by living forms.

Because our daily experiences of our own living are so extensively and intimately geared to technology, and because so many of us are too far removed from what is truly biology, the growth not only of our agricultural crops but even of those non-agricultural is viewed as if it were a technological matter which we could readily manage. In the argument for that, there is often cited the hydroponic tank with no more than water and a collection of salts of the inorganic or the ash constituents of the crops to be grown. But we have not demonstrated the hydroponics as means of growing very many kinds of crops, save for those which are mainly a vegetative, cellulosic mass carrying much water, sugar, and starch. Tomatoes, potatoes, spinach, flowers, and similar crops whose reproduction potential has not been tested for a series of generations of growth under hydroponics, have been the demonstrators of this procedure. As a challenge to the hydroponic technology using the flowing, very dilute, often replenished, inorganic solutions, let us ask the proponents of this method (who are probably opponents of the highly organic soil as a necessity for crops) to grow one crop of mushrooms in their hydroponic tank as a substitute for the rotted manure of the mushroom bed. The crop growth by hydroponics, claimed to be rapid, is no match for the speed with which the mushroom mycelia literally run through the bed and grow the mushroom crop.

But, as a beginning and for a good start in our understanding of what makes things grow, the hydroponic idea is a very helpful demonstration. It uses the water as a means to dilute the inorganic salts. It obviates the danger of too much salt. It permits renewal of the salt supply, since only by an enormous amount of water under such required dilution could enough salts be delivered to mature the crop. Water, however, is the medium for ionization of the salts to make their elements active for root entrance. Soil areas of crop production must contain both water and fertility compounds. Dry soils with salts in excess are the saline and alkaline areas with no crops. Hydroponic technology uses solutions so dilute that it duplicates the laws of gaseous behaviors and does not duplicate the soil where within root-reach the nutrient supply dare not be in highly concentrated salt form but yet must be large enough in quantity and in active form to mature a significant crop.

Soil, as the assembly line, is then far different from hydroponics. So is the mushroom bed with its rotted manure. Decaying organic matter in the soil, similar to the clay there, is a colloid on which absorbed nutrient elements are held, and from which they are exchanged to the plant roots. Also for the nutrient release, by the decay of the organic matter in the soil, the increasing rate of this process is timed to be highest when the seasonal conditions suit the speediest growth of the crop. Nature has synchronized these two performances, *i.e.* the decay of the residues of past crops and the growth of a new crop, by making the increased rate of decay of the organic matter within the living soil provide the means of increased nutrition of the crop above the soil. Hence, the cause of the crop growth is a living soil under nature's management. Crop growth is not the result so much then, of a technology under man's manipulation. Rather, it is an exhibition of the biology of Mother Nature.

Organic decay is an agency for the increased weathering of the disintegrated rock. By it the living soil makes the dead rock elements become active to support more life. Our thinking has not pushed forward our understanding of what makes things grow. Our comprehension of those processes has not gone much beyond the "solution" idea of hydroponics. We have not yet seen the soil as the handful of dust into which the moist breath is blown by the weather and can mean the creation of life. There is reason then why for so many folks there is as yet no concept of "a living soil." Hence, there can be no living soil in their vision when so commonly "We are down on what we are not up on."

That the soil is living may well be illustrated in trying to bring about a loose soil structure in a flower pot or in the putting green of a golf course by mixing peat, sawdust, or other cellulosic matters with the soil, and then discovering that the potted plant or the grass crop does not grow well as a consequence. Very often the plant or crop turns yellow. The grass appears to be "burning out" and fails in spite of good rain or applied water. The farmer experiences the same with the damage to a fall-seeded wheat crop after turning under much straw of a preceding wheat or oat crop, or the stubbles of a matured soybean crop. The wheat crop following the turning under of such cellulosic organic matter, supposedly to enliven the soil, is said to be "burned out." On the contrary, it is apt to be "starved out" for the nitrogen taken away from it by the living soil's crop of living microbes. These are in competition with the grass sod crop of the golf green or with the wheat crop of the farmer or with the plant in the pot, not so much for water as for nutrients.

The living soil must, first of all, be balanced nutrition for the microbes, the major life of the soil. This life in the soil is the soil's primary crop that must be properly fed. It eats at the first table set in the soil. The grass crop, or any other supra-soil growth, eats at the second table. The high carbohydrate contents of the sawdust, the peat or the straw are not carbohydrates of energy value to the plants. Plants use sunshine energy and chlorophyll to make their own energy foods by photosynthesis. But plowed under and buried into the soil, those highly carbohydrate substances are energy food for the microbes with too little nitrogen or protein added along with it or stored in the soil to balance this large allotment of carbon. They draw that nitrogen supply in the soil down far below the level required for nourishing the competing crop with nitrogen. Thus the living soil given too much of only energy supply in the organic matter and too little growth-promoting nitrogen or protein with it, feeds even the microbes with a poor diet. As a consequence, their competition with the crop means just that much too poor a diet for the latter. The agricultural crop is thus "burned out" and must be a poor one because it was on a truly living soil. But that living soil was one not fertile enough to feed two families, namely, first the microbes under Mother Nature's management, and second, the crop plants under human nature's management.[2]

Nutrition from the soil for microbes and for the plants may be under not only a shortage of any element, but also under imbalances in regard to combinations of many of the nutrient elements when we manage the soil as only a technological procedure that dumps on fertilizers, whether organic or inorganic, in the belief that "If a little is good more is better." This policy of generous applications of even the supposedly insoluble limestone rock as a soil treatment has now shown itself a case of poor biology though it might be considered good economics and excellent technology. Fortunately, the microbial life of the soil tolerates any shocks of imbalance in soil treatments better than they are tolerated by our crops. The living soil can stand up under shock better than the crop can. Hence, the naturally higher levels of organic matter in our virgin soil and the accompanying much larger numbers of highly active microbes, have been what might well be called the "constitution" of the soil.

This term implies about the same as the doctor indicates when in speaking of his patient he says, "He has a good constitution." By that statement the doctor merely designates the biological capacity of his patient to survive in spite of, rather than because of, the doctor's technological treatments. Our soils of high organic matter contents have thereby had "good constitutions" through the protection of which the commercial fertilizer prescriptions have been successful rather than because of the knowledge of their biological function and behaviors in the soil exhibited by those prescribing them. If then we are to grow good crops of nutritious food, a good grass agriculture feeding our livestock, a fine lawn, or an excellent putting green, which can continue to grow while we cut it back often, it is well to build up the soil in organic matter as well as in the inorganic chemicals. That means a good soil constitution to grow the grass in spite of, if not because of, the able superintendent and all he tries in hoping to make the grass grow continually.

Growth of any vegetation is always promoted by cell multiplication (except in some cases like the watermelon in which what seems to be growth occurs because the cells are only expanded by putting in more water). Any cell multiplication calls not for carbohydrates, not for fats, but for proteins delivered regularly, and all else usually accompanying the proteins. Proteins are also required for protection against disease, and for reproduction of the species. If the growth of a grass in a pasture, on a lawn, or on a golf green is to be maintained, the soil's assembly line must be delivering fertility steadily with nitrogen and all other required helps for protein production coming both prominently and regularly. Any protein synthesis calls for many life processes supporting it. They need not be merely in gear or running. Instead they must all be doing so in complete integration, coordination, and interaction with each other. It calls, therefore, also for many intrasoil conditions like aeration, relative moisture, limits of temperatures, and others as well as certain supra-soil conditions for the processes to run the plant's assembly line of making carbohydrates, proteins, fats, vitamins, etc., from the elements and compounds to be truly growth. "Better" pasture grasses are not necessarily "better" as feed for the animals because they make more mass and more complexity of the protein. Better grasses must make more protein to protect themselves from diseases. They are also makers of protein in seed as their method of reproduction in place of multiplying by cuttings, rhizomes and other vegetative means of keeping the species surviving. We must see the plant struggling to grow itself, to protect itself and to multiply itself. We must help it in those objectives of its own survival first and its services to us second.

In this there is a basic principle, namely, that the grasses in their growth are a living body. There are many requirements to be satisfied if the physiological processes within the plant are to be maintained at a high level. Also, only as those functions are more numerous and more complex do we have vegetation that is apt to be called "better." It can be such only as the soil is "better" in its fertility supply, in the moisture, in the air, and in the biological dynamics which keep it living and active in all that a soil does when it grows a plant. To keep on growing is the plant's struggle for which we give it all too little support via the soil.

First of all we like grasses best, whether pasture, lawn or golf green, that keep on growing regularly. But we clip grass back and give it little chance to grow tops by which to build reserve nutrients into the root system. That root system is therefore shallow. Regrowth after every clipping back calls for nutrient reserve in the roots and a high level of fertility for protein-making since only protein synthesized within the plant results in plant growth. Instead, we dodge that nutritional responsibility to any plant that can serve us. We start to search for another grass as if grasses could be found that will tolerate starvation coming via the soil. Only as the soils are living providers of the soil fertility and an environment which keeps grasses producing protein—not just vegetative bulk—can a crop be expected to be kept on living, especially if pruned back regularly by the cow or the lawn mower.

The imbalance of fertility for a shallow-rooted crop is common if we expect to grow it by a hydroponic procedure with a dead soil serving as only the site for the demonstration. Salts and water are too much of a shock treatment. That kind of treatment represents much of what is man's struggle to make grasses grow themselves. But after composting the fertilizer salts with the organic matter to let the microbes take the shock and bring about their own quick recovery, as is true in the compost pile, the composted and transformed salts combined with the decayed plant residues represent a new constitution for the soil. Such composted matter put into the soil represents better microbial liberation of fertility, more water retention, regular temperatures and a timing of the rate of decay by the season to keep grasses growing.

Naturally there are some climatic limitations for truly "living" soil. One must therefore appreciate man's possible error in his high hopes to grow certain grasses where he fails to observe that nature never grew them. Bowling on the lawn is common in Great Britain. The game of golf rose to its height in one section of that country. Pastures are the ideal of the Herefords, the Aberdeen Angus, the Shropshire, the Clydesdale and other animals with British sounding names, as real grazing. But when grasses are moved out of that setting as for example southward even within the north temperate zone into high temperatures and spasmodic distribution of rainfall, they are no longer "naturally" on what is truly "living" soil for them.

While we may think technology so readily under control of human nature, we dare not forget that the soil as a creative manifestation by Mother Nature is biology and not technology. Industry may readily exercise control of what it does, since it deals only in technology. But agriculture cannot exercise much control since it deals mainly in biology. Managing the soil is not just technology. It is also biology since the soils that truly feed us, that grow proteins, and that keep crops growing will do so only if they are truly living and not dead soils. They must be considered (a) in their climatic setting (b) in relation to the physiology of the crop they are to nourish, and (c) the biochemical as well as chemical services at all times in the growing season if their assembly lines are to put out the maximum for our pleasure and profit by the growing things.

TO KEEP THE SOIL A "LIVING" ONE

Some studies of the effects of incorporating organic matter regularly into the soil were undertaken by the Missouri Agricultural Experiment Station as far back as 1917.[1] *Agricultural Experiment Station Research Bulletin Accumulations* told us how much organic matter needs to go into a cultivated soil annually, if that soil is to maintain "the standard of its living" which it exhibited when broken out of its early sod. This record of the "living" soil has too long remained hidden.

Under natural climax crops all the produce of the soil is left on it. This decays in place and the return to the soil serves to build it up for its higher living, as measured by the accumulated nitrogen, the index of protein, or the living contents of cells. It is helpful to know just how much of the organic matter grown on a soil needs to go back annually to keep the living soil actively and healthily so. If the garden plot, or the field, is to be kept high in its organic matter content while its crops are hauled off, how much additional soil area must there be supplying the organic matter to keep it so? Then also, there is the question whether organic matter is the only addition to the soil needed to keep it living.

Beginning with 1917, some plots of Putnam silt loam soil were kept free of crops and of erosion under screen covers. Each plot was tilled once annually to duplicate the plowing and preparing of a seed bed. One series of plots was given no other soil treatment; a second series turned some dry, chopped red clover hay into the soil at the rate of two and one-half tons, or the equivalent of 106 pounds of nitrogen per acre; while the third series had the same additions, but these were applied after the tillage to leave the organic matter on the surface of the soil for its remains to be turned under by the tillage of the next year. Chemical measurements of the total nitrogen of the soil were made annually at tillage dates from 1918 to 1932 inclusive, or for a period of 15 years, in order to determine the changes in the soil's supply of organic matter during that period.

For this study it was necessary to import the clover as a growth from some other soil if we were to study the addition of the organic matter as an effect separated from that of the growth of the crop on the same soil. This allowed the microbial activities within the living soil to be measured in the absence of effects from the growth and organic additions of the roots of a crop. It aimed to determine the effects of added plant tops when the soil made no expenditures in plant production. Its only expenditure was in growing a microbiological crop, the one living within, and at the expense of, the organic matter of the soil.

The following are some of the basic facts that exhibit themselves via this soils study:

1. The increases obtained in the soil's nitrogen content when given the annual additions of clover differed by only the small figure of 3%, according as the clover was left on the surface or was mixed into the soil during

simultaneous applications and tillage. Since this advantage of 3% was in favor of the organic matter left on the surface, we are told thereby that the surface application did not volatize or leach any more than the incorporation into the soil.

Measured by the soil's increased store of nitrogen coming from the atmosphere via legumes, the surface application of organic matter, according to nature's plan, was more effective than man's practice of mechanically incorporating it into the soil.

2. Even with these heavy applications of nitrogen in leguminous organic matter, the soil's store of nitrogen was increased by no more than 20% (one-fifth) of the annually applied nitrogen. However, when this increase is corrected for the annual decline of the soil's store of nitrogen under tillage and under no additions of organic matter, the effects of adding the clover, for keeping the living soil actively so, approach an improvement by 33% (one-third) of the nitrogen applied annually.

3. For the untreated soils there was an annual loss or a decline in the store of nitrogen. This was equivalent to the upbuilding effect from one-half ton of clover, as demonstrated on the treated plots. Hence, this soil, living under fallow, requires one-half ton of clover (dry weight) annually merely as a "maintenance ration."

4. There were neither losses nor gains of nitrogen in the subsurface layer of the soils given no additions of organic matter. But, below the surface soil where the clover was incorporated, the subsurface gained more nitrogen than the corresponding lower layer under the area where the clover was left on the surface.

This tells us that its incorporation mobilized the nitrogen more rapidly into the subsurface soil. It suggests that applying organic matter as a surface mulch may be a more efficient use of its nitrogen as fertilizer for crops, so far as keeping a larger active store of nitrogen in the soil's surface layer is concerned.

5. These facts were obtained from a soil to which mineral dust was added naturally from the atmosphere by the prevailing winds, which brought it out of the southwest at the rate of 1,000 pounds per acre annually. This figure was obtained from the dust collectors for the study of the loessial deposits, such as the river bluffs, which came from the drier areas in the Missouri River's flood plain.

The dusts consist of naturally pulverized but unweathered rock minerals, according to examinations under special microscopes. These minerals have doubtless been a factor in the upbringing of nitrogen by organic matter on these shallow soils, underlain as they are by a plastic, hydrogen-saturated clay subsoil in which a slight increase in nitrogen resulted under addition of clover to the surface soil. What the nitrogen increase would have been in the absence of the additions of this natural rock fertilizer—so common in the loessial soil area, like the cornbelt—must remain a conjecture so far as this study went.

These studies of nearly five decades ago served to measure for us the two natural forces in "soil construction," namely (a) the regular offering within the soil of unweathered, mixed, rock minerals; and (b) the annual additions of the leguminous or highly nitrogenous organic matter. The microbial digestion of the organic matter serves to weather the rock minerals more rapidly and to release their insoluble nutrient elements of microbial combination with organic compounds as more favorable plant nutrition in ways we do not yet fully comprehend.

These studies measured also the forces of soil destruction in the same soil under man's failure to return organic matter to it. By balancing these two accounts of construction and destruction against each other, we have the clear picture of the difference between man's management of the soil and nature's, when she builds climax crops of plants, animals and man for their healthy survival. It is the weathering of the natural minerals by the maintenance of a generous supply of organic matter that keeps the living soil actively so, as these studies have so clearly demonstrated.

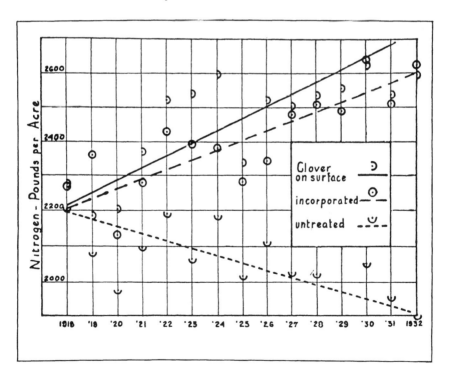

SOIL'S RESURRECTION IN THREE YEARS

During the first 10 or 20 years of the present century, the scientists studying soils and plant nutrition emphasized two main factors. They were concerned about mineral breakdown within the soil as the source of the inorganic nutrients for plants. And they were even more concerned about the return to the soil of barnyard and green manures which were considered the agency by which the living soil maintained its productivity. That is the soil's source of internal energy.

One of the pioneers among the scholars of soil science and plant composition at that time was Dr. Cyril G. Hopkins of the University of Illinois. His plans for maintaining "soil fertility and permanent agriculture"[1] called for close cooperation with nature. His research aimed to comprehend the underlying mechanisms by which the essential elements within the inorganic rock particles of the soil are broken out; how they are present as a reserve in the soil, yet can be available in sufficient quantities for plants during the growing season; and how the organic matter returned to the soil functions to increase availabilities of the inorganic nutrients and to contribute organic nutrition to crops. He envisioned nature "making bread from stones."[2]

As early as 1909, Dr. Hopkins pointed to soils deficient in decaying organic matter as those on which chemical fertilizers demonstrated their interactions. He was confident that decaying organic matter released inorganic elements from the mineral particles. He undertook research with his staff, aiming to learn what amounts of potassium in the soil could be made usable for crops by starting with the insoluble residue of a productive soil. That residue had been produced after treating the soil by strong hydrochloric acid at 212 F. for a long period and then washing it free of solubles by distilled water. That was the treatment employed in the laboratory for removing anything that might become soluble for plant use.

In one of his early experiments [3] enough of such insoluble residue was prepared to fill three pots. Then, with two similar pots of normal soil for comparison, the following treatments of the insoluble residues were set up. To one pot (number 2) there were added calcium carbonate, calcium phosphate, calcium sulfate, magnesium sulfate and iron chloride. Then another similar pot (number 3) was given that same list of treatments, but with ammonium nitrate in addition. Then a fourth pot (number 4), which duplicated the second and its treatments, was given also sodium ammonium phosphate and sodium ammonium acid phosphate to supply soluble nitrogen and phosphorus.

Those soils were seeded to inoculated red clover and rape in 1910. The clover failed, but small rape plants started and were soon turned under as the first addition of organic matter. Pot number 2, as the first of the insoluble residue series, was given 0.2 gms. of potassium sulfate, some ammonium phosphate and ammonium nitrate. Then also, since these three "residue" pots were in a bad physical condition, each was divided into equal parts to which acid-treated and washed quartz sand was added to give duplicate pots of half sand and half insoluble residues. These six pots, along with the normal soils, were planted to red and alsike clovers.

During that first year as much as 6½ grams of dry matter from one pot resulted. It contained 22.5 mgs. of potassium, when the total potassium applied was about 1.4 mgs. before leaching. The lowest crop yield was 0.5 gms. dry matter, containing twice as much potassium as was initially added. The crop residues were returned to the soil.

The crop grown in 1911, the second year, was better than that of 1910. It was harvested on August 9, and again on December 21. The crops per pot of residue soils ranged from 11.33 to 30.33 gms. dry matter. The organic matter was returned to the soil.

The crop of clovers in 1912 was still better. The tops harvested separately ranged in weights of dry matter per pot of residue soils from 25.25 to 41.07 gms. and the weights of roots from those ranged from 10.47 to 26.80 gms. The potassium contained in the tops ranged from 90 to 157 mgs. per pot. That in the roots ranged from 21 to 25 mgs.

Since not over 6 mgs. of potassium had been added to the pots 3, 3a, 4 and 4a from 1910 to 1912, it is significant to note that the total potassium in the crop of 1912 alone from those four pots was 529.2 mgs. of which 523.2 mgs. or nearly 99% must have come from what was considered insoluble residues of the soil.

As a consequence of these experimental results, Dr. Hopkins told us the following as facts. "The results indicate that after two years of green manuring, sufficient potassium was liberated from the insoluble residue to enable the clover to be benefited by the lime and phosphate fertilizers so as to outyield the crops on the normal soil to which no such fertilizer had been applied. Potassium can be liberated from the inexhaustible supply naturally contained in the normal soils of Illinois."

Dr. Hopkins contributed much research work to support his belief in the importance of green manuring and all other means of maintaining a high level of active organic matter in the soil to further decomposition of the soil's minerals as sources of plant nutrients. His ideas about soil fertility and permanent agriculture are well worth reconsidering as hidden ideas among unopened books.

BETTER SOIL—BETTER SECTIONS

In making microscopic studies of plant tissue we are thinking mainly of anatomy. We are looking for differences in size, shape, wall thickness and particular arrangement of the parts. We are also thinking about the possible functions the microscopic part serves in the life and growth of the larger tissue mass. We are not prone however, to think in the converse and to imagine how any changes in the physiology of the tissue may be modifying the anatomy or the appearance of the cells.

Some studies of the nutrition of soybean plants on soils deficient in calcium and the same soils well supplied in this respect emphasized the importance of better soil for better plant nourishment and thereby for better sections. Less fertile soils made poor microscopic sections. The fertile soils made good sections of the plant roots and stems.

So much has been said about acid soils for so many years that this problem was attacked in the belief that in condemning acid soils we were probably laboring under erroneous reasoning. It seemed highly probable that when calcium carbonate, applied to the soil, gives better legumes while it also reduces the degree of acidity, we are reasoning that the change in acidity of the soil renders the beneficial effect when it might well be the application of the calcium as a provision of better nourishment of the plant, that is responsible. Under stimulus of this hypothesis, soils of very acid nature were treated with compounds of calcium other than the carbonate and therefore without effect on the reaction of the soil.

Attempts were made to detect differences in the anatomy of the plant tissue as revealed in microscopic sections. Micro-chemical tests too were undertaken. Soybean plants had been grown on acid soil without treatment and on the same soil given calcium sulfate. The sulfate seemed logical since Boussengault, the French scientist, had used gypsum or calcium sulfate on the soil for the legume, red clover (*Trifolium pratense L.*) as early as 1843 and found this soil treatment beneficial to the crop growth. The parts of these plants grown in soil low in calcium and in the same soil relatively high in this respect were used for microscopic sections.

Chance would have it, that sections were first attempted of the plants grown under calcium deficiencies. Used as green sections for chemical studies as cut by the hand microtome, they were so mutilated that the technique of handling them was immediately discredited. When, however, sections of the plants grown on calcium treated soil were similarly handled, they were excellent specimens. Later when these same plants were studied as microscopic sections made in the usual complete embedding and staining technique, it was clearly evident that the fertility of the soil was at the foundation of these differences. Sections, cut at most any thickness of ten microns or less, of the calcium-starved plants showed the tissues so badly torn to suggest many defects in the technique. Sections from the calcium-fed plants were good even when cut very thin with the same technique. Here was evidence that the soil that grows the plants, more than the techniques of operating all that centers about the microtome, determines how good the sections are.

We know that soil acidity is a nutrient deficiency and that by plant starvation in terms of soil fertility the whole physiology of the plant is disturbed. Thereby the "stability" of the anatomy in terms of the microtome knife, is also disturbed. Since calcium plays a role in the cell wall, physiologically speaking, and is a mobilizer of many other nutrient elements like nitrogen, phosphorus, potassium and others into the plant, we can see why the anatomy of the plant will reflect the physiology of it.

In making sections of plant tissue, it is well to be cautious about blaming the technique when "ragged" sections result. It may be that the plant "grew that way" while suffering "hidden hungers" for some essentials coming from the soil. Even in plant microscopy we can say that the better the soil the better the sections.

SCHEDULE OF SOIL FERTILITY DELIVERY AND CROP GROWTH

Just how much inorganic nourishment a crop takes from the soil (per week, month, or season), and to what extent that contribution of mineral breakdown from the soil's reserve will result in different parts of the plant as very clearly presented for the mineral-rich, high-protein crop of alfalfa as early as 1897. Professor John A. Widtsoe reported a rare assembly of facts about the soil fertility required, and about the differences in chemical composition of the plant as potential nutrition for animals, in Bulletin number 48 of the Utah Agricultural Experiment Station.

Professor Widtsoe's data deserve recollection and repetition for emphasis. They show the pronounced variations in the plants as crop yields and as nutritional values, according to the age of the plant. Reading his report at this date will be enlightening. A critical study of his data will help one appreciate the spring season as the naturally favorable birthdate of the young of grazing animals.

Dr. Widtsoe's report lends itself to review by discussion in two parts, namely, (a) soil fertility taken during periods of growth of the crop (alfalfa) and (b) soil fertility and crop quality by seasonal periods. We shall consider the subject accordingly.

Since alfalfa is a perennial forage crop, and permits of several cuttings during a single year, it is significant to note that each period of plant growth taken as a cutting for hay is a cycle of development and physiological changes from youth of the plant to its maturity, as it were, for each cutting.

Let us examine, first, the yields of the crop as growth (increase in dry weight) per week and month in terms of the whole plant; then, also in terms of the separate plant parts, as leaves, stalks and flowers (see chart). For the first 12 of the 16 weeks (May 4 to August 4) there is a steady increase in the dry weight of the whole plant. Then for the next four weeks (the last one-fourth of its growth period) there is a decrease.

The weight of the stalks takes the same graphic pattern of increase for the respective dates; but for the last quarter of the growth time, the weights are constant rather than on the decrease.

The weights of the leaves do not give such a rapidly rising curve as the one for the weights of the stalks, or of the whole plant. The leaf increase in weight ceases three weeks before the cessation of growth as bulk by the stalks and the whole plant. These facts point to the late increase in bulk of the whole plant as being due mainly to that of the stalks. The latter represent storage of carbohydrates, and reflect the photosynthetic activities of converting water from the soil and carbon dioxided from the atmosphere into sugars, starches, cellulosic and other fuel substances. Those are the aspects that contribute tonnage per acre only, so commonly the economic interest in crop growth.

Leaf growth depends on the biosynthesis of proteins by the leaf itself while simultaneously carrying on photosynthesis of carbohydrates. It is the increase in proteins that grows more leaf surface to catch more sunshine. It is important to note in the illustration that the increase in mass of leaves continued for but nine of the 16 weeks. Cessation of leaf growth though, came but two weeks after the start of flower production, or after the beginning stage of reproduction.

The weights of the flowers reached their maximum at the same date as the stalks and as the entire plants. One can see this shift in the weights of leaves connected with the biosynthesis of proteins for growth of the flowers, their fertilization and their activities in providing the seeds as means of reproducing the plants and preserving the species. Here we see the shift in physiology from one of the vegetative increase in bulk to one emphasizing proteins for reproduction. This shift registers in the decreased mass of the whole plant. Likewise, the threat of it is shown two or three weeks (flower start) before the leaf weight drops.

This physiological shift becomes a shock, as it were, to vegetative increase. It is triggered when the pollen (male cell) is dropped from the anther to be caught on the stigma, grown down into the ovary, and fertilizes the egg for production of the seed. This conception releases many new hormones and other catalytic agencies to terminate the vegetative physiology and give activity and emphasis to reproduction. This brings about the termination of more yield or tonnage output.

Even though plants are monoecious organisms, they are shocked decidedly when the separate female part demonstrates the act of conception. Some distinct physiological changes occur. The plant, initiating reproduction, experiences some changes in body biochemistry, as does the bride taken suddenly by some strange symptoms and a disturbing surprise.

We need to remind ourselves—with emphasis—that the soil's contribution of fertility, or plant nourishment, must precede the growth of the crop. The germinating seed sends its roots down into the soil first, and then, later, the plant top up into the air. Hence, when the total amount of ash elements going into the alfalfa crop are measured by time periods, it should be expectable (though possibly surprising) that the total ash in the crop reaches its maximum by the seventh week in a plant's life history lasting about 16 weeks. The maximum of its fertility must have been mobilized from the soil into the young crop of alfalfa (see chart) before its season of growth, or its life, is half spent. The ash data are reported graphically only for the crop as a whole for comparison with the amounts of the crop's yields as bulk of the different plant parts.

The additional fertility data by Professor Widtsoe emphasizes the facts also that (1) the maximum ash content of the leaves was reached by the sixth week, one week earlier than for the plant as a whole; (2) that declined to a total of almost a third by the end of the season; (3) the maximum ash of the stalks occurred at the seventh week, determining that for the plant as a whole; (4) the ash content of the stalks declined but little from that date to maturity; (5) the maximum ash in the flowers was not reached until the 12th week, the date of maximum crop bulk.

One needs but glance at the graphic report by Professor Widtsoe to realize the simple fact that the soil must already be a dynamic force at the time the crop is started. The soil must have made its major nutritional contribution before the first half of the crop life is gone. The leaves, as the photosynthetic and biosynthetic power, must have their store of fertility in stock and in action by the time three-eighths of the crop life is gone.

All of this was emphasized before the close of the 18th century, yet we are slow to appreciate the simple fact that the soil is the power of creation of all living substances and must be highly dynamic when we make the planting.

In summary, then, a forage crop like alfalfa increases its yield of dry matter for three-fourths of its growth period, or season. It attains its maximum by the 12th of the total of 16 weeks. Such was the schedule when the weight of the entire crop as bulk was the measure. But when the weight of the leaves was considered, the maximum yield was attained three weeks earlier, or by the ninth week of growth.

Since the leaves carry out both photosynthetic and biosynthetic activities, the photosynthetic activity makes the increase possible through extended leaf surface via photosynthesis of proteins as living substance. In the early portion of the plant's life, the extension of leaf surface, the increased photosynthesis and the enlarged bulk dominate. But in the later period, the activities of the leaves shift away from vegetative output to the reproductive one of seed formation, when the proper degree of maturity in the plant's schedule demands.

The reproductive action calls heavily on the proteins. They are not a direct result of photosynthesis. They are an output of the plant's life processes using carbohydrates, in part, for energy and also as starter compounds from which to synthesize the proteins. The elaboration of that living substance demands also extra and early fertility from the soil.

Although the continued increase in yield extended itself through three-fourths of the life period, it required that the highest supply of fertility be delivered to the plant before scarcely half of the growth had taken place. This demand comes through the life processes which are building the proteins, our life-supporting foods, much more than from the photosynthetic processes that pile up carbohydrates, which are only fuel foods.

That the delivery of fertility by the soil is most closely connected with the output of quality nutrition in proteins for animals, by a crop like alfalfa, will be quite evident if we will notice the schedule of the concentrations of albuminoids (the flesh-formers, the important part of "crude" proteins) found in the alfalfa plants and its correlation with their fertility uptake from the soil (see graph).

We previously reported that the highest yield of leaves occurred in the ninth week of the 16 week session. But the high nutritional quality, the highest concentration and yield of the albuminoids in the leaves, occurred in the sixth week of this same length of growing season. The albuminoids at their maximum preceded the measurable amount of flowers. This fact emphasized the shift of that form of protein from vegetative increase to reproductive output. It is indicated by the drop in the graph for albuminoid content of leaves during the seventh week. Simultaneously, there is a decided rise in the graph for albuminoids in the stalks, which suggests they are en route from leaf to flower and caught in the stalk of the plant.

ALBUMINOIDS

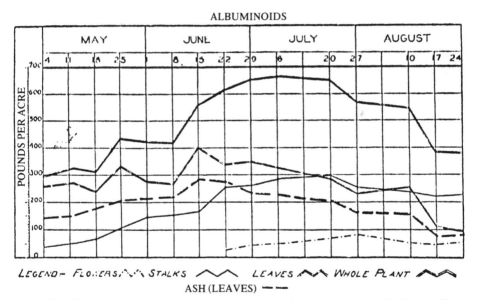

The shift of the form of protein from vegetative increase to reproductive output is illustrated here in Dr. Albrecht's raw note graph.

It is also in the seventh week that the albuminoids—in both the stalks and the plants as a whole—are not much below the maximum for the entire season. The growth period, from as early as the fifth to the seventh week, points out several marked physiological activities and changes. These include (a) the maximum supply of albuminoid protein in the leaves and its mobilization from them and (b) its services for the increase in the crop yield from 3,500 pounds at the fifth week to more than 6,000 pounds per acre by the 12th; and (c) the initiation and production of the flower crop, for the plant's reproduction and the survival of the species by the formation of seed. But most important for these dynamic aspects of crop growth is the delivery of the fertility which reaches its maximum in the synthesizing part of the plant (that is, the leaves) by the sixth week (with a sharp rise from the fifth week as shown in the graph), and reaching its maximum in the entire plant by the seventh week of its season of 16 weeks.

For many observers, crops are like Topsy in the novel, *Uncle Tom's Cabin,* who said, "I wasn't born, I just growed." Little thought is given to the decided shifts and changes in the plant's life processes during the growing season. Much less is it generally realized that the success of crop production depends on the activities of the living soil, through the dynamics of which the crop's nutritional quality is controlled. Yet as early as 1897, Professor Widtsoe reported the data by which these facts, and more, were clearly revealed. Much knowledge about nature remains hidden in unopened books.

SOIL ACIDITY (LOW pH) SPELLS FERTILITY DEFICIENCIES

Acidity is a common soil condition in many parts of the temperate zone. It occurs where the rainfall gives water enough to go down through and to wash out much of the fertility. In general, if the rainfall is high enough to provide plenty of water during the crop growing season, there will also be enough water, with its carbonic acid, to leach the soil or to give hydrogen in place of much of its supply of plant nutrients, and thereby make it acid.

Acid soils differ in their degrees of acidity, expressed as negative logarithms or what are known as pH values. Accordingly, then, a higher degree of acidity is represented by a lower pH value, or figure. This merely means that as more hydrogen has come in, less fertility or other positively charged nutrients are left there. Timbered soils of the eastern United States are acid; also those of the eastern edge of the prairie are sour. Acidity is a natural condition where soils have had rainfall enough so they have been growing much vegetation. Such soils have therefore been subjected (a) to a leaching force taking the fertility downward, and (b) to the competitive force of the vegetation with its roots taking the nutrients upward. In the latter case those nutrients are built into organic combinations of them above the soils of the forests and within the surface soils of the prairies. Consequently acid soils have distinct surface soil and subsoil horizons in their profiles. They are naturally low in fertility, especially in the subsoil, and have been growing mainly carbonaceous or woody vegetation. It is no small soil's problem to have such soils grow protein supplying, mineral rich, highly nutritious crops.

Natural soil acidity is in reality then, mainly a shortage of fertility in terms of many plant nutrients reflected in the physiological simplicity of the vegetation. This is the situation because the soil has been under-cropping and leaching for ages. This was true before we took over to intensify these fertility-depleting effects. This, then, is the condition of the soil that prompts the common question, "How can we grow mineral rich, fertility consuming forages, like the legumes, of good feed value for such high powered, protein producing animals as cows?"

It was the growing agricultural science of the early decades of the 20th century that brought liming of the soil back as a more general agricultural practice. We cannot say that liming was an art carried over from colonial days. It had been pushed out when fertilizers came into use. Liming the soil has become an extensive practice under the encouragement of an embryo soil testing service. That service was guided by the belief that the applications (a) of limestone, which is a carbonate of calcium; (b) of hydrated lime, which is an alkaline calcium hydroxide; or (c) of quicklime, which is a caustic oxide of calcium, are all beneficial for crop growth because each of these is ammunition in the fight against soil acidity, or against the high concentration of hydrogen in the soil, or the soil with a low pH figure, as the degree of acidity is now regularly expressed.

This struggle to drive the active hydrogen ion, or acidity, out of the soil was aided by the technological advancements giving us instruments and equipment that measured the hydrogen ion to a finer degree than known before. The ease and speed with which soil acidity could be detected and measured encouraged the widespread testing of soils. This activity discovered soil acidity almost everywhere in connection with extensive agriculture. Through the help of the pH-measuring gadgets we were impressed by the apparent universality of soil acidity. Only a few humid soils were not seriously stocked with acid.

We discovered that for acid soils, in general, the productivity was lower as the degree of acidity was higher, or as the pH value for the soil was a lower figure. From such a discovery we might expect to conclude—even though it was later found to be the wrong conclusion—that the presence of the large concentration of hydrogen ions in the soil, or a certain low pH value was the cause of the poor crops. This conclusion would be expected also from the bigger troubles in growing the mineral rich legumes of higher feeding values and of more physiological complexity through which these values alone are possible.

The extensive use of limestone in the cornbelt has now multiplied itself into the millions of tons of these natural rock fragments that are annually mixed through the soil. This increased use was prompted by the belief (a) that limestone is beneficial because its carbonate removes the acidity of the soil, and (b) that soil is most productive if it is neutral, or when it has no active hydrogen ions in it. Under these beliefs (now known to be poorly founded), we have become belligerent foes of soil acidity. Limestone has become the ammunition for fighting this supposed enemy hidden in the soil. With national financial aid, we have been prone to believe that in putting limestone on the soil we can follow the old adage which says, "If a little is good, more will be better." We are just now coming around to a fuller understanding of how nature grew crops on the acid soils before we did and that crops are not limited to growth within certain pH values when they are well nourished by ample, well-balanced fertility.

Only recently have we recognized the fallacious reasoning behind the conclusion contending that it must be the presence of acidity in the soil that brings crop failure when liming lessens both (a) the degree of and (b) the total of the soil acidity while making better crops at the same time. While the convenience of soil testing gadgets for refined points of pH was encouraging, this erroneous belief about soil acidity was an error. It was the diligent study of the physiology of plants of the colloidal behavior on the clays growing them and of the chemical analyses of them all that finally pointed out the errors of such hasty conclusions. It indicated that the presence of soil acidity is not detrimental, but that the absence of fertility, represented by the acidity, is the real trouble. On the contrary, some acidity can be, and is, beneficial.

We now know, of course, that in applying the limestone, which is calcium and magnesium carbonate there is possibly some reduction of the degree and the total acidity by the carbonate portion. At the same time there is applied also some calcium and some magnesium—nutrients highly deficient in the leached soils—to nourish the calcium-starved and magnesium-starved crops. These nutritional services come about both directly and indirectly. We have finally learned that it is this better nourishment of the crops, rather than any change in the degree of acidity, or any raising of the pH value, of the the soil that gives us the bigger and better crops. Unwittingly we have been fertilizing the crops with calcium simultaneously while fighting soil acidity with the carbonate, the hydroxide, or the oxide of lime.

Regardless of our ignorance of how lime functions we have unknowingly benefited by using it. However, an erroneous understanding of what happens to crops and to soil when we apply lime, cannot successfully lead us very far into the future. We dare not depend forever on accidents for our good fortune. We cannot continue to grow nutritious feeds under the mistaken belief that we do so merely by changing the degree of acidity, or by the removal of the soil acidity through the use of plenty of any kind of carbonates on our humid soils. Wise management of the soil to grow nutritious feeds can scarcely be well founded on facts so few and so simple.

Should you decide to demonstrate for yourself the truth of what has been said above, you might apply some soda lime, or sodium carbonate, to acid soil. This will increase the pH of the soil. It will reduce its total acidity. But while this soil treatment will rout the enemy, *i.e.* soil acidity, and raise the pH toward 7.0, it will still not give successful crops. Merely removing the acidity by a carbonate does not guarantee the successful growth of the crop.

As proof that it may be calcium as plant nourishment that is the helpful factor in liming a soil, one can repeat Benjamin Franklin's demonstration and apply calcium sulphate, that is, gypsum, to the soil. One might even apply some "Dow Flake" a calcium chloride. Either of these calcium-carrying compounds will make the soil more acid; either will lower the pH decidedly. In spite of this fact and because they add calcium, the gypsum and the "Dow Flake" will improve the crops on the initially acid soil either left so, or made more acid. We are now resurrecting the ancient art used by Benjamin Franklin, for whom liming the soil was a matter of fertilizing it with calcium sulphate, and not one of fighting soil acidity with calcium carbonate.

While we were fighting soil acidity, we failed to notice that most of the populations of the world are concentrated on acid soils. They are not in the humid tropics, where the soils are not acid or where the clay doesn't adsorb much hydrogen or even much of any nutrient cation. Nor are they on the arid soils that are alkaline (high pH values)—a reaction opposite to the acid (low pH values). Soils that are not acid are not necessarily the supporters of many peoples. Yet in fighting soil acidity we labor under the belief that if a soil were limed to the point of driving out all the acidity, such a soil should be highly productive.

We now know that even while a soil may be holding considerable acidity or hydrogen, it may be holding also considerable calcium or lime. To a much smaller extent of its exchange capacity, it is also holding nutrients other than calcium. Among these are magnesium, potassium, manganese, and others. But these in total are held in much less quantity and by less force than are either the calcium or the hydrogen—the former a nutrient and the latter a non-nutrient cation, or a positively charged ion. Should we put on lime or calcium enough to drive all the acidity out of the soil, that is, to make it neutral or to bring it to a pH of 7.0, by putting calcium in place of the hydrogen, all the other nutrients would be more readily driven out than would this acid-giving element.

Liming the soil heavily, then, does not necessarily drive out only the acidity, i.e. the hydrogen cations. Instead, it would also drive out all other fertility cations except calcium. It might load the soil with calcium so completely that it could offer only calcium as plant nourishment. Plants would then starve for other nutrients even though on a neutral soil. Plants on such a non-acid but calcium-saturated soil would be starving for all the same nutrients, except calcium, as they do on the acid soils. Making soils neutral by saturating them with calcium does not, therefore, make them productive. This is the situation of some of the neutral (pH 7.0 and higher) semi-arid soils of our western states. In our struggle against soil acidity we need to remember that neutral soils are not the productive soils. Instead, productive soils are the acid yet fertile ones that feed us and nourish the major portion of the other peoples of the world.

By considering the increasing degrees of soil acidity simply as increasing deficiencies of fertility, we find in nature, in general, that as the degree of acidity is higher (pH figure is lower), the adsorption or exchange capacity of the soil is saturated to a higher degree (larger percentage) by the positive ion, or cation, hydrogen, with this higher saturation by hydrogen, there are more hydrogen ions per unit of exchange capacity active or not held inactive by the soil; consequently the degree of acidity is higher. The acid is stronger. There are more hydrogen ions to make contact with the measuring electrode, and the pH value is therefore lower.

The same holds true for the degree of saturation of the soil's exchange capacity by calcium, or magnesium, or potassium. As the degree of saturation by any one of these nutrient cations goes higher, more of it is active in making contact with the plant root and in getting into the growth activities of the plant. These cations are nutritional helps coming from the same source as the hydrogen cation, namely, the soil colloid. The hydrogen coming from there is not. Because we have had the gadgets to measure the hydrogen, we have emphasized the pH, or the presence of a certain degree of acidity. We have not emphasized the absence of all the many fertility cations resulting because the hydrogen has replaced them on the negatively charged exchange complex or colloid of the soil. We have not had simple gadgets to measure them.

If, then, we should have a sandy soil, for example, (low in clay content and thereby low in exchange capacity) with a low pH value or a seriously high degree of acidity, or hydrogen saturation, this would conversely represent a low degree of saturation of its exchange capacity by calcium, magnesium, potassium, and other nutrient cations. Accordingly, then, the addition of but a small amount (two tons per acre) of limestone (calcium and magnesium carbonate) would move the pH value up decidedly or shift the degree of acidity to neutral.

This is similar to changing the degree of heat of a cup of scalding hot coffee by putting an ice cube into it. Here a little ice lowers the degree of heat very much where there was little total heat. With the sandy soil's low exchange capacity there could not be much total hydrogen, even if the degree of activity by it is high; consequently, the pH is changed decidedly toward neutral and the acidity is completely removed. The exchange capacity is loaded very highly, in turn, by the calcium or magnesium of the limestone. Then, accordingly, these two nutrients become highly active in plant nutrition to make legume crops succeed well where on this sandy soil they may have previously failed.

By doing no more than using the gadgets, in this case, to measure the change in pH (or in the degree of acidity), resulting from liming the soil, one would conclude readily that the crop grew better because the pH was changed or the acidity was neutralized. One would not concern himself very commonly about the increased amounts of calcium, magnesium, and other nutrient ions which became so much more active to nourish the plant better. We have no simple gadgets to measure these effects; hence we attribute the crop improvements to the wrong causes. Grazing animals probably make no such mistakes in their choices of forages, judged according to nutritional values in terms of calcium and magnesium, rather than in terms of pH of the soil.

If, on the other hand, we should have a heavy clay soil (high in exchange capacity) with a seriously low pH value, or a high degree of acidity, and conversely, of a low degree of saturation of its exchange capacity by calcium, magnesium, potassium, and other nutrient cations, the addition of the same amount of limestone as was applied to the sandy soil would not change the pH value or the degree of acidity significantly.

This would be similar to dropping an ice cube of carmine solution into a bathtub of scalding hot water. The cooling effect would not be recognized, but the coloring effect would. Because the larger exchange capacity and larger total amount of hydrogen would keep almost the same amount of it active in spite of the relatively small amount of limestone, there would be no measurable change in the pH of the soil as it is commonly sampled and tested. Yet the calcium (magnesium) carbonate would react with the soil to be adsorbed by it on the soil's colloidal complex. It would exchange from there to the plant roots to improve the legume crop, even if much active hydrogen left in the soil maintained the pH of the soil near the initial value. There would be focal points of calcium (magnesium) in the soil (significantly so if the limestone was drilled) to exchange these nutrient cations more actively to the plant roots than before the soil was limed. Hence the two tons of limestone on the clay soil, initially considered of seriously low pH value, may not have changed the pH, although it established the legume where it failed previously.

Thus clover may be established on the sandy soil by two tons of limestone where the pH was changed to a decidedly higher value. Also, clover may be established on the clay soil by two tons of limestone where the same pH value was not changed significantly. Plant behaviors tell us that the changes in the pH values are not contributions to the improvement of the crop growth. On the contrary, it is the liming as a remedy of the fertility deficiency in its application of calcium (magnesium) for the crop, and not the change of the pH or degree of acidity by the carbonate that is the responsible factor in crop betterment. Different soils may differ widely, then, in the extent to which their pH values (or degrees of acidity) are changed by soil treatment for growing better crops, when it is the deficiency of fertility—and not the degree of acidity—that is the cause of the trouble on so-called "acid" soils.

It was just such a case of confusion about what pH really means and how liming the soil serves plants as cited above, which put a county agent of Missouri into an embarrassing predicament many years ago. This occurred when the campaigns for "Lime for Clover and Prosperity" and "Lime for Legumes and Livestock" were at their height. A farmers' meeting under his leadership was held one autumn day on a farm where the soil was about to be prepared for wheat serving as a nurse crop for red clover. The crowd assembled at the first field on the river hill, a windblown bluff of very fine sandy loam. After testing the soil and finding it seriously acid (of low pH figure), it was agreed that, according to this pH report on the soil, two tons of limestone per acre were needed to grow red clover.

The farmer crowd then moved down into the river bottom to the second field, made up of a heavy clay soil. This soil, under acidity test, revealed the same degree of this trouble. The same amount of limestone per acre, two tons, was deemed necessary as for the field of fine sandy loam.

After both fields had been plowed the two tons of limestone per acre were applied. The soils were disked, the wheat was seeded and followed by the clover seeding the following early spring. The clover stands in the wheat stubble the next autumn were excellent in both fields.

This was reason, and considered a good setting, for another farmer meeting on liming and soil acidity. This one started again with the fine sandy loam soil, and the test of its pH to reveal the absence of acidity and the good clover there, supposedly because the pH value of the soil had been changed to that of neutrality. But in the second field, with its clay soil, the degree of acidity under retest was the same as before the limestone had been applied. Yet the crowd observing this test was standing in an excellent stubble crop of red clover. The county agent was in a predicament. Here the liming treatment of the soil established clover in the second field without changing the pH of the soil, when on the first field he had just pointed out that liming the soil established clover because, as he erroneously explained, it had changed the degree of acidity, or raised the pH of the soil. The pH of these two soils was not shifted to the same extent, nor was the acidity changed by the same degree; yet the clover shifts were the same, namely, from failure to good stands.

That plants are not "sensitive to, or limited by, a particular pH value of the soil" was demonstrated by experiments at the Missouri Agricultural Experiment Station some years ago. The clay fraction was taken out of the Putnam silt loam, and electrodialized to make it completely acid (replacing the nutrients by hydrogen) which gave it a pH value of 3.6. Six lots of this soil were set apart. Each was titrated with limewater to rescue its acidity to a certain particular degree, or specific pH figure. The lots represented the following series of pH values, namely, 4.0, 4.5, 5.0, 5.5, 6.0, and 6.5.

Enough clay was taken from each lot of this series of clays to represent .05 milligram equivalents (M.E.) of exchangeable calcium per plant for a total of 50 plants, and put into pans of equal amounts of quartz sand. In a second series, enough clay from each lot was taken to provide .10 milligram equivalents (M.E.) of caclium per plant in each of the six pans of sand, or doubling the amounts corresponding to the different pH values in the first series. A third series of these same different pH values of the soil was set up similarly, except that enough clay was used to provide .20 milligram equivalents of calcium per plant, or four times as much calcium in each pan as in the first series. Thus the three series were triplicates in pH values of the soils, but there was more clay, more adsorptive-exchange capacity, and more exchangeable calcium by two and four times in going to the second and third series from the first.

Observations of the soybean crops grown on these pans suggested different so-called "sensitivies to pH values" by this crop. By observing the first series containing the least amount of clay in the sand (the most sandy soil), and thereby the least amount of calcium for the crop (.05 M.E. per plant), one would have concluded that soybeans are sensitive to a pH of 5.5 but are not so to a pH of 6.0. Had one observed only the second series, the corresponding figures in one's contention would have been pH 5.0 and 5.5 But had only the third series been open for observation, one would have put the "sensitivity" value at pH 4.5 and not at pH 5.0.

Here, then, a lower pH value (or a higher degree of acidity) by as much as ten times was the difference in sensitivity brought about by offering four times as much exchangeable calcium as nutrition for the plants. This was brought about merely by giving more clay, a heavier texture, to the soil at the same degree of acidity in the series, or at the same pH. More exchange capacity offset the significance erroneously ascribed to the pH.

Still more significant as the change in the pH values of the clay-sand soils as the result of growing the soybean plants on them. The three more highly acid soils of pH values, 4.0 4.5, and 5.0 in the three series had all become less acid. The growth of the crops had made their pH values in these nine cases move upward, or shift toward neutrality. The three less acid soils of pH values 5.5, 6.0, and 6.5 in the three series had all become more acid in consequence of growing the crop; or this crop growth had moved the pH values downward in these nine soils, away from neutrality. These shifts in pH values were as much as 1.5 pH, where the original pH values were 6.5. The soils in these instances were made 32 times more acid by only the partial or limited growth of the crop. Surely, then, when the growth of the crop, or the activities of the plants by way of the roots' contact with the soils make these soils 32 times more acid, one would scarcely say that it is the pH of the soil to which the crop is sensitive, or that a crop will grow only when a certain restricted pH or degree of acidity of the soil prevails. Plants are very sensitive to minute degrees of fertility deficiencies, but certainly not to degrees of acidity of very wide ranges.

Liming the soil, then, is a matter of putting active calcium and active magnesium into the acid soil, or even into one that is not necessarily acid. These two elements need to be in certain ratios of their respective degrees of saturation of the exchange capacity of the soil, if that soil is to grow legumes or protein rich crops. For calcium, this may well be 75%, while for magnesium it may well be near 10%. For potassium the percentage saturation of the exchange capacity of the soil occupied may be from 2 to near 5. Just what percentage the other cations, especially the trace elements should occupy has not yet been specifically suggested. We need, then, some gadgets to measure the activities of the calcium, the magnesium, the potassium, and other nutrients. Instead of becoming so serious about the pH of the soil, we need to become much more serious about pCa, pMg, pK, etc., since these are activities of the nutrient ions and would help us get a picture of the dynamics by which these move toward the plant root for entrance there and nutrition of the plants.

Since the hydrogen ion, a non-nutrient, is positively charged, as are the nutrients calcium, magnesium, and potassium, it is significant to consider hydrogen along with these as the combination representing almost the total exchange capacity of the soil. From this total capacity the ratios of the percentage saturation of that capacity by the nutrients (and also by hydrogen, a non-nutrient) may be calculated and adjusted by fertility treatments for most efficient plant nutrition.

The pH, then, serves to suggest the degree to which the total potential stock of nutrients in the soil has been replaced by hydrogen, a non-nutrient; but, it gives no suggestion as to which nutrients are grossly deficient or to what degree the nutrients are imbalanced. It is not an indicator of what kinds or amounts of fertility are required to make the soil productive, and has therefore been a hazard to keeping soils productive and in nutritional balance. Undue emphasis on, and attention to, the pH of the soil to the extent of disregard of the soil's fertility saturation for plant nutrition suggests itself as a case where "a little knowledge can be a dangerous thing."

OUR SOIL FERTILITY—ONE OF THE ALLIED POWERS

The soil, with its fertility or its chemical productive power, has suddenly come in for our serious attention. The dwindling supplies of commercially processed foods have given us a quickened interest in home gardens, home killed meats, and other food products coming to us more directly from the land. We are coming to appreciate the soil more as we are wondering how to make that food factory provide more of those products which we can grow and process by ourselves.

Fortunately, the soil has been enlisted in war service, and more for its greater fertility per acre than for the more extensive acres of it. It is enlisted decidedly nationally now that many are making more intimate contacts with it this spring. Its international enlistment will also be appreciated when in the final settlements we face the global food problem as our responsibility as part of a global people.

The fertility of our soils may well be considered the resource that paid the bill for much that we, considered as individuals or as a youthful nation, have enjoyed in what very properly must be called "past" prosperity. It was the payoff in the form of squandered potentialties to our soil—so generously encouraged by the unearned increments form farm investments—that brought us to a rather jittery condition in the depression following the first World War. The financial structure built on these unearned increments and false land values collapsed suddenly when farm values had to be based on soils rather than sales.

For many years in the early decades of this century, our soil fertility was going abroad in the form of food products to give us gold in exchange. Meantime we were trying various political and economic devices only to arrive at the conclusion that gold, after all, is inedible. International relations have come to such an impasse now that, under the title of lend-lease, our soil fertility is going abroad at a still greater rate. Paradoxical as it may seem, we are at this same moment looking to the formation of a western hemispheric union for its post-war isolation. This union aims at the exclusion from use by some Europeans and some Asiatics of that last significant store of unexploited soil fertility in Argentina in particular, and South America in general. It is now realized that South America has become the bread and meat basket for the axis countries when meanwhile by international trade rearrangements they were gradually walled out of the fertility supply in the northern half of our hemisphere.

National attention has been going to our soils for their services, but many of those services have been as pawns on the chessboard in an international political game. The soils coming in as controllers of the international breadbasket are about to take over the great global game now in progress. They may play some nations into famines, while others still feast, unless all of us soon learn more about our soils. The concern for ourselves in the many and less cogitated moves about the political board may well bring us to consider our soils with their larger fertility supply for maximum services to ourselves first and then also to the greatest number of others. Surely we can begin looking to the soil early so that through this one of the Allied powers as a natural means there may eventually come a more satisfying and permanent solution of our problems. The call for attention to our soils is urgent and will become more so as the war continues.

Within less time than two decades, numerous national, almost catastrophic, experiences have made us soil conscious. The maximum of floods and the worst of droughts in our history befell us. The first World War, under need for intensive food production, gave us the maximum soil exploitation and subsequently the worst dust explosion. Fluctuations in land values reshaped our whole national economic structure in a sudden and tremendous financial depression that reshuffled the cards for a new deal, particularly in matters economic and social. These experiences, with little cramping of our dietary style, gave us soil conservation on a national scale, at least so far as soil removal by erosion is concerned. It brought us to accept the struggle of keeping our soils at home.

A second World War is now the occasion for even greater food production, but fortunately as yet under extensive soil conservation against erosion even if it is occasioned at tremendous costs to the federal treasury. It is focusing our attention on the real and fundamental property of the soil that needs conservation, namely the fertility, or the producing power, within as well as the mere bulk of the soil. This war may well bring soil conservation against fertility depletion as the first war brought soil conservation against erosion. It is the fertility of the soil that enables nature to grow cover and make natural rather than mechanical conservation against erosion possible. It is the fertility that determines how much food we can produce and how nutritious it can be. It is the supply of fertility that determines whether mineral-rich, proteinaceous foods or whether mineral-deficient, carbonaceous products are the output of the land. Our nutritional level and our stamina rise with the fertility supply of the soil.

Soils in some regions are exposing their internal weakness. In others they are demonstrating their strength. Limited transporation of foods, and a more intensive live-at-home policy will soon reflect the differences and shortages in the fertility in different localities through our own health troubles. Rationing under point systems and other limitations in our dietary habits will bring the words "soil fertility" into the list of household terms and into common conversation. It will likewise give meaning to soils in a global way much as our soldiers and their experience gave us other global concepts.

Fortunately, we have the belt of the so-called "chernozem" soils, as the Russians call them, including Kansas, Oklahoma and Texas as the southern half of the belt, and Nebraska, the Dakotas and Minnesota as the northern portion. This is our great reserve of soil fertility, or our reserves in good possibilities which we have yet to throw into the conflict. It was the "chernozem" soil belt of Russia that set the axis in reverse in their movement eastward, or their "Drang nach Osten." Doubtless our chernozem soils can set in reverse their movement westward.

If food is to win the war and write the peace—and food is fabricated soil fertility—a tremendous power of good rests on the hand of the lowly dirt that holds the pen. By the stroke of its fertility there may be saved, or starved, the millions of humans according as the dictates come, or do not come, from soils still fertile enough to share themselves extensively. That stroke must also be guided by a spirit that is still unstarved of its freedoms as well as by soils unexhausted of their productive powers. Surely our recent progress in appreciating our soil and in the knowledge of its conservation for wise use will undergird our hopes for international democracy and our plans toward that end. The soil may be the supreme power among the Allied forces as they move toward final victory.

REVIEW: SOIL, GRASS AND CANCER

The title of this book, *Soil, Grass and Cancer,* is more complete when followed by the subtitle statement, namely, "Health of animals and man is linked to the mineral balance of the soil." The author is a member of the Academy of Agriculture of France. He has charge of the instruction at the National Veterinary College of Alford.

The translation is by Catherine T. M. Harriot and Dr. Henry Kennedy, secretary, Irish Agricultural Organization, Society Ltd. There are 267 pages of text of 66 short chapters on different subjects presented with two or three appropriately headlined subdivisions per page. Consequently, each idea is presented briefly and concisely to lend the book to intermittent reading. The more than 100 references are well cited in the text, indicating the author's study of, and familiarity with, the research reported in more than one language. By the digestion of that assembly of facts in relation to his own experience that resulted in his success with his rational grazing of grassland, he links soil science, biochemistry, plant physiology and medicine in a broad approach to biological matters as only a closely-observing and intelligent farmer can. The more technical chapters are so labeled for the choice of the reader.

This book of late 1959 is a sequel to his *Productive de L'Herbe,* Flammarion, 26 Rue Racine, Paris, 1957 and its translation, *Grass Productivity,* by Crosby Lockwood and Sons 1959.

In its practical aspects, this publication encourages soil conservation under grassland farming with details of its profitable management equal to that of arable farming. That is clearly presented with facts and figures of layout of areas, grazing systems, soil treatments, and animal behaviors to be observed from their more efficient services as harvesters of grass.

In the more extensive and technical discussions, the roles of the different inorganic elements are presented as those fail to serve in nutrition because of deficiencies and imbalances. Emphasis is given, in particular to the trace elements copper, iron, iodine, zinc, molybdenum and magnesium, as parts of the cell's enzymes, and other biochemical compounds serving in the body processes.

Thus the soil is considered the foundation of health via nutrition. By means of that ultimate basis, the cells of the microbe, the plant, the animal and the human body build the health of themselves through their protein defense mechanisms for digesting foreign proteins before such invaders digest their victims in what we call "infectious diseases."

The author emphasizes the observations of the animal's struggle for its own good health, via proper nutrition. His diagnoses of ill-health consist of search for failing biochemistry because of deficiencies and imbalances of essentials coming from the soil through grass. For him, infections are merely the symptoms of such to be prevented by bringing the physiologies of the plant and animal into proper relation with the fertile soil.

His able management of the health of cattle, according to this principle, through 13 years of his "rational" grazing system on his farm in northern France and his study of biochemistry lead him to connect the insufficient soil and deficient grass with the degeneration of cell functions, called cancer. He visualizes this as a degeneration, in agreement with Warburg and others, because of deficiencies and imbalances in nourishment which inhibit the highly oxidative cell processes and the removal of byproducts. Shortages of the trace elements and the enzymes they support, like the catalyst to remove hydrogen peroxide, a byproduct of respiration, are suggested as a causative condition of this cell irregularity in its growth and metabolism.

When, (1) copper serves to put iron into hemoglobin; (2) this element is depleted from the blood stream of cattle grazing grass fertilized with nitrogen to give lowered milk output; (3) variable copper in the blood stream suggests itself as a test of this trace element in the soil; (4) low copper supplies in the liver and blood reduce the catalase activities of body cells; and (5) both copper and iron must be present in proper relations to let the latter reduce anemia; he emphasizes this as an illustration of the several trace elements in their biochemical roles for healthy warm-blooded bodies. Mr. Voisin presents in provocative form what more and more other observing farmers, agricultural scientists, veterinarians, dieticians, and doctors are accepting as logical. They will read with interest what he says in seeming contradiction to conventional beliefs. They will appreciate the able support for his projected thinking, which he has assembled from the scientific literature and his own trials. Mr. Voisin moves our thinking away from emphasis on relief for ill-health by artificials, and toward attention to good health by building it through a sound nutrition that starts with fertile soils.

SOIL HUSBANDRY

For thousands of years we have said, *"Creation started with a handful of dust."* As for "What's new in soil husbandry?" most significant is the new thinking and concern about what's in that dust, or soil, that makes things grow.

1. More elements coming from the soil are proving to be essential. The list of inorganic, or ash, elements coming from the soil for the nutrition of plants, animals and man is getting larger. For a long time the chemists considered the soil's contribution to creation to include seven elements for plants and nine for animals and man.

The three additional elements for all life as its combustible bulk, namely carbon, hydrogen and oxygen, come from the air and water. Nitrogen, calcium, phosphorus, potassium, magnesium, sulfur and iron come from the soil for plants except as some nitrogen can be taken from the gaseous supply in the air. New knowledge of requirements from the soil now adds the elements manganese, boron, copper, zinc and molybdenum. For animals, our limited knowledge would remove boron and molybdenum from that list but add sodium and chlorine, common salt.

We are now talking about these newer five as "trace" elements because they are required in almost unmeasurable amounts, or so small as to be mere traces. They were not appreciated until persistent irregularities in the health and the reproduction of animals, coupled with finer chemical tests, brought first the theoretical consideration and then the demonstration of their essentialty.

More significant is their essentialty in the process of creating proteins rather than carbohydrates. Through proteins they contribute to the growth of the body rather than to providing energy or fuels. Their shortages in the soil show up first as a deficiency for legumes, the better forage feeds. They seem to be tools in the life processes more than materials of construction. Because we do not know how they function, but, nevertheless, know of disaster in animal and human health through their absence from the soil, our animals must provide the experimental tests for their shortages in, and successful applications on, the soil.

More than 100 fertilizer companies now have them available in their fertilizers. They may well be going on many of our soils as tests of shortages through their benefits and as a kind of health insurance.

2. The nitrogen deficiencies in our soils are becoming more grave. While lime, legumes and livestock are a combination once considered equal to the task of upkeep of the soils in organic matter and nitrogen, too few legume crops have been plowed back into the soil for that. While legumes may fix

nitrogen, they have not built up the soils in practice. Their protein nitrogen has gone to make protein in livestock and moved off the farm instead. Livestock does not create protein but only assembles it. Consequently, our soils are going lower in nitrogen in spite of our talk about lime, legumes and livestock for soil building.

Fortunately, the chemical conversion of air nitrogen into fertilizers has given us salts of nitrogen to demonstrate what extra nitrogen in the soil will do. It has given increased bushels of corn per acre through more ears per acre—rather than larger ones—by more stalks per acre in heavier rates of planting. It has given more protein per acre too, and higher concentration of it in both the grain and the ensilage from the stalks.

More fertilizer nitrogen on the soil has come to mean less purchase of protein supplements in feed to balance the value of corn as such. The yields of wheat and the protein concentration in it as "hardness" or "softness" are also subject to the amount and season of fertilizer nitrogen applied on the soil growing it.

3. Deficiencies in the soil of more of the essential elements are expectable. Agricultural production is no longer a matter of merely planting seeds and expecting them to rustle through the soil for their nutrition as we once turned out a flock of sheep or a herd of cattle on the plains for muster and droving of them later in the year. Instead, crop production is the problem of having available in the soil all the elements in balance required for plant nutrition so the crop as feed and food will have all the elements and compounds required for animal and human nutrition.

Not only the one element, nitrogen, must be coming as raw material from the soil for creative services, but phosphorus, magnesium and all the others, including those called "trace" and those still unknown.

Chemical testing of the soil is telling us of shortages of elements previously never suspected. We must be open-minded for new ideas about the fertility, the power of creation in the soil. Seemingly simple elements are the raw materials that the virgin supply in the soil, or our addition of them to it as fertilizer, must put on the assembly line of agricultural production at the starting point in the soil.

That the soil fertility is a consumable natural resource, and that we must search out and use all possible means of supplementing it, is one of the newest concepts gaining ground in soil husbandry. That it is the active fertility of the soil that is mobilizing all that is agricultural is also new in our thinking.

SOME IMBALANCES, DEFICIENCIES AND DECEPTIONS
VIA SOIL AND CROPS

All of us are ready to grant that any living body must be nourished if it is to survive. But we do not grant so readily that the soil is the producer of that nourishment. We might accept the latter as true for the nourishment of microbes, or plants, or animals. But we have not been well enough informed to grant that man, as another animal, is also limited by the soil, even though he is not fixed in one place. He refuses to grant that he too must fit himself into the biological laws of nature, so well exemplified by other life forms below his. Instead, he assumes that he might take over the control of nature.

In pursuance of that ambition, man has lived according to the behavior pattern suggested by Col. C.L. Boyle, who said, "For generations, the conquest of nature has been accepted as man's prerogative, but man is a part of nature, it being his essential environment and unless he can find his rightful place in it, he has poor hope for survival. Man's present behavior often resembles that of an over-successful parasite, which in killing its host accomplishes also its own death. Man's environment is the whole natural scene, the earth with its soil and water, its plants, its animals. In many places these have reached a natural balance which man disturbs at his peril."

By failing to see that man must fit into the soil pattern just as any other life form fits into that great scheme, man has about destroyed all the surface soil. He has left nothing that would still represent the original soil patterns of nature to guide his maintenance of the soil according as nature would make her recommendation or she would maintain it. Man has not heard the "Voice of Nature" in these respects.

If we study the geography of primitive man, it is interesting to note that he seems to have been located in areas of lesser rainfall, or in regions of even occasional famine, if Joseph's story may be taken as an indication. He was located for survival where the winds mixed the soils by dusts blown in, by mineral matter delivered by the waters in their river floods. With his high requirement for fertility essentials from the soil, naturally the soils which supported man as a primitive had to contain all the essential, both major and minor, inorganic nutrient elements. They had to offer the calcium, the magnesium, the potassium, the phosphorus, the copper, the zinc, the manganese, the cobalt and all the inorganics which we now know are required in the nutrition of the warm-blooded, high protein bodies, like man, his flocks and his herds.

In those primitive locations man's numbers would soon reach the saturation point or the population limit set by the area. The population problem of too many of the primitives did not reach very large numbers in any locality before it pushed some of them out. Accordingly as technologies were introduced, man was compelled to colonize other areas under the struggles involving him in serious and bloody wars. He ventured out only short distances each time because, as he went away from the soils which had been guaranteeing a survival, he moved to those which would not be so much of a guarantee unless he had lifelines reaching back to the soils where he had learned, by experience, that his survival was possible. He moved, then, into areas where primitive man had not been, and very probably because the nutritional level of that soil was not equal to the fullest requirements for his survival without some lifelines reaching to other more fertile areas.

If we study the growth of the populations as numbers of the human species on the earth—plotted as a graph in relation to time—we find that the curve fits exactly the same laws which are demonstrated when we drop a single microbe into a large quantity of sterile nutrient medium and count the microbes as they multiply and populate the limited volume of that food source. In that microbial demonstration we have the biotic, or the sigmoid, curve shaped like the letter "S." With but one microbe put into a large volume of medium at good incubation conditions, the growth or multiplication of the population at the outset is relatively slow. But soon it increases until the numbers of microbes seem about to reach infinity. At that moment, the curve is rising almost vertically. But soon it turns toward the horizontal and the increase in numbers ceases. That upper, horizontal part of the curve demonstrates the increasing food troubles for the rising populations. Those troubles may, in part, be brought on by accumulated waste products. But more commonly they are due to the decreased food supply. Just as such microbial population curves level or flatten off, so many of the human population curves have already flattened off in the world's older areas of exhausted soils under extended and intensive use.

At this moment in our population problem in the United States, we are apt to emphasize various political situations. We seem to have forgotten the serious biological situation of man in relation to his foods, particularly in supply of proteins. A look at the curve of the population of the United States during several decades of the past leads us to believe that we can go on increasing our population forever at the rate of one percent per year without ever dreaming that our curve of population must flatten off as those of all populations eventually must. We do not imagine that it might drop suddenly, or have partial rises as recoveries, and that it never can go back up to the maximum height again with the favorable health conditions of the once maximum.

We have excellent examples in some of the older countries where the population curves have flattened off long ago and where their struggles for *lebenstraum* have been quite evident for some time. In the United States, we are in the vanguard among the populations of the world. But we are about to get around the world to the starting point in the ancient East or in the Orient from which apparently, the earliest population took off for the westward march of multiplication in the open territories. Our ancestry was a part in the dash to the open country to the west across the Atlantic and farther. We scarcely appreciate some of the significant historical facts connected with problems of feeding the many in the expanding populations. We scarcely think of that as the situation when General Douglas MacArthur completed that westward march around the world and was held up politically in what would have started the second circuit of food search around the globe by the hungry human populations.

The streams of human population have always flowed from arid soils to humid ones. Those flows occurred only as the technologies helped in the travel and as they lengthened and maintained the life lines reaching back from the newly established peoples, when they had gone to less productive soils without first considering those as guarantees of food for health. Moved to those newer soils, we indulge as populations in an agriculture of which we speak as "specialized" when it would be more fitting to say "limited." It is limited because the soils are not complete enough in respect to the list of essential inorganic elements in their fertility supplies; nor are those supplies large enough in their stores of individual elements; nor are those soils amply stocked with organic matter to represent higher potentials of proteins in plants and all else associated with them to guarantee the health of humans and other warm-blooded species, both wild and domestic.

Each new soil, as we discovered it, originally had its climax of virgin vegetation and, in case of more fertile soils, had also its climax of animal life. But in the absence of animals there, we did not observe that fact as a report telling that the vegetation was mainly of carbohydrates and of too little protein for warm-blooded bodies. On such soils, the fertility may be imbalanced so far as the plant's nutrition is concerned and thereby the plant products are apt to be imbalanced so far as their services in the nutrition for the animals is concerned. When those so-called "newer soils" are seeded to legumes for protein production, all crops behave physiologically like non-legumes, their pedigrees not withstanding. The deficiencies in the soil fertility make the plant practice a kind of deception. Plants, then, so handled are, nevertheless, a kind of hypocrite. Their appearances in quantity may be deceptive of their low nutritional quality.

Unfortunately, we have looked at our lands in terms of only two dimensions, namely length and breadth. Under the campaign against soil erosion by the early Soil Conservation Service, we were introduced to a third dimension, namely the depth of the surface, the living soil. We need to see also now, however, the fourth dimension, namely the inorganic and organic fertility as that represents the power of the land in the creation of the living forms of animals and man by the way of that living soil.

The climaxes of the virgin vegetation, and even the natural recovery of vegetation on some of those soils which we have abandoned and turned back to nature after we had worn them out, tell a significant fertility story if we can see the land in terms of soil and of that resource in its cycle. The virgin climax may be grass that feeds the cattle. It may be trees such as hardwoods that feed our deer. Or it may be the conifers that starve them. It may even be legume trees, like the mesquite, which cattle and other animals refuse to browse, save under threat of starvation.

Natural climaxes of vegetation represent various stages of soil development. At first that development is a case of soil construction, building up to the potential of the more complex proteins. More soil development under more rainfall and higher temperatures thereafter, represents soil destruction. With this there comes (a) the decline in the crop's nutritional output from proteins for growth, protection and reproduction, (b) less and less yield, (c) more pests and diseases, (d) vegetative reproduction rather than one by seeds, and finally (e) crop failures. In our use of the soil, we have too often disregarded its lesson about the health of any plant. Much less have we considered the term "health" so carefully discriminated as to emphasize those qualities of a particular plant species resulting on a particular soil because of a particularly well-balanced fertility. The seed catalog seems to decide what crops will be planted when the decision should rather be made according to the soil as nutrition for the crops that are expected, (a) to grow, and (b) to deliver nourishment for man or beast. As a consequence, under crops making higher feed values and taking more out of the soil more speedily, the drop in soil fertility was disastrous on even the fertile soils within the time of one human generation without any alarm for us. Both the quantity of crop and its quality as nutrients soon decline faster than the fertility of the soil indicates even if followed by chemical inventories.

The declining yield as quantity of crops is readily recognized. But the decline in nutritional quality might be seriously ahead of a noticeable decline in quantity (of yield). The decrease in quality, therefore, is apt to go unrecognized. During soil exhaustion there are shifts in the ratios of the amount of nutrient elements in it due to consumption of the supplies of some elements relatively more rapidly than of others. This means shifts in the dietary balance of the plant's nutrition. Consequently, it means increases in the products of photosynthesis, namely the carbohydrates going upward, but a shift downward in the products of biosynthesis, namely, the proteins.

Some elements in the soil go out of balance with more seriously disturbing effects than others. Among these are the monovalent elements or the more soluble elements, especially, nitrogen and potassium. Then since calcium and magnesium, as divalents, are also more soluble, especially when they are in the form of salts of carbonic acid (bicarbonates), they, too, shift in their ratios to others in the soil and cause wide variation in the carbohydrate—protein ratio of the products grown within the crop. Thus the changing ratios of fertility elements are the cause of the changing nutritive ratios (carbohydrates to proteins) in the feeds we grow to make these represent the fattening and not the truly feeding of the growing animal, (including the human).

Such variations in the plant compositions are a part of the natural ecological pattern of crops on soils under construction by lower annual rainfalls and also on soils under destruction by higher rainfalls. Such is the result with fertility exhaustion either by the natural weathering processes or by intensive cropping. The case can be nicely demonstrated by single cropping continuously on a soil even in experimental tests. Here, then, are the deficiencies and imbalances in the soil fertility which compel the crop to practice its deception on those who judge the soils only by the amount of bulk that any crop might grow on them.

When we feed only to fill and to fool, we neglect the animal in terms of real health and natural protection against invasion by foreign proteins like the microbes. Should we be surprised, then, at the increasing animal "diseases" and degeneration, exhibited in failing conception and in the production of midgets or dwarfs as the resulting births without potential future growth? If we emphasize the production of crops only for fattening castrated males, naturally, we cannot expect the animal species to survive. The streams of life cannot be expected to flow in spite of us when our attention is so completely focused on economics and technology in place of on the basic biological laws of nature, by which animals, plants and microbes must live.

In the nutrition of plants, the ample presence of calcium has connected this element with protein production, particularly by the legumes. If we are to grow proteins, we lime the soils under higher rainfalls. But the soils must also provide potassium if the legumes are to make the sugar which the plant converts into proteins by its own life processes. Then also, the calcium and potassium must be in certain quantitative ratios if they are to balance the plant's own nutrition even for its production of the carbohydrates. Even legumes grown on a soil low in calcium and magnesium, may behave physiologically as a non-legume. They may make mainly carbohydrate bulk and little protein.

Imbalances, then, in soil fertility as nutrition gives plants which are unable to build proteins and the protein-like compounds, including the antibiotics, by which this type of growth protects itself. Diseases and pests then plague those same crops which in the virgin, ecological climaxes were protecting themselves when there were no commercial pesticide sprays and no similar poisons.

Recent researches suggest that nutrition of the plant through balanced soil fertility may be more of a prevention against fungi, bacteria and insects than we appreciate. Studies in potato scab demonstrate the fact that correcting this tuber damage may be a matter of the fertility balance between calcium and potassium by which the resulting plant's own processes possibly bring copper, etc., from the soil amply as the antibiotic agents when the former two fertility elements are in the proper balance of ratios.

We are apt to emphasize the economics under the sale of poisons and sprays more than we are to indulge in careful studies of plant nutrition for prevention of diseases. That this is the situation, was illustrated at the scientific meeting only this past holiday season in the agricultural section of the American Association for Advancement of Science. In their program dealing with "biological and chemical control of plant and animals pests" the first session covered recent advances in chemical control measures. Another part of the program was devoted to "inherent resistance to pests" including animal diseases, plant insects, and diseases of field and horticultural crops. In the twenty-four well-prepared papers which were presented at four sessions, it is significant to note that "one paper covered the relation of host nutrition to pest reaction." Unfortunately, as this program had it, only about four percent of our thinking goes to the concept that plants are sick from imbalanced or deficient nutrition and thereby become the victims of microbes in the form of fungi or bacteria and even of our insects, while the 96% of our thinking emphasizes the poisoning of the enemy rather than the building of healthy plants by fertile soils.

We fail to realize how the latter type of thinking may be a case of growing poor nutrition for ourselves and our animals as food instead of better nutrition by guiding the nutrition of the plant for its own health and protection against its diseases and enemies. We are slow to see that the soil must undergird our health. We are still slower to see the imbalances, the deficiencies, and the deceptions in our crops in relation to this old truth of good nutrition as the basis of good health, for any form of life.

OLD SANBORN FIELD

The little professor through the years, with soil auger in hand and with students following behind him at a dog trot, had almost worn a path from his classrooms in Waters and Mumford Halls to "Old Sanborn," the small eight acre experimental field within this city's [Columbia, Missouri] boundaries.

His actions were by no means unusual in this placid community long accustomed to professors, where education is the common currency. If he had been carrying a blunderbuss instead of the soil auger, it would hardly have caused an eyebrow to raise.

Presently, he came to Plot 23. He stopped suddenly, gave it a cursory survey. He could recite its history backwards and forwards, every year of its existence since 1888, or since J. W. Sanborn, the stormy, crotchety dean, had established this land as "rotation field." During all these 57 years this plot had been unfertilized, Albrecht knew, and had constantly been cropped to timothy alone.

Now, back in his lab on this August day, 1945, less important things, such as conferences with professors and meetings with fertilizer executives, could all wait. He had something more important to do. He had this package of soil to mail, without delay, to his old-time colleague and former University of Missouri faculty friend, Dr. Benjamin M. Duggar, the botanist.

"What has Albrecht sent me this time?" Duggar no doubt said on receiving this bit of Missouri crust. "He's probably outdone himself this time."

The botanist was to find that his own words were truly prophetic, and that Albrecht "had outdone himself" and all other men up to that time for the laboratory soon was to reveal that the sample from Plot 23, Sanborn Field, University of Missouri, contained the first golden mold from which aureomycin was obtained. Thus, this was the beginning, the starting point, of the now world-renowned antibiotic similar to penicillin.

4

SOIL ORGANIC MATTER

Soil organic matter, along with the mineral content in sand, silt, clay and water, has much to do with which particular texture of soil will be preferred for a certain phase of gardening or field crops. Discussion has been previously presented to emphasize the differences in the soil's nutritional services to plant because of differences in soil's mineral texture.

When a soil is sand it is made up of more than half sand. Ths same figure holds for silt if it is a silty soil. But the soil takes on decidedly in its nutritional services to plants and microbes when the two preceding figures are interchanged and present the organic fraction. It would be a great blessing to all nutrition, that is, microbes, plants, animals, and man, if all our soil could contain 5% organic matter. In Missouri the average figure of this component for all soils is as low as nearly 2%.

Productive soils must have minerals, that is, rocks as aggregates of minerals, decomposing or separating their inorganic compounds and setting free the elements of these compounds. These elements must go into action, some into solution, and some adsorbed in the clay, to move their own energy so they may be taken up by the plant root. If soils are to be productive they must be more than a pile of pulverized rock with water poured over it. They must have some organic matter. This must support the microbes. The soil must be a truly living soil.

Even when nature starts off with volcanic ash, freshly belched from the hot interior of the earth and scattered as dust, there is eventually some single plant taking a foothold on it. After one plant grows for one season to make seeds, more plants grow during the next, because the death of the first plant and the decay of its small amount of organic matter contribute to the inorganic soil helpful organic compounds which start building the soil for better plant growth. Each succeeding season makes its additions of organic matter. This better plant growth results from the soil's own kind of organic matter carrying its own selection of the particular combination of inorganic fertility which grows its own particular species. By returning the organic matter with the ash elements combined in it to the soil, each season builds up and retains more inorganic fertility in an organic combination improved in the amount taken from the soil during that season. Each year returns more extensively the specific organic matter which should represent the reconstitution of the same species of plant more rapidly than is possible in any other setting.

Thus nature—in man's absence—has grown each of its various separate plant species into what is called an *ecological climax,* or where one crop fits healthily and profusively into a particular location. It fits there better than any other kind or species would.

In such a pure, healthy stand of a virgin crop we have emphasized the inorganic fertility, such as calcium, magnesium, potassium, phosphorus, sulfur, iron and all the trace elements so well balanced for the crop in that ecological climax. But we have forgotten the residues returned annually for their specificity of the inorganic compounds serving so directly in the nourishment of the new crop each year. We must think more than of just *ash* as plant nutrition if we are going to duplicate nature's performance in growing abundant vegetation, which naturally protects itself from fungus or bacterial afflictions, or from annihilation by insect ravages, and reproduces itself by putting forth seed abundantly.

The home gardener has always started his soil preparations with the application of animal manures and of composts. The history of gardening is built on organic matter. The tempting tastes and delectable qualities of vegetables rest more in that simple fact than we appreciate. High quality of vegetables will not tolerate much salt content of the soil growing them.

Yet in applying soluble fertilizers with the seeding we are offering the prospective plant the maximum of solubles at the seedling period when within the seed's storage is the maximum for takeoff, even in the absence of soil. The seed is also designed to put roots into the soil in search of nourishment even before it puts out stems, leaves, or the showy plant part. Such fertilization placed near the seed at the time of planting offers less and less of itself for plant nourishment as the roots go deeper or farther from the point of this soil concentration. Can such a situation be as satisfactory as scattering through the soil the decomposed matter from the decaying roots of the previous crop? Or as the crop residue plowed and cultivated into the soil?

Organic matter dropped naturally onto the cultivated soil surface for a continuous natural cropping to annuals, or left under the canopy of perennials, soon serves to loosen the soil to significant depth. It serves to invite the many small forms of life, like worms and insects, to incorporate the leaf mold into the soil to a significant depth. It opens the soil to the maximum for action by all the microbial forms living within the soil and dependent on the atmospheric oxygen for their respiratory activities of organic combustion.

Undisturbed by man, and with the organic matter going back to the soil annually while the crop keeps growing into a better exhibition with each successive year, we see how nature builds healthy, insect free crops into a climax. These are the crops which we should take as the ideal for our own crops if we expect them to give us nutrients.

As soil managers we may well ponder nature's plan of putting back into the soil the maximum of organic matter. In this she is doing much more building of the organic than she is of the inorganic fertility of the soil. Her practice is just the reverse of ours in this respect. It may well challenge our thinking more about organic matter in the soil, which will be better for our crops and for us too.

FERTILITY AND CROP NEEDS

"Sunshine, we say, makes the crops grow." So, as the days become longer, comes the growing season. After midsummer, with the shortening of days, there is the gradual closing of this season. Considered so simply, we are prone to believe that growth is due wholly to sunshine applied to plants as light and heat. We forget that all plants depend on the soil, the organic content of which indicates the season by timing its decay and delivery of its active fertility with relation to the temperatures the sun affords.

The light of the sun functions through the chlorophyll—the green enzyme of leaves)—to produce the sugars, starches, and other carbohydrates. These are produced more abundantly as the longer days give more light. Carbohydrates are truly the plant's food, just as they are part of the food used in our bodies. In the plant, too, they give energy by being respired in the cells. Sunshine energy serves to create sugar which becomes energy food in the plant cells. Plant cells truly grow or increase their living tissues (proteins) in the absence of light by growing at night as well as by day. Growth is the result of the cell's conversion of some carbohydrates into proteins, while other carbohydrates are turned into energy for that process. Carbohydrates are starter compounds into which nitrogen, sulfur and phosphorous are combined to bring about the living, protecting and reproducing tissues which we include in the terms *proteins*. These are not synthesized by the sunlight. Proteins are biosynthetic and not photosynthetic. It is their nitrogen content in particular by which proteins are distinguished from the carbohydrates.

Heat applied to any of nature's chemical reactions serves to double their speed for each 18 F. (10 C.) increase in temperature. Thus the season's growth comes about because of the rising temperature which speeds the plant processes, providing, of course, that the soil offers increasing amounts of both organic and inorganic fertility along with the advancing season.

The increasing amounts of fertility of the soil timed with the mounting temperatures of the advancing season, depend on the increasing rate of decay of organic matter in the soil. This is the activity by which the crop growth of the soil is determined. It is timed with the rising temperature to increase more of its released inorganic elements and organic compounds for increased plant nutrition. It is the real cause of the more rapid plant growth through more abundant plant nutrition from the soil, and not so directly from the sunshine. This increasing decay in the soil is, then, synchronized with the plant growth, since it is the cause of it.

Tillage speeds the decay processes to hold the nitrate amount at higher levels when the supply of organic matter allows. The organic matter of the soil is the major support of crop growth. The decay releases nitrogen, sulfur and other elements serving the plant in its manufacture of proteins from part of the carbohydrates. Such release results from the microbial struggle to get their energy foods and food for growth while they "decay" or digest the organic residues.

Fortunately, this element remains chemically inactive when combined in soil organic matter at the lower temperatures under which the microbes are inactive. But its decay starts in and undergoes mounting rates of change from organic to inorganic form in ammonia and nitrates, both taken readily by plants. This process of nitrification, then, is in a large measure the seasonal support or control of natural plant nutrition and growth, since it means protein which is life to the microbes first and to the plant second. It is the organic matter that gives release also of much carbonic acid from microbial respiration of the carbon simultaneously with the release of the nitrogen. This increase in the soil acids speeds up the breakdown of the rock fragments and their minerals to release more active inorganic fertility. This means more efficient protein construction for better plant growth.

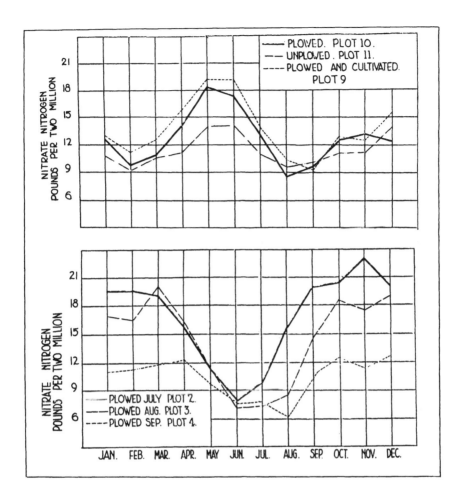

The study of the soil's nitrogen supply in the form of nitrates tells us that wheat, corn and other crops including those in the garden, grow not only because the light and heat of the sun fall on the plant's leaves, but because the sun's heat is applied also to the moist soil. This brings on more rapid organic decay to recycle the fertility elements, especially the nitrogen, in higher speeds and amounts by which the more rapid crop growth is determined, provided the nitrogen is in balance with larger supplies of other fertility essentials. Plants, along with soil microbes, struggle to get proteins, or to live. Only as the seasonal conditions offer the chance to make more protein can there be more growth of the crop. Such is the natural seasonal cycle bringing about crop growth. That cycle is timed according to plant growth, since it is the natural supply of active fertility coming from the decay of the inorganic matter in the soil.

"CONSTITUTION" OF SOIL

In a severe illness we place faith for recovery in the help of the physician or surgeon first. But if hope grows dim and they too become concerned, they offer consolation by telling us that we have a good constitution. Fortunately for many a patient, his recovery depends on his *constitution,* or what may be defined as his ability to survive in spite of the doctor and not because of him.

Any living soil must also have a good constitution in the form of an adequate supply of organic matter, preferably grown much as it occurs in an ecological climax of nature. By the presence of that organic phase, the microbial activities are the soil's metabolic processes by means of which it recovers from chemical shocks, like heavy applications of salt fertilizers. Through the combination of organic matter, as energy and growth foods, and the microbes multiplying as successions of hidden crops themselves, the soil keeps on living and nourishing our crops in spite of us doctors of the soil more than because of us. Heavy dosages of chemical salts dare not be used as fertilizers with the planted seeds because of the danger of killing their growth and thereby giving crop failure. The placement of such salts in the soil—far enough away from the seeds to escape that damage—is challenging the crop engineer's mechanical ingenuity. This fact is indicated by the variety of planting and seeding machinery offered now with special fertilizer attachments. If such salts will damage the seed, shall we not consider what a shock such concentrated application must be to the microbial life in the soil area surrounding the seed and the growing seedling?

Fortunately, the microbes, the organic matter and the clay of the soil can and must take the shock if there is to be a forage or vegetable crop saved for us. Yet under such soil treatment, we are not much concerned about keeping the microbial forms growing and thus more organic matter going into the soil as its constitution. When we dose ourselves with aspirin, for example, as relief from fevers, headaches and other symptoms of our body's more deeply-seated troubles, we dare not forget that the relief is bought at the price of shocking and overloading many organs and their processes in disposing of the drug. These processes are called upon to decompose, or resynthesize, the drug chemically in the liver; to carry it in the bloodstream; to pass it through the kidneys (not without possible damage); and eventually to eliminate it in the urine, the skin or by other routes. In the soil body, too, the biochemical processes are similarly marshalled to overcome the shock of heavy salt dosages much as the human body must overcome them from drugs.

The first body part of the soil that helps to reduce the salt damage is clay. It absorbs the component parts of the salts in order to take them out of solution and reduce their damaging effects. Not in doing so, other essential elements held in the clay for microbial and plant nutrition, may be put out of retention as help to the crop. And the clay becomes imbalanced by the excessive stocking with the few applied elements replacing the extensive natural combinations of both known and unknown essentials already in it.

The soil's second shock absorbing help is the supply of decaying organic matter. This is the more effective defense against salt injury to planted crops, and against serious imbalance in the clay's essential or nutrient elements. Fertilizing or salting the soil's organic matter brings about different processes by different kinds of microbes coming into dominance. If one change in the soil's chemical condition is brought about by fertilizer treatment, there will be some bacteria, fungi or actinomycetes favored especially. They will grow rapidly and will dominate. Some of the salt is taken into their bodies, recombined with the soil organic matter and reduced in its salting effects. Following that change in the soil conditions, some other species will profit by the resulting products and will dominate and bring about another step in the chain of processes absorbing the shock. These successions of domination by different microbial crowds continue as long as there are organic matter reserves and salts left to feed new generations, coming about every hour in the growing season, and thus representing the *active constitution* of the soil. It is because of the soil organic matter and its guarantee of the microbial processes by these shock troops that our field and vegetable crops, following salt treatments of the soil, live so often in spite of us rather than because of us.

Fortunately, not all fertilizer salts are so severely disturbing or dangerous. Least dangerous among them are those carrying salts of phosphorous. This element, changed from rock to soluble acid combinations in fertilizer production, combines quickly with calcium, iron or aluminum in the soil to become less soluble. The chemist says, "It reverts." While it is not so shockingly dangerous, it is correspondingly difficult to keep it in a form available to the plants. We therefore need to apply it more generously for its fertilizing services.

More disturbing are the salts of nitrogen, either in the ammonium or the nitrate forms. The same is true of salts of potassium. The increasing concentrations of these two elements going into the modern fertilizers have brought on increasing trouble in placing such salt in the soil at safe distances from the seed at planting time. When mixed fertilizers were used some 50 years ago under the label of 2-12-2, (2% ammonia, 12% of phosphoric acid and 2% of potash), there was little shock danger as compared with what is considered the lower concentrations today of 12-12-12, with as much of each of the two dangerous salts as of the one less dangerous. It is significant to note that the present annual consumption of fertilizers is showing an increase mainly in those states where the soils are still higher in organic matter. Where the soils are lower in this respect and in fertility in general, which brought fertilizers into practice in these sections many years ago, there has been a decline in the annual use of mixed fertilizers. Shall we finally come to believe that this means such concentrated salts are safe treatment only where there remains enough organic matter for the living soil to survive in spite of the soil doctors?

There is still hope, however, for our use of commercial fertilizers when the soil organic matter and the microbes working it over can take up the shock to the soil well ahead of the crop, and so prohibit the salt damage. This fact suggests that we can compost the salt fertilizers with most any kind of organic waste—even sawdust—either in a pile above the soil or in a mixture within the soil, well in advance of the crop that would be hurt by salts applied directly with its seeding. Also, we can grow green manure crops, give them heavy fertilization, and turn them under to bring the fertilizers to harvested crops, after the fertilizer salts are worked and reworked into the organic matter supplying the crop, by rotting as an organic fertilizer. Salt shocks are taken up safely when given first to this fertilization crop and then to the microbes when the extra organic matter is put back into the soil.

Yes, we can use salt fertilizers if we have organic matter enough in the soil by which it and the microbes give the soil a good healthy constitution to stand up under occasional necessary prescriptions of salt treatments by the soil doctors. But we must maintain a living soil, and this is possible only if the organic matter is well maintained in it.

MOBILIZER OF INORGANIC SOIL

Since plants at their best growth, in what we call a natural ecological climax, reach that freedom from weeds in a pure stand and self-protection against diseases and insect pests only after their residue returns of many successive generations have accumulated their effects, we certainly ought to look to the many organic matters as well as the inorganic ones that will serve as fertilizers of our soils. Good gardening has always called for plenty of manure applied regularly. One might well believe that there are benefits from returning organic matter to the soil, because just that much more ash material is in the cycle of growth and decay, to be supplemented by the annual increment coming as addition from the mineral reserves in the soil. All of this means more inorganic fertility for growing the next annual crop. We emphasize only the inorganic elements in that cycle, like calcium, magnesium, potassium, phosphorus, sulfur and other ash elements. We do not point out the organic compounds like amino acids, carbohydrates, ring-carbon structures and others, which are given back to the soil in crop residues as help in growing better as well as bigger crops.

Nor do we imagine that the organic compounds may be the agency through the chemical combination with which some of the essential inorganic elements are more efficiently moved from the soil into the roots of the plants. That decaying organic matter may supply organic compounds going into the plants, and may carry the inorganic elements along in an organo-inorganic combination, is a rather unique phase of plant nutrition only recently recognized, hence considered new. It is spoken of as *chelation*. We have long viewed the movement by the inorganic nutrient elements from the soil into the plant root as due to their high concentrations on the clay or in the soil solution. Like a mathematical equation, we habitually read from left to right, or we emphasize the need for raising the concentration of the fertility on the clay to drive that reaction to the right, or into the root. We forget that an equation is the same truth when read from right to left. We have not considered the possibility of lowering the concentration in the root as a way of increasing the gradient in that direction by such means, or a means of aiding the root in its moving the elements more effectively into the plant through better use there.

We have not envisioned the plant as it might have organic compounds—of its own synthesis or absorption from the soil—in its roots which are literally taking the fertility elements away from the collodial clay rather than having the clay thrust them into it. That organic compounds in the roots are serving in that fashion has recently been established by experimental demonstration. Plants are their own chelators, if their roots combine organic substances with those inorganic from the soil for mobilization of the latter into the roots more efficiently.

Emphasis has recently gone toward the commercially synthesized compound ethylene-diamine tetra acetic acid (EDTA) as a ready combiner with iron. Prepared in the laboratory, that combination as a whole is absorbed by, and translocated within, the plant to cure its chlorotic condition. More iron moves under such chelation than is moved in solution or otherwise from the soil into the plant without the EDTA. The unique service of this complex EDTA compound as a chelator, or organic combiner with the inorganic, to move more of the latter from the soil into the crop, was demonstrated by P.C. de Kock of the Macauley Institute for Research, at Aberdeen, Scotland. He grew the sunflower plant with the root system divided between two containers, supplying the iron in one and the EDTA in the other, only to get healthy plants by that combination. They become chlorotic if only the EDTA was omitted from that arrangement. What particular interest his test has in connection with natural organic matter of the soil, was his demonstration by means of the same technique that a water-extract of peat used on the one-half of the root system as a substitute for the EDTA served similarly to improve the plant's absorption of the iron by the other half of the roots and to prevent chlorosis. Without the treatments by the peat extract, the plants became chlorotic.

Such facts establish a rather unique function for soil organic matter, when by its decomposition it gives compounds which need be taken up by only some of the roots and thereby serve to help other roots—which are neither nourished by nor even in contact with it—to take up more inorganic elements, like iron, from soil area not stocked with any organic matter. This suggests that a few focal points of decaying organic matter in the soil may render more extensive benefits for better nutrition from the inorganic part of the whole soil than we appreciate.

Dr. H.E. Hampton of Texas demonstrated by his research at the Missouri Experiment Station that merely putting legume bacteria on the roots of soybean plants made these take the inorganic nutrient elements off the clay to a larger degree of exhausting that supply than they were taken by uninoculated roots of similar plants. The inoculated soybean plants, which were producing more protein from atmospheric nitrogen through inoculation, were literally taking the fertility away from the clay. They suggested that inorganic fertility was taken and held by the inoculated not with a greater energy than was true for the roots of the less proteinacious soybean plants behaving (in the absence of nodule bacteria) physiologically like nonlegumes.

When iron is so insoluble, but yet is chelated within the roots by EDTA which was fed into other roots (and also into the plant tops) of the system than those in contrast with the iron, we can visualize that other less soluble elements, like phosphate, might be chelated too; that might be expected, since that element serves more effectively in plant nutrition when it is plowed under with leguminous green manures or barnyard manure.

COMPOST FOR THE SEA OR THE SOIL?

We have seen the problem of the disposal of kitchen waste by mechanical disintegration, and the interest in composting organic wastes and all else one connects with the need to return to the soil for maintenance of its fertility all of the organic results of its productivity. In facing the problem of kitchen food wastes, we are concerned—at first thought—only with disposal. Refuse of this kind accumulates very rapidly, especially with shells of seafoods or rinds of watermelons. The idea of flushing this through the drain into the sewer, by means of mechanical disintegration, takes hold quickly as a convenience in disposing it to the streams and to the sea. But it neglects the necessity of maintaining the cycle of growth, death and decay right in place of all organic materials, if soils are to be maintained in productivity, rather than simply mined and destroyed.

Kitchen gadgets for disposal eliminate the garbage man. But we need to consider garbage disposal in terms of its potential in maintaining soil fertility . . . by return of the organic matter as a help in plant production, rather than the return only of the ash or of the chemical salt equivalent. So, while the enthusiasm for mechanical disintegration may carry the wastes to the sea, we need to consider the mechanical disintegration as a secondary effect of microbial decomposition of these wastes in the compost heap. Thereby, and through the balancing of the microbial diet by the addition of chemical fertilizer salts to the composting, a fertilizer of balance in terms of both inorganic and organic essentials for plant growth may well be made. This is, then, truly "conservation of soil fertility" in action, rather than in lip service only.

Rather than being a case of biological shock of salt application to plant roots in the soil, this salt shock is transferred to, or taken up by, the soil microbes in the compost heap by using the fertilizer salts there. Those salts are combined with less active organics. They may be chelated, or made more effective, for plant use—and may give play to many unknown factors in soil productivity. While household conveniences are always welcome, it is well that the matter of composting our wastes for return to the soil—to become soluble and to be reused there, rather than to be made soluble for disposal to the sea—be given more serious consideration and wider practice. Plants reach a climax in maintaining a pure stand of the species when they grow in the place where their own wastes, or they themselves, are completely returned to the soil. Man may be considered in the same light of better survival, as a species of life, if he will return all his waste to the soil, rather than primarily to the sea. Because of the idea of turning, more and more, to the idea of returning our organic wastes (along with chemical fertilizers) to the soil for soil fertility maintenance, we want to add our encouragement . . . in the scientific study of the potential for production of higher nutritional quality in crops when the return of this organic matter is more completely brought about.

INCLUDES MUCH "ET CETERA"

The pig, like other animals, teaches us by example rather than by propaganda. Since we are not prone to mimic what might even appear as wisdom in the behavior of a lowly animal, it has taken us almost a half century to become a nation of carrot eaters. During all those years the pig was selecting yellow corn with its precursor compounds of vitamin A in preference to white corn, deficient in those. Scientists refused to put much stock in the farmers' report years ago about the pigs' choices connected with the higher nutrition qualities of those selections. So the pig was eating yellow corn for all that the scientists listed as food values "et cetera" (and others). The pig selected for the "et cetera" much more than possibly we realized. It has been those "et cetera" compounds, in connection with nutrition, which science has been discovering more rapidly in the years since the first vitamin was found. More and more essential organic compounds are being listed under the category of "essential." More and more hormones are classified by their functions and chemical structures. New antibodies against disease are coming to light and late ones are replacing earlier listings. Organic chemistry is the field of extensive elucidation of what must have been in the food as "et cetera" when we said, "The requirements for our nutrition are the carbohydrates, fats, proteins, inorganic compounds, et cetera."

For plants, the study of soil fertility about a half century ago listed the essential elements to the extent of only ten. These included: carbon, hydrogen, oxygen, nitrogen, (all originally from air and water, but also from the soil as organic compounds) phosphorus, potassium, sulfur, calcium, magnesium iron, "et cetera" (all from the minerals of the soil initially but also from the organic compounds grown on and returned to the soil). In that day of ash analysis of the plants to be matched against the inorganic fertility elements of ash coming from the soil minerals, not much emphasis was put on "et cetera." But with the addition to the plants' requirements of the trace elements, namely: manganese, copper, zinc, boron, molybdenum, chlorine and cobalt for the blue-green algae, "et cetera," we are realizing that our listing of essential inorganic elements is not a matter in its finality. Rather, our minds must be open to the possibility that natural processes may be using qualities of other elements so small that they escape our methods of detection and accurate measure. As late as June 1958, there appeared a report that "Additions of organic materials to soil will influence the availability of the trace metals to plants."

Unfortunately, in teaching facts of nature we omit the "et cetera" all too often. We are prone to emphasize what we have listed and what we know. We are more anxious to exhibit our wisdom than to admit our ignorance. Yet the admission of the latter about things natural would not belittle us. Rather, it would extol nature and all that we need yet to learn if we are to cooperate with her in managing agricultural production (creation) more successfully for the survival of all the species of life we like to see propagated. By example, nature has been teaching us that a crop without man's aid or interference grows to a climax of pure stand, of little disease or insect attack and of fecund reproduction through the help of the accumulated organic matter built up from its own remains year after year. Because we do not know the specific organic compounds in the soil going into the crop and causing the weed exclusion, the absence of fungi and insect pests, or the high seed yields, we close our minds to the remarks of the man who emphasizes the use of more organic matter because he believes it is the cause of these advantages in the survival of the crop in its ecological climax. We say, "He has no scientific proof that soil organic matter, or the practice of what he calls *organic gardening and farming* can give healthier crops with larger yields of higher nutritional values."

In our scientific thinking we are apt to omit "et cetera." In their unsophisticated view of the growing things, the practical gardener and farmer magnify that "et cetera" part. The simple fact that we do not know specifically and to the accuracy accepted as the standard for scientific reporting, should not prohibit our starting the growth of our knowledge from empirical matters in which there is still so much "et cetera" beyond what little we know. Such a method of propagating knowledge in practice preceded by centuries the published knowledge we include in what is called "science."

It is unfortunate, that with so much emphasis on the science of academic and classroom origin, we are prone to believe that organized knowledge about nature (which is a common definition of science) coming from observation, experience and practice in agriculture, is not to be trusted as truth or as fact. But even the scientist's offerings of organized knowledge meet with skepticism and refusal of acceptance when he, for example, extols the use of salts of nitrogen because they make the crop so much greener, grow so much taller, and even be richer in crude protein. Such a scientific exhibition meets with skepticism from nature herself, that is from grass-eating animals like the cows and the rabbits. The former refuse to eat such grass if the nitrogen comes from their own urinary droppings. The latter refuse to eat the grasses fertilized with only the salts of nitrogen common in fertilizers.

Such is a case where nature, as it were, closes her mind to the claims of the scientist, satisfied as he is to measure the high nitrogen content of the forage resulting from soil treatment with nitrogen salts and to claim it of high protein content. Animals are skeptics of his claims. They classify them as propaganda. Apparently the animals know more clearly and accept more readily the scientist's "et cetera" than they do his specific listings. Unfortunately, much is emphasized as science for only its monetary values. Too often the "et cetera" are not listed or mentioned because they do not contribute to the collection of fees and profits accordingly. We are made gullible on one hand by much that is claimed to be science, yet on the other hand, we are often made so skeptical by it that we are prone to exclude all empiricism until so-called science in commerce establishes the details of its potential value by continued repetition in announcements.

Organic matter in the soil is an illustration of that situation. Through empirical knowledge of experience and practice, its services to the crops are known to be very valuable. But through fear of diseases emphasized in study of fungi, and bacteria found on crops, the use of decaying organic matter is not considered as near a sanitary fertilizing procedure as is the use of chemical salts. We have built up a fear of "germs." Because organic matter, like manure, cannot be reported as carrying certain specific organic substances in specific percentages, and serving in specific plant functions, we say it cannot be shown to be a true fertilizer. Its use is not considered a fertilizing act, but it is viewed as only a case of disposal of a barn waste. But the pioneer guano user of our South insisted that the bird dropping from Chili were superior as fertilizing help for his crops to the saltpeter from the same place. About 50 years ago, one of the present day producers of commercial fertilizers distributed the company catalog with claims for their "pure animal matter fertilizers," and pointed out (with plant illustrations) the injury by the salt fertilizers when applied with the wheat seeding.

Because we do not have enough scientific explanation of the particular functions all this is serving in organic fertilizers, and since they are not abundantly available for sale at a profit, there is not much propaganda to bring us to study their effects. Our minds are, therefore, closed to the enthusiasm of one who is an organic gardener. Even if the healthier plants in an ecological climax are examples of crops organically grown, and if animals are teaching us, by example, that fertilizing with nitrogen salts in their own droppings does not necessarily mean more choice protein, though it may mean more nitrogen in the crop, we are slow to realize that organic matter may make many of the same contributions made by commercial fertilizers' "et cetera." We do not yet appreciate the "et cetera" as something that may be better nutrition in what is yet unknown to us but well known to nature.

Perhaps the day is not far distant when, instead of growing crops for their maximum removal from the soil in that form, we shall grow crops for their organic matter to be returned to the soil on, say, half or less of our cultivated areas. By that we can go fifty-fifty with nature and use the organic fertilization to let us work with nature in maintaining living soils rather than work against her to maintain dying and nearly dead ones.

FARM MANURES HELP MAINTAIN IT

The use of fossil organic fuels in their various forms, like coal, kerosene, gasoline, and other volatile, readily combustible materials for agricultural power, to replace that of horses and mules, has brought about the highly exploitative attacks on the natural reserve organic matter of our surface soils. This has resulted for two reasons: (a) more power and speed are applied to the tilling of the soil more deeply and vigorously to hasten the combustion of the reserves of microbial energy materials; (b) less organic matter is returned in the animal feed residues as manure, modified and improved as nutrition for the soil microbes and plants by the addition of the chemically more complex and varied waste products of the animal's physiology.

The first of these reasons has been widely recognized as an unavoidable result of the high labor costs demanding such speed to raise the output per man. The second reason has been generally disregarded. Manure handling has always been considered a distasteful sanitary chore incidental to keeping animals housed and penned, more than it has been appreciated as an essential, biochemical contribution to the nutritional quality of feeds and foods grown on manured soil. Also, it simultaneously does much to maintain the organic matter in its fertilizing services.

Chemical studies were made of the soils after 67 years of (a) no manure on one set of plots, and (b) six tons per acre annually on another. Each set in such contrasting pairs had been under cropping to (a) wheat, (b) corn, (c) timothy annually, and also to (d) a four-year rotation of corn, oats, wheat and clover and (e) a six-year rotation of corn, oats, wheat, clover and timothy. From these data, it is clearly evident how much the use of barnyard manure has contributed to help in the upkeep of the organic matter supply in those soils. Under cropping to wheat continuously, the manured plot of soil has 2.4% of organic matter, when the unmanured one had only 2.1%. The former was three parts richer over 21 parts, or higher by one-seventh. Under corn continuously, the manure plot was higher in organic matter after 67 years by four-sevenths. Under timothy sod continuously, the increase figure was nearly one-third; under the four-year rotation, it was over one-third; and in the six-year rotation, one-fourth, or next to the lowest, which was the soil under wheat. These were the effects from using manure when in all of these cases the entire crops had been removed and no crop residues were returned.

As additional significance, there is the help from barnyard manure in the maintenance of the inorganic part of the soil fertility. This was shown by the ash analysis of the soil for phosphate (phosphoric acid, P_2O_5) and for some of the cationic essential elements, namely: calcium, Ca; magnesium, Mg; and potassium, K. It is also significant to note the help from manure in keeping up the soil's exchange—absorption capacity (cation exchange capacity)—in which the organic matter is more active than the clay. Also the lowered soil acidity resulting from the use of manure, as measured by the amount of exchangeable hydrogen, in the soil after 67 years, deserves attention as a modified soil condition not commonly appreciated in connection with this soil treatment. Contrasting values in each of the above cases of the elements cited for manure and no manure, show clearly that manure has fertility values we do not commonly emphasize.

TABLE I
Soil Composition—Due to Barnyard Manure after 67 Years.
Sanborn Field, Columbia, Missouri

Crop	Treatment	Organic Matter %	Phosphoric Acid, lbs/A	Essential M.E. Ca	Mg	K	Cation Exchange Capacity M.E.	Hydrogen M.E
Wheat	Manure	2.4	189	2140	306	348	16	8.5
	None	2.1	77	1900	360	312	16	9.5
Corn	Manure	2.2	202	3350	565	414	17	6.0
	None	1.4	62	2600	462	239	15	8.0
Timothy	Manure	3.0	201	2650	216	273	15	4.9
	None	2.3	15	2100	140	144	15	4.8
4-Year	Manure	2.7	151	3850	245	307	18	4.8
Rotation	None	2.0	38	3230	258	240	17	4.9
6-Year	Manure	2.5	94	2600	210	233	16	4.5
Rotation	None	2.0	22	2866	108	113	16	4.6

After nearly three score and ten years of manuring, this treatment demonstrates that, in the matter of soil maintenance, it has values for (a) upkeep of the supply of reserve organic matter; (b) holding up the soil's content of phosphorus even when manure is relatively low as a fertilizer for this essential element; (c) preserving the supply of active potassium; (d) maintaining the exchangeable magnesium; (e) preserving the supply of active calcium; and (f) helping to hold down the excessive concentration of acidity as hydrogen. Manuring the soil has been doing these things for years under merely the belief in it as a good practice, and long before science gave us these few tabulations of what we can prove in favor of farm manure. In the organic matter of the soil as part of the nutrition of microbes, plants, animals and man there is still much in the realm of good practice and much remains yet for science to prove and to explain.

POSSIBLE POISONS NATURALLY

The organic matter in the soil represents the death-end processes of the organic remains of previous crops. They are giving up the inorganic parts which initially come from the soil. Those parts were the original mineral starters and directors of the chemical synthesis by the plants of their combustible selves. We commonly assume that organic matter in our crops, grown naturally, is always good nourishment for warm-blooded bodies, and always beneficial manure for microbes and plants when plowed under. Whether that is true depends on (a) climate, in general; (b) season, occasionally; (c) the plant species, in particular; and even (d) the soil. These factors may disturb the natural processes in the cycle of growth, death and decay enough to give poisons from organic substances in the soil. The processes may also be perverted from their normal by man's management to give poisons of our own making.

Poisonous organic matter may occur in the soil because we use highly poisonous organic chemicals as crop protection. We forget that putting them in the soil or on the crop, to protect against insects, fungi, bacteria and weeds, is also an application of them to the soil for possible poisons to the microbes and to the crops we grow, supposedly to be nourished, not poisoned, via the soil. Poisons put into the plant's living system may be a case of dangerously poisonous herbage and of turning under poisonous organic matter for the microbes or even for the following crop. The more powerful we make the poisons, especially those recently designed in terms of the complex carbon-ring structures with their additions, the more resistant, in general, those chemicals are to decomposition via natural chemical and biochemical processes in the soil and in the bodies and cells of the various living forms. It was this ring-carbon structure, like carbolic acid, from coal tar distillates, that was one of our first antiseptics. It serves well in killing bacteria. It is concentrated in the bark of trees. In passing from these to be recovered in coal, it suggests that it is chemically more stable, or permanent, than we appreciate.

While "more and better chemicals" are apt to breed confidence in better protective chemical services to crops, we need to be reminded that organic reactions are not completely predictable. What we call "better poisons" for plants, insects and microbes may bring on unknown side-reactions deceptively harmful to animals and man.

The crops are poisonous sometimes because the plants take up too extensively some poisonous elements from the soil in certain climatic settings. This is more common in areas of low rainfall, because the rocks and minerals have not been significantly weathered into soil. The two elements, molybdenum and selenium, will serve to illustrate the case of their concentrations in the herbage to be poisons to animals and man consuming the herbage and the seeds. Molybdenum in higher concentrations in the forage brings on excessive cathartic effects with emaciation and then death of the animal as the final result. Yet this is an essential element, especially if legumes are to grow root nodules and use nitrogen from the atmosphere in building their higher protein concentrations. Only fractions of an ounce of molybdenum per acre is the difference between success and failure of the legume crop. Likewise, only ounces in excess spell poison. Unfortunately, no soil tests commonly used give warning of such danger. Selenium, not considered a fertility element, is also taken excessively by crops in areas of lower annual rainfall. It accumulates too high concentrations in the plant tissue and in the seeds of some species. Certain geological conditions in the soil's origin contribute to the danger. Animals may discriminate against plants growing where the fertility is imbalanced, but their self-protection is not so discriminatory in case of selenium as an inorganic poison within the organic matter eaten.

That a plant species which grows on ordinary organic matter may have some varieties which grow food, while others grow poisons, is well illustrated by the mushroom. The distinguishing characteristics are not common knowledge. The crop is one of the fastest growing ones we raise. That speed is possible because the mushroom builds itself more from the only partially decayed organic matter synthesized by other crops. It suggests that all crops might be users of organic compounds more extensively than we realize, and susceptible to taking up poisonous organics as well as beneficial ones.

The early drug business was built up on herbs, extracts of plants and other organic materials grown naturally for their drug value. The pioneer studied his plant medicines. Even wild animals know theirs. Medicines and poisons from plants give their names to the labeled jars on the drug shelf too numerous to recount here. We need to remind ourselves that drug plants are naturally more numerous on the highly weathered soils of the wet tropics. Some narcotics will illustrate by listing, for example, quinine, opium, caffein, morphine, codiene, atrophine, digitalis, etc., all coming from plants, including larger plant groups among which some farm crops and weeds may be varieties. Organic poisons and drugs are common but our emphasis on those from the chemist's laboratory have made us forget those from plants. Farm crops carry drugs and poisons too. They develop these in some cases because of their disturbed growth. Sweet clover is an excellent legume for green manure effects in supplying corn with nitrogen. But corn grain grown after green sweet clover is turned under will not be taken by hogs if they choose corn grown where sweet clover grew to maturity and only the dead crop residues were turned under. Green sweet clover so used produces the drug dicumoral, an anticoagulant of blood. Other legumes, the crotalaria, grown in the south have varieties with poisonous effects. Cows offered these in cafeteria style will discriminate amongst them.

Some of the farm grasses and grains may grow poisons because of seasonal irregularities or even partial crop harvest by cutting. The rye will grow the ergot in place of a grain. Bluegrass does likewise. This is a fungus giving the powerful drug, ergotamine. Animals fed on grains or bays carrying the ergot become stiff, lose their hooves and eventually die. The common sorghums, also grasses, if cut and allowed to regrow produce a poisonous alkaloid acting via hydrocyanic acid. In these cases most of the poisons contain a complex carbon structure with nitrogen linked into it. However, this kind of nitrogen is not the amino form, characterizing the proteins for which every life form is struggling. Yet in measuring the crude protein contents of these crops we merely digest them in sulfuric acid, collect all the nitrogen, multiply it by 6.25 and call all of it protein. We are only coming around to realize that what organic matter we offer as nourishment to all the life forms, from the lowest to the highest, may possibly be poisons, even naturally.

POSSIBLE POISONS OF OUR OWN MAKE

We take it for granted that a growing plant, like corn in the field or in the garden, will be feed or food. We certainly do not expect it to be poison. Nor would we imagine that the nitrogen in the decaying organic matter, making its cycle of going from the dead plant remains to the living plant tissue, might be the dangerous element. We would not anticipate decaying organic matter to put poisonous nitrogen into the water we drink from our wells. The biodynamics of the living soil are also assumed to behave regularly. We forget that the climatic forces, the inorganic and the organic parts of the soil, and the particular growing crop, all operate under carefully integrated conditions to give what we know as normal crop growth of high food value. We can scarcely imagine that decaying organic matter, setting free its nitrogen in the soil to feed microbes, plants, animals and man, might be thrown out of integration to turn that nitrogen into poison for the entire upper part of that biotic pyramid. We may be growing crops in which the nitrogen is not a part of the protein but is poison of our own make.

Only slowly are we learning enough about the soil to appreciate how seriously some small changes in the growing conditions can affect the physiology of the crop. We may appreciate the complex physiology of our bodies, but we do not imagine that the physiology of the plant is very near the equal in complexity and delicate operations of its many required processes for healthy plants. During the high temperatures of 1954 in Missouri from late June to mid-September, unusual heat and drought operated through the soil organic matter to give disasters because we grew poisonous corn crops. The heat stunted the corn plants to make them represent death, not feed, for the animals. Man, too, was the victim in a few cases. But that dry season with its disasters brought our studies to explain why and how those resulted. Animal deaths from ensilage had been reported a few decades ago as *forage poisoning*. Corn stalk disease for horses and cattle was the label for autumn and winter troubles 40 years ago. The theory of the causes remained to suggest explanation at this late date.

Temperatures reached their maximum of 113 degrees F. in the early part of July. That high heat was sufficient to change the green color of the leaf to white in that end portion where the deficiency of nitrogen is regularly outlined when the corn is said to be fired by the drought. The absence of soil moisture, allowing the soil as well as the atmospheric temperatures to mount so high, was changed but briefly by a two-inch rain in early August. That set the rewetted soils into increased microbial activities in decaying the organic matter. That stepped up the conversion of nitrogen into the highly oxidized saltpeter, or the nitrate form. This salt naturally moved up into the plants. But since the activities by the enzymes in the leaves had been disrupted as the result of that living protein's pasteurization, the unaltered nitrates accumulated in the stalks. Chemical analyses of the internodal sections of them showed that there were increasing concentrations of nitrate nitrogen in going from the top sections toward the lower ones of the stalk. Even in the dry stalks in the field in January, dangerously high concentrations of nitrate (and nitrite) nitrogen were still present according to the chemical tests.

Those disrupted soil-plant activities concerned with the nitrogen coming from the soil's organic matter prompted the intense study because of the sudden deaths of cattle grazing the corn fields in September, and of men making ensilage, in due season, from the heat stunted corn. When cattle had grazed the injured corn plants in July or even in early August without deaths, it was most disturbing that the damaged plants should threaten with an epidemic of "silo-filler disease" caused by dangerous nitrous-nitric oxide fumes in silos after a day's operation of ensiling such corn fodder in September. At that time the California research by Dr. Went (later of Shaw's Botanical Gardens of Missouri) had not yet reported that high temperatures for tomato plants cause abnormally high nitrate concentrations in the plant tissues to disrupt fruiting. Nor had anyone ever seen yellow fumes roll out on the opened silo to flow to the ground to kill the vegetation to the leeward. We had not thought much about the freshly ensiled plant matter carrying on its anaerobic respiration in place of the normal aerobic one to give the reduction of the nitrates to nitrous oxide. We need the shocking experiences of the death of animals and man to bring the dynamics of soil organic matter to our attention.

As far back as 1918, there was some research by the Illinois Agricultural Experiment Station on animal deaths at certain seasons from feeding them ensilage. There had been deaths during some late winter seasons when the animals were feeding on the dry stalks in the fields. These reports, coupled with the experiences in 1954, are now pointing up the nitrate production in the soil from the oxidative decay of the soil organic matter (more lately from fertilizer nitrogen) particularly during drier seasons when the high temperatures disturbed the physiology of the plants. No such cases are on record for 1958 with its unusually favorable seasonal distribution (possibly excess) of rainfall in Missouri. Some animal deaths from their licking of nitrate fertilizers for salts through even a knothole have also contributed to the explanation. All the factors, viz: climate, soil, plants and animals need to be considered when such experiences are so disastrous.

Excessive nitrates naturally present in the soil in Kansas in March 1948, where no fertilizer nitrogen was used, were deadly to babies whose milk formulae had been made up with shallow well water carrying enough nitrates to be deadly. A dry autumn and early winter did not prohibit accumulation of nitrates in the soil. A heavy winter snow on which late March rains fell was rapid movement of ample water through the soils and into the wells to carry the dangerous nitrates from the soil into the wells with deaths for two babies. A third one was rushed to Kansas City where it was literally resurrected, as the report of the newspaper had it, on Easter Sunday. We have now learned to live with excess of nitrates so far as medical emergencies like these are concerned. We are now in position to be on guard when high temperatures may be reason for plants to accumulate them, or when droughts—and those broken by rainfall—may also move excessive nitrate nitrogen from the soil into the plants without their change of it to protein there.

AND MAN-MADE POISONS

Experiments using varied fertility of the soil under crops have demonstrated that plants protect themselves against insect and fungus attacks according to the balance of that fertility for suggested protein production by the crops.[1] Yet it is still a prevailing practice and belief that we should expect insect pests and fight them with powerful poisons. We have given little thought to the simple fact that we can nourish the plants so they will build their own protection (thereby also better nutrition for us when we eat them) according as we manage the fertility of the soil growing them.

Since insect poisons, such as DDT—in chemical name, 1,1,1-Trichloro-2,2-bis (p-chlorophenyl) ethane—have been used now for over a decade in agriculture on orchard and annual crops, with the latter grown on both the untilled and the plowed soils, it is timely that the research stations are giving us data on what the living soils are doing to destroy the residues of these powerful organic poisons so widely used in sprays, and conversely, what these deadly poisons intended for pests on the plants are doing to destroy the lowly life forms within the soil.

The very chemical structures of the DDT, and of other chlorinated hydrocarbons or similar sulfonated aromatics representing most of the recent deadlier poisons, suggest that these might be expected to persist unchanged in the soil, or as residues on food and in contact with any kind of matter. Since carbolic acid, or phenol, of allied chemical structure with but a single benzene ring, was one of the first antiseptics, it has been under study for many years to learn if there are any microbes which destroy it, as well as that it should seemingly destroy most all microbes. Only in a few instances, and under rarer conditions, has it been reported that some microbes suggest their breakdown of this carbon ring compound. If phenol is not broken down significantly in the soil, then we might well expect that these more powerful poisons, carrying combinations of several such rings with chlorine, sulfur and side-chains of carbon attached, would not be oxidized or changed much in the soil. That is the expectable, even though the surface layer of the soil is commonly considered a kind of universal crematory for most anything to the plants without their change of it to protein there. That condition may result even from the decay of natural soil organic matter. It should be more expectable if heavy applications of fertilizer nitrogen, as imbalance with other fertility elements, are used. We must know the nutrition of the plant as well as the fertility of the soil, since even the soil organic matter which is usually a safety factor in nature's nutrition of the crop, may prove to be poison under abnormalities in the crop's physiology as we manage the soil. organic that we consign to it for destruction and disposal. Some recent studies on the persistence of DDT gave reports for soils in various conditions and for time periods of ten or more years. Some turf plots in Cleveland, Ohio, were treated with this poison for Japanese Beetle in 1945 at three different rates. The soils were sampled in 1955 for recovery of this applied poison. The results are given conveniently in the table below.

Recovery of DDT in the Upper 6" of Silty Clay Loam Turf Plots in 1945 Treated 10 years previously.

DDT Applied Lbs./Acre		DDT Recovered	
	PPM	Lbs./Acres	Percent of Amount Applied
12.5	0.77	1.36	10.9
25.0	2.04	3.52	14.1
37.5	3.89	6.72	17.9

It is significant to note in these data that, even after ten years under the turf, as much as 10% of the original application was recoverable, and that was true for the lowest rate of the treatment. This tells us that this poisonous compound persists unchanged in the soil. It cannot be decomposed readily by the microbial life there. It renders, then, no food service to these lower life forms. It is significant to observe also from the data that the percentage recovery is higher as the application is heavier, i.e. a bigger share of the dose remains unaltered when that is heavier.

Soil samples taken in some two dozen orchards in the same studies by E.P. Lichenstein[2] where the sprays were used in successive years for as long as ten or more in the midcontinental states with soils of higher organic matter, there were pronounced accumulations of this powerful organic poison. After applications over periods from 9 to 11 years the DDT was still present in the soil in amounts ranging from 93.5 to 106.0 ppm in Indiana; 38.6 ppm in Ohio; 36.6 ppm in Missouri and 1.5 to 38.3 ppm in Michigan. In a total of 14 orchards tested, the average recovery was 26.6% of the total amounts applied, and 237.0% of the average annual application. These data tell us that, rather than serving to destroy this poison, the soil is retaining it against removal by rainfall or leaching, and against microbial oxidation or other chemical reactions resulting in loss of its lethality, or deadliness. The annual destruction by the soil falls far short of the annual application. The soil, like the human body, suffers from an accumulation of DDT poisoning. This is an attendant danger not so apt to be appreciated when the poison is used to destroy insects on the vegetation and not within the soil.

Similar studies on the accumulation of this organic poison in cropped soils, also in the cornbelt, growing various field and vegetable crops, showed serious amounts likewise. Of two dozen soils tested, the recovery from the surface layer of 6 inches amounted to 15.5% of the total applied, and to 61.2% of the average annual application. The concentrations remaining in the soil ranged from 0.38 to 4.6 ppm. Just what this accumualtion means is not apt to be fully appreciated. But it emphasizes its danger when this poison is accumulating slowly, for example, also in the fatty tissues of the human body, and gives varied symptoms of its lethality when body stress calls on that reserve energy store to consume it but liberate its stored poison content into the system. Then, also we dare not forget that organic compounds of similar chemical structures, applied to seeds, are taken up by most any plants. They can be expected to be taken by plant roots from the soil for many years after application, due to their unchanged persistence there, according to these data. That they would not be altered much by life processes within the plant might well be expected when the many varied microbial processes of the soil do not transform them during periods as long as a decade. Shall we not expect such poisonous organics to be accumulating in the crop's organic matter?

Reasonably mature judgment in behalf of our own health would arouse skepticism about consuming vegetables grown on soil poisoned for plants in our aims to poison only insects, and poisoned still more by spraying the plants directly. Shall we take chances on fighting a few maurauding insects today at the possible price of our own lives at some later date through the delayed action of lethal accumulations in the soil, and in the plants as well as in our bodies?

Natural organic matter in the soil is considerable protection against the deadliness of man-made organic poisons in an extensive chemical family including such names as aldrin, dieldrin, chlordane, lindane, toxaphene, methoxychlor, benzene, hexachloride and others. The soil organic matter absorbs them, so that they are less destructive to insects in contact with the soil, according to the report by the Wisconsin Experiment Station testing the poisoned soil with banana flies.[3] The clay of the soil exercises a similar but less pronounced absorptive effect. The silt and sand as separates exercise much less of such action on them. Accordingly, then, nature offers more protection for the insects against our attempts to poison them according as the soils are richer in organic matter, or are more fertile in this commonly neglected soil property. But conversely, the poisons will be more effective as we deplete our soils more of their natural organic matter. Also, but much worse on soils lower in natural organic matter, these man-made organic poisons neglected as residues within the soil will be more available to the plant roots and absorbed more readily into the plant tissues to make them more dangerous, or lethal as foods and feeds.

Highly organic soils, like the mucks required more than 25 times as much lindane and aldrin, for example, as were required by sandy soils, to be lethal under tests with banana flies. As the natural organic matter of the tested soils was higher, more of each of these poisons was required for lethality. Unfortunately, the reduction of effectiveness of the poison by the soil organic matter was due to only a physical effect, since the poisons were recovered by chemical extraction. Again, the emphasis for safety goes to the soil's content of natural organic matter as its "constitution," or as the prominent factor in ameliorating the damaging effects of these powerful man-made poisons. But while this protective service to some degree is a natural matter, we are making the poisons of so much higher lethality and are using amounts large enough to go far beyond the soil's protection of the insects. We cannot expect, then, to be protecting ourselves when such practices and poisons suggest their accumulations in the soils, in the crops, and in our bodies.

Instead of trying to kill insects marauding our crops, probably because of depleted soils, and thereby unwittingly poisoning ourselves, why should we not consider modifying the fertility of the soil as nutrition for the plants to enable them to ward off the insects, as the same plants must have done to survive before we domesticated them? Plants so nourished and so protected via the soil will not only give simultaneously larger yields per acre but higher quality as nutrition when consumed as feeds and foods.

MAN-MADE ORGANIC SUPPLEMENTS

In considering the soil, we commonly look at its organic matter as nature's supplement to the inorganic, or the mineral parts, for growing nutritious feeds and foods. But for folks unduly enthusiastic about the *organic* part, the use of *inorganic* salts is considered a doubtful treatment of any soil for better crop growth. Yet, the very soil itself consists of the inorganic rock substances—of rock and mineral origin—becoming soluble salts by which the creation of the organic part or the crops is possible. The inorganic part came first. The organic came second. The former supplements the latter, and vice-versa. But, among either there may be some kinds which may be injurious to the growing plants which, in their turn, may even be poisonous feed for animals, which live by consuming such organic creations.

Feeds have long been calling for supplementations of both the inorganic and the organic kinds. Among the inorganic supplements there have been the elements sodium and chlorine in common salt; calcium and magnesium in limestones; calcium and phosphorus in bone meal and inorganic phosphates; iron in ferrous sulfate; copper in a similar combination; zinc also as sulfate; cobalt similarly; and iodine in potassium iodide. The list may be extended. For many years too, feeds have been supplemented with the organic materials of higher nitrogen contents serving as "crude" protein supplements. Through the addition of such to the animal ration, the gains in the body weight of the animal per unit weight of consumed feed were increased. Very recently, instead of the crude proteins as feed supplements, use has been made of one or two of the amino acids—separated parts of the protein—to give decidedly more growth per unit of the carbohydrates as well as per unit of the "crude" protein eaten. More recently also, use has been made of specific man-made organic chemical supplements which do not finally become parts of the body tissue. Instead, they are simulated hormones of laboratory synthesis serving to speed up, or *whip* as it were, the cell growth and animal gain in weight into a higher rate. The synthetic female hormone of wide use in animal feeding, known as diethylstilbestrol is a good example. Only very small amounts need to be used because of the powerful—and potentially dangerous—effects of this laboratory attempt to duplicate the natural female hormone of body origin.

It is well to remember that a body, of either sex, generates hormones of both male and female effects, but with decided dominance of that one corresponding to the particular sex responsible. We would not expect plants to create, by their own growth, similar organic compounds which will, when consumed by the animals, serve the same as hormones of animal origin. Such is, however, the fact reported by Dr. H.S. Bennetts of Perth, Australia, when sheep consume the common clover, *Trifolium subterraneum,* grown in that country so extensively. Unfortunately, this legume—serving as the ration's supplement to the non-leguminous forages—destroys many sheep by bringing on urinary calculi (kidney stones), prolapse of the uterus, and other troubles for which no simple or effective relief has yet been found. Here there is excessively rapid growth of only a part of the anatomy, and a very decidedly disturbed condition in the excretionary function because plants produce a hormone duplicating the disasters reported for the artificial hormone, diethyl stilbestrol. These observations raise the question whether the production of sex hormones by the animals is not determined by the particular forages which the animal is taking. In practice, when the early fall growth of forages serves in this pre-breeding season as a "flushing" operation for increased conception, might that not be a case of giving the "nature-made" hormones?

The Kansas experiment station reported at *Livestock Feeders' Day* on May 21, 1953, on some feeding trials with sheep given stilbestrol, the man-made hormone supplement used as a tissue implant rather than via the digestive system. This was one of the 25 or more projects in animal feeding presented on that occasion and reported in their circular Number 297.

They reported that, "Gains were approximately one third larger in the lambs receiving the hormone implants. The rate of gain was not increased by giving a second implant after 70 days of feeding." Very significant is their further report that, "Where all the lambs received the hormone, the increased rate of gain was apparently due to greater feed consumption and the amount of feed per pound of gain was actually just as high, or a little higher, than in the lot of lambs receiving the same standard ration and where only half of the lambs were given implants." That the lambs given stilbestrol were not healthy is clearly indicated by the deaths of some, and by the report that, "A smaller percentage of lambs given stilbestrol was selected for slaughter as compared with those given no implants. Abnormal development of the reproductive organs was found in the wether lambs given the implants and these abnormalities were capable of producing prolapse of the rectum as well as symptoms of urinary calculi. A high incidence of these difficulties has been reported in several commercial feed lots where the lambs have been given stilbestrol implants."

They report and illustrate also the enlarged prostate glands when they emphasize "the almost enclosed lumen of the urethra of the lamb given two implants. While these animals had shown no external, visable symptoms of distress, it would appear logical that further closure of the urinary passage might result in symptoms similar to those produced by blockage of the passage by urinary calculi." The possible serious effects of the indiscriminate use of this hormone-like material in lamb fattening should deter any commercial feeders from using it until further work has indicated that it can be used safely without danger from heavy losses."

Since the chemical structures of the sex hormones resemble closely those of the coal tar distillates, reported responsible for skin cancers of mice, it would seem well that such unusual growths of the tissue of the sex organs provoked by stilbestrol should be examined to learn whether they represent malignancy in this animal tissue. Just what such condition in animals means for their meat as food is also a matter that ought to disturb our confidence in our own good health by eating animals that appear to be quite far from good health before slaughter. Much is still unknown in the creative processes of growing things when man-made supplements for increased rate of growth disturb the living processes to the potential destruction of the very organism itself. Instead of those growing things representing the natural survival of those most fit for their environment, they suggest man's attempts to keep the unfit alive. Much is still unknown about the nutritional values, or dangers, to the human consuming what he grows in his struggle to solve his problems of the proteins. Shall we not emphasize "nature-made" organic matter more and "man-made" organic supplements less?

EUROPEAN COMPOSTS REALLY "MAKE" MANURE

European agriculture, like that in most older countries, finds people living close to the animals and the barn. Livestock there is an integral part of the farm and of the family, much as we think of a dog, a cat, a pet pig, or a pet lamb. The barn and the house are often under the same roof; they may be a continuous building, possibly arranged in a quadrangular structure surrounding a central area often spoken of as the "Hof." We would consider it the barnyard. Under such arrangements the barn wastes are piled up in the "Hof" while being put through the process of "making manure" as the European farmer speaks of it. This "Hof" is the center of all other barnyard activities to say nothing of including those that we might not put in the front yard. That the farmer under the older civilization in some of those older countries should conserve the animal wastes and all other organic refuse so zealously seems strange to many American visitors. They brand him as a *peasant* for having what seems untidiness, if not even unsanitary practices, so close to the house. Little do they realize that the production of food is so closely linked with the conservation of the fertility coming from the soil in the crops, and especially with the nitrogen of soluble form in the animal urine.

Most rigid conservation of the fertility element nitrogen has been a requisite for the existence of agriculture on many of the older soils. Those countries have grown old and their soils have fed them all these years because their farmers used the compost as a big help in the maintenance of the soils. They must maintain their soils in fertility but particularly in nitrogen, the distinguishing element synthesized by crops into compounds of protein and of growth, capacity in contrast to those for the laying on of animal fat. Livestock is a part of the soil conservation pattern and fertility rotation scheme in older countries because the cow has always gone ahead of the plow there. She assayed the soils and her selection of them was nutritional security for the people following with the plow. She is power, she is some milk, and eventually she is meat. Because of her long life of labor before she becomes meat, however, we can understand why she is eventually served as sausage whereby some mechanical helps lessen the problem of mastication. In addition, she is a help in returning to the field much of the soil fertility and the organic matter taken from and grown there. By living as long as she does, she becomes the means of keeping much of the fertility rotating or going back to the soil. Ten years by one cow making a total of ten cow-years in that way will haul off the farm much less time and phosphorus in the bones and less nitrogen in the muscles than we do, for example, in ten cow-years made up of ten yearlings sold off the farm. Yearlings haul off the fertility built into their bodies before they have lived long enough to rotate much fertility back to the soil. They are consumers and removers of soil fertility. The old cow is rotator of it while doing other services besides making milk and meat as food.

Much of the European world has lime-rich soils. This is shown by the lower rainfalls that have leached them less and the extensive use of alfalfa, or "lucerne," as it is called there. This crop on well-limed soils is the means of taking some nitrogen from the air and building it into protein of the plant tissue. By using this as feed, the cow has a means of rebuilding her protein as she wears it out of her body and passes this original air nitrogen to the soil. Since it comes from the animal in highly soluble and volatile form in the urine the farmers of older countries use the bedding carefully and wisely to catch and preserve the liquid manure most completely.

If you should observe a French farmer carefully, you might find him bedding his animals with some coarse reed-like material cut from swamps that was dry enough in the summer to permit this harvest. Then you would find him adding some leaves collected from the forest. If you should ask him why the particular combination he would explain that the leaves, if used alone, pack too tightly to absorb the liquids, and the reeds, if used alone, do not compact readily enough. But as a mixture, the reeds are broken by trampling and the leaves intermingled with them make a bedding that is an effective absorbent. Experience of a long time has developed this art of blending even the constituents that go into an efficient bedding for the animals in some of these older agricultures.

To the European farmer who may be met cleaning the stalls and taking out what we call stable manure, this refuse is not strictly manure. To him it is more nearly a barn waste which he composts in order to "make manure," literally out in his frontyard, in what is the center of the barnyard or the "Hof." To him this barn product, or what we call stable manure, is not classified under that name. It must first be composted to really "make manure." Putting manure into the soil is a matter of providing a balanced ration for the soil microbes first and fertilizing the crops afterward. In feeding farm animals we demand a certain nutritive ratio, or a certain ratio of carbohydrate to protein. Since microbes can use materials of wide diversity, their demand is for carbon as energy in a certain ratio to nitrogen needed for growth material. The farmer of the Old World who composts his farm wastes knows the proper carbon-nitrogen ratio of the manure that must be obtained by composting before he turns it into the soil for them. When he is "making manure" as he speaks of this process of composting the barn waste, he is preparing a suitable diet for the soil microbes in order that they may live by it and yet make it serve to nourish his crops.

The mixture coming from the barn is an unbalanced microbial diet. It has a surplus of straw or woody material. It has too much energy foods for these microscopic life forms. Hence if this were turned into the soil they would balance it as their diet themselves by taking more soluble nitrogen, for example, or mineral elements from the soil. This microbial activity of feeding themselves properly would thus be competition with the crop for the nutrients in the soil. As a result the crop would be the loser. The microbes eat first. This is what happens to our corn when we turn under strawy manure ahead of planting it and then find it turning yellow or "burning out" as some farmers speak of such damage.

The farmer of the Old World making compost knows that he can't afford to run the risk of damage to his crop. In the prevention of it, he piles the material from the barn and all other organic refuse into a flat pile and looks after its proper moisture and air contents. There the microbes multiply rapidly because of plenty of carbon. This is consumed rapidly enough to cause the pile to "heat," as the farmer says it, or to burn off the carbon which escapes as gas while the nitrogen and other fertility elements are retained in building microbial products. When the pile has gone through the heat, the carbon-nitrogen ratio has become narrow enough, through loss of carbon to the air, so that it is a microbial diet which will give off nitrogen as the next set of them consumes it for the carbon as energy source. It is then that it is ready to go on the soil. It is only then that it will give something to the crop rather than take the fertility elements away from it. It is only then that it is truly a "manure" or truly a fertilizer, as the farmers of older countries use that term. Collecting the animal manures from the barn is merely the beginning of "making manure" in these older countries. It is the composting process that is included in the term "making manure."

When the nitrogen supply is so limited, and when crop production for feed and food is so dependent on this element of nutritional service to plants, animal and man, one can see why the compost heap finds a place in the European front yard. The size of the farming business and thereby the wealth of many families under this older agriculture can truly be measured by the size of the compost heap. Older countries may seem to have strange practices with reference to their soils, but under each of these seemingly odd things we may well expect some significant principle that has kept up the productivity of the land and helped in providing survival. It was the keeping up of the land in terms of its fertility that has allowed their soils to grow old gracefully and thereby their civilizations to last so long and to do likewise.

ORGANIC MATTER MAKES "HEALTHY" SOILS

Nature produces her mineral-rich, high protein crops only where there is a deep, dark-colored surface soil nourishing a crop of microbes on a generous supply of organic residues grown in place. Through that combination the microbes, as the primordial crop, serve to balance soil fertility potential for crops of more nearly constant nutritional services to the life forms fed by them. We do not yet appreciate the truly living soil, reflecting its degree of development of the rocks into creative potential according to the climate, all pictured in the profile of less than three feet of depth. Of that, the highly organic surface horizon buffers our shocking mechanical and chemical treatments, and yields nutritious crops in spite of, rather than because of, our management of it.

Just 40 years ago, Dr. H.L. Shantz, an outstanding taxonomist and ecologist, sketched a diagram of the depths of the surface soils of profiles under increasing rainfalls and differing crops as one goes from arid western United States eastward to the humid area. Arid soils have little organic matter and truly surface soil. The microbial activity within the semi-humid soils of the midwestern United States causes rapid decay of the protein-rich organic matter grown there. It releases the combined organic nitrogen, which is rapidly transformed into readily adsorbed ammonia and later into a soluble nitrate form whenever the soil moisture permits. The proteinacious vegetation in consequence offers itself for decay as a microbial diet with a narrow carbon-nitrogen ratio (the same ratio exhibited, for example, in the rapid spoilage of meat). This ratio reflects the high degree of activity of all the other fertility elements along with the nitrogen that contributes to the high protein content of the grasses.

These grasses include wheat, in which the high protein of the grain's endosperm, as well as the germ, is associated with the so-called hardness of the kernel. Nitrogen is put into the starch storage part of the grain because it is picked up by the roots from the greater depth of the surface soil later in the plant's growing season. This occurs after the germ has been laid down and the plant roots have followed the moisture removal downward in the deeper fertile profile. This suggests a high mobility of the soil's nitrogen, even under moderate moisture. All this is possible only because the fertility (much of it wind blown as surface deposition) produces a vegetation high in protein which serves as a well-balanced diet for rapid multiplication of the microbial forms that maintain the cycle of vegetative growth and decay. So, too, the high state of activity of the whole list of essential, mineral-rock elements favors the generous fixation of atmospheric nitrogen by both the free living microbes in the soil and those in the nodules on the roots of the legumes, naturally prominent in the mixed flora.

The combination of the high level of inorganic fertility, the rapid growth of protein-rich vegetation, and the speedy turnover of the fertility from the crop back to the soil, and vice versa, in the midcontinent and the West, means that the subterranean flora is held down by the shortages of carbon as energy food. This life within the soil is not in competition, then, with the crop plants for the nitrogen and the inorganic fertility supplies of the soil. Instead, the soil microbes prepare the fertility for the wheat crop. The shortage of bulk production as carbohydrates by crops is due to the shortage of water, that is, rainfall. But the scanty precipitation leaves within the soil the active offerings of both the inorganic and the nitrogenous organic fertility, by reason of which the meager rainfall is the indirect cause of protein-rich vegetation of lesser bulk per acre. It emphasizes itself as "grow-food" for healthy survival of all species fed by it.

Equally illustrative of the above basic principles, but in the negative for healthy life forms, is the physiological behavior of the microbial flora in the soils of the eastern United States with its opposite effects. The eastern soils, highly developed and leached under the higher temperatures and rainfalls keeping the soil profile permanently moist, support a carbonaceous vegetation of low protein, such as the forests. Forest litter, resting on top of, rather than within, the soil (as is the case with the matted grass roots of the prairie sod), has a wide carbon-nitrogen ratio. On decay, it furnishes a microbial diet deficient in growth essentials and unbalanced by excessive carbon. This diet does not encourage the soil flora and fauna to multiply rapidly; hence, breakdown of the litter is slow, and it accumulates on top of, or only partly within, the soil layer.

There is, then, only a shallow surface soil. Its oversupply of energy food for the microbes, together with the *deficiency of growth food,* leaves them ready and waiting for any nitrogenous and inorganic nutrients that may become available. Such a condition makes the microbes competitors with the growing crop plants for the fertility available within, or applied to, the soil. It is illustrated in practice by the plowing under of straw or woody vegetation which is so hazardous to a succeeding crop planted too near this tillage operation.

The crop cannot be highly nutritious in defiance of the microbes that eat first.

The ecology of our crops in the United States, growing our longer-lived cattle in the western midcontinent and fattening our shorter-lived pigs in its eastern part, tells us how nature managed the living soil as the quiet force in control of that arrangement, so successful long before we even recognized it. Our early soil-plant scientists pointed, as example for our management, to the fertility renewal in wind-blown rock-minerals and their development into ample fertility by organic matter returned for active microbial life that must be the forerunner of all the other crops by the soil, if they are to be healthy followers in that train.

ORGANIC MATTER—UNDER TIME AND TREATMENT

Sanborn Field of the Missouri Agricultural Experiment Station provides an excellent opportunity to study the properties and performances of organic matter in the soil. The latter reports the microbial activities or the life of the soil. The field was laid out in 1888, at a time when barnyard manure was the major fertilizer. Pressing questions then were "How much manure shall we apply per acre? Where in the crop rotation should it be applied? What crops should make up the rotation in contrast to a crop grown continuously on the same land?" Many of the original plot treatments, aimed to answer those questions, are still being followed.

Since the field is about to experience its 75th crop, or anniversary, it may be helpful to note the chemical changes in the organic matter of the different plots as indicators of the biological activities in the soils during the first two quarters of a century, and learn how these suggest the expected "life" in the soil to testify at the end of the third quarter. These reports may increase our appreciation of the organic aspects of the soil, so seriously neglected in research and being so rapidly depleted. Since the soil organic matter is a major natural resource in determining the higher qualities as food and feed values which our soils produce, its continued depletion becomes most serious. Since any living matter is distinguished by its chemical substance called "protein," and since this is characterized by the element nitrogen connected with carbon (both combustible), the chemical analyses of the soil by ignition served to measure these two life essentials in the soil at the end of the first 25 years. The data from such measures made on the soils of six of the plots on Sanborn Field, at two quarter-century periods, are reported in the accompanying table.

Only those soils under continuous cropping are cited, in order to eliminate irregularities due to changes in the crop during such a seemingly short period as a quarter of a century in the life-span of a living soil. Only two crops, and both of grass species, namely, wheat and timothy, are cited.

The soil treatments used were commercial fertilizer salts and barnyard manure. The latter was applied at two different rates: six (short) tons and three tons per acre per annum. The wheat crop involved annual plowing and additional soil tillage. The timothy plots were plowed occasionally at intervals of about six years, but represent maintenance of a grass sod. According to the data, these two different soil treatments emphasize clearly (1) the serious depletion of the soil organic matter under continuous wheat as a tilled crop; and (2) the opposite effect, or an increase in the soil organic matter by the untilled soil or sod-crop of the non-legume, timothy. The table divides itself naturally into two parts exhibiting these separate facts. The changes in the amount and kinds of organic matter are shown by varied values of both carbon and nitrogen, the two indices which must be considered in combination. If the soil organic matter increases, certainly the nitrogen as the index of living tissue must increase, if we view the living soils in terms of microbial performances or processes. The carbon may increase merely as if it were a charcoal, or non-living matter. It may also decrease while the nitrogen is increasing due to different quality or chemical compositions of the organic matter, shown by increases or decreases in the carbon-nitrogen (C/N) ratio.

Under the wheat crop, all soils showed decreases in nitrogen as the years went by. These declines were most rapid where commercial nitrogen alone (Plots 20 and 30) (see accompanying table) and commerical mixed fertilizers (Plot 2) were used for 25 years in the former and for 50 years in the latter. Instead of building up the soil's nitrogen, these additions of it in salts lowered the soil's supply most decidedly. Simultaneously, the carbon loss was relatively much higher where nitrogenous salts were used singly (plots 20 and 30) (see accompanying table) than where mixed fertilizers were applied (plot 2). In contrast, the soil under timothy sod gained in carbon whether given manure or not. However, it lost nitrogen when nothing was returned, but gained in this element and in organic matter in general when barnyard manure was applied.

That the nature of the soil organic matter was also changed is shown by the changes in its carbon-nitrogen ratios. Here again, the nitrogenous salt fertilizers disturbed this ratio most (wheat). The ratio was increased, not because the amount of carbon in the soil increased, but because the amount of nitrogen became decreased. Hence, there was less living organic matter. This substance may still have energy, or fuel values, but not much value for sustaining life. Hidden in the data of soils "living" during the two quarter-centuries, and long before so much nitrogen was available in commercial fertilizers, are the cold facts telling us that single element additions of fertility

Carbon and Nitrogen Contents (Also Carbon-Nitrogen Ratios of
Soils Under Continuous Cropping to Wheat and Timothy.
Sanborn Field, Missouri Agricultural Experiment Station

Plot Number	Cropping Periods	Crop, Soil Treatment	Carbon %[1]	Nitrogen %	Ratio C/N[2]
		Tilled Soil, Continuous Wheat			
2	1st 25 yrs	Wheat com'l	1.13	0.107	10.5
	2nd 25 yrs	Fertilizer	1.02	0.100	10.3
5	1st 25 yrs	Wheat 6 T Manure	1.52	1.40	10.8
	2nd 25 yrs	Wheat 3 T Manure[3]	1.27	1.19	10.6
20	1st 25 yrs	Wheat 6 T Manure	1.38	1.45	9.5
	2nd 25 yrs	Am. Sulfate	1.07	0.081	13.2
20	1st 25 yrs	Wheat 6 T Manure	1.61	1.71	9.4
	2nd 25 yrs	Sodium Nitrate	1.30	0.094	13.8
		Sod Soil, Continuous Timothy			
23	1st 25 yrs	Timothy, No.	1.32	1.41	9.4
	2nd 25 yrs	Treatment[4]	1.45	1.35	10.7
22	1st 25 yrs	Timothy 6T	1.69	1.77	9.5
	2nd 25 yrs	Manure	2.04	1.95	10.4

[1]Percent of Dry Soil. [2]Ratio of carbon to nitrogen in the soil. [3]Tons per acre of barnyard manure. [4]Save periodic plowing of both plots after plot 23 became foul with weeds.

are not maintaining our soils. Nitrogen, in particular, is even destructive of the virgin or reserve organic matter still remaining (or built up) in the soil. They tell us also that while chemical data give suggestions of slow changes, those under tillage of the soil announce forcefully that they seem deadly sure.

"Shall we be able to recover if the soil organic matter goes much lower?" is a very significant question. It is even more so in view of the fact that nature arrived at her climax crops only by returning *all* of the organic matter grown in place. Time and future treatments of our soils will eventually give the answer.

CHANGES IN QUALITY OF SOIL ORGANIC MATTER

In a previous discussion of the properties and performances of soil organic matter on Sanborn Field of the Missouri Experiment Station, the chemical analytical data showed the serious decline of the quality of organic matter in the soil during a 25 year period. The depletion of this important dynamic part of the soil was pronounced under no more tillage than that for a wheat crop. There was a marked loss of nitrogen, even under a continuous sod, in a timothy crop unless manure was applied. This loss of nitrogen, under removal of timothy hay and no soil treatment, took place even though there was an increase in the carbon of the soil. Accordingly, by using carbon as the basis for determining the soil organic matter, one falls into serious error, since the quality of the organic matter cannot be a constant if the carbon is under accumulation while the nitrogen is under depletion and both are its major components.

The extensive changes in quality (as well as quantity) of the original matter of the soil under various treatments is an outstanding fact established by this old experiment field. The use of commercial nitrogen only on wheat did not maintain (much less increase) the soil's stock of it. Quite the opposite, it reduced it by nearly 45% in 25 years. This resulted from using either ammonium sulfate or sodium nitrate. Yet, during that same time, the carbon reduction by either of these salts was near 20%, or less than half that of the loss of the nitrogen supply. When both nitrogen and carbon are constituents, such shifts in chemical composition suggest an approach to coal, an organic

TABLE 1
Soil Organic Matter After 25 and 50 Years
Lignin as Percent of Total Organic Matter[1]
(Sanborn Field)

Plot Number	Crop Soil Treatment		Organic Matter(%)	Lignin (%)
2	First 25 yrs	Wheat, Com'l	1.94	
	Second 25 yrs.	Fertilizer	1.75	39.5
5	First 25 yrs.	Wheat 6T Manure	2.62	
	Second 25 yrs.	Wheat 3T Manure	2.18	48.9
20	First 25 yrs.	Wheat 6T Manure	2.37	
	Second 25 yrs.	Wheat Am. Sulfate	1.84	46.1
30	First 25 yrs.	Wheat 6T Manure	2.77	
	Second 25 yrs.	Wheat Sodium Nitrate	2.22	50.5
23	First 25 yrs.	Timothy, No	2.29	
	Second 25 yrs.	Treatment	2.49	40.5
22	First 25 yrs.	Timothy 6T	2.91	
	Second 25 yrs.	Manure	3.51	48.8

[1] Calculated from carbon of soil.

matter of little support of microbial activity.

In an attempt to establish that fact about changes in quality of the organic matter under tillage and cropping, a test was used on the soils under wheat and timothy to measure the lignin part, or the degree of lignification as it changes toward coal-like lignite. The data for the lignin in percentage of the soil organic matter is assembled in table 1. Also given here are the quantities of organic matter after 25 and 50 years, based on the carbon by calculation.

According to the data, it is important to notice that the lowest percentage of lignin, or the more nearly complete destruction of this highly carbon part occurred where more complete fertilizers were used for the 50 years. This suggests that the extra fertility elements helped the microbes digest even the lignin. The highest percentage of lignin remained where sodium nitrate was the soil treatment for the last 25 years. Manure additions, seemingly, served also to retain a higher percent of lignin in the organic matter, even while the soil's supply of it was declining seriously. Manure with its high nitrogen content, in contrast to other elements, acted much like nitrogen salts to emphasize the lignin part and bring about an organic matter of less microbial activity or service to crop growth.

That these soils were not really dead, but only starved for organic matter, was demonstrated under laboratory tests of their transformation of applied green manure nitrogen for its accumulation as nitrate nitrogen. Samples of the soils under wheat and timothy were given (1) no treatment, (2) organic matter (leguminous), (3) limestone, and (4) organic matter and limestone.

TABLE 2
Nitrate Nitrogen (Pounds per 2 million) Accumulated in Six Week Test

Laboratory Treatment	Wheat Continuous	Timothy Continuous
None	59	48
Organic Matter	52	110
Limestone	102	104
Limestone Plus Organic Matter	172	183

When kept under proper moisture and incubation for six weeks, the accumulated nitrate nitrogen was trebled and quadrupled by the applied combination of organic matter and limestone (table 2).

Hidden in the soil's experiences of this old field, now approaching 75 years, are the following facts:

1. We are starving the soils into low productivity by neglecting to supply active organic matter.

2. We are not building organic nitrogen into the soil, but are depleting the supply of it more rapidly by adding only commercial nitrogen.

3. The remnant organic matter has changed in its quality to be more carbonaceous or coal-like and more deceptive in value when considered in the services the active organic matter renders to give nutritional quality to foods and feeds.

4. In our haste to look ahead we miss much without an occasional look back.

SOIL HUMUS . . . CHELATOR OF INORGANIC ELEMENTS

Nature does not divide the chemical reactions of microbes, plants, animals and man into what was once called the *inorganic* chemistry and the *organic*.

Instead, she carries on the chemistry of living matter (biochemistry) by reactions between large molecules containing both the ash elements (inorganic) and the combustible ones (organic). Because the science of chemistry began with the inorganic compounds, familiar to more persons now, and then came along later with organic chemistry, we are not prone to envision these *two kinds of chemistry joined* in the soil and in the growth processes of all life forms.

In what has recently been called *chelation,* we recognize that biochemistry is often a case of the organic molecules combining with, or enshrouding, the inorganic ones. By this action there is little separation into ions—the common behavior of inorganic salts—in water to allow them to conduct electricity. Thus, we do not see the larger living parts mobilizing—and managing—the dead ash elements. The biochemical action is mainly a molecular one, and between much larger units to give slower rates of reaction. These make time a fourth dimension of the organic and living processes.

It has now been established that the fertility elements, like calcium, magnesium, phosphorus, iron and others, are moved from the soil into the plant root as insoluble parts within larger organic molecules. Also, the same elements are moved about within the plants in similar combinations, or chelations, of themselves as non-ionic parts within a large organic one. Then too, the nutrient elements taken from the soil by the one kind of chelator compound may be shifted into other chelator molecules before they have moved very far up through the plant stem. In these natural facts we recognize now that organic molecular compounds are taken from the soil into the plant as its nutrition as well as, or (possibly) better than, the plant takes from solution the same ions, namely calcium, magnesium, phosphorus, iron and others broken out of rock minerals by natural weathering processes. We now recognize the plant's intake of nutrient elements from the soil as both the soluble ionic forms and also their chelated combinations into large organic molecules.

These chelator services were first demonstrated by feeding the chelator compounds already combined with an element or by demonstrating the chelator uptake in one part of the root system and its effect on the chelation and mobilization of the elements from some other part of the soil by other roots of the plant. In similar experiments, the humus extracts from ordinary cultivated garden or field soils served as well to chelate and mobilize within the plants the fertility elements from the soil. The research separation of the humus from soils on Sanborn Field at the Missouri Experiment Station and the chemical analyses of it from soils under various crops and soil treatments demonstrated clearly that calcium, phosphorus and even silicon were insoluble and non-exchangeable parts within the humus, (table 1).

TABLE 1
Humus (Percent in Soil) and Its Content of Nitrogen, Carbon, Calcium, Phosphorus and Silicon Under Manuring and Different Cropping for Fifty Years. (Sanborn Field, Mo., Expt. Sta.)

Crop	Soil Treatment	Soil Humus%	°N%	C%	Ca%	P%	Si%
					Humus Content		
	Manure	3.280	7.40	14.15	2.24	0.710	6.05
Corn	None	3.218	3.45	8.76	2.12	0.448	3.34
	Manure	4.712	7.09	14.11	1.71	0.648	3.44
Timothy	None	3.314	5.52	16.51	1.71	0.842	2.82
	Manure	3.958	5.34	18.09	2.74	0.724	5.70
Rotation	None	3.322	4.99	17.07	1.56	0.808	2.16

°These symbols refer to the following order of elements, N-Nitrogen, C-Carbon, Ca-Calcium, P-Phosphorus and Si-Silicon.

Viewed as a collodial chelator of plant nutrients, humus appears more important in providing a better balanced plant diet of fertility elements than if viewed as a random ionic mixture taken from the soil solution. This balance value of humus has come about from the digestive activities of microbial life forms. It brings us to see that:

1. Plants can be fed by organic matter seemingly more effectively than by inorganic matter only, and . . .

2. The organic matter, like humus, holds the inorganic elements as the insoluble, yet available, nutrition in more favorable balance for nutrition of both microbes and plants.

HUMUS . . . SOIL MICROBIAL PRODUCT

In a chemical study of the varied nature of the organic part of the soil, the methods required for extracting the humus fraction for detailed analyses suggest some of its properties. The methods consist of leaching the soil first with an acid until no more calcium appears in the leachings. This removes the exchangeable, or absorbed, cations from the humus and clay, the collodial parts of the soil. It also makes acid-humus and acid-clays. Hence, any calcium or other cations found by later analyses of the humus must have been a part within the humus and within the clay molecules and not merely adsorbed on their surfaces. Calcium, for example, would scarcely be available from this humus to the plants unless the organic part was first altered (as we expect from microbial digestion of it) to put the calcium into more available, but not necessarily soluble, ionic form.

After being leached with acid, the soil is treated similarly with distilled water until it is acid-free. It is then shaken in an ammonia solution. This separates the black, collodial humus from the soil as a suspension of ammonium-humate. This is poured off, more ammonia washing is given to it, and the resulting humus suspension is aerated and finally made acid to permit filtering off the precipitated humus. This product is washed, dried, and weighed to learn the fractional parts of the soils it represents. These percentages are given in the table. The weights of the humus fractions of the six different soils represented from over three to nearly 5% of the dry weights of the soils. The humus separates were analyzed for their nitrogen, carbon, calcium, phosphorus and silicon, also reported as percentages of the humus and given in the table.

It was quite evident from the analyses that the manure served to maintain

Some Chemical Elements in Ratios to Each Other According to the Soils Under Manuring and Different Cropping for 50 Years (Sanborn Field, Mo. Agr. Expt. Sta.)

Crop	Soil Treatment	Ratios					
		CN°	C/P	C/Si	N/P	Ca/P	Si/Ca
	Manure	1.91	19.93	2.32	10.42	3.15	2.71
Corn	None	2.54	19.95	2.62	7.70	4.73	1.57
	Manure	1.99	21.77	4.10	10.94	2.65	2.01
Timothy	None	2.99	19.60	5.85	6.53	2.04	1.64
	Manure	3.38	26.36	3.17	7.37	3.78	2.08
Rotation	None	3.42	21.12	7.81	6.17	1.94	1.38

°These symbols refer to the following order of elements, C-Carbon, N-Nitrogen, P-Phosphorus, Si-Silicon, Ca-Calcium.

a higher humus content in the soil. Its benefit was not significant in connection with continuous corn, but amounted to 40% difference in the case of timothy grown continuously.

Manure held the nitrogen content of humus high by differences as much as doubling it. The manure held the carbon of the humus higher under corn and rotation, but not under timothy. These facts suggest the more coal-like nature of the humus under the two crops given tillage, and similarly high degree of carbonization of this organic fraction where timothy was given no fertility return as manure. The chemical analyses of the humus calculated in ratios between them (see table this page). These ratios suggest the low quality of the humus as microbial nourishment after extended cultivation of 50 years. The ratio of the carbon to nitrogen (C/N) tell us that, as a microbial diet, the wider ratio means less nitrogen or *grow-food*. Also, according as that ratio approaches 2.00, going from the larger figures, the more nearly are the measurements reporting mainly microbial bodies rather than much additional organic matter. Hence, the data suggests the high stability of the chemical nature of the humus after crop removal and increasing deficiencies in fertility.

The calcium within the humus, reported either as percentage or as ratios to phosphorus and to silica, does not vary widely because of manure additions, save in the case of crop rotation. That no treatment has caused the humus to be low in calcium and that manure has given higher calcium is evident in both of these measurements. But most decidedly noticeable in the data is the small variation of the phosphorus in the humus, save where no treatment and cropping to corn continuously were combined. In that case the ratio of calcium to phosphorus was lower; while for timothy it was higher for manure over no treatment. This raises the question whether the phosphorus as a nutrient element is so seriously deficient after 50 years that any available fraction of it is quickly taken by microbes for use in energy metabolism or in growth of cell tissue. Its ratio to carbon fluctuates very little, while its ratio to nitrogen does so to a greater degree. These facts suggest that the phosphorus in the soil organic matter (to say nothing of it as inorganic forms) is limiting the bacterial action in mobilizing the carbon and nitrogen in connection with itself as an active nutrient. Consequently, the soil is less for crops in both quantity and quality as nutrition for higher life forms.

After 50 years of cropping (a) these soils have gone down decidedly in their organic matter; (b) their seasonal cycle transforming it is at a low level; (c) their mobilization of the inorganic essentials into plant roots is reduced by less chelation services of the microbes; and (d) there is a failing natural balance of the plant diet of humus in both ash and organic parts. Are not such conditions reasons why crops on such soils are of low quality in (a) their value as food and feed; (b) their self-protection against pests and diseases; and (c) their capacity to reproduce with high yields; all of which the gardener boasts about when he applies organic matter plentifully in his practice of what he calls organic gardening and farming. Apparently we need more than chemical data on soil humus and more than 50 years of experience, hidden in the records, before we realize how rapidly tillage and salt fertilizers have burned out the soil organic matter, and how slowly it can be restored. Restoration of the soil becomes more difficult once it has gone too low to produce a crop of healthy soil microbes which must be fed first before the soil will feed any other living form.

THE VALUE OF ORGANIC MATTER

The declining numbers of acres left for growing crops, and the dwindling supply of soil fertility, are bringing home to us the necessity of properly fertilizing our soils. The tonnage of available barnyard manure has long been insignificant as a source of fertilizer supply. Gradually we are coming to realize the basic fact that our soils are being rapidly worn out, because of our old concept of using them as a source for cash crops rather than as a means of growing crops completely to nourish our animals and ourselves. Organic matter, such as animal and plant manures and accumulated virgin soil, has always been the most desired form of fertility for growing our crops, and thereby in turn to feed well our farm animals and ourselves. Now that we have mined most of the original organic matter supply, to say nothing of the inorganic, we are debating the question among ourselves as to whether we can produce good foods and feeds from our crops when they are grown without organic manures to help fertilize them.

Soil itself originated from the rock minerals. In trying to learn what the soil feeds to the plant, we made a list of the inorganic elements found in the plants after reducing them to ashes. Inventories of the inorganic elements in the plants were then matched against inventories of the soil's similar contents. Such knowledge built up the inorganic concept. This knowledge also is serving well for our testing of the soil's needed supplies as against the growing plant's contents; for we have learned that a growing plant contains 13 or more essential inorganic elements which move into the crop from the soil. By the help of such tests, we make our decision when buying needed chemical fertilizers to act as supplements to the incomplete plant and animal matter of the soil.

Success to date in improving the yields of our crops, by means of commerical fertilizers, has naturally emphasized the crop's need of inorganic nutrients from the soil. Unfortunately, such success in some instances has made us prone to discredit the value of both plant and animal manures. It has encouraged us to believe that manure is worth no more than the total of nitrogen and inorganic elements it contains. Yet tests have shown otherwise when plants are grown by hydroponics, or water culture. The growing of plants in pure water, to which has been added the chemical equivalents of the manure's ash components, is not the equivalent of growing them in rotted manure itself. Organic processes in general, however, and most biochemical reactions, do not give such speedy comparative performances. Even some inorganic reactions, particularly those including the element silicon, making up such large molecules as the clay, are slow and sluggish. Only lately have we become able to build up organic compounds like the synthetic fibers (rayon, vicara, orlon and others of industrial output) to substitute for those created naturally. Something of this sort may later become applicable for soil use.

Plants will grow when fed on strictly inorganic elements in water, but that fact is no refutation of the possiblity that such a seemingly good diet for plants might not be a better one if supplemented by some organic compounds. The limitations of hydroponics indicate how much such plant growth procedure differs from that of plants growing in the soil. Hydroponics may grow the plant, but this is not a process necessarily duplicating those activities involved in growing plants in the soil, even insofar as inorganic nutrients are concerned. Consequently the fact that plants can be grown with reasonably good yields, on wholly inorganic materials, does not prove that plants, if grown by different dynamics within the soil, may not take from the soil some organic compounds serving best for plant nutrition.

The pioneer farmer looked much to the organic matter of the soil to produce the crops for feeding his young animals. Early sales of commercial fertilizer, particularly in the South, met with resistance due to the farmers' just contention that bird guano from South America helped their crops more than they were helped by Chile saltpeter. Now we find that the antibiotics are doing wonders for us. Water extracts of the organic matter in soils serve as growth hormones in the laboratory for test plants. Hogs have long had the habit of rooting. They have been grown more rapidly under experiment if allowed on pasture, or if fed some sod soil or its equivalent in antibiotics, as compared to strictly dry lot feeding. Isn't it then time that we open our minds to the possibility that organic compounds, as well as inorganic, may be needed for better plant and animal nutrition, and for superior reproduction of their respective kinds? Mushrooms are a food crop that grows by feeding wholly on organic matter. They grow in the dark; consequently they do not use energy directly from the sunlight. For energy, they must absorb organic compounds, and burn them or respire them. They create living organic matter by using dead and decaying matter.

Some field tests have been conducted at the Missouri Station on the use of various kinds and combinations of organic and inorganic fertilizers for growing field corn. In these tests corn was grown on three plots treated as follows: (1) limestone, (2) limestone and phosphorus, and (3) limestone, phosphorus and potassium. On these three experimental plots sweet clover was grown as a green manure crop, then plowed under ahead of the corn. As a control, corn was also grown on three comparable plots which received exactly the same inorganic fertilizer applications (1,2, and 3), but in this case the sweet clover was allowed to occupy the plots for the entire season. The sweet clover plants grew to maturity and produced seed; the seed was harvested and the remaining plant residues were then plowed under in the fall to be followed the next season with a corn crop. As a result of these treatments and applications, higher yields were obtained when larger and more complete combinations of inorganic fertilizers were used as in plot number 3. However, there was no significant difference in corn yield between using the sweet clover planting, earlier in the season as a green manure crop, as compared with letting it mature. The grain grown on each of these plots was harvested and later put in separate compartments of self feeders, and made available to hogs. The hogs voted, as manifested by their appetite, in favor of organic matter in the form of mature sweet clover residues (plus the fertilizers used in plot number 3), as compared to the clover as an immature green manure crop.

Recent research by Dr. Francis.M. Pottenger, Jr., of Monrovia, California, points out that differences in the way the feed was handled or processed, for the animal making manure from it may be reflected as corresponding differences in the character and manner of growth by the plants and their seeds on soil fertilized with such manure. For example, some dwarf bean plants were grown on the sand of various pens into which cats had buried their dung for the two preceding years. The pens included cats fed alike in all respects except for differences in their milk, which included: (a) condensed, (b) evaporated, (c) pasteurized, and (d) natural (raw) milk. At the end of the tests, it was clear that the four different kinds of milk, fed to the cats, produced different growth effects on the bean plants which had been fertilized by these various cat dungs in the sand pens. Dung from all the cats that were fed heated milk produced only sparse plant growth. On the other hand, dung from cats fed the natural (raw) milk produced such fertile soil that a dense, healthy plant growth resulted.

The first weed growth later was removed, and the pens were then seeded to the ordinary white bean of dwarf growth habits. It was most surprising to note that in all six pens, in which the buried dung was from cats fed the heated milks (condensed, evaporated and pasteurized), the bean plants grew only as dwarf plants. But in the two pens in which the buried dung was from cats fed unheated milk, the bean plants grew, not as dwarf plants, but as pole beans with their vines going to the top of the screened sides of the pens. Here is an illustration that organic compounds, as well as the inorganic elements, may be traveling in cycles: first, from the soil into the plant, for their build-up into more complexity there; then into the animal, for possible digestive simplification there and later, through the excretions back to the soil, for another cycle of nutritional service. It is particularly significant that the illustration cited relates to the amino acid tryptophane, which is the major deficiency protein of the corn grain. When the effects from fertilizers on soils are measured only by yield variations in vegetative bulk, recorded as tons and bushels, there is little chance that we shall recognize crop differences demonstrating the varying effects between the use of inorganic and organic fertilizers. Our animals, however, tell us that the crop's nutritional quality reflects the different organic and inorganic compounds feeding the plants. When we learn to measure the crop's responses to soil fertility by more than bulk values and ash differences, then the contributions of the soil, both organic and inorganic, to plant nutrition will be more correctly realized.

ORGANIC MATTER BALANCES SOIL FERTILITY

Soil tests, attempting to measure plant nutrition, have demonstrated that the high quality of the crop depends on what may be called a "balanced diet" offered to the plants by the soil. In its first aspect, that diet consists of the required insoluble, but available, inorganic elements. The amounts of several of those have now been specified within fairly reliable ratios for balance.

YOUNG SOILS SOON GET OLD (SANBORN FIELD TESTIFIES)

When the young soil in Sanborn Field was plowed out in 1988 and put under different treatment in the many plots by the Experiment Station, Professor Sanborn left several with continuous cropping and no soil fertility return. These had the entire crops, both grain and straw, removed.

We can get a picture of some of the indicators telling us that soils become old, or how productivity declines, by studying the wheat yields of Plot 9. Nothing but the wheat stubbles were put back as organic matter. The grain grown there was not used as seed. Consequently there was no fertility applied save some very small importation of it via that route. Early plowing in the fall also reduced the chance for weeds to serve as catch or cover crops.

The wheat yields during the last 30 some years, plotted as a graph and illustrated herewith, show there the mean grain yield has been going down slowly to indicate the declining soil fertility. But more significant is the evidence of the declining rate of the chemical dynamics within the soil for release of active nutrients from either the inorganic supplies in the mineral reserves or from the crop residues as organic ones. The rise of the yield curve in nearly alternate years fairly regularly, and its corresponding schedule of fall suggest that this soil's chemical and biochemical activities are not ample to get it ready by the October seeding when it gave a yield in July. This soil now requires a "barren" year, or low yield year, to rest and to get itself ready for a yield the next year. This behavior of the soil body is a clear illustration that it is getting old, more frail and is slowing down.

NUTRITION AND THE CLIMATIC PATTERN
OF SOIL DEVELOPMENT

The nomad found his good nutrition when his cow went ahead of his plow. His herds were biochemists assaying and selecting the soil as guarantee of their growth and reporduction via proper nourishment. They were not measuring its production as tons and bushels per acre under economic pressures. Their nomad owner plowed it with assurance of its delivery of the requisites for his good nutrition. But modern technolocial means put the plow ahead of the cows. They pushed agriculture away from more fertile soils under animal selection and into the fringes of fertility. There single crop specialization flourishes under hidden hazards for, and deficiencies in, nutrition.

The climatic pattern of soil development of the United States emphasizes the fertility of the mid-continent for protein production and nutrition of high order. This was once buffalo territory, and later the hard wheat and beef cattle area. Less rainfall and insufficient soil development to the West limit production in balanced nutrition. More rainfall and excessive development of the soil to the East represent greater nutritional problems in its delivery of mainly carbohydrates under the criterion of, and economic emphasis on, bulk. Basic to this varied food synthesis by the plants is the pattern of the chemical fertility of the soil.

Our national pattern delineates the ecology of the soil microbes, of the native and crop plants, of the wildlife, of the domestic animals, and of man himself. We have been late in seeing ourselves and other life according to the variation in nutrition determined by the fertility pattern of the soil. Geographic arrangements of draftee rejections, of tooth troubles, and of diseases more generally have not yet been viewed as the possible result of nutritional deficiencies going back to the soil. Whether we can see a world pattern of control by the soil seems to await the day when not only deficiencies in nutrition but hunger in terms of failing bulk compel us to recognize that the soil is in control.

Those specifications hold more particularly for the ash-rich and protein-rich crops, like the legumes.

The clay and the humus are the parts of the soil responsible for the concept of "insoluble, but available" nutrients. Of those, the calcium, magnesium and potassium have been fairly accurately determined as desirable amounts required in a soil to prevent deficiencies of them. Sodium, as the alkaline element, and hydrogen, as the acidic one, have been listed as *tolerable* amounts or ratios, above which they would be injurious. These are the positively charged elements. They are held as insoluble, but available, ones by the col-

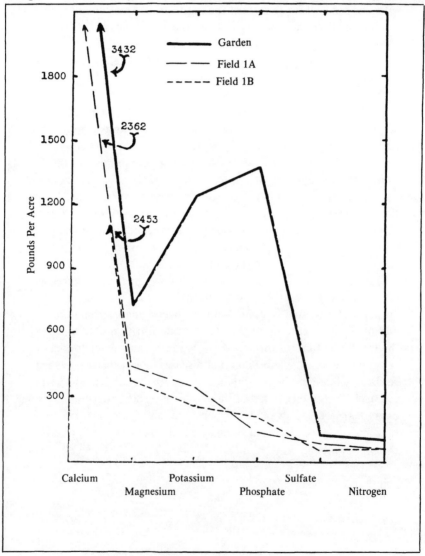

lodial (glue-like) humus and collodial clay. By means of their adsorbing capacity, those two parts of the soil filter those soluble elements out of solution. They hold them as "insolubles," much like the water softening compound takes soluble hardness out and holds it.

But those first four essential, adsorbed elements are given up to the plant root when it comes along and exchanges hydrogen, or acidity, for them. The hydrogen does not serve as a nutrient from that source. These elements are insoluble in rainwater going down through the soil, yet they become available ones, so far as the plant nutrition is concerned. The soil's capacity for holding positively charged elements, or cations, is measured by soil tests. That property is called the "cation exchange capacity", (CEC). It is specified in terms of "equivalents of the hydrogen." The amounts of each of the five elements (calcium, magnesium, potassium, hydrogen and sodium) held by the exchange capacity, are also measured. They are specified as their percentages of that total capacity.

The desirably balanced plant diet, according to experience to date in soil testing related to plant nutrition, would have the available calcium represent 60-75% of the soil's exchange capacity; magnesium, 10-20% and potassium, 2-5%—all so balanced to prevent deficiencies. Then it would have sodium take up 0.5-3% and hydrogen less than 10% to avoid excesses of these two. Trace elements are significant for plants in such small amounts that our measures yet designed are too unreliable to warrant specifications of them for either soil or crop. In its second aspect, the plant diet includes organic compounds. The organic matter is nature's main means of giving the "balanced" property in the soil for growing plants as contrasted to growing them in the highly diluted solutions of salts of the nutrient elements used in the practice of "hydroponics." Soil tests of farms in Lancaster County, Pennsylvania, the home of the Garden Spot of America Organic Club, give the evidence for the truth of that statement. For years, that county has practiced using both barnyard and green manures for building up the soils in organic matter. Much use has been made of limestone, rock phosphate, glauconite (green sand marl), granite dust and other natural mineral applications to the soil. Those practices are showing, according to the soil test data, that organic matter is the safety factor against excesses of elements in soil treatments, or upsets and imbalances in the plant diets resulting in low quality of the crops as feed and food.

The soil test data from the more than 80 acre farm of Mr. and Mrs. Willis K. Killhefer of Manheim, Pennsylvania, may well be one of several that could be taken as examples. They grow wheat, corn, tobacco, red clover, soybeans, grasses and an excellent garden with vegetables and flowers in wide variety, but high quality. They market their crops via cattle and chickens to

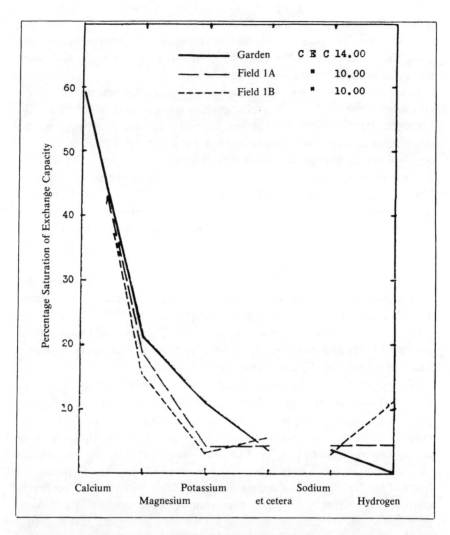

give human food products mainly as milk and eggs. Such a plan of management calls for purchase and import of concentrates to supplement the generous yields of forages, ensilage, hay and bedding. But all those result in the larger amounts of manure managed carefully to maintain fertile fields, but particularly a more fertile garden considered "so essential for the health of the family." It is the garden, managed by machinery insofar as possible like the fields, that speaks for organic matter to balance plant diets for crop quality.

Its soil tests tell us that one builds balanced soil fertility successfully by using generously of organic manures and natural mineral fertilizers, and enough so to be satisfying even where the crop quality goes under critical taste inspection regularly by the entire family. The garden lies alongside the road as "front" to the house and farmstead. There are fields on either side of the garden which suggest, in advance of soil inspection, that all three are of the same soil type. Consequently, differences in the values found by soil tests for the garden and fields must be due to the generous manuring and treatment with minerals. The test results exhibit the two fields as very much alike. But they show that the garden is decidedly higher in all the values measured by test, yet those are well balanced as plant nutrition. This is true even after the soil's total exchange capacity (CEC) in the garden has been increased during the years of organic manuring by 40% over that of the adjoining fields. That has increased the available fertility in the garden accordingly.

The test results, or measured amounts of the available fertility as pounds per acre, i.e., per 2 million pounds of soil, are shown in figure 1. The different elements are listed along the base line. Their pounds per acre are shown along the left margin (going upward). It is significant to note that the values for the garden soil (solid line) are far higher than those for the two adjoining fields. They are particularly higher for the phosphate and the potassium. At first sight, the curve for the garden as pounds per acre appears a bit erratic, especially the potassium. But when one considers (a) that the organic matter of the garden soil was increased by nearly 70% above that of the fields, and (b) the mineral treatments were separate applications, should one not anticipate possible imbalances? Yet, quite contrary to such anticipations, the test values in figure 2, reporting the percentages of saturation by the elements of the exchange capacities of three soils, show that they are each in like balance according to desired standards as we now have them. Even if the values of the total exchange capacity for the garden went up 40% over that of the fields, because of its increased organic matter, each of the elements increased accordingly and none went out of balance. Nature's balance by organic matter transcends man's by soluble means. According to the report, there was little that the professional soil tester could specify as deficiencies or necessary treatments. About all he could recommend was to keep on with the past *natural* practices as this farmer in the Garden Spot of America had been using them for many years. He had followed nature's methods of providing balanced diets for growing nutritious crops and had not fallen into any errors as far as man's knowledge to date could determine.

5

MYCORRHIZA

MOBILIZERS OF ORGANIC PLANT NUTRITION

Mycorrhiza is a term first used about 75 years ago. It refers to the many fungi in close contact with—and entering into—the plant roots growing in virgin soil or in soil with ample organic matter. It has long been a question whether the fungi are "friend or foe."

The term *mycorrhiza* carries the concept that soil fungi are symbiotically nourishing plants by the products of decomposition of the organic matter in the soil on which these microbes live. The plant roots are in close contact with the mycelia (threads) composing the fungi. These are the major microbes bringing about the early stages of decay of the fibrous, organic substances going back to the soil from vegetation grown on it.

Hidden away in the laboratory notebooks, microscopic slides, recorded observations in the field, glass house and laboratory, as well as in the visions and theories of a botanical naturalist of more than fourscore years, S.C. Hood, Hood Laboratories, Tampa, Florida, there is much to clarify the natural organic nutrition of our crop plants. Hood has collected, arranged and logically organized many facts about the dynamics of soil organic matter as it functions indirectly in plant nutrition via fungi, and by direct uptake through plant roots.

Fungi isolated from plant roots and grown on laboratory media, listed in the order of survival under declining soil fertility.

Left: As nodular excrescences formed by fungi within them. (Fraxinus americana, white ash.)

Right: Gliocladium

Left: As outer net enshrouding root of Scutelaria integrifolia, an harbaceous or shrubby plant of rock gardens.

Right: Trichoderma viride

Left: As outer net of Basidiomycetes and undernet of smaller fungi on root of Galax aphylla.

Right: Fusarium

Living plant roots in suggested symbiosis with soil fungi.

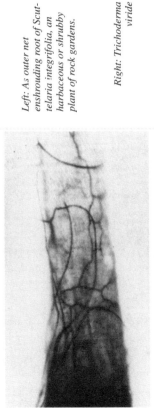

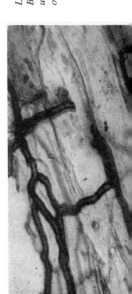

The latter is now an expanding concept. It will welcome the support of Hood's reports. We are turning more attention to uptake through plant roots, with more appreciation of organic matter serving naturally during the past ages, since commercially-produced organic chelators are known to have moved and circulated iron, phosphorus, magnesium, etc. inside the plants. This attention was encouraged decidedly when organic extracts of soil were shown to duplicate the biochemical services of these proprietaries.

But the concept that fungi, living on decaying organic matter and in intimate contact with the inside and outside of the root, move organic nutrient compounds from the soil into the plant is one which many folks say just ain't so. This contradiction may be a confession of ignorance when the facts of careful research have been established to tell us more widely that "it *is* so."

Hood's records with their collection of many natural facts may well be cited in a series of articles to follow. These will be of particular concern to the multitude of organic gardeners who have seen the benefits of composting, organic fertilization and other similar practices in growing edible crops of more nutritional quality; and who are aware of the resistance to diseases and pests shown by crops grown on organically rich soils.

Ever since 1888 we have known that Rhizobia, the bacteria cooperating with plant roots in the specifically formed nodules, nourish the legumes by converting inert gaseous nitrogen from the atmosphere into plant proteins. Here, microbes in symbiosis with plant roots have synthesized the proteins required to supplement the carbohydrates so readily compounded by sunshine energy but so incomplete as nutrition for the plant serving as food for higher life forms. No doubt the legumes built up the ability of the virgin soil to support higher life forms with proteins. We must remind ourselves that legume crops are successful only on soils that are rich in both the organic compounds and the inorganic elements like calcium, magnesium, potassium, phosphorus, sulfur, iron, manganese, copper, boron and possibly many others, known and unknown, necessary not only for plants but for animals and man. These essentials must be provided to man by the plants.

It is the dynamic organic matter that gives us the so-called "height of the growing season." This results from microbial processes attuned with rising temperatures, coupled with ample soil moisture to feed the plants more generously. It is a consequence of a doubling of the rates of living processes for every 18 F. in temperature. It is not due to the plant's biochemical response to temperature alone. Increased nutrition is the reason for it.

This seasonal activity of decaying organic matter is dominated by the fungi. They precede the bacteria. Hood's research has demonstrated that *the roots of the non-legume plants, too, are cooperating with soil microbes for better nutrition and growth in terms of proteins.* However, *the microbes are the fungi in symbiosis with the roots, but only in soils which, like the virgin ones, are rich in decaying organic matter.*

We are slow to envision fungi in organically rich soils carrying on decay in order to obtain their own necessary energy foods and proteins while simultaneously extending their filamentous structure from the soil to, and into, the roots of plants as ministration to the latters' struggle for more protein through this symbiotic relation benefiting both plant and fungi.

Because of the widespread belief that germs are dangerous, we have closed our minds to their universal benefit through their bringing about decay of organic matter. Hood points to nature's "recoil" or "striking back," through declining food values and health, at our disregard for soil organic matter in which fungi become helpful microbes below the surface of the soil. Likewise, we fail to recognize these same fungi on organically poor soil when they have moved to the surface as parasites, and we combat them with poisons. We hope to bring out of hiding Hood's thinking in connection with better soils for better nutrition.

MISCONCEPTIONS PERSIST

That organic matter serves directly and indirectly via soil microbes in nutrition of plants is well shown by the studies of S.C. Hood. Some of the facts reported in his recent manuscript[1] deserve wider acquaintance. We need very soon to be concerned with the high rate at which we are burning out the organic matter of the soil and thereby lowering the nutritional qualities of what we are growing. "Before we can have a clear concept of any symbiotic reactions between soil fungi (mycorrhiza) and plant roots," says Mr. Hood, "it is necessary to remove some current, though ancient and venerable, errors. For many years those errors were accepted as proven facts. They even served as premises for pseudo-investigations.

"Some errors were so firmly implanted into our botanical thought that even when later investigations repeatedly had shown them to be errors, the new evidence was widely ignored. Some errors refuted more than 20 years ago are still included in recent textbooks and taught in classrooms.

"The oldest and most persistent of these errors may be referred to as the Liebig Complex. Over 100 years ago Justus von Liebig announced that plants needed from the soil no more than proper amounts of nitrogen, phosphorus and potash in water-soluble forms.[2] This announcement came at a time when soil exhaustion had become a major problem. A few years later phosphate rock was discovered in South Carolina, and later in Florida, the phosphorus of which was made soluble by treatment with sulfuric acid. The huge nitrate beds of Chile saltpeter provided soluble nitrogen, and the Stassfurt mines of

Germany, the soluble salts of potassium. There was soon started the expanding industry for the mixing and manufacturing of chemical salts of commercial fertilizers to provide these new kinds of so-called plant foods.

"While the Liebig theory of autotrophic[3] plant nutrition was promptly accepted in America by farmers and scientists, probably due to its extensive promotion by fertilizer manufacturers, the acceptance in Europe was much less complete. Many scientists there demonstrated by experiments that some form of organic matter was needed for large yields and higher quality. Most of the European farmers continued to use barnyard manure and composts.

"McCarrison, a British doctor in India, found in 1924[4] that plants grown on fields fertilized with manure were richer in vitamins and other substances than those grown on chemically fertilized soils. *Animals fed,* he reported, *on fodder from manured fields were healthier and more resistant to disease than those fed from mineral fertilized fields.* In 1930[5] Rowlands found that rats fed on clover from manured fields gained almost twice as fast as those fed on clover from mineral fertilized soils. Ressel and his workers showed in 1933[6] that the organic substances of the soil stimulate the growth of plants and increase the yield. He concluded that no mixture of chemical fertilizers can be as effective as manure in maintaining a high yield of crops. But six years later, 1939[7] Leong found that barely fertilized with manure had twice as much vitamin B-1 as that fertilized with chemicals. In 1953[8] Lebedev found that lucerne grown on fields fertilized with manure had 81 milligrams of carotene per kilogram, while on fields fertilized with chemicals there were but 27 milligrams.

"In 1961[9] Krasilnikov reported a summary of the research work of a number of scientists who proved that chemical fertilizers alone did not give as high a yield as when manure was used. The active principles of humus and compost are not the mineral nutrients, but the organic substances and the biologically active metabolites of the microbes. It was found that this new wonder chemical plant food was not entirely satisfactory. According as the soil organic matter was increasingly exhausted by its use, the yields and quality of crops were lowered. Lowered quality was recognized, in general, except in the case of the vegetable crops. Even today, inferior produce of that type is forced on the consumer because that alone is offered in the markets. Only when the yield is reduced is any trouble recognized."

MISCONCEPTIONS PERSIST

Earlier, we told of the studies made by S.C. Hood of the Hood Laboratory, Tampa, Florida, regarding symbiotic reactions between soil fungi (mycorrhiza) and plant roots. Since it is our desire to acquaint the reader with additional previously unknown facts which were related to the author in a recent manuscript, we now continue with Mr. Hood's comments.

"The fact was finally accepted that organic matter is needed for soil maintenance," Mr. Hood continues. "The scientists gravely assured the farmers that organic matter was required by the soil to improve its tilth and conserve soil moisture. This was as far as their thinking had gone. Yet the soil's need for organic matter as nutrition of plants was a fact established by the ancient Romans and long since forgotten. It was Vero, a Roman, who said, *'Any permanently successful agriculture must be founded on livestock.'*

"In the meantime, the market gardeners persisted in their use of barnyard manure as long as it was available from nearby city stables. When the horses disappeared from the cities, they turned to the use of chemical fertilizers with disastrous results to both yield and quality of their produce. For 60 years this writer has known a number of old market garden areas in the northeastern states, some of which had been growing vegetables for 100 years. The soil productivity was maintained by the liberal use of horse manure from the nearby city stables. The vegetables were of the highest quality. When manure was no longer available, gardeners turned to chemical fertilizers with the result that in a few years the poor quality of their produce was so prominent that it could not compete with the better quality of what was shipped in from newer soil regions. Some of these old garden lands have later been taken over by the suburban sprawl and others have been abandoned to weeds for many years.

"In the South, where most of the better lands have been worn out years ago by cotton growing, and their limited amount of virgin organic matter all but exhausted, there was little livestock and that was on the open range. The cotton, corn and tobacco farmers depended entirely on chemical fertilizers. While the cotton lint is a product of photosynthesis, it is produced on a bed rich in proteins. The yield was low and most of the farmers expected nothing more. Corn is mainly a carbohydrate crop, and tobacco has become so changed by cultivation that it is largely a chemical product. In recent years it has been established that small amounts of about a dozen elements other than nitrogen, phosphorus and potassium are needed for complete plant nutrition and, at last, this fact has been reluctantly accepted.

"About a year ago a learned professor from one of our large western colleges of agriculture presented an article in one of our most popular magazines in which we held up to ridicule all those who try to maintain their soil productivity by the use of manure, compost and mulches. All that was needed, according to his claims, was chemicals. This was in the enlightened year of 1962. A few months after, the same magazine published another article in which the same propaganda was put forth in a different dress. Is there an organized campaign to quiet the already large number of people who realize that there is something wrong with the quality and nutritive value of our commercially produced food plants?

"Another error, associated with the Liebig Complex, is the claim that all nitrogen-bearing materials in the soil must be changed to nitrate or ammonium salts before their nitrogen can be taken up by the plant. There is also the related claim that only small and simple molecules can pass through the cell walls of roots.

"The acceptance of these errors in basic facts," says Mr. Hood, "blocked all true studies of plant nutrition. All investigations were based on the current erroneous ideas. Many elaborate studies were made of the conditions necessary, and of the pathways followed to convert the plant residues and soil materials into the simple water-soluble components available to plants."

And thus the misconceptions persist.

FACTS ABOUT THEIR MAGNITUDE

"When we make a careful microscopic examination of a portion of the living root of a plant," says Mr. S.C. Hood, "we'd find a net of small fungus. It may at first thought appear like an insignificant thing. However, when we understand the quantities of the mycelical fiber and surface area of the fungus in the limited soil volume encompassing a single plant, we begin to realize their importance.

"In 1937-38, H. Dittmer[1] reported his quantitative studies of a single winter rye plant, four months old. On this, he found a total root length of 377 miles, of which 80% or 275 miles were feeding roots. The root hairs on that single plant numbered 14.5 billion with a fibrous length of 6,214 miles. Their surface area was 4,704 square feet, or more than a tenth of an acre. The combined length of roots and root hairs amounted to 6,990 miles and the combined surface area, to 63,784 square feet, close to 1.5 acres; all this for soil contact and exchange within the root zone of a single plant. Winter rye has an unusually large system of roots and very fine ones. Probably the plant examined was a more robust one. Similar quantitative studies have been made on other plants by other investigators. While other plants do not equal the rye plant, their roots are also of great lengths and extensive areas. In an acre of winter rye, or meadow grass, the total area of roots and root hairs may well exceed 30,000 acres, one-third of which is covered by a net of fungus mycelium with additional area in soil contact. We may well keep the figures in mind as we proceed to the consideration of the relation of the soil fungi to the plant roots.

"In his 1961 summary of the work of some 20 investigators, *Soil Microorganisms and Higher Plants,* Krasnilikov[2] reports on the qualities and quantities of exudates by plant roots. These researchers found growing roots to exude inorganic elements, sugars, many amino acids, a number of organic

Kind of Soil	Plant	Depth Examined	Ratio: Numbers in Rhizosphere Numbers in Control Soil
PODZOL	Rye	0-20	300
		40-60	800
		60-100	1700
	Clover	0-25	630
		40-60	1000
		60-100	2000
CHERNOZEN	Lazern	0-25	50
		40-60	200
		60-100	270
	Wheat	0-25	20
		40-60	150
		60-100	300

ones, vitamins, biotics, antibiotics and many other organic compounds. It is, therefore, to be expected that the root surface is utilized by fungi as a feeding ground. Denidenko was cited to have found a single corn plant which, during its vegetative period, exuded 486 milligrams of organic substances when the nutrient solution remained unchanged. When that was changed seven times during the growth period, 2.3 times as much, 1,136 milligrams, of organic substances were exuded.

"In 1921 Lyon and Wilson of Cornell Experiment Station[3] found that during the entire vegetation period the roots of plants exude up to the equivalent of 5% of the weight of the total organic matter of the plant. These exudates from growing roots consist of a wide assortment of organic compounds, especially carbohydrates. This fact explains why many investigators found a concentration of microorganisms in the rhizosphere and on the plant roots.

"At the New Jersey Agricultural Experiment Station (1929) Dr. Starkey[4] demonstrated that different plants have different influences on the accumulation of microorganisms in the soil, with the number in the rhizosphere many times greater than in soils at a distance from it. For beet plants, he found 427 million bacteria per gram of soil of the rhizosphere, but only 8.2 million in the control soils. Correspondingly for clover, he found 11.32 billion in the rhizosphere, in contrast to 6.6 million in the control soil, or more than 1700 times as many. For wheat his similar values were 13.4 million and 22.8 million respectively.

"In his own research, Krasilnikov studied 27 crop plants and trees in a wide range of climate and soil conditions. He found, also, the numbers of microbes hundreds and sometimes thousands of times greater in the rhizosphere than in the control soil. He presents the following table showing that the above kinds of ratios increase as the roots go deeper into the soils, whether these be the more weathered podzol or the scarcely-weathered chernozen; and that in the same soils the microbial concentration in the rhizosphere of legumes is higher than on non-legumes. The higher rate at greater depths is due to reduction in the numbers within the control rather than to an increase in the rhizosphere. It points out that the organisms follow the roots as incentive to occupy greater depths into the soil.

"The data on the growth of microorganisms deals usually with only actinomycetes, mycobacteria and bacteria," states Mr. Hood. "It is a well established fact that soil conditions favorable for the growth of bacteria also promote the growth of fungi. This fact explains why fungus species consistently inhabit the roots of plants, only they have been little studied and emphasized for their significant connections.

"When we search out the subject of compounds produced by root-inhabiting fungi, we find extensive literature and great masses of data, but little attempt to organize all these facts about fungus products into usable information. Hundreds of organic compounds have been isolated from media in which various fungi have been grown. Among these are compounds similar to those of plant root exudates, namely, biotics, antibiotics, auxins, enzymes, amino acids and a great number of miscellaneous ones. These were produced by fungi and exuded into the media, into their root contacts and into the soil surrounding the fungi. To this writer it is very significant that the majority of these compounds of fungus production are of the aromatic chemical group, or extensive carbon-ring compounds.

"In discussing the production of these aromatic compounds at some length, Cochrane showed the probable pathway by which Neurospora and Claviceps produce the three amino acids containing the benzene ring in their chemical structure, viz., tryptophane, tyrosine and phenylalanine. He discusses, also in detail, the synthesis of other amino acids by various fungi.

"The old idea associated with the Liebig Complex, namely, that only small and simple molecules can pass through the cell wall and root membrane, has now been entirely disproven; but vestiges of it still remain for many dealing with salt fertilizers. Much research work on nutrient uptake by roots has been done with tagged, or radioactive elements incorporated into complex organic compounds.

"By that experimental technique, and others, it has been proven that such complex organic molecules as indole, vitamins, antibiotics and amino acids pass from the soil into the plant cells and to other parts of the plant without much change of chemical structure and with change into other molecules equally complex. Much of such work has been summarized by Krasnilikov.

"The whole subject of symbiosis between fungi and plant roots may be summed up, so far, in the following statements."

1. Plant roots exude compounds utilized by the fungi growing on them.

2. The fungi, in turn, exude many compounds which are utilized by their host plants.

3. This mutual relation is almost universal in the plant world. We have found it existing in every plant we have examined which was growing on virgin soils. The only exceptions we found were plants of a weed nature growing where natural conditions had been disturbed by man.

REVELATIONS OF SPECIES

"Microscopic examination of the small feeding roots of any plant growing on a virgin soil," says S.C. Hood, "will show a network of fungus mycelia over the root surface. The thickness and density of this net will vary with the plant and the soil conditions. On most herbaceous plants it consists of two layers. The outer one is made up of mostly brown or gray septate (sectioned) hyphae spreading over the root surface and sending strands into the surrounding soil. This outer layer is made up of mostly Basidiomycetes. There are often tangles of mycelia in the surrounding soil, cotaining small rhizomorphs (root-like bodies) which present different forms and colors, according to the species represented.

"Mingled usually with the Basidiomycetes in this outer layer are hyphae of Rhizopus. They are easily identified by the large size and curious U-form of branching. There may be also Mucor, Cunninghamella or other phycomycetes mingled in with others.

"Then beneath this outer layer of mycelia of mainly Basidiomycetes and Rhizopus, there is an underlayer of very small, glassy hyphae very closely appressed to the root. These fungi are so small and inconspicuous that they are often overlooked. Careful staining is required to make them microscopically visible. They like to follow the groove between epidermal cells where they are especially difficult to demonstrate. This inner, or second, layer consists mostly of the species of Fusarium, Trichoderma and Gliocladium, though others may also occur there.

"We have isolated 47 genera from the roots of plants.[1] Most of these species are of only occasional occurrence. Many are parasites on the aboveground portions of the plants and probably developed from spores which fell to the ground and germinated there.

"There are also usually present Penicillium and Aspergillus, the latter being most abundant in later autumn. There are others of the scavenger class. We are of the opinion that Fusarium, Trichoderma, Gliocladium and Basidiomycetes, when the latter is present, are the important fungi in this fungus-plant symbiosis, or mycorrhiza (see illustration).

"As we go from the richer forest soils, where the fungus flora is very abundant in amount and species, to the soils of less and less organic matter, we find the fungus growth greatly reduced in both amount and kind. The Basidiomycetes are the first to be absent, and then one group after another is missing, until, finally, in the exhausted and near-barren soils only an occasional Fusarium remains.

"There are some plant species of a weed nature, the first to colonize a bit of barren waste, that often grow on this type of soil but without fungus associates. The same is also true of many of our cultivated plants, that is, they may grow on very poor soils but without mycorrhiza. On rich soil these same plant species soon pick up their fungus symbiont. Nelson-Jones and Kinder[2] tell us that the majority of plants have fungi on their roots. The fungi are useful but not indispensable. In such cases they aid the nutrition of the plant, the plant grows better, and more readily adapts itself to new locations.

"In our studies we found Trichoderma viride, one of the symbiont fungi, present on 54% of all roots collected in North Carolina. On roots of trees of Florida it, or its relative Trichoderma glauca, was found on 60% of them. It was found on roots of 315 herbaceous plants as Florida collections. On experimental corn plots in North Carolina it was found on from 20 to 100% of the roots, varying according to the methods of soil fertilization used.

"Trichoderma viride occurs on plant roots as a very fine under-net of hyphae, one micron in diameter, and very closely appressed to the root surface. It is hyalin or glassy, and difficult to demonstrate. It occurs also as a parasite on many of the Basidiomycetes where it is impossible to be detected unless a conidiophore can be seen. It is also a parasite on many of the Phycomycetes, especially on Rhizopus and the larger Mucors. In culture it does not attack either Fusarium or Glicocladium, but grows intermingled with them in harmony. It was found by Weinding[3] to be parasitic on Rhizoctonia solani. He stated also that it attacks most Basidiomycetes. A fungistatic compound was isolated from Trichoderma viride by Brian[4,5] and later a second compound, *viridin,* both of which were found lethal to some fungi and ineffective on others. Weinding[6] isolated *gliotoxin* from Gliocladium. None of these compounds was tested on plants.

"This writer holds to the opinion," says Mr. Hood, "that the genera Fusarium, Trichoderma, and Glicladium are the major important ones in this fungus-plant roots symbiosis and that the compounds produced by them are used in the economy of the plants. It is important that tests be made on higher plants, using the compounds produced by fungi, either in pure state or by growing the plants with pure cultures of them. This would answer many disputed questions on the role of symbiotic fungi in the economy of higher plants.

"It has been fully demonstrated that this symbiosis is not involved in the process of photosynthesis, since the production of fiber and other carbohydrate materials goes on whether fungi are present or not. It is, therefore, a fair hypothesis that this fungus-plant root symbiosis of mycorrhiza promotes the production of amino acids for the building of the protein molecules."

PARASITE OR SYMBIONT ACCORDING TO SOIL NUTRITION

"The dividing line between symbiosis and parasitism is very narrow. There is some reciprocal crossing. We have yet to find any evidence of parasitism by these root-inhabiting fungi when the host plant was growing on virgin, undisturbed soil. But we have found cases when the host was growing on cultivated land and on some cultivated crop plants, showing that *plants on cultivated soils are of lower resistance.*

"The following report is pertinent to this discussion. There was a grower of lilies in Delaware County, Pennsylvania, raising Formosanum lilies from seed, selling the seedling bulbs by mail. His small, backyard business was producing 15,000 to 20,000 bulbs per year—possible on a small area. He had much trouble with basal rot of the young bulbs, caused by Fusarium lily, which often took 50% or more of the crop. He consulted the lily experts at Pennsylvania State College and at Beltsville, Maryland. He was told that Fusarium lily was a very active parasite and there was nothing he could do except get new soil each year.

"This advice showed that these experts had little knowledge of either the distribution of this fungus or of its adaptability. The grower secured new land, even virgin land, on which no lily had ever been grown, nor had lilies been grown in the vicinity. Yet he still had considerable loss; and it was very heavy on a second-year crop.

"The grower measured the pH of his soil to a depth of six inches, added enough dolomitic limestone to give the soil a pH of 7.0 to that depth, and added pulverized gypsum at the rate of 500 pounds per acre. This was applied in the fall and mixed well into the soil. On the crop the following year, planted in the usual manner, there was but a very small percent of rot. He had realized that this plant, native to alkaline soils of Formosa, had been transplanted to and grown on the acid, podzol soils of the Eastern states until it was of low resistance. He gave the lily a soil suited to its physiological needs and simultaneously a slightly alkaline medium in which Fusarium, at least this particular acid-soil type, does not thrive. It had been noted that there was no basal rot when this lily was grown on limestone soils.

"The *Fusarium oxysparum* is very versatile, as are all groups of that genus. They are present almost everywhere as saprophytes in the soil and as inhabitants of plant roots. They have been found in some form in almost every soil where fungus surveys have been made. Five species of Fusarium were found by Hodges[1] in the soils of forest nurseries of the Southern states, while *fusarium oxysparum* was present in all ten states and *F. salani* in five of them. Six species of Fusarium, with *F. oxysparum* and *F. salani* most common, were found in Georgia by Miller.[2] Fusarium of 20% occurrence in Florida chrysanthemum fields was found by Jackson.[3] *F. rodeum* in the soils of the Nevada test site and *Fusarium sp.* in the soils of Death Valley were reported by Durrell and Shields.[4] Occurrence of this fungus up to 43% was found in the soils of Iraq by Yousef-Al-Doory et al.[5]

"Normally, this genus is a peaceful saprophyte in the soil, and a beneficial symbiont on plant roots. When this fungus encounters a root poorly nourished, a plant of low resistance, it can readily become pathogenic. If this pathogenic relation is allowed to continue, the fungus builds its pathogenic potential and becomes an active parasite. This contention may not be in line with prevailing thought, but it deserves consideration in the light of our observations."

SOME FIELD OBSERVATIONS

We can see wildlife about us, and readily appreciate its value. But soil fungi are hidden in the dark underground. "They are so small that they can be seen only with the aid of a microscope of high power," says S.C. Hood. This dedicated researcher has furnished us with additional information, as follows:

"There are more kinds of plants underground than grow on the soil's surface, and they are just as important as those we see about us. In fact, it is these tiny underground plants that have made possible the growth of the higher ones. They decompose the dead material. They change it into organic matter to make the more fertile soils on which the higher plants can grow. They make available the reserve mineral elements of the soil. Last, but not least, they enter into a symbiotic relation with the roots of higher plants and supply them with many important compounds.

"It is probable that this symbiotic relation began when the first primitive plant forms left the primordial sea and took to the land. There were primitive forms of fungi and algae, both of which had developed in the water. When cast on dry land, as separates, both were helpless. The fungi could not make carbohydrates. The algae could not secure mineral nutrients from the rocks. But united in a partnership, both could survive. The algae made carbohydrates for both, and the fungi extracted from the rocks the mineral elements needed by both.

"This close relation between these two persists to the present in the lichens, the first builders of soil. As the higher plants developed into their complicated structures, they retained some of this early interrelationship. They are still dependent on their associated fungi for development, especially chemically. Many botanists may not agree with this statement and consider it too highly simplified. We reply that botanists have made the above situation too complicated.

"These filamentous, underground plants form a cobweb-like growth throughout the soil and over roots. They are so slender that should we twist together 500 of the larger ones, we would have a rope no larger than a human hair. There are some fungus hyphae so small that it would require 3,000 strands to make a hair-size rope. This is the reason why the study of them has been neglected and their importance has only recently become recognized. We have made many examinations of crop plants grown under the usual methods. No extensive study of the singular effects of commercial fertilizers was made. However, some of the observations of the effects of such, as well as microscopic studies of plants in the treated fields, are suggestive.

"There is in western North Carolina a large and beautiful estate on the eastern slope of the valley of the French Broad River. The soil is a typical sandy, clay loam of that region. The estate is operated as a summer camp for 200 girls under care of the requisite staff. For some years the estate managed a garden for supplying the camp kitchen and grew most of the usual necessary vegetables, including asparagus and berries.

"The garden was operated under strictly organic manuring. They managed also a riding stable and large flocks of chickens and turkeys. Consequently, they had abundant manure for direct use and for making compost. Raw rock phosphate and basic slag were supplements. No sprays or insecticides were used, save Bordeaux mixture on the tomatoes for control of bacterial blight. For our studies, we were given free run of the place, with permission to take any specimens. Full advantage was taken of the courtesy.

"Evidence is acumulating to tell us that, with the rapid depletion of soil organic matter by salt treatments as fertilizer, quantity production may still hold on long after quality as nutrition has been lost."

PROTEINS, AMINO ACIDS AND BENZENE RINGS

"In the course of our studies," says S.C. Hood, Tampa, Florida, "we have found many statements in biochemistry which have a bearing on the subject of mycorrhiza as a fungus-plant root symbiosis. Basic principles in that science hold as true for more than one form of life."

Mr. Hood further observes, "It is a well-established fact that health is most fully assured by a properly balanced diet. What are the chemical compounds in food which promote health and resistance to disease? What are the substances lacking in our present day foods, because of which lack certain serious ailments become rampant; or poor health conditions result, which should be regarded as a national scandal? We are cognizant of the claims that *life expectancy* has been lengthened by 20 years, and more. But that is the result of the high mean value of the statistics due to the reduction of infant mortality, hence only an increase at the beginning or youthful end. There is no significant increase of *expectancy* after the age of 50 years or more.

"Our doctors and health officials have done an excellent job. Our agricultural producers and research workers in the experiment stations have been so concerned with the production of quantity in relation to market economics that sight has been lost of the biotic aspect of food as support of living species in good health. We must look to changes in the soil and modified aspects accordingly, and to soil and crop management for assignment of much of the blame for lowered food quality. We have not learned the simple truth that naturally fertile soils are expendable, before we know fully what originally made them truly creative of healthy species, including man.

"Most individuals in our population over 50 years of age recognize the fact that vegetables offered in the markets are lacking in flavor and quality. The younger folks have probably never known what good produce was like, unless they have had access to that from home gardens. There is no doubt about prevailing deficiency in quality, but just what is that deficiency? This is the question concerning situations that should occupy the concern of our research institutions, if there be such that are not handicapped by financial grants committed to political entanglements.

"Pointing toward deficiencies of proteins and amino acids in the realm of nutrition, there is a significant statement by Polczar and Reid.[1] *Analogues of tryptophan and phenylalanine block coli-phage formation; ethionine and methoxine appear to reduce the rate of influenza virus (strain PRB) in tissue cultures, whereas ethionine inhibits the Lansing strain of poliomyelitis virus growing on embryonic brain tissue. This statement suggests that disease resistance, as least so far as viruses are concerned, lies in the realm of amino acids illustrated by tryptophan and phenylalanine as compounds of benzene ring structures or modifications of such.*

"Albrecht[2] emphasized the importance of tryptophane. It is important not only as nutrition to promote the health of animals, but its breakdown in the digestive tract provides compounds active in promoting growth and health of plants also. Sheldon[3] et al emphasize the importance of tryptophane in animal nutrition, and by culture experiments with forage plants show the effects of the soil's mineral elements on the tryptophane content of these plants.

"We know that tryptophane, tyrosine and phenylalanine are the amino acids containing the benzene ring in their chemical structure. It has been shown that this ring portion is not broken down in the digestive tract of animals. The first of these three amino acids is voided as indole (fecal odor) and may be taken up as such by the plant, where it is changed into the well-known plant hormone, indolacetic acid. This action may be performed also by the microflora of the soil and the acid given to the plant in completed form. This latter is probably what occurs under naturally fertile soil conditions."

S.C. Hood, of The Hood Laboratories at Tampa, Florida, pointed out the deficiencies of proteins and amino acids in the realm of nutrition resulting from the poor quality of our foods. He remarked that disease resistance, so far as viruses were concerned, lies in the field of amino acids—particularly *tryptophane, tyrosine* and *phenylalanine,* which contain the benzene ring in their chemical structure.

	PODZOL SOIL	
	Non-sterile	Sterile
Gliotoxin	10 days	16 days
Viridin	8 days	16 days
	ORCHARD SOIL	
Gliotoxin	2 days	7 days
Viridin	1 day	1 day

This ring portion is not broken down in the digestive tract of animals. Tryptophane, for example, is voided by the animal as indole, and this, when taken up by the plant, is changed into the well-known plant hormone, *indolacetic acid.* Under naturally fertile soil conditions, this same action also may be performed by the microflora of the soil and the acid given to the plant in completed form.

Dr. Hood presents interesting facts concerning the soil microflora as well:

"According to Cochrane, indole and acetic acid are produced by certain fungi, actinomycetes and bacteria. *Neurospora crassa* produces an enzyme which synthesizes tryptophane from indole. Claviceps carry on the synthesis of tryptophane. Also, gliotoxin produced by *Trichoderma viride* is believed in its chemical structure to be a reduced indole nucleus.

"It is believed that many of these compounds produced by fungi of the soil are unstable. Wright[5] found that *Trichoderma viride* produced 40 milligrams of biotoxin per gram of soil after 14 days of incubation in culture. Jeffries[6] tested the stability of some of those compounds and in tabular form showed that their introduction into an orchard soil was stable for but a few days, while in a podzol the stability lasted many days longer.

"The work of a number of investigators, cited by Krasnilnikov, on the antibiotic substances produced by the microflora of the soil proves that these complex organic compounds are taken up by plants without change. He reports that actinomycetes, bacteria and fungi, which grow in the soil and in the rhizosphere of the plant roots, saturate this zone, or microfoci, of the soil with the products of their metabolism, including antibiotics. Also, he reports that these micro-plants enter the higher plants through their roots and exert their action there.

"Accordingly, it is evident that the concentration of antibiotics in the soil, when these are formed under natural conditions, will be lower than concentrations used as treatments by artificial introduction. However, under natural conditions, these substances are continually formed and, therefore, one would assume that their entrance into the plant is continuous during the whole vegetative period. In other words, microbial antagonists are factors which naturally increase the resistance, and non-susceptibility of plants to infections.

"Since it has been demonstrated that the large, complex, organic molecules of antibiotics and other metabolites of the soil microflora are taken up unchanged by the plant roots, it would be of great interest to know the roles they play in the economy of the plant.

"It has been shown that the majority of the compounds produced by the fungi and other microflora of the soil have one or more benzene rings as basic chemical structure. *'What is the ultimate fate of this ring inside the plant?'* is a very logical question. Is it possible that these aromatic rings are used in the synthesis of the three amino acids—tryptophane, tyrosine and phenylalanine—and is it also possible that the lack of tryptophane in our food plants (so well established) is due to the shortage of fungi and soil organic matter needed for them to provide these basic materials? Such inquiry is in advance of any bio-chemistry establishing it as fact, but in the brashness of ignorance and curiosity, we are presenting the theory."

Hood has given us his extensive observations and critical reports on studies of the symbiosis of soil fungi with plants, both legumes and non-legumes. He points out, forcefully, the facts that he finds such symbioses dependent on: (a) the presence of soil organic matter; (b) the absence of fertilizers as salt treatments of the soil; and (c) the absence of executive cultivation accompanied by fertility depletion. Accordingly, the failing symbioses of the fungi and plant roots are an early index of declining values in our crops of field and garden as nutrition of quality.

EARLY BELIEFS LATELY CONFIRMED

The preceding paragraphs on mycorrhiza reported S.C. Hood's studies, microscopic and otherwise, of living plant roots intimately associated with living fungi, with seeming benefit to both on natural soils. Just how those benefits are brought about is not yet elucidated. While it is now granted that bacteria in nodules on roots of legumes are a case of symbiosis (mutual benefits), there is still some hesitation to consider the same true for fungi on the roots of non-legumes.

As early as 1903 Ludwig Jost[1], a distinguished plant physiologist, was already familiar with fungi as well as bacteria so intimately associated with plant roots for benefits when he told us, "Possibly, however, the fungus aids in the absorption of materials of the ash, and does not supply the needs of the higher plant for nitrogen at all. Fungi make very heavy demands on such materials, and since they collect these very rapidly they are vigorous competitors with flowering and seed bearing plants.

"Higher plants are able to grow far better in humus which has been deprived of the fungi naturally present. A mycorrhizal union occurs especially in such plants which live in humus or which, for other reasons, exhibit feeble inflow of minerals. Hence Stahl assumes that these plants make the fungi contribute to their wants in that respect, turning antagonistic neighbors into efficient assistants . . . The function of the fungus, however, according to Stahl, consists not merely in the absorption of nutrient salts from the soil, but also in the transformation. He comes to this conclusion from noting that the majority of mycotrophic plants do not contain in their tissues certain waste bodies, such as calcium oxalate, which is associated with the assimilation of nutritive salts."[2]

Even if we cannot outline the physiological modus operandi through which the association of mycorrhiza are helpful to the latter, or vice versa, the benefits of fungus to plants have recently been demonstrated by experiments and reported for yellow poplar trees by F. Bryan Clark[3] (1963) of the Central States Forest Experiment Station at Redford, Indiana.

"Studies begun in 1959, designed to show effects of various soil factors on tree seedling growth," says Clark, "clearly indicate that endotrophic mycorrhizal fungi are important for the vigorous growth of seedlings of the yellow poplar, or tulip tree (*Liriodendron tulipifera L.*). Uninfected plants infected with the mycorrhizal fungi were large and vigorous.

"In the yellow poplar studies, samples of undisturbed soil were taken in one-gallon tin cans driven into forest soil. The large plugs or cores in the tin containers served as excellent media for growing seedlings with soil structure essentially undisturbed. The sample site is in a mixed hardwood stand in southern Indiana. The soil is classed as a Wellston silt loam and the pH is about 6.0.

"Autoclaving and gassing with methyl bromide were used for sterilization. Both small plugs of natural soil and macerated roots of forest-grown yellow poplar seedlings were used to supply inoculum for sterilized containers. About two to three grams fresh weight of macerated roots were added to each container. Sections of roots used for inoculum were examined and found infected with endotrophic mycorrhiza.

"Yellow poplar seeds were germinated in trays and planted into the undisturbed soil. The seedlings were grown on a 14 hour day under artificial light for 12 weeks. Distilled water was used for watering.

"Seedlings were recovered (for weighing at the close of test) nearly intact from the containers by soaking and washing. Examinations of the root systems for mycorrhizal fungi were made by Dr. Edward Hocskaylo, plant physiologist, USDA Forest Service, Beltsville, Maryland.

"These were the three treatments of the soil into which the seedlings were planted, viz., (a) undisturbed forest soil, (b) sterilized forest soil and (c) sterilized forest soil inoculated with yellow poplar roots.

"Growth differences among the various treatments were outstanding. The fresh weights of roots and tops averaged 1.6 grams per seedling in sterilized containers. In contrast, seedlings from unsterilized containers and those unsterilized and inoculated with macerated yellow poplar roots averaged 7.7 and 9.0 grams respectively. Microscopic sections of the root systems revealed that the seedlings from sterilized containers were non-mycorrhizal, while seedlings from unsterilized and sterilized-inoculated containers were mycorrhizal.

"It is interesting to note that the influence of the fungus was not effective immediately. At seven weeks there was no height difference between seedlings in sterilized and sterilized-inoculated containers. Evidently the organism or host plant must reach a certain stage of development before the mycorrhizal infection becomes effective."

We are not able to find much research on such matters dealing with the organic matter decay within the soil by which fungi as well as plants are nourished. Perhaps when processed organic wastes of urban origin come under higher sales pressures, rather than being catalogued for pollution prevention as they apparently are mainly now, grants for research will help us see that it is the organic matter, and not commercial salts, in the soil by which both fungi and food crops are nourished and that thereby may be serving symbiotically to help nourish each other in close contact much as nodule bacteria and legumes do.

6

THE CALCIUM CONNECTION

LIMESTONE—THE FOREMOST OF NATURAL FERTILIZERS

Liming the soil has long been an agricultural art. It has now become a modern scientific agricultural practice. Putting ground limestone on the soil may well be viewed as a case of an old practice that has now come to a newer scientific understanding. It is only recently that scientific facts have given us comprehension of the soil and plant relationships that underlie the services which the limestone renders for the crop.

Limestone has always been associated with the production of leguminous plants. They in turn have always been considered good feed for young and growing livestock. We are just coming around to realize that the calcium supplied by limestone is a fertilizer, as the ancients probably also considered it. Calcium is, in fact, the foremost one of all the nutrient elements for animals and man that can be put into the soil to help it grow bigger crops, giving us better nutrition through them.

We use limestone to supply calcium, rather than to remove soil acidity. Acid, or sour soils, have long been known to be low in productivity. Seemingly like spoiled food about which we say, "It is poor food because it has soured." so we have come to consider "soured" soils as poor soils. This reasoning has appeared sound because we found that limestone, which reduces the soil acidity, also makes better crops. As a consequence of the observation of these two simultaneous results, namely, reduced soil acidity and better crops from applying limestone, our soils have been widely tested for their degree of acidity in the belief that the acidity was the cause of the soil's low productivity. Limestone has been the ammunition in the war on acid soils.

During our belligerency toward soil acidity, a very important fact escaped us. It was the recently recognized one, namely, that while the carbonate part of the limestone is removing the acidity, the calcium going with the carbonate is serving to nourish the crops. Delicate electrical instruments and refined chemical tests helped us to detect and measure the acidity, or the activity of the hydrogen ions that is the cause of it. Since hydrogen is the most active of all elements, and since there are more hydrogen than any other ions in the universe, we might well expect this to be the first one of which the activity would come under such accurate measurement. This attention which was focused so sharply on soil acidity resulted in disregard of the declining and deficient soil fertility.

Unfortunately, neither calcium nor any other plant nutrients have as yet submitted themselves to any such minute evaluations. As a result of these facts, the hydrogen ion or soil acidity has held prominence. This prominence resulted because hydrogen could be easily detected and conveniently measured, and not because of knowledge of its activities in the soils or in the plants. Its presence in the soil did not call attention to the absence there of the calcium, the magnesium, the potassium, and the other plant nutrients, all of which are more deficient as hydrogen is more abundantly present.

It was necessary, therefore, to use the physiology of the legume plants and to study their growth and chemical composition when they were produced on soils of which the acidity was nearly neutralized by limestone, or calcium carbonate, in contrast to these properties of those grown on soils likewise given the plant assay method that revealed the forms of calcium sulphate and calcium chloride, neither of which reduces the soil acidity. It was this plant assay method that revealed the fact that soil acidity is in reality a deficiency in soil fertility. It is a soil situation wherein the hydrogen of no nutrient service to the plants has come into combination with the clay to take the place of several nutrients that are there in productive soils. This method demonstrated also that legumes will grow on a soil that is acid provided it supplies amply the fertility or stock of plant nutrients needed.

Unwittingly we have carried calcium as a fertilizer along when we were applying its carbonate as the remedy for soil acidity. The same has also happened for our unrecognized benefits in "correcting the acidity of commercial fertilizers." More fortunately, however, the dolomitic, rather than the pure calcium limestone, has been the "neutralizer for fertilizer acidity." Consequently, both calcium and magnesium have been coming along with the nitrogen, phosphorus and potassium (N, P, K) in fertilizers, though probably more because dolomite has higher "neutralizing value" than because of the planned desire to add these two extra nutrients for which no additional fertilizer charges are made. This is a case where calcium has been going ahead of—while going along with—the other fertilizers, even though it was not regarded as such in the designing of commercial fertilizers.

The fact that calcium has been the major component of a fertilizer, like superphosphate for example, has reacted to the pronounced benefit of lateritic or red soils so common in the South. These soils have little absorbing or exchanging capacity. Consequently they do not absorb or retain much hydrogen or acidity. There has been no "war on soil acidity" in the South. There is, however, a serious need for calcium as a fertilizing help in better animal and human nutrition coming from the soils and as a help for those plants which synthesize the proteins and other chemical complexes of higher food values. While tropical soils do not invite the use of limestone in a war on their acidity, they do demand limestone to supply calcium as a fertilizer in its own right.

Ash analyses of plants leave confusion about the services of calcium. Unfortunately for the services which mineral nutrients coming from the soil render in the plants, the chemical analyses ignite them to destroy their organic combinations. Such procedures measure mainly the percentage of the ash constituents in the dry plant tissue. This gives no concept of the many organic compounds of plant construction into which the calcium, for example, may have been combined, or in the syntheses of which this nutrient plays an important part. It leaves mainly the idea that the plant hauls either a large or a small load of calcium and other minerals from the soil.

Ash analysis is no measure of the functions performed by the chemical elements. It fails to point out in what period of plant growth the calcium and other minerals are taken from the soil in major or minor amounts. It has not given calcium its decided importance in the very early life of many plants. It has not emphasized the help of calcium in moving other nutrients into the root of the plants, which Professor A. C. True of the University of Pennsylvania has called a "synergistic effect." It has given undue importance to potassium, for example, as a fertilizer for potatoes because of emphasis mainly on the potato tubers. It has left unemphasized the facts, (a) that the tops of the potato plants carry more calcium than does a legume crop like red clover, and (b) that lime may be necessary as a fertilizer for potatoes more often than commonly surmised. It is such incomplete chemical analyses, with their attention to the ash constituents only rather than to the more complete organic compounds, that have given the confusion about potato scab in relation to soil acidity, instead of its connection with deficient nutrients, even with respect to calcium.

Ash analyses may measure the mineral elements of soil origin, but such measurements fail to mean much when the more efficient function by the plant in synthesizing important compounds is not necessarily dependent on a larger amount of one single plant nutrient taken from the soil. Unfortunately, such chemical measures do not inform us as to what constitutes the properly-balanced supply of all nutrients at any time, nor how that balance must be modified for highest plant efficiencies in different periods of growth. It is such ash analyses that have failed to classify calcium as a fertilizer of even greater deficiency on many soils than are phosphorus and potassium. Yet both of these latter two are so common in and emphasized by the mixed goods of commercial soil treatments, the calcium contents of which get no mention on the label or in the sale.

Soil acidity must be removed by fertilizing with calcium, plus other nutrient elements. That soil acidity should have come under condemnation by the recent scientific attacks on it seems strange, now that we look at the pattern of life on the globe and find it most concentrated, not on the neutral and alkaline soils, but rather on the acid soils bordering those that are calcareous. Agriculture has reached its high food output by the help of grazing animals. Grasses as feed for grazing animals are most common and most nutritious on soil developed under moderate annual rainfalls. Grasses grow under a distribution of rainfall which leaves a droughty period of the growing season that spells destruction of the trees but not permanent extinction of the grasses. Such rainfall distributions develop acid soils but do not leach the soils of their adsorbed supply of calcium and other bases. Such rainfalls gave us the prairies that are acid soils but that are also stocked with plenty of calcium, as was the virgin soil of the corn belt. Man and his companion animals for his support have multiplied most rapidly and concentrated themselves most highly, not on soils that are neutral, but rather on those that are acid in their reaction. Yet we have recently gone forward under the belief that soil acidity is highly detrimental and should be completely neutralized. Scarcely have we cherished the thought that soil acidity might even be beneficial, as the locations of higher concentrations of populations and their better agricultural support suggest.

When soils are a temporary rest stop of rocks and minerals on their way to the sea and to solution under increasing rainfalls encouraging their faster travel in that direction, we must credit carbonic acid as the natural agency that is mainly responsible for the rock and mineral decomposition. When carbonic acid breaks down the rock, another kind of acid, namely, a soil acid must of necessity be the result. Nature has long been using acid reagents to decompose rocks and minerals of which the end products are nourishment for vegetation. But it has only recently been recognized that the soil acids or clay acids in our productive soils are the agencies that are weathering rocks and minerals to release their nutrient contents to the absorbing clay and thereby for exchange to the growing crops. Soil acidity is an integral part of the chemical mechanisms within the soil by which the mineral reserves are broken down to fertilize the crops.

Surely, then, we must recognize in these facts the need for the soil to be acid. At the same time we must recognize the necessity for that soil to contain mineral reserves, among which limestone is the foremost. This must be there to provide calcium for plant nourishment while this stone is being decomposed on contact with the soil acid. In such a concept of the function of soil acidity, its partial removal is a means of fertilizing the soil and crop with available calcium through the service of this acidity in breaking it out of the limestone rock. Viewed in this light, the application of limestone to the soil is a case of applying calcium as a mineral fertilizer for its mobilization from inert rock form to active form on the clay by means of the acidity of the soil. Surely, then, we would not remove from the soil this mobilizing agent and thereby lose its valuable services.

Can we use too much limestone on the soil? Now that the soil acidity is considered a means of decomposing the soil minerals to make their fertilizing contents available to plants, it is evident that a productive soil is one which contains not only hydrogen or acidity, but one which is also supplied with the elements that are nutrients or fertility. Just as our application of limestone is a means of letting the soil acidity mobilize the stone's contents of calcium, so many other minerals with fertility contents may be applied to the soil and made available by the soil acidity. Rock phosphate is an example. Other minerals may come into use later as fertilizers under this same category. It was from a mixture of such rocks and minerals that soils were originally developed to form the clay residues and to load these with the many nutrients that give our productive soils.

When the plant roots are exchanging their hydrogen or acidity to the clay of the soil for its fertility contents, we may well visualize the fact that they might remove these so completely that the soil becomes infertile and highly acid. Then if we should put limestone on such an acid soil until all of its acidity is removed, would this make it a highly productive soil because it was now neutral, and because that neutrality was obtained by loading it with nothing but calcium, of which the associated carbonate in the limestone had neutralized the acid after the calcium had displaced it from the clay? If a soil is neutral but completely saturated with only one element—even if it be a plant nutrient ever so extensively taken by plants and animals as food—is that soil going to be any more productive than when completely saturated with the non-nutrient hydrogen that makes it very acid? Alkaline soils are not necessarily productive merely because they are not acid. They are often deficient in some elements of fertility, just as acid soils are deficient in some. Thus a very acid soil made completely neutral by liming as the only treatment becomes a hazardous condition in that the acidity, or hydrogen, on coming originally into the soil, displaced too completely many other nutrient elements as well as the calcium. Very acid soils, then, need other fertilizers besides the calcium we provide by applying the limestone.

Calcium has been the foremost deficiency in fertility on extensive soil areas. That limestone has been the most effective fertilizer is indicated by its use to the total amounts of more than ten million tons in the state of Missouri, for example, in less than ten years. The amounts of all other fertilizers used has not been one-fifth that of the limestone during their maximum use. But now that the calcium shortage in the soil has been remedied to strengthen that one weak line, the next item representing the next weakness will need to be strengthened.

On soils limed now for some years, the potassium deficiencies are being indicated more commonly by crop symptoms. Corn stalks are not so strong and may break over. The ears of the corn are less solid or more chaffy where heavy liming is used to grow legumes that are turned under as green manure. Heavy liming and consequent reduction in the degree of soil acidity are bringing on deficiencies of manganese. This deficiency in the crop may possibly reach greater importance as liming is more generously used, and when we recall that perosis of chicks is caused by deficiencies of manganese in their ration. Manganese, commonly considered among the minor nutrients, takes on major importance if its deficiency in the soil can reflect troubles in the animals by way of the crops they consume.

Boron and iron, too, are demobilized when the acidity of the soil is much reduced. Alfalfa, root crops, some vegetables and other crops require more boron than may be found available in a soil that has been given heavy dosages of limestone. Whether the excessive carbonate or the excessive calcium is responsible for the trouble has not yet been learned in all these cases. Nevertheless, the trouble is prevented by caution against believing that if a little limestone is good, much more of it will be better. Calcium used alone is not able to offset the shortage of other nutrient elements. Plant nutrition demands calcium in generous amounts for its direct services, and also for many benefits it exercises in mobilizing other nutrients. Nevertheless, soil acidity is also required. It, too, has much mobilizing power for nutrients toward which excessive calcium and neutrality of the soil exercise quite the opposite or a demobilizing effect.

Calcium must lead the parade for other fertilizers. Calcium plays a prominent role in—and is always associated with—protein production by plants. Amino acids, the building blocks of proteins, are not synthesized by animals and humans. They are the synthetic product of plants and micro-organisms but most commonly by those kinds of these producers for which liberal supplies of lime are requisite. Animals and man are always in the struggle for proteins. On the contrary they obtain carbohydrates more easily. On the calcareous soils of the prairies, rather than on the lime-deficient soils cleared of their forests, do we find production of animals less difficult. Animals are grown on the former and fattened on the crops from the latter. By the same token do we have poor reproduction and growth of animals on soils that, through crop removal and neglect, have been depleted of their calcium and the other fertility elements that are associated with it in fertile soils. Lime is first on the list of needs for soils that are to be kept high in animal production.

It was on those soils containing acid properties in the surface horizon, but calcium in their deeper layers, that the bison originally supported himself. It is on these same soils that production of beef and mutton rose to the magnitudes of which we boast. It is on the soils of greater deficiencies in calcium and other fertility constituents where the hog of mainly fat output is the king. Humans, too, may be fitted into the soil picture with more tooth troubles on calcium-deficient soils, as the draftees for the Navy demonstrated. Calcium, which constitutes 40% of limestone, makes this rock an important fertilizer for the soil in service to man as well as to plants and animals.

Limestone is no longer merely a soil conditioner in terms of the control of the degree of soil acidity. It is the provider of the foremost element for fertilizing effects. It is the mobilizer of other nutrients. It is the catalyzer in the process of synthesizing proteins. It has been delivering these services ever since it was a part of the art of agriculture, dating back some 40 centuries. But, unfortunately, only recently have we realized that calcium is only one of the essential nutrients needed by plants and that many others must come along with it for most efficient crop production. Nevertheless, when animal and human nutrition are taken as the goals of crop production, calcium heads the list of the nutrient elements and stands out as the one demanded in largest amounts from the soil. In terms of human foods for their quality dependent on the soil, limestone is the contributor of calcium and is the synergistic agent for other nutrients; which services make it the foremost of the fertilizers.

LIMESTONE—A FERTILIZER

Making liming pay better ought to have more attention now that we are using this soil treatment to feed calcium to plants rather than to fight soil acidity. This shift in purpose of liming points to possibilities in reducing the labor and financial load. Serving the single year needs of a crop for lime to make it better feed for livestock ought to be more encouraging than trying to remove completely a soil condition arising from many years of soil neglect.

Better feeding values in forages and healthier animals on soils treated with lime are recognized now that we have learned more about the services of calcium, or lime, to plants. In evaluating feeds as they supply proteins, carbohydrates, minerals, and vitamins one might not readily comprehend how calcium is connected with any of these items except, possibly, the minerals. But we know that calcium goes right along with nitrogen, the key item in protein. More nitrogen goes into plant protein only as more calcium is supplied by the soil. Then, too, phosphorus, which like nitrogen is also a part of the protein, is moved into the crop through addition of lime to the soil. This helps us to understand how calcium makes protein, even if it doesn't come through as a chemical part of this nutrient complex. Lime in legumes is the force that moves phosphorus from the soil and nitrogen from the air, so the plant can run not only its protein and mineral factories, but also can be a better factory for possibly other complexes, such as vitamins, which make the big differences in the feed from limed soils when its full value is reflected in the animals that eat it.

We are so accustomed to thinking of legumes taking nitrogen from the air that we can scarcely imagine that they could fail in this process. Careful chemical studies show that unless they get lime liberally they don't use air nitrogen. Can you imagine that soybeans could grow to be almost two feet high without taking nitrogen from the air? Would you believe that even some of the nitrogen and minerals in the seed were lost back to the soil by this crop? Under such soil conditions the resulting legume forage crop has less minerals and less protein in it than was in the seed at planting time. This has happened on soil too low in lime. Only when liberal lime allotment was offered by the soil and taken by the crop were the minerals from the soil and the nitrogen from the air moved into the crop to make it a real feed in place of so much woody packing for the poor animal's paunch. Lime must get into the plant and serve there as a tool in fabricating the complex substances the plants make out of nitrogen, phosphorus and other plant nutrients.

Thus, legumes can be feeds, not merely because their pedigree labels them as such. Rather they are nutritious according as they have calcium within their plant tissue to help carry out their plant functions, and not necessarily because the lime application has corrected soil acidity. Feeding plants lime makes it possible for them to feed the animals with forage of nutritious value.

Young plants must get lime early in their life. This was demonstrated in studies by Dr. H. F. Rhoades, now at the University of Nebraska. When soybeans were started ten days in limed sand and transplanted to soil, they grew much more successfully than those transplanted from unlimed sand. Young plants without lime often die and look as if they had been hit by a fungus to make them "damp off." Raising the delivery of calcium to the plant removed this "disease," so when plants are "taken" by fungus disease it may not be so much the epidemic as it is a lack of vigor.

Have we been thinking enough of the health of the plant as it depends on our supplying its needs in soil fertility, of which calcium is the foremost item? Good feeding of the plants enables them to resist disease. Haven't we possibly been throwing seed away, complaining about the failure of plants to fight off disease; haven't we been purchasing disease-combating chemicals in place of recognizing this situation as indicating a fertility so low, first in lime, then in phosphorus and even other nutrients, that the soil delivery of those nutrients is too slow in the spring? In such cases the seed supply presumed to carry the plant into the warmer part of the growing season becomes exhausted before the soil delivery of nutrients is in higher gear. In place of taking up a fight against plant disease, perhaps we might well look to lime for help in "eliminating" weak plants by making them healthy and thus "immune" to disease because they are well fed.

LIME THE SOIL TO CORRECT ITS MAJOR FERTILITY DEFICIENCIES

Liming the soil, so that this practice can build up the fertility reserve of calcium (and magnesium), has gone unappreciated all too long. Instead, we have persisted in the erroneous belief that the benefits to crops from liming result from the reduction of soil acidity by the applied carbonate. We are gradually realizing that our productive soils, under annual rainfalls abundant enough to give larger crop yields, must contain more of calcium (and of magnesium) in the exchangeable (available) form than any other fertility element. The laboratory gadgets for measuring soil acidity in degree—and in total—have absorbed our interest so completely, and for all too long a time, that they kept us from recognizing the services by limestone in the nutrition of the crops in the field. We failed to connect the activities and ratios of the fertility elements, exchangeable and active, in the soil with the nutrition of the plant. We were oblivious to the facts (a) that calcium is one of the elements which the growing plants must find in the soil very early, and (b) that it seems to serve in setting up the conditions by which the other nutrient elements and compounds are mobilized into the roots for crop growth. We are gradually coming around, however, to see that by liming the soil we are fertilizing it with the two major nutrient elements; namely, calcium and magnesium. Accordingly, this practice is taking on a new classification and a greater significance.

Now that we view most of the plant nutrition processes as a case of the positively charged elements held on the clay exchanging from there for the non-nutrient hydrogen, or acid, coming from the plant root, the extensive soil testing is pointing out that crop production requires larger amounts of the exchangeable calcium in the humid soils than of any other fertility element. Calcium is especially important in the production of proteins. These are the only compounds capable (a) of giving cell multiplication or growth, (b) of protecting the plants against disease, etc., and (c) of reproducing them by seeds. It is required by legumes for this reason more than for the "suitable degree of soil acidity" of which the carbonate of calcium might have been the producer. Lime is important because its calcium (and magnesium) nourish the crops.

In order to appreciate just how much exchangeable calcium a productive soil contains, let us consider the soil test results from a good silt loam, a corn-belt soil like the Marshall of north Missouri or Iowa. This has a total exchange capacity of near 18 milligram equivalents. This figure tells us that such a soil could hold by adsorption, and for possible exchange, 18 milligrams of active hydrogen—a non-nutrient and acid—per 100 grams of soil, or the equivalent in other positively charged ions. This would be 18 pounds of hydrogen per 100,000 of soil or 360 pounds of hydrogen per plowed acre of 2,000,000 pounds. For good crop production, it is considered well that about 75% of the soil's exchange capacity should be taken by calcium, and from 7 to 10% by magnesium. These make up the maximum two of all the nutrient elements held by the adsorptive and exchange capacity of the soil, or nearly 85% of the total capacity. For potassium, the next item in order, the figure is 2 to 5%. This leaves but 10 to 16% of the soil's exchange capacity for all the other necessary positive ions of nutrient services to the crops.

In terms of pounds per acre of soil of plow depth, or 6 to 7 inches deep, these percentage saturation values as replacements in equivalents for hydrogen or acidity represent (a) 5400 pounds of calcium, (b) 302 to 432 of magnesium, and (c) 280 to 700 pounds of potassium. Even with these amounts occupying the soil's absorbing power, it would have capacity remaining to hold the other nutrients in ample amounts, especially the trace elements, and then also some capacity for hydrogen, or acidity, as the favorable soil condition. Plants are nourished better in the presence of some soil acidity. Let us note that the amount of exchangeable calcium in this series is more than ten times the maximum of the nearest amount of any one of the others. By finding such calcium values in terms of the requirements for plant nutrition, we begin to get some basic concept of the importance of liming for the calcium supplied to feed the crop rather than for the carbonate incorporated to fight the soil acidity.

All of this may well serve to classify the liming of our humid soils into the category of farm operations more technical than those of merely dumping any kind of limestone on the land, and of proceeding under the belief that "If a little is good, more will be better." It puts liming into the group of skilled operations calling for a clear-cut diagnosis of the soil's condition before treatment is undertaken. Testing the particular soil for its shortages in calcium and magnesium in order to build up its supplies of these by either a calcic or dolomitic stone, or both, makes liming a prescribed nourishment of the crops. This is a treatment different from one of using the carbonate of any stone, regardless of whether calcic or dolomitic, merely to reduce the degree,or the total, of soil acidity.

Viewed from the vantage point of plant nutrition, liming the soil becomes the application of fertility elements of quantities nearly ten to twenty times as large as any of the other elements commonly used in commercial fertilizers. It becomes then a major fertilizing performance. Surely under such large amount applied according to soil test, and under the concept of lime as our foremost fertilizer, the business of limestone production and distribution should feel itself playing the major role in maintaining the fertility and productivity of our soils. Unfortunately for the liming of the soils, as for the other fertility restorative treatments, its services in food production for all of us, rather than for profit only to the farmer, are not yet recognized nor appreciated. The 85% of us in the urban portion of our population do not yet feel any obligation to help resources coming to us gratis from out of the rural area. We are set up in urban commercial businesses and industries of which the laws, economics and taxation procedures are so formulated under carefully lobbied legislation that our capital investments in them are self-perpetuating. Even for the minerals or rocks taken out of the limestone quarry, for example, the owner-investor may be allowed a depreciation, or depletion, figure as high as 15% of the income. For the owner-investor in an oil well, it may be a larger amount. The capital investment in these mineral businesses is soon recovered.

But for the mineral fertility taken out of the soil and delivered in the crops to the urban population without charge for it, there is as yet no economist or authority on taxation suggesting the justice of a depletion allowance to the landowner, or investor in that kind of real estate, for the perpetuation of his capital in his farming business. His investment in the minerals in the soils for the food production for all of us is being liquidated gradually under an economic thinking (or the lack of it) which contends that the farmer is thereby taking a profit. On the contrary, he is compelled to throw his financial, and our national, security by installments into the bargain every time he makes a sale of his products. Those of us on the urban receiving end of that transaction get those installments gratis and flush them into the sea. We are parties to the crime of soil fertility exploitation, but yet are crying against the rising costs of living. We are slow to see that such short sightedness (or absence of any sightedness) in our economic, agricultural, and other policies toward the fertility resources in the soil are undermining seriously our national security. All this is the more serious with a growing pressure on the soil's production potential by our own increasing population to say nothing of that by the rest of the world calling on us to share that potential with them.

Liming our soils deserves consideration as an operation undergirding our future security in food, and particularly those foods of high protein content. We have long known that lime is needed for legumes. We are slow to see that need as one for the production of protein, rather than the tonnage, yield of the crop. It is lime via that route that gets us our meat, milk and eggs. Viewed in this light, one cannot escape the question whether we dare expect the farmer to continue liquidating his fertility assets under the false concept of taking a profit and at the same time ask him to purchase large amounts of calcium and magnesium to aggravate his rate of liquidation all the more. Isn't it about time that as a basic agricultural policy we design the required machinery of economics and taxation to guarantee the self-perpetuation of the farmer's fertility capital which must feed all of us, both urban and rural?

Perhaps now that the fertility restoration by liming the soil is moving itself into the more exact category of soil chemistry for the nutrition of our plants, our animals and ourselves, should not the maintenance of the soil fertility and thereby of agricultural industry be interpreted by the same views in economics and taxation as those prevailing in other industries?

Perhaps we can bring about self-perpetuation of our soil fertility capital under the agricultural business in the rural areas in the same manner as perpetuation prevails for monetary capital under all businesses in our urban centers. If that situation is consummated, then liming the soil for calcium's sake will become big business by meeting the major needs in our soils; namely, lime and other fertility-restorating helps through which there can be guaranteed greater national food security for the future of all of us.

How shall we get lime or calcium into the plant and how much will it take? If all that we needed to use were that which gets into the crop, the figure would be less than 150 pounds of limestone a ton of clover hay produced, or less than two-thirds of this figure for a ton of soybean hay. We still can't get the lime into the plants by external application. We can't rub it on. It must come through the roots and they must take it from the soil. Delivery to the plant by this soil route is far more effective when a little of the soil is heavily loaded with lime, than if all of the surface soil has the limestone thinly scattered through it. Non-legumes such as bluegrass and redtop, as well as legumes, get their lime or calcium much more effectively if the upper two inches of soil are heavily dosed than if this same amount of limestone is mixed into the soil to a depth four times as great. Soil that has become sour has a tremendous power to hold lime. Plants can't take from it all the calcium it has. Studies to date give a low efficiency in lime recovery by plants unless the lime is used so as to saturate the soil in the root feeding zone. We are then forced to think of the practice that loads a little of the soil completely rather than all of the soil only partially, if the investment in limestone is to give us maximum return.

Studies of the practice of drilling limestone as a fertilizer have demonstrated that as little as 600 pounds on a soil needing more than 2 tons to sweeten it can establish sweet clover regularly in a rotation, though more limestone is better. The stand of sweet clover from drilled limestone holds out against winter-killing when that sown without limestone fails. The composition of the crop in terms of forage feed, and its effects as a soil-improver on the corn crop following, are all evidence that giving the crop its calcium without neutralizing the acidity is coming to be the real function of liming, and that economical and effective use of limestone means that it may well become a fertilizer in our thinking and in its use.

The art of liming is old. The science of it is new. Our science has led us astray and we are just now getting back. Nature always has been consistent in demonstrating the effects on plants by liming, but we have not been so consistent in explaining how these effects came about. We have looked to the wrong one of two things going on at the same time, as the real cause. When we use limestone we put on calcium combined as a carbonate. The carbonate neutralizes the soil acid. We have misconstrued this phenomenon as the cause of plant improvement when we should have been thinking of the addition of the calcium to the soil as the caustive factor. Since sodium carbonate which removes the acid doesn't help the plants, while calcium chloride helps the plants but doesn't correct the acidity, we know now that liming is not a matter of fighting soil acidity but one of giving the plants calcium, their much-needed nutrient on our humid soils.

Thus, we can put liming into the fertilizer category and look to lesser applications per acre to serve its fertilizing function. But we must remember that nature has been taking the lime out of our soils for many years and a teaspoon dosage now won't do the work completely. We need to give many of our soils a heavy liming to offset this neglect and then we can go to regular lighter applications of 1,000 pounds an acre by drill in place of tons by spreader. As we go to using lime to feed plants so they can feed and protect our animals against starvation fevers, we see prospects of making this operation economical enough in money and labor costs so we will adopt it for use as regularly as we scatter a legume seeding.

BLAST FURNACE SLAG—A SOIL BUILDER

The term *conservation* implies so much, and is taking on so much importance, that many folks are asking whether the soil might not be built up in fertility by using some of our industrial wastes. Numerous inquirers, interested in soil organic matter, have asked about city garbage, and septic tank sludges recently. Also, inquiries have come in concerning the value of blast furnace slags, the wastes from making steel. Such slags should be considered, though their variation in composition demands that one know something about them, and about the fineness of the materials. They are the residue from putting limestone, feldspars and other minerals in with the iron, to serve as fluxes, to purify it. The carbonate part of the limestone burns off to let it become quicklime, calcium silicate, or calcium phosphate, and other combinations possible at those high-furnace temperatures.

Slags are the rock-like residues dumped out after the molten iron has been drawn off. They are of fertilizer value, therefore, as carriers of phosphorus as well as calcium, with much of the latter in silicate form. In making some steels, manganese and other "trace" elements are often present, too, in this complex silicate rock. Sometimes the hot-rock is slaked and granulated by spraying with water, or it may be cooled and crushed. Either treatment aims to make it serve as a lime substitute for soil building.

Since, like many other original rocks, it is a silicate, therefore, it weathers down slowly. Its use is, then, a case of adding "sustaining" fertility to the soil rather than as a "starter" fertilizer. By its decomposition it adds not only calcium, some phosphorus, and "trace" elements, but also some silica. This is a clay-builder for the soil which would be helpful on sandy soil with "too little body," or not enough capacity for adsorption and exchange of nutrients to the plant roots. In the slow reaction, by this kind of "lime," there may be more of a safety factor than when lime carbonate is too generously used under the belief that "if a little is good—more will be better." Since we lime soils now to supply calcium (and magnesium) as fertility, rather than to remove the acidity, the blast furnace slag has been shown by tests to be a good way of building up the soil in calcium (and magnesium). We can, therefore, practice conservation with profit by using this waste from the steel mills to build up the soil.

The fineness of the slag, into which it is ground—as for limestone—becomes a factor in its rate of being effective in crop nourishment. Also, its lime content (calcium and magnesium) must not be too low (preferably near 45%) if its effects are to follow more promptly after its application on the soil. These may be greater because it is not so much of a reagent to reduce the soil acidity as it is an active silicate providing calcium. Combined as a silicate rather than as a carbonate, it is more of a "buffer" in that it does not bring on, or permit, sudden shifts in the degree of soil acidity under heavier applications of it. In terms of the microbial life of the soil, its application is no "shock" because of any "salting" effect. Yet it stimulates (a) nitrification, as the change of ammonia nitrogen to the nitrate form; (b) the speedier oxidation of the carbon compounds; (c) the fixation of nitrogen by microbes living independently of the legume plant roots; and (d) all the other biological soil processes which distinguish a "live" soil from a "dead" one.

The employment of blast furnace slag as a fertilizer for the fields, and as an aid in composting, has been a practice in the "art" of agriculture by some folks long before recent scientific studies, tests, and partial commercialization gave its use greater sanction as a soil treatment—using this accumulating waste from the dump heaps of steel mills. We can use such material not only for true conservation but also with assurance that it builds up the soil for more nutritious crops.

DRILLING POWDERED AGRICULTURAL LIMESTONE

Recent additions to our knowledge of sour soils and of the requirements for successfully growing legumes, indicate that the practice of applying two to three tons of coarsely ground limestone per acre in order to grow certain legume crops bids fair to undergo modification. The well-recognized necessity of liming the soil long in advance of seeding the legume crop is evidence of the sluggishness with which the common agricultural limestone becomes effective. Though relatively insoluble, limestone becomes much more soluble when extremely finely divided. The wider recognition of this fact and the fuller understanding of the functions of limestone in growing legumes are contributed to the impending changes in our liming practice. It has been recently emphasized that the one of the beneficial effects of liming is due to the fact that it supplies the element calcium. Sour soils present a problem not only because of their sourness, but also because of their deficiency in this plant nutrient. This suggests that the lime of the Romans and other ancient agricultural nations may well be called "forgotten fertilizer." Laboratory studies and field trials suggest the fitness of this newer cognomen, when they demonstrate that 300 pounds of finely ground. limestone. drilled with the legume at seeding time, is enough to establish red clover, sweet clover, and other lime-loving plants on soils giving tests of two to three ton lime requirement. Farm trials in cooperation with the Missouri Agricultural Experiment Station, dating from 1926 and in gradually increasing number, suggest the wisdom of giving consideration to finely ground limestone as a fertilizer as well as a soil-sweetening agency.

Trials of limestone of different fineness have always indicated that the extremely fine material is the most important part of the limestone. Early experimental data by the Pennsylvania Agricultural Experiment Station and others following have pointed out that only when limestone is ground finely enough to pass a hundred-mesh sieve, does its effectiveness approach that of the soluble hydrated lime or quick lime. During the early development of the agricultural limestone market, the product offered was of widely varying fineness, for the problems of crushing the stone prohibited much else. It was a by-product. Now science points to the need for a specially prepared material whose effectiveness demands that it be very finely ground. At present with newer types of stone-crushing machinery which can produce at low cost a limestone ground finely enough to pass a hundred-mesh sieve, and with an entire rearrangement of our economic household in progress, we may well contemplate changes in our liming practice. We may well consider this powdered limestone ground finely enough for most of it to pass a hundred-mesh sieve as the standard product for general use. Its economy is an especially weighty argument for its adoption, since its rates of application are low enough to cut the cost of material to one-half, and the amount handled to one-tenth. Savings in cost of transportation, the convenience of handling a bagged product, and the reduction of the labor of application to a one-man basis instead of a community affair, will direct attention to this newer practice of using the powdered or hundred-mesh limestone.

The powdered limestone must be drilled into the soil. The old methods of spreading limestone broadcast will not suffice. By drilling it, certain areas within the soil are given a concentrated application from which the plant may take its supply of calcium, while adjacent soil areas are not subjected to the radical changes in chemical and biological conditions that would be created by complete neutralization of acidity. The fertilizer drill presents itself as the logical machine for drilling this fine limestone, and wherever it is available its use is recommended. The scarcity of fertilizer drills in some sections of the country raises the question,"Why not drill it with an ordinary grain drill?" The problem of distributing limestone powdered finely enough to pass a hundred-mesh sieve has recently been given some attention in the hope of learning something about its drillability, and the possibility of drilling it with a regular grain drill, as well as the fertilizer drill. The tests reported in this

TABLE 1

Fineness of Powdered Limestone Used

Mesh of test screen	Per cent caught on test screen	Per cent passing through test screen
40	2.0	98.0
60	0.3	97.3
80	1.1	96.6
100	1.6	95.0
200	16.8	78.2
300	46.2	32.0
Through	32.1	

paper indicate that the ordinary grain drill may help solve the distribution problem created by the change from coarsely to finely ground limestone in agricultural practice.

A test was run on the fertilizer distributing part of a superior combined grain and fertilizer drill equipped with the finger or star-wheel type of fertilizer feed. The stone, furnished by the Columbia Quarry Company and

TABLE 2

Rates of Delivery of Hundred-Mesh Limestone by Different Drills

Superior Drill (Fertilizer Side)*			McCormick-Derring Drill (Grain Side)**			
Fertilizer gate opening	Fertilizer rate, lb	Limestone rate, lb	Oats rate		Limestone rate, lb Throats	
			pecks	lb	open	closed
3	115	86	4	32	106	116
5	200	163	6	48	182	200
7	300	233	8	64	225	245
9	400	284	10	80	242	329
12	490	361	12	96	242	354
15	550	390	14	112	266	371

Superior Drill (Grain Side)***		
Gear	Oats rate, quarts, per acre	Limestone lb per acre
3	81	192
5	108	217
9	162	288
13	216	316

*Gear 6.
**Fluted-roll, force-feed type. Agitator in grain box.
***Internal double-run, force-feed type. Set for oats. Homemade agitator in grain box.

ground by a crusher using air draft to separate the fine material had the sieve analysis as given in table 1. The method of testing consisted in filling the fertilizer hopper with the powdered stone, hauling the drill with a tractor for a distance equivalent to one-tenth acre, collecting the stone delivered by each delivery opening in a separate container attached just below the drill box, weighing this, and making calculations on the acre basis. The distributing fingers were set at the high speed (gear 6), and the test run with different gate openings. The results are shown in table 2, which compares the amount of stone delivered to the amounts of fertilizer that would be delivered according to the sowing table furnished with the drill. The weight of stone delivered in the test varied from 70 to 81% or an average of 75% of that given in the fertilizer sowing table for the different gate settings. It should be borne in mind, however, that the sowing tables for fertilizer furnished with a drill, can be only approximately at best as different fertilizers vary considerably in weight and drillability. In drilling finely ground limestone through a drill, the rate of application can be determined approximately by noting the acreage covered, as indicated by the drill surveyor, while a known amount of material is drilled.

Attempts were made to drill fine limestone through ordinary grain drills, both of the internal double-run type and of the fluted-roll type of force feed. It was found that this fine, fluffy material would not feed through. Tests were next run on a McCormick-Deering drill equipped with agitators. The drill was of the double-rod type, with three-finger spider stirrers on the lower rod and with two-arm paddle throats beneath the fluted rolls open, and with them closed. The results are shown in table 2. The tests indicate that this drill can be easily made to deliver 200 to 350 pounds of this powdery material by setting it the same as for 6 to 12 pecks of oats per acre. Since it would be difficult to get agitators for some of the older grain drills, a homemade agitator was made and tested in a Superior grain drill, this particular drill being equipped with the internal double-run type of force feed. The agitator was made essentially as follows: A one-inch gas pipe was run lengthwise on top of the drill hopper and mounted in improvised wood bearings. The outer end of this pipe was equipped with a crank so that the pipe could be oscillated back and forth in its bearings. Vertical arms were attached to this pipe and allowed to project downward beside each of the drill runs in the bottom of the hopper. The first design of this agitator failed to work because these vertical arms did not work in close enough proximity to the wheels which carry the seed through the runs.

During the test, the agitator was worked back and forth by hand twice for each revolution of the ground wheel of the drill. Very little effort is required to operate the agitator, and doubtless wood blocks bolted to wheel spokes could be made to operate it. The results of the test are given in table 2, and indicate that the internal double-run type of force feed will drill fine limestone when a suitable agitator is used in the drill hopper.

With coarse limestone for our past experience, the opinion naturally arises that the drilling of limestone through the regular seed runs of grain drills will cause excessive wear and consequent inaccuracies in subsequent drilling of grain and seed. The trials reported here did not include tests on this point, though such are contemplated. The finely ground limestone, however, is widely different from the commonly used, coarsely ground agricultural limestone. This finer material is impalpably fine, and resembles flour more than it does the common agricultural limestone. Its fluffy nature and ease of agitation through failure to pack as does the coarser material suggests that any wear on the drill by such material would be relatively small. Further, it is of neutral reaction—neither acid nor alkaline—with no corroding effect on metal. While there may be some wear, the seriousness of this remains to be established by experiment or experience. In all of the trials there was a surprising uniformity in the rate of delivery per spout, and calculations based on the lowest spout rate and the highest spout rate were never widely different. The variations were certainly within the limits of accuracy commonly demanded in such farm operations.

The results of these trials as given in table 2 indicate that present drilling machinery will distribute the finely powdered limestone effectively and in rates that easily accommodate the amounts suggested by soil experiments with this fine limestone.

DRILLING FINE LIMESTONE FOR LEGUMES

The importance of limestone as a soil treatment, especially for legumes, has come to be widely appreciated, but its use has not become a general practice. The labor required to deliver and to apply two or more tons of 10 mesh material per acre is often too large to fit into the farm scheme except at periods of slack labor. Moreover, the maximum effectiveness of this coarsely ground material is delayed until six months or a year after its application. Finally, the wide variation in the quality of such stone available, especially in its content of material fine enough to pass a 40 mesh sieve and be effective during the first season, gives a correspondingly wide range in its effectiveness and in amounts necessary for good results. All these are handicaps in the wider adoption of liming as a regular farm practice and they have pointed to the need for a simpler method. This has been found in the plan of drilling smaller amounts of the more finely ground limestone with the seeding of legumes. It should not be understood that the plan of using larger amounts of ordinary limestone is not as valuable as ever, but the use of fine limestone permits liming under many conditions where heavy liming is not commonly practiced.

According to the common conception of the function of limestone, it is applied to the soil as a means of removing, or correcting, soil acidity. Experimental studies at the Missouri Experiment Station, however, show that limestone, or calcium carbonate, renders two services. One of these is the removal of the soil acidity that is accomplished by the carbonate part. The other is that of supplying calcium as a nutrient to the plants. In the past, emphasis on the removal of acidity has so completely overshadowed the importance of supplying the much needed calcium for plants, that this latter function of lime has not been fully appreciated. Experiments have shown, however, that in terms of better plant growth, the application of calcium to the soil is more important than the removal of acidity. Compounds of calcium other than its carbonate, which do not remove soil acidity, will often serve in place of limestone. Conversely, however, carbonate compounds that will remove the acidity but do not contain calcium do not have significant influence on plant growth. Since limestone is the cheapest source of both calcium and carbonate, such other compounds have not been substituted for it and these facts were not observed in practice. Thus, in using calcium carbonate to remove the soil acidity, the calcium needs of the plant have nevertheless been met without ascribing to the limestone application this particular and important function.

Studies on calcium as an important nutrient for legumes have shown that the amount of this element required by these plants is large in comparison with the needs of non-legumes plants. For 25 bushels of wheat and a ton of straw, only 5 pounds of calcium are needed. For 50 bushels of corn and a ton of fodder a like amount must be provided. To produce two tons of clover hay—about the crop that might be expected on 50 bushel corn land—the soil must supply 80 pounds, or 16 times as much calcium. A two-ton hay crop of soybeans, often considered able to grow on sour soil, requires 55 pounds of calcium. Legumes make large demands on the soil for calcium in comparison with other crops, and for this reason they represent the first group of crops to show disaster from a depleted supply of calcium in the soil.

In terms of the amount of limestone required to supply this required calcium, however, the figure is small. Pure limestone contains 40% calcium, or 40 pounds per hundred, hence a crop of 50 bushels of corn and stover would take calcium from the soil, equivalent of only 12 1/2 pounds of limestone. Red clover, a much heavier feeder on calcium, would take for a two-ton crop, the calcium that would be supplied by 200 pounds of pure limestone. Soybeans at the same acre yield would need about 150 pounds.

Thus the actual calcium needs of the crop can be supplied in relatively small quantities of limestone if it can be delivered to the plants in such a way that they can use it fully. In respect to the crop of needs of calcium, therefore, we may think of limestone in terms of pounds rather than tons, provided this is delivered to the plant in usable form.

When the limestone needs approach such small figures per acre the liming treatment becomes similar to that of applying fertilizer. Then, too, since it becomes a matter of getting the lime, or calcium into the plant, it further approaches fertilizer in the matter of providing limestone of ready solubility. Limestone is similar to fertilizer in still another respect, namely, that the effects of the lime are marked in the early life of the plant. Experiments have shown that legume plants given lime are larger and more able to take nutrients from the soil in their early life, when given access to lime for only the first ten days of their growth and then transplanted as seedlings to acid soil, than when lime is withheld. Also they are more active in forming root nodules and earlier as well as superior in nitrogen fixation.

As a rock, limestone is usually considered insoluble, yet this is not the whole truth when one recalls the numerous caves dissolved out of limestone by running water. When finely ground, of course, limestone becomes more soluble in the same way that powdered sugar dissolves more quickly than rock candy, yet both are the same chemical composition. When limestone is ground into a powder that is fine enough to pass a sieve with 100 holes per linear inch, or 10,000 holes to a square inch, its action in the soil is practically as rapid as that of the water soluble forms of lime, namely, quick lime and hydrated lime. The finer grinding of limestone with this resulting increase in solubility make it behave like a fertilizer in speedy effects.

By drilling finely ground limestone into the soil at the time of seeding the crop, the approach to fertilizer is still closer in method of application and in use by the small plants in their first stages of growth. The effectivenes in starting legumes by drilling these smaller amounts which do not remove the acidity of the entire soil layer, points to the fact that it is not necessary to correct all the soil acidity before legumes can be grown. Finely ground limestone has started sweet clover on soil whose degree of acidity was quite high, (pH 4.9, requiring more than two tons of coarse limestone on a silt loam), and this acidity was slightly changed in no greater distance than two inches from the drilled stone. Even with heavy applications of limestone, legumes succeed when not all the soil acidity has been removed. In fact it has often been observed that clover will succeed in consequence of applications of coarse limestone on soil whose test after treatments still shows considerable acidity. Such soils are evidently delivering enough calcium to the plant for successful growth even though they are still acid. When plants can be transplanted from limed to sour soil and are better there because of the short early period in the presence of limed soil, and when nodules are produced in the soil at some distance from the streak of limestone applied by the drill, as has been common observation, it is clearly evident that lime can serve the plants without neutralizing the acidity in the entire soil area. It is highly probable that it would be disastrous to plant growth in other respects if many soils were suddenly neutralized completely. Potato scab is encouraged by neutral soils and the potato grower may well consider fine liming as a means of growing legumes for organic matter addition to his soil without bringing on the scab disease that results from correcting the acidity completely. Excessive liming has given bad effects in a sufficient number of cases to lead us to believe that some degree of acidity is desirable. Under such circumstances limestone behaves as a fertilizer in that it supplies the calcium needed by the plants, and can be handled on this basis in farm practice on many soils without necessarily completely neutralizing the soil.

If limestone is to be rapid in its action it must be finely ground. Much pulverized, or powdered, stone is now available as a consequence of improved methods of separating this fraction during grinding. Likewise channels that formerly consumed such output are now using less, so that it is available at prices more conducive to agricultural use. Some quarries are providing stone of such fineness that all of it passes the 100 mesh screen, while many have 40 mesh, or 30 mesh, stone. These latter contain no particles larger than those which will pass screens of such size and usually have about one-half, by weight, fine enough to pass the 100 mesh screen. These also lend themselves to drilling better than the 100 mesh material which does not flow through machinery easily.

The regular 10 mesh stone commonly broadcast at heavy rates might also be drilled according to this plan but it contains such a small portion of finely ground powdered stone that it is slower in its action. If larger amounts can be drilled so as to put into the soil as much powdered stone as is added by the finer material, similar results may be expected. Such large amounts cannot be handled so easily through the drill, nor with so little wear on the machinery. It seems doubtful economy to drill the coarser stone in place of the 40 mesh and finer material. For drilling purposes and effective results the finer stone should be considered.

Beside limestone, there are other compounds which can supply calcium and are often available. Acetylene plant waste is a form of very finely powdered lime hydrate that on drying and exposure to air will change to calcium carbonate. It will serve effectively as limestone, though its fluffy nature prohibits easy drilling unless there is an agitator in the drill box. Lime tailings, residues from burning lime, are another by-product that deserves consideration. Lime hydrate in the commercial form will also serve. It carries as much calcium in 74 pounds as limestone does in 100 and one will need only three-fourths as much of this as of limestone. Granulated quicklime may also be used, but is not as convenient to handle because of its caustic nature and like the hydrate may disturb germination if put into close contact with the seed in the soil. About 56 pounds of this are equivalent in calcium value to 100 pounds of limestone. When quicklime air slakes completely and changes from the stone to the powder form, it may also be used. Then it has no weight advantage and 100 pounds are required for the equivalent of 100 pounds of limestone. It also has the same chemical composition. Its fineness introduces difficulties in drilling it effectively. Other kinds of lime and lime wastes may be considered and can be evaluated on basis of their calcium supplying power. Many of these miscellaneous forms of lime deserve more consideration as a soil treatment.

If smaller amounts of finely ground limestone are to be successful in supplying plants with calcium and establishing the crop, the limestone should be drilled into the soil. Broadcasting such small amounts as 500 pounds per acre is not significant in its effects. Yet when this same amount is drilled, each drill row represents small soil areas where the limestone is concentrated and the soil along the row is more highly saturated with lime. Experimental studies show that the higher the degree of saturation of the soil by lime, the more readily does the plant secure the lime. Thus, the plants find in the drill row this favorable condition for supplying lime and will grow there. As is true for wheat and other drilled grains, so it is true for legumes— their establishment in the drill row only usually means plenty of plants per acre and a good stand.

Finely ground limestone need not be drilled deeply. It moves slightly downward in its reaction with the soil. Even if put right on top, it will be fairly effective but in this case the wind scatters it to reduce its effects. It is unnecessary, however, to make the drilling operation a heavy load by setting the drill deeply into the soil. If a quiet or non-windy time is chosen, the drill can be run shallow, the limestone delivered in a very narrow strip into the soil with light cover, and narrow, highly-loaded streaks of soil through the field provided. There the plants can early find their needed lime supply and get off to a good start. This early growth is essential in the life of the clovers if they are to get their roots down into the lower soil and establish themselves in competition with the nurse crop of wheat or oats for the soil fertility and moisture. Only as they do so can they survive the summer and make a paying crop later. Lighter applications of limestone cannot be promptly beneficial if scattered enough through the entire surface soil. They can be helpful, however, if drilled into the soil.

Since fine limestone is considered much like a fertilizer, naturally the season for drilling it might be expected to be that when the legumes are seeded. It has been found a good practice to drill the limestone in the spring when the clovers and other lime-loving legumes are sown. The fertilizer attachment of the grain drill will deliver the limestone, while the grass seed attachment delivers the seed. In this way one operation over the field completes the seeding. If the drill is not run into the soil deeply, the seed may be delivered down the spout and the seeds and limestone put into immediate contact. If the seeds are covered too deeply by soil or heavy droppings of the dry powdered stone, the germination and stand may be disturbed. The seed delivery spouts on the drill may be detached from the sprouts leading down to the drill shoe, and the clover seed scattered on the surface of the soil. The seed spouts may also be extended to scatter them behind the drill, where they will fall into the drill furrows immediately over the limestone and be covered well enough by the first rain.

When drilling the fine limestone in the spring season, it should be done as early as possible because of the well known need for seeding clover early. This is sometimes impossible because the soil is too wet to permit going over it with the drill, and the wait for suitable soil conditions delays the seeding until the nurse crop is so large that the clover will be smothered out, or fail because of moisture shortage. It is not necessary that the limestone and the seed go on together, provided the soil is not cultivated or disturbed between these two operations. Consequently, the fine limestone may be drilled during the winter when soil conditions permit. The broadcast clover seeding may follow at the proper date. This will serve practically as well as drilling the two together.

As heavy applications of coarse limestone are often made in connection with wheat seeding in the fall, so the drilling of the finer limestone may also be done at this season. The limestone may be drilled like a fertilizer directly with the wheat. Since the wheat and limestone cannot be mixed and seeded together through the grain section of the drill very successfully, the stone should be put on with the fertilizer attachment. Limestone so applied in the fall will be effective the following early spring when the clover is seeded broadcast in the customary manner. If fertilizer is to be applied for the wheat this may be mixed with the limestone and both put on at the same time. Such a mixture may also be drilled with the clover seedings. There is no serious danger from the interference of one with the other. On the contrary, there may be improvement in the effect of the fertilizer as a result of the presence of the limestone. Likewise, for the limestone effect on the wheat, this will not be detrimental but may be helpful. Inoculated soil may also be mixed with the limestone as a means of inoculating the following clover seeding.

As for the time when fine limestone may be drilled most conveniently and effectively, the fall seeding season is a good one where wheat or barley is the nurse crop. If oats serves as such, the limestone may be drilled similarly with the oats in the spring and the clover broadcast later. When the legumes are seeded alone, then the limestone may well be drilled at their seeding season.

"How long will the fine limestone last?" is a common question when one contrasts this method with that of broadcasting a heavy application of coarse material that is effective to the legume crops in more than one round of the rotation. Legumes are the first among the crops to need lime, consequently, the fine stone is drilled with the legumes. The effect will last longer than this one crop if the soil is not disturbed. Sweet clover has reseeded itself after a start with fine lime, showing that the effect can carry over to the third year. When only the small soil areas represented by the drill rows are treated and the ground plowed afterward this small amount of limed soil is too thoroughly scattered through the great soil mass to lend much effect. When the next legume crop comes around in the rotation another limestone treatment should be used. Because broadcast heavy liming is an arduous task and represents a significant investment, one naturally hopes that its effects will last a longer time than for one single year of rotation. Drilling the fine lime is a simple, one-man operation of moderate cash outlay and it might be considered as a part of the treatment for every legume seeding.

The most effective method of drilling fine limestone is by means of the fertilizer attachment on the grain drill. This will handle limestone effectively though one cannot expect even this machine to operate without attention. One must always make sure that the stone is not failing to get down into the distributing machinery satisfactorily. It is also necessary to learn the rate of delivery. Some careful tests have shown that very fine limestone was delivered at only three-fourths of the rate as given for the particular set of gears and gate opening specified for that of fertilizer. If one is to drill 500 pounds of the finer stone it may be necessary to set the machinery at a higher figure than that for fertilizer delivery.

The ordinary grain drill without fertilizer will distribute fine limestone if some agitating device is used. Some grain drills are already made for, and can easily be equipped with, an agitator in the grain box so that they will serve to drill fine limestone. In testing such a machine with 100 mesh limestone, it delivered 200 pounds per acre when set for six pecks of oats, and 350 pounds per acre when set for 12 pecks. Another drill equipped with a home-made agitator tripped by a block on the wheel, delivered slightly less than 300 pounds when set for 9 pecks of oats. Such machinery is not as convenient as the fertilizer section of a grain drill, but will serve and can be used to drill the stone. As coarser stone is used, the wear will be greater, but this is not a serious matter and should not prohibit drilling limestone by this method. It is important, however, that the drill be cleaned thoroughly thereafter.

As the declining fertility of our soils becomes more widely recognized and the use of fertilizers to replace it becomes a more general practice, the fertilizer drill will be a more common machine for applying limestone as well. In respect to farm machinery, the fine limestone drilling methods will fit into the already common stock of farm equipment and call for no special machinery of limited use.

It is not uncommon experience in Missouri to find that an application of limestone alone does not secure a stand of clover. This has been true with heavy applications of limestone, but has come under more careful observation and with more emphasis in trials with fine limestone in conjunction with fertilizer treatments. Clover requires more than limestone for its successful stand and growth. It is true that liming increases root nodule production and, through the nodular bacteria, helps the plant to get its nitrogen from the unlimited supply in the soil air. In respect to this one nutrient, beside calcium, liming increases the supply of nitrogen for the legume plants by their improved nitrogen fixation. Limestone cannot substitute, however, for soil shortages in phosphorus, potassium, moisture or any other items required for plant growth. The addition of phosphorus to limestone has shown itself beneficial. The addition of potash is also noticeable in its effects so that on many soils of the state, the level of this nutrient is so low as to deserve consideration. Farm manure will supply some of this shortage and should often be used for this reason in conjunction with liming for a legume stand. Resistance to drought by clover was increased as limestone was supplemented with other treatments, possibly because these produce greater plant vigor and a deeper tap root. These illustrations indicate that more liming is often required, and that if fine limestone has been drilled with the clover seeding which fails, that failure should not be wholly ascribed to the fault of the fine liming method. Rather, some other soil deficiency may be responsible. The fine liming method will supply the needed calcium, and will increase nodule production and consequent nitrogen fixation, but it cannot take the place of other requisites for this crop. When used alone fine lime should not always be considered as a guarantee for a good stand and crop of clover.

As the soils in the regions of great rainfall and heavier crop production have become low in lime—now being especially recognized by clover failures—so have they also become correspondingly low in other nutrients not so grossly removed by plants. The soil deficiency in these is just as disastrous since the crop is impossible unless each of the required nutrients is amply supplied. The use of fine lime drilled with wheat has sometimes improved the wheat crop, pointing out that the soil was low in calcium even for wheat, and doubtless for corn and other crops that require but small amounts of it. Liming ahead of corn has improved this crop, probably by indirect as well as by direct effects through the calcium supplied. Oats have sometimes been improved by liming and reports of improvement in soybeans from limestone drilled with them are not uncommon. Its benefit on oats and wheat nurse crops, suggest similar effects from it on barley serving the same purpose, especially since barley is the most sensitive of the small grains to the lack of lime. The low supply of lime that may be disastrous to the extent of complete crop failure for legumes, is therefore injurious to many other crops.

This declining supply of soil fertility may be responsible for clover failure where it is grown with a nurse crop as contrasted to success where grown alone. The fertility supply of the soil may not be sufficient for two crops. Illustrations are not uncommon of clover in wheat drilled around shocks of corn fodder. In such cases the clover may be large next to the shock where nutrients were leached from the fodder into the soil by rain, while farther from the shock where no wheat was drilled and the clover grew alone it will be somewhat smaller. It will usually be still smaller within the wheat crop. The improved growth of clover around the shock from which the added fertility was leached into the soil, points out that the fertility of the soil is low for clover, but especially so when it must grow in competition with the wheat for this limited fertility supply. Farm experience in growing clover alone successfully is testifying to this situation. When grass takes alfalfa, this is also a testimony that the fertility level will not meet the high demands for good alfalfa that would smother the grass. We are expecting too much of many soils when we seed a nurse crop and clover too, and expect both to succeed on the low level of soil fertility offered them.

This declining fertility level is evident in spite of the fact that a liming treatment, especially a heavy application, helps much in making other plant foods more effective. It is now known that liming helps the plants to obtain more potassium. Also it is instrumental in making a phosphorus treatment more beneficial. On limed land phosphorus is usually more effective than on unlimed soil. Lime also helps the plant to get nitrogen. It aids the plant in making much better use of the limited supplies of these other nutrients. It does not add these to the soil, hence the already low supply will be more rapidly depleted by liming. If, however, clovers can be grown and larger crop yields result, the restoration of the fertility should be quickly undertaken when this soil need is fully appreciated. As we use more limestone, attention must likewise be given to other deficiencies of soil fertility which this practice will help bring to our notice, and for which limestone cannot be a substitute.

To date the drilling of the finer limestone has been tried with successful results by farmer cooperators in many parts of the state. The soil types represented include the following: Boone, Cherokee, Crawford, Decatur, Edina, Gerald, Grundy, Knox, Lebanon, Marshall, Memphis, Oswego, Putnam and Summit silt loams; the Shelby and Lindley loams; Clarksville and Baxter gravelly loams; Lintonia fine sandy loam; and Wabash clay loam. By no means have all soil types been included in this rather extensive list, but those of level topography, heavier subsoil and significant degree of acidity have been grown to acid sensitive crops by means of lighter applications of limestone drilled on them. They testify to the success of this practice on those soils most difficult to seed to clover. Not only red clover, but sweet clover, and in some cases, alfalfa has been started by this treatment. Unfortunately, liming cannot offset bad seed, summer drought or infertility, but it can care for the calcium deficiency, or lime need, on many of the prevailing soil types in the state.

In terms of cost of the limestone, the drilling of a quarter ton of finer limestone is less than that of broadcasting two tons of 10 mesh material per acre. With the price of the former at $5.00 per ton at the quarry and a delivery charge of $1.00 per ton within a radius approaching a hundred miles. A 500 pound, or quarter ton application should call for a cash outlay of $1.50 per acre. For two tons of 10 mesh material such a cash outlay would allow only 75 cents per ton delivered on the farm. Costs of this coarser material have usually been much greater than this, so that drilling finer limestone should not exceed—and will usually be less than—the per acre cost of coarser material at the two ton rate.

In terms of the labor of distribution, the drilling method effects a real saving. To drill 500 pounds per acre on 20 acres is a one-man labor load, totaling five tons of material, while the corresponding labor load of 40 tons broadcast might require the help of the neighbors. It is this labor requirement that should be considered as the significant advantage of the finer limestone, and that makes this method lend itself to bringing limestone to soils where the other method might mean too great an initial cost. The smaller amount of limestone means less initial cash outlay; it permits the stone to be hauled to greater distance from railroads or delivery points, and makes possible liming within the farmer's own labor. The one-man labor load and smaller amounts of stone required make delivery possible at any time with storage for later use. When its use becomes more widespread, the stone may be stocked more generally by local dealers and thus still greater economies effected. Under such conditions, its costs when used regularly in every rotation should not exceed the costs of heavier applications of coarser stone applied less often.

This method of handling the liming need of the soil reduces it from a complex problem of large cash outlay and extensive labor, to a regular farming practice that can be geared into the routine farm program without its disruption. On such a basis the drilling of fine limestone may be accepted as a regular part of the legume seeding whenever it comes around in the rotation just as fertilizing should be a part of wheat seeding. Under such conditions more legumes can be successfully grown, more fertility restored to the soils and higher profits returned by the land.

LIME FOR BACKBONE!

The business of farming depends much on using the soil as the main factory. Our attention has been so completely absorbed above the soil that the real basis of "growing things" has not been commonly examined on each farm for its possible success and security. With animals playing a larger part in the final accounting of profit and loss, however, we are beginning to recognize the possibility of doing something to feed our animals better by treating the soil with some added fertility. And animals tell us, unfortunately, that as meat producers they are not as certain of profit today as they used to be not many years ago.

Much of this uncertainty may be traced right back to the declining fertility supply in the soil. When a 70% calf crop cuts into the margin of safety in the farming business, we are inclined to blame the bull. We have been told that he is "half the herd." When only one animal needs to be sacrificed to correct a 30% trouble, we are apt to dispose of the bull and pin our faith anew on another one that may not give us even a 70% calf crop. Reproduction is a delicate physiological performance. The fecundity in it, by both female and male, is influenced more by the soil than by the pedigree. Soils with depleted fertility and producing forages that are consequently deficient in minerals means that shy breeders and aborters will be more numerous. Losses through those channels alone, if corrected, may push the balance sheet in the farming books from the loss to the profit side.

During wintertime, feeds that are mainly of fuel value are not of great help in foetus production, which demands calcium and phosphorus in liberal amounts. When a cow calves and goes into milk production, the demand on her body for daily delivery of calcium and phosphorus goes even higher. Some soils are too deficient in these nutrients to enable the cow to go through the pregnancy period without developing acetonemia in late stages. Should she carry her foetus-building business through under strain, by sacrificing much of her own skeletal calcium and phosphorus for the offspring, she may yet break down in milk fever when the demand for the minerals arises.

"Pregnancy disease" among ewes is similar testimony when those with twin foetuses are more commonly taken with it. Rickets in calves, in spite of sunshine for vitamin D and of ample volume of milk, are occurring on soils from which the fertility has been highly exhausted. This exhaustion has reached a degree where the product of the milk is not necessarily of unvaried food value, which, even in milk, depends on the soil from which it is produced.

Animal deficiencies are pointing their fingers back to the soil and not to the drugstore. Plants given calcium and phosphorus via soil treatments do more than convey them to the manger. Plants manufacture essential food products, many probably still unknown as to composition and bodily service. They may be the means of making the animal sleek in the spring before the soil factory runs out of its raw materials. It may be the lack of these that gives us poor animal appearance commonly ascribed to fly troubles by August.

Fortunately for better feeding values in the grains and forages for our livestock, and in the vegetable and animal products for human consumption, we are gradually putting the essential nutrient elements, calcium and phosphorus, back to the soil in a larger soil improvement program.

Calcium and phosphorus, or limestone and phosphate, as their compounds are called, need to become household words in the soil fertility list. There is no substitute for them, except as we will accept starvation. Lime needs to be used more often. Lime or calcium is first of the items on the chemical list in the business of farming. It has gone ahead of nitrogen now that we know that the legumes given calcium and phosphorus can serve us to run nitrogen-fixing plants on every farm.

Though plants and people may be mainly carbohydrates and fats, both of which originate in fresh air and sunshine, it nevertheless takes some soil minerals to put a backbone into them—so badly needed by all of us now. It is soil and its mineral output that makes us "personalities rather than puddles." As fast as we realize that what must be put into the soil determines what we get out of it, we can optimistically view the future. The soil is still our best support. It is still the basis of our biggest business.

ITS THE CALCIUM . . NOT THE ALKALINITY

Normal development of plants like any other growth performance, is distinctly a matter of proper nutrition. Nodule production on the roots of the soybean plant and its use of nitrogen from the atmosphere to let this crop serve as a protein-producing, and a nitrogen-fixing factory on the farm, are determined in the main by the nutritional levels or the fertility conditions of the soil.

Of the 14 chemical elements required to construct plants, 11 must be supplied by the soil in case of the non-legumes. One less, or 10 are demanded from the soil by the legumes. The legumes, in the same manner as the non-legumes, use carbon, hydrogen and oxygen provided by air and water. In addition, and quite different from the nonn-legumes, they can take a fourth nutrient—nitrogen—from the air provided they are operating in cooperation with the proper bacteria on their roots commonly supplied as inoculation.

Much of the attention to the behaviors of legume plants and their accompanying bacteria has centered about the fact that legumes can draw, on the weather, as it were, for four of their nutrient requirements, while non-legumes are limited to three. Little attention has gone to the fact that legumes must still obtain ten (possibly more) nutrient elements from the soil. Demand made on the soil by the legumes for these elements is greater than by the non-legumes because the mineral content of legume forages are of higher concentrations. These demands are more significant because on these increased mineral content drawn from the soil fertility store there depends the effectiveness with which the root nodule producing bacteria will work.

Because the soybean can go, via bacteria, to the atmosphere for its nitrogen supply, we must not fix attention so completely on this escape from one responsibility as to forget the ten others that still lie in the soil. Studies to date have not given sufficient importance to all the soil-borne plant nutrients as these influence inoculation, nodule production and nitrogen fixation by legumes. Critical attention has gone to some, namely: calcium, phosphorus, magnesium and potassium, the four most prominent in the soil fertility list. Consider the importance of these in connection with the soybean.

Since long ago the art of agriculture has been pointing to the need for lime by many soils if they are to grow legumes. Nodulation of soybeans is generally improved by the practice of liming. It is only recently that science has begun to understand the function of liming for better cooperation between the plants and the bacteria. The scientist's first suggestion as to the role of liming soils in giving better legume growth was that lime was effective because it removed soil acidity.

This explanation is about to lose its adherents, in the face of the accummulating evidence that liming serves because it supplies the plants with calcium, one of the foremost soil requirements for both legumes and non-legumes.

Legume bacteria, too, have been considered sensitive to soil acidity. Failure of inoculation has often been ascribed to injury to the bacteria by the soil sourness. Successful inoculation, or ample nodule production, however, involves more than the idiosyncracies of the plant and bacteria. It involves, most decidedly, the soil as it nourishes both of these properly and sufficiently to make their joint activities result not only in a crop of larger tonnage but one of increased concentrations of proteins and minerals.

Since the soybean must be provided with its specific nodule bacteria when seeded on a soil for the first time, naturally the practice of inoculation of the seed is a recommended one. Failure of inoculation to produce nodules in many instances has brought blame on the bacterial culture, which, like water over the wheel, was past recovery or beyond defense when once distributed throughout the soil. It seemed a logical hypothesis that defective plant nutrition because of soil fertility deficiency might be prohibiting effective inoculation.

In order to test the nutritional value of liming for the soybean plants as compared to the role of lime in neutralizing soil acidity as these two effects encouraged better nodulation, calcium as a chloride was drilled with soybeans in comparison with similar drilling of calcium hydroxide. Though the latter neutralized soil acidity while the former did not, but treatments brought about effective nodulation, deeper green color and larger plants of more stable cell structure. The nodules were not necessarily located in the soil areas into which the calcium compound was deposited. Roots in the acid soil areas bore nodules. Here was evidence that liming was improving the results from inoculation because lime was providing calcium.

In order to separate the nutritional value of calcium for the plant from those for the bacteria, more detailed tests of the soybean and its calcium needs were undertaken. It was readily demonstrated that calcium was more important than magnesium or potassium in the early life of the soybean plant.

A deficiency supply of calcium encouraged attacks on the plants by a fungus resembling "damping off," and brought failure of inoculation.

To determine the minimum amounts of calcium required per plant for effective establishment of the stand, calcium was used in the solution form and in the form absorbed on colloidal clay. The latter method permitted variable amounts of clays at different degrees of acidity (pH). It thus permitted controlled amounts of calcium at any pH or degree of acidity desired. These trials demonstrated that the soybean's early growth was dependent on a significant supply of calcium more than on a particular degree of soil acidity. Nodulation could not result later unless liberal levels of calcium were provided early to carry the plant to the inoculate age. More detailed separation of the calcium as a nutritional element from its role in modifying the soil's reaction as this influences nodulation was undertaken by using clay neutralized to different pH values or degrees of acidity through titration with calcium hydroxide.

Constant amounts of calcium were provided at different pH values by taking the proper amount of clay at a particular pH. Thus by placing these different amounts of the clays of different pH values into sand for soybean growth, there were provided soils of variable pH but of constant supplies of exchangeable calcium. Plant growth and nodule production showed clearly that even though the soybeans reflected their response to differences in soil acidity, they reflected far more their growth and nodulation response to the amount of calcium provided.

Nitrogen fixation, or an increase of nitrogen in the crop over that in the planted seed, did not occur even in a neutral soil unless the supply of calcium was ample. It occurred in acid soils containing liberal supplies of exchangeable calcium. Here, then, was distinct evidence that if inoculation of soybeans is to be effective in making this crop serve for soil improvement, the soil must deliver calcium to these plants.

We may well imagine competition between the soil and the plant for the lime. The absorbing power of the soil for nutrients like calcium, potassium, magnesium and other substances is appreciable. It was demonstrated by means of better soybean growth, nodulation and nitrogen fixation, that placing the calcium on a small smount of soil to saturate it highly is more effective than is placing it on much soil to increase the soil saturation only slightly.

These effects from variable degrees of saturation of the clay by the plant nutrient demonstrated similar results regardless of whether the variable calcium was accompanied by acidity or by neutrality. The soybean growth proved that it was not the acidity that disturbed plant growth, but that it was the deficient soil fertility commonly present when soils become acid. Likewise it demonstrated the more efficient use by the plant of the applied calcium in a soil more highly saturated by it. It also suggests a higher efficiency for drilling soil treatments than for broadcasting them.

That calcium is needed for the legume bacteria as they live independently of their host has become a well known recognized fact. With limited lime supply they become abnormal, and fail to inoculate. But given plenty of calcium, they grow well and are effective inoculators.

Unless both the plant and the bacteria have access to calcium, effective inoculation cannot be expected. Lime for a legume—even an acid tolerant plant like the soybean—plays a helpful role because it nourishes the plant rather than because it removes soil acidity. Even an acid soil must supply lime for successful inoculation and growth of the soybeans.

Phosphorus, like calcium, is a requisite if soybeans are to be active in nodule production and in nitrogen fixation. But its importance and behavior are closely related to the amount of calcium. Unless calcium is amply supplied, soybeans are poorly nodulated, and are poor nitrogen fixers for soil improvement. In fact they may even lose phosphorus back to the soil, so that the final crop will return less phosphorus when harvested than was in the planted seed.

That magnesium should be helpful toward better soybean inoculation has not come to our attention because relatively little magnesium is required by the plant, and most soils are not seriously deficient in this nutrient. This element is effective on soybeans, but probably indirectly as well as directly. It makes calcium more effective and thus illustrates the fact that fertility elements work together. These effects suggest an interstimulation among the elements, so that the final results can not be considered merely as additions of the values of their effects when applied singly.

Improved inoculation may be also dependent on the potassium supply in the soil. Experimental studies demonstrated increased nodule production and better growth as potassium deficiencies of the soil were remedied. With more liberal amounts of potassium, however, particularly in contrast to the amount of calcium, inoculation may be less effective and give reduced nodulation and nitrogen fixation. Excessive potassium in relation to calcium makes the soybeans produce more tonnage, but they fix less nitrogen and become more clearly non-legumes than legumes. They move into the class of woody vegetation and out of the class of vegetation with high protein content of high nutritional value as animal forages.

Inoculation, or the introduction of nodule bacteria with the seeding of the soybeans, is not necessarily a practicce that will compel the plant to accept the companionship of the bacteria. The latter cannot use cavemen tactics. Rather, the plant and bacteria will unite in their efforts toward getting their necessary nitrogen out of the gaseous supply in the atmosphere only when the soil provides liberally of all the nutrient elements required by both the plant and the bacteria.

Successful soybean growth on soils of declining fertility can not be guaranteed simply by the introduction of a fed particular pedigree microbes. The plant must first be healthy because it is well fed with calcium, phosphorus, magnesium and other soil-contributed elements. Unless it is well nourished by the soil, the inoculating bacteria will not associate with it to give it the one distinguishing character so desirable in legumes, namely, nitrogen fixing capacity.

Inoculation, or the introduction of the bacteria, is no substitute for the high levels of soil fertility that are demanded for successful legume crops.

PURPOSE OF LIMING SOIL AN ENIGMA

More than a quarter of a century ago, 400 samples of 21 different soil types of Missouri tested for exchangeable calcium showed a close relationship of the amounts of this insoluble but available plant nutrient to the soil's capacity to give good crops yields. That was also the time when limestone (calcium carbonate, and calcium-magnesium carbonate) was applied extensively for the purpose of reducing soil acidity, or raising the numerical value of the pH *i.e.* the degree of acidity of the soil. The pH value as a soil test report was easily obtained by special laboratory equipment. But measuring the exchangeable calcium (or magnesium) was a tedious manipulation. However, the latter related the soil to potential crop production, while the pH was a technical expression, not so readily connected with the nutrition of the crop plants.

At that early date, the evaluation of the soil types with their arrangement in order of decreasing production of crops and livestock and their similar classification as an arrangement into six groups, A,B,C,D,E,F—by the soil surveyors—showed a close agreement with their decreasing amounts of exchangeable calcium by soil test as set forth in the accompanying table. The more productive soils supplied calcium in this exchangeable form of plant roots in quantities three times as great as did the poorer soils. The total

Soils Arranged in Order of Decreasing Productivity Shows a Closely Similar Order for Their Amounts of Exchangeable Calcium.

Groups	Soil Types	Exchangeable Calcium, milligram equivalents per 100 gms. soil
A	Marshall	14.80
	Summit	12.64
	Grundy	12.71
B	Knox	11.32
	Pettis	10.86
	Crawford	10.68
	Chariton	10.21
	Eldon	8.99
	Oswego	9.19
C	Putnam	8.89
	Bates	7.86
	Memphis	6.22
	Hagerstown	5.91
	Lindley	8.64
	Union	6.64
D	Cherokee	5.57
	Baxter	5.57
	Gerald	3.82
	Boone	7.59
E	Lebanon	5.51
	Clarksville	4.29

Mo. Agr. Expt. Sta. Bul. 387, p. 85, 1937. Report for year ending June 30, 1936.

quantities so active were large enough, and the differences between soils were great enough, for an accuracy of measurement which left no doubt about it.

Measurements of the clay-humus in the soil made possible the evaluation of the degree of saturation of that part of the soil from which the calcium (and magnesium) are exchanged. Thus, soil testing for calcium moved itself more closely toward indicating potential nutrition of plants, especially the legumes as producers of proteins. The term "pH" expresses the concentration of hydrogen as an active ion, separated out of any compound. Like the calcium and magnesium, it too is a positively-charged ion. Hence, any of these three can exchange for any other on the clay-humus colloid. Unfortunately, the hydrogen is not a plant nutrient coming from that source, while calcium and magnesium are. So when the hydrogen from cropping, weathering, leaching, etc. replaces the calcium and magnesium, we say the soil becomes "sour" and the crop fails. But the real cause of legume failures is the "going out" of the nutrients, calcium, magnesium, potassium, etc., the presence of which makes the soil non-acid, and not by the "coming in" of the hydrogen by which it is made sour or acid.

When those two exchanges or soil phenomena occurred simultaneously with the legume failure the soil's increased acidity was quickly recognized. We made the error of considering the soil acidity, the hydrogen concentration, the cause of crop failure when it was the fertility deficiency of calcium (and magnesium), or the failing plant nutrition, that was responsible. The validity of this conclusion was experimentally established by preparing a purely hydrogen-saturated clay and then separating lots of it as a series of increasing degrees of saturation by calcium. Half of these were prepared to give a series of increasing calcium saturation with reciprocally decreasing saturation by hydrogen or with decreasing degrees of acidity.

The other half of the lots was a series given barium to just replace the decreasing hydrogen or to approach the neutral condition for all of the lot. This gave increasing saturation by calcium and reciprocally decreasing saturation by the non-nutrient barium. These clays were added to sand in such amounts as to supply constant totals of exchangeable calcium per pot or sand-clay combination and were planted to soybeans. They resulted in literally duplicate series of crop growths according to the differing saturation by calcium that resulted, irrespective of the presence or absence of the acidity as shown in the accompanying illustration. Thus the enigma of the purpose of applying lime was solved long ago when such experiments told us that the benefit from liming the humid soil comes from its nourishment of the crop by calcium, and not from its reduction of the soil acidity by the carbonate acconpanying the calcium in the limestone. Seemingly this truth is still much hidden in unopened reports.

CALCIUM AS A FACTOR IN SEED GERMINATION

That the soil should be a factor in determining the percentage germination of seeds may seem an overemphasis of the soil's service in plant growth. When the ash content of a plant is approximately only 5% or, as maximum, 10%, then this is a relatively small contribution by the soil. But when growth as a synthesis of carbon-dioxide and water into compounds by means of sunshine energy will occur only after the soil has made its seemingly small contribution, this diminutive offering mounts in its importance. Since the major part of the nutrients from the soil enter the plant in the early phases of its life history, it seemed logical to determine whether variation in soil fertility, particularly of calcium, might not register its effects so early in plant life as even to influence the percentage germination of the seeds of a crop like the tomato, for example, which is not commonly considered a calcophile.

The tomato seeds were planted in ordinary greenhouse flats at increasing rates, starting with 14 seeds per row, or a spacing of 1 inch between the seeds, and increasing to 5, 10, 15, and 20 times this number per consecutive row. The rows and the rates were duplicated in the second of the flats. The soil treatments used consisted of (a) none, (b) calcium chloride, (c) complete fertilizer, and (d) calcium chloride plus complete fertilizer. These treatments were duplicated by duplicate flats.

Three trials, each with a growth period of approximately 4 weeks, were carried out in February, March, and May, respectively. The soil treatments were mixed as chemicals and ground with fine quartz sand so as to provide sufficient bulk for uniform distribution by hand in the bottom of the rill. Water was sprinkled on the applied fertilizer, the flats were covered. Observations of the early plant appearances were made and the growth with possible disease studied. After 27 to 29 days the counts were made of the plants per row.

TABLE 1

Plants produced and percentage germination represented thereby with increased rate of seeding.

Seeds planted per row	February		March		May		Mean	
	Plants	%	Plants	%	Plants	%	% of seeds planted	%
14	6.6	47	7.7	55	9.3	66	56	100
70	21.3	30	22.5	32	41.6	59	40	70
140	21.0	15	30.5	21	69.1	49	28	48
210	13.7	6	34.7	16	89.6	42	21	35
280	21.7	7	40.8	14	93.8	33	16	30

When the number of plants produced (table 1) is considered in relation to the number of seeds planted, regardless of soil treatments, a decreasing germination with increased rate of seeding is clearly demonstrated. These data represent a combination of all the soil treatments with 12 cases in each growing period and 36 cases in the mean. The mean is expressed for the plants as percentage of the seeds planted and also as percentage, assuming the plants in the lowest seeding rate as representative of the viable seeds of the lot. The large decrease in number of emerging plants with the increased rate of seeding was observed in the counts of the individual rows as well as in the summation of the data.

TABLE 2

Percentage germination as influenced by soil treatments.

Seeds planted per row	No treatment		Calcium only		Complete fertilizer		Calcium/ fertilizer	
	Plants	%	Plants	%	Plants	%	% of seeds planted	%
14	7.6	54	9.3	66	6.8	48	8.0	57
70	27.9	39	36.5	52	20.8	29	29.1	41
140	35.6	25	51.6	36	28.6	20	45.1	32
210	40.3	19	64.5	30	32.1	15	50.0	23
280	48.1	17	66.7	23	32.6	11	57.1	20

These observations raise the question as to the soil condition responsible for the decrease in germination, when careful attention was given to such items as provision of ample moisture, as covering the planted flats with a thin surface layer of quartz sand, and other means of providing optimum conditions for germination. There is an improved germination with the advance in the season, but all three trials suggest that there is some soil factor which may be sufficient for the limited seed numbers but becomes insufficient for their increasing numbers.

That some soil factor, such as a nutrient element, is responsible herein is suggested when the same data are assembled to show the variable germination in relation to the different soil treatments, as presented in table 2.

It is significant that the complete fertilizer applied and watered well into the soil for 3 days in advance of the seeding should give the lowest germination of all the trials. This fertilizer addition may be credited with an injurious effect, since the numbers fell below those for the soil without treatment. When the calcium, which was a chloride and not in an acid-neutralizing carbonate form, was added along with the fertilizer, it served to offset the injury.

It improved the germination beyond that in the untreated soil. This improvement was relatively greater as the seeding rate was larger. It was most startling, however, to find that the introduction into the soil of calcium chloride alone gave the highest percentage of plants from the seeds planted.

Such increases suggest a possible significance of calcium in the soil for better seed germination. Its effects can not be ascribed to changes in soil reaction. It must be related to the role of calcium as a nutrient, and gives the calcium of the soil an importance for possible attention in practice in terms of exceedingly small amounts for significant benefits.

NOW WE KNOW LIME IS A PLANT FOOD—
NOT MERELY A TREATMENT FOR ACIDITY

For bountiful production in agriculture we must always work with, not against, the stern laws of nature. Sciences are doing much to help in our understanding of nature's ways in the growth of our crops, our livestock and ourselves. But this knowledge still is not complete enough to keep us free from occasional but significant errors.

Such errors most often come about when we try to move too quickly with programs designed to change the habits and thinking of large groups. If we allow time for individuals of the groups to learn and understand basic principles, such errors are not too likely to occur. Then, the new behavior will be the result of changes by each individual—not just because he joined the group. Campaigns dealing with farm production changes may suffer from lack of sufficient understanding at the outset of basic natural forces.

The campaign for liming the soil based on the slogan, "Fight soil acidity" is an illustration. We have added to our understanding of how the soil serves to nourish the plant via its roots. Thus, we ought to be rethinking the wisdom of the idea of fighting soil acidity to the point of getting rid of it—of making the soil "neutral."

Serious disturbances, even disasters, in crop production, followed by irregularities in animal feeds on those crops grown on "neutralized" soils, indicate fighting soil acidity with carbonate of lime in limestone is not in accordance with natural facts of plant creation.

The cry, "Lime the soil for legumes," was well received by the public, followed by such slogans as "Grow legumes to build up the soil." Both of these farm slogans now are being reconsidered for the serious errors delaying activities for better food production. Soil exploitation rather than soil restoration was increased.

While legumes have the ability to fix nitrogen (they can take nitrogen from the free supply in the air as well as the limited supply in the soil) we find they do not necessarily carry out this philanthropic service to the soil. They are not always using atmospheric nitrogen merely because they are growing.

There have been no measurements of nitrogen fixation by legumes growing in the field that are accurate enough to tell us just how much nitrogen is taken from the air by a legume crop. Also, even if a legume takes nitrogen from the air to make plant growth, that nitrogen is made a part of the plant tissue, more in the tops than in the roots. This nitrogen is not made a part of the soil to any extent unless the entire crop is sacrificed on the spot and plowed under. We are now learning that acidity of the soil is not to be blamed when legumes fail to grow on those soils that have become highly acid from the forces of nature. Soils where the rainfall is high, particularly where virgin forests once grew but have been cleared, fail to grow these protein-producing, nitrogen-fixing legumes because these crops do not find enough fertility.

The missing soil nutrients were lost because acidity, or hydrogen, came in to replace them. Decaying or "souring" forest litter made much acid for that effect. The growing trees were setting free acidity or hydrogen from their leaching rainfall. These soils were growing only wood when the pioneers took them over. Shall we expect legumes planted there to make much more than woody tissue even if they grow there? Plants grow because they can put acid out of their roots thru respiration. Plant growth is possible because plants trade that acidity to the soil and take fertility in exchange. If there is acidity present along with plenty of fertility in the soil, then plants grow better than if that fertility is not accompanied by any acidity.

We now are coming to see that had we known more about how plants feed with their roots in the soil, there would have been no "war" on soil acidity. Instead, each of us would have undertaken our separate responsibilities to rebuild our soil first with calcium supplied with limestone. That work might well have started 25 years earlier. Perhaps we would have lime to supply magnesium, too. Had we looked upon increasing soil acidity as nothing more than decreasing soil fertility, we could have believed our soils are declining in supplies of all nutrients, including the trace minerals now so disturbing as to their possible needs.

Only as our understanding of the natural behaviors and natural laws of nature increases, will we farm more effectively on the soil that provides the creative potential for farming. For creation of farm products we need to supply the soil with the fertility for which plants trade their acidity.

SOIL ACIDITY IS BENEFICIAL

Only recently have we come to appreciate the services of soil acidity in mobilizing—making available—many of the nutrients in the rocks and minerals of the soil.

When we learned that soils are less productive in giving us legumes and other protein-rich forages, according as they become more acid—either naturally or under our cultivation—we came to the conclusion that soil acidity is the cause of this trouble. We now know that a plant puts acid into the soil in exchange for the nutrients it gets. It is that same acid held on the clay that weathers the rock fragments and serves to pass their nutrients on to the clay, and from there on to the plant. The coming into the soil of excessive acidity is merely the reciprocal of the going out of the fertility. Nature's process of feeding the plants, and thereby the animals and us, is one of putting acidity into the soil from the plant roots in order to break out of the rocks what nutrients they contain for nourishment of all the different life forms.

When we put lime rock on the soil as a fertilizer supplying calcium to our legume crops, we know full well that this rock reacts with the acid-clay of the soil. The acid goes from the clay to the lime rock which, being calcium carbonate, breaks down to give carbonic acid while the calcium is absorbed or taken over by the clay. While the calcium goes on to the clay to be available there for the plants, the carbonic acid decomposes into water and carbon dioxide as gas. Since this gas escapes from the soil, this escape takes away the acid, or, as we say, "it makes the soil neutral." The benefit to the legume crop from the application of this lime rock to the soil does not rest in the removal of this soil acidity. Rather, it rests in the exchanging of calcium as a nutrient to the clay which was holding the acidity or hydrogen, a chemical element that is not of direct nutritional service.

Soil acidity has been breaking potash rock down chemically too. During all these past years the potash feldspars have been undergoing weathering attacks by soil acidity. On this rock the acid clay carries out its weathering effects in the same way as it does for lime rock, except that it trades acid to the feldspar and takes potassium unto itself in exchange. Magnesium rock, as we have it in dolomitic limestone is also broken down by the acid clay. By this same process the clay becomes stocked with magnesium. This is then more readily exchangeable and available to the plant from the clay than it would be if the plant root were in direct contact with the rock fragment itself. By exactly the same mechanism we can expect phosphate rock to be made available for the plant's use. It is in these processes by which the acidity of the soil is beneficial. If the soil contains the two colloids, clay and humus, which can hold acidity, and then if that soil has scattered through it fragments of lime rock, of magnesium rock, of potassium rock, of phosphate rock or in fact of any rock with nutrients, it is the soil acidity that mobilizes to the clay the calcium, the magnesium, the potassium, the phosphorus, or all the other nutrients respectively for rapid use to the plants. This is nature's process of providing plant nutrients on the clay of the soil in available form. By it Nature has stocked our moderately acid soils with fertility. It was that condition of our virgin soils that prompted population to seek new lands in the first place.

SOIL ALTERS CALCIUM DIGESTIBILITY IN LEAFY GREENS

That the green leafy vegetables of the goosefoot family (spinach, Swiss chard, beet greens, and New Zealand spinach) do not increase the concentration of their calcium according as the soil is more heavily limed—as is true for the leafy vegetables of the mustard family (kale, mustard greens and turnip greens)—has been previously pointed out. Nor do those of the goosefoot family carry as high a concentration of calcium as do any of the mustard family group. The difference in the calcium concentrations between these two families are much more magnified when one considers differences in their nutritional availability of this essential inorganic element. The calcium in the four kinds of goosefoot greens cannot even be digestively utilized in the diet, according to good authorities, because of the large amounts of oxalic acid formed and present in these plants.

This organic compound of plant origin combines with the plant's calcium and also with the magnesium to convert these into insoluble and indigestible oxalates. In sharp contrast, according to these authorities, the calcium, for example, in the mustard greens, turnip tops and the kale is almost completely usable since these of the mustard family are practically free of the oxalates which make the calcium and magnesium indigestible. In some experiments using soils controlled as to both their available calcium and their degree of acidity (pH values) while growing spinach, we made the startling discovery that the spinach grown on the more acid soil had higher concentrations of the inorganic elements, calcium and magnesium, and also of the organic compound, oxalate, than were those found in the spinach grown on the less acid or nearly neutral soil.

But even at these higher concentrations, those amounts of the calcium and the magnesium added together were more than sufficient to neutralize the oxalic acid by forming oxalates and to leave some extra calcium and magnesium in other forms than this indigestible combination of them. The spinach plants on the nearly neutral soil failed to take enough calcium and magnesium from the same soil's supply to offset the oxalic acid produced within the plants. Therefore, they could offer no digestible calcium and magnesium when these greens were put into the diet. Also, on the nearly neutral soils, the application of varied amounts of extra calcium to the soil failed to change the concentrations of calcium within this green leafy vegetable significantly.

When the four goosefoot greens were grown on nearly neutral soils and chemical analyses made of them for their (a) calcium, (b) magnesium, and (c) oxalate, their high concentrations of oxalates were most noticeable. Even though the calcium in the soil was increased through units of 5, 10, 20 and 40, while the magnesium in the soil was held constant, these four leafy greens each produced more than enough oxalic acid to make both the calcium and the magnesium insoluble and indigestible. This is quite different from what would have been the case had the soil been varied in its available calcium while kept at a more acid reaction, which results when calcium in the gypsum rather than in the limestone or carbonate form is used. The chemical results of these greens as carriers of calcium and magnesium in combination with the oxalates when grown on nearly neutral soil under variable calcium supply are shown in the accompanying chart.

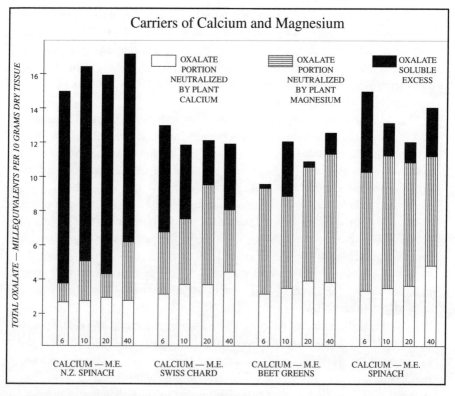

Probable disposition of oxalate in New Zealand spinach, Swiss chard, beet greens, and spinach when grown at variable levels of calcium.

In only the best greens was the combination of calcium and magnesium almost enough to overcome the detrimental effect of the oxalic acid in making these two essential elements wholly insoluble and indigestible. These data tell us that not only the amount of calcium in the soil but even the degree of soil acidity comes in to determine whether the green leafy vegetables will give us the "mineral" elements, calcium and magnesium, in a digestible form. Only slowly are we coming to realize that the condition of the soil, as well as the kind of crops, determine the nutritional value of what we grow and eat.

WE CAN GROW LEGUMES ON ACID SOILS

Legumes are almost an indispensable forage for the dairyman. They are high producers of his raw proteins, or the amino acids from which his cows produce the milk proteins. Legumes can use, both from the soil humus and from the atmosphere, the nitrogen that characterizes the chemical composition of these life-carrying substances. But unfortunately legumes are feed crops not grown so universally. We have ascribed their failure to the acidity of the soil. Whether this diagnosis of the trouble is correct may be questioned. It deserves reconsideration in the light of our better understanding of the soil and its interactions with the plants.

Acidity is a common soil condition in many parts of the temperate zone. It occurs where the rainfall gives water enough to go down through and to wash out much of the fertility. In general, if the rainfall is high enough to provide plenty of water during the crop growing season, there will also be enough water to leach the soil of much of its supply of nutrients and to make it acid. Timbered soils of the eastern United States are acid. Those of the eastern edge of the prairie are also sour. Acidity is a natural condition where soils have had rainfall going down through them and where they have been growing much vegetation. Such soils have, therefore, been subjected to a leaching force taking the fertility downward, and to a competitive force of the vegetation with its roots taking the nutrients upward. There they are built into organic combinations of them. Consequently acid soils have a distinct surface soil and subsoil horizons in their profiles. They are naturally low in fertility and have been growing mainly carbonaceous or woody vegetation.

Natural soil acidity is in reality, then, mainly a shortage of fertility in terms of many plant nutrients. This is the situation because the soil has been under cropping and leaching for ages. This was true before we took over to intensify these effects. This, then, is the condition of the soil that prompts the common question. How can we grow mineral-rich, fertility-consuming forages, like the legumes, of good feed values for such a high-powered, protein-producer like the dairy cow?

Applications of limestone, and other compounds carrying the nutrient calcium, to acid soils are known widely to be beneficial soil treatments for legumes and other crops. This was known even to the Romans, who used lime as a fertilizer on their soils. Much later in general, but yet early in our own colonial history, it was reported that Benjamin Franklin used gypsum or land plaster on clover with good improvement of this legume crop. Right here on our own soils the ancient agricultural art of liming the land was practiced for the benefit of better crops as feed. Here the sulfate of lime, or gypsum, which does not take away the acidity of the soil was making better clover. We have forgotten this unusual wisdom about soils among the many bright ideas that came down to us from this colonial sage. We may well go back and look carefully and critically into it now. We need to ask ourselves, Why can't we grow legumes on acid soil when Franklin grew them better by putting on calcium sulfate? This was a soil treatment that not only failed to reduce the soil acidity but even made the soil more sour.

It was the growing agricultural science of the early decades of the twentieth century that brought liming of the soil back as a more general agricultural practice. We cannot say that liming was an art carried over from colonial days. It had been pushed out when fertilizers came into use. Liming the soil has become an extensive practice under the encouragement of an embryo soil-testing service. That service was guided by the belief that the applications, (a) of limestone which is a carbonate of calcium, (b) of hydrated lime which is an alkaline calcium hydroxide, or (c) of quicklime, caustic oxide of calcium, are all beneficial for crop growth because each of these is ammunition in the fight against soil acidity, or against the high concentration of hydrogen in the soil.

This struggle to drive the hydrogen ion, or acidity, out of the soil was aided by the technological advancements giving us instruments and equipments that measured the hydrogen ion to a finer degree than known before. The ease and speed with which soil acidity could be detected and measured encouraged the widespread testing of soils. This activity discovered soil acidity almost everywhere. Through the help of the measuring gadgets we were impressed by the apparent universality of soil acidity. Only a few humid soils were not seriously stocked with acid. We discovered that for acid soil, in general, the productivity was lower as the degree of acidity was higher. From such a discovery we might expect ourselves to conclude—even though it was later found to be the wrong conclusion—that the presence of the large amount of hydrogen ions in the soil was the cause of the poor crops. This conclusion would be expected also from the bigger troubles in growing the proteinaceous, mineral-rich legumes of higher feeding values.

The extensive use of limestone in the corn belt has now multiplied itself into the millions of tons of these natural rock fragments that are annually mixed through the soil. This increased use was prompted by the beliefs (a) that limestone is beneficial because its carbonate removes the acidity of the soil, and (b) that soil is most productive if it is neutral, or when it has no active hydrogen ions in it. Under these beliefs (now known to be poorly founded) we have become belligerent foes of soil acidity. Limestone has become the ammunition for fighting this enemy hidden in the soil. We are just now coming around to a better understanding of how nature grew crops on the acid soils before we did. We are now beginning to understand what limestone really does when it makes better crops.

Only recently have we recognized the fallacious reasoning behind the conclusion that it must be the presence of the acidity in the soil that brings the crop failure when liming lessens the soil acidity and makes better crops at the same time. While the convenience of soil testing gadgets encouraged this erroneous belief about soil acidity as an enemy, it was the diligent study of the physiology of the plants, of the colloidal behavior of the clays growing them, and the chemical analyses of all these, that finally pointed out the errors of such hasty conclusions. It pointed out that soil acidity is not detrimental, but is in reality beneficial.

We now know, of course, that in applying the limestone, which is calcium carbonate, there is possibly some reduction of acidity by the carbonate portion. At the same time there is being applied also some calcium—a nutrient highly deficient in the leached soils—to nourish the calcium-starved crops. This nutritional service comes about both directly and indirectly. We have finally learned that it is this better nourishment of the crop rather than any change in the degree of acidity of the soil that gives us the bigger and better crops. Unwittingly we have been fertilizing the crops with calcium while fighting the soil acidity with the carbonate, the hydroxide, or the oxide of lime.

In spite of our ignorance of how the lime functions, we have benefited by using it. However, an erroneous understanding of what happens to the crop and to the soil when we lime cannot successfully lead us very far into the future. We cannot continue to grow better feeds under the mistaken belief that we do so merely by the removal of the soil acidity through the use of plenty of carbonates on our humid soils. Wise management of the soil to grow nutritious feeds can scarcely be well founded on facts so few and so simple.

Should you decide to demonstrate for yourself the truth of what has been said above, you can apply some soda-lime, or sodium carbonate to the acid soil. This will reduce its acidity. But unfortunately for you if you are a foe of soil acidity this soil treatment will rout the enemy but will still not give successful crops. Merely removing the acidity by a carbonate (of sodium rather than of calcium, in this case) does not guarantee the crop.

As proof that it is the calcium as plant nourishment that is the helpful factor in liming, one can repeat Benjamin Franklin's demonstration and apply calcium sulfate to the soil. One might even apply some "Dow Flake," a calcium chloride. Either of these calcium-carrying compounds will make the soil more acid. But in spite of this fact and because they add calcium, the gypsum and "Dow Flake" will improve the crops on the initially acid soil left so. We are now resurrecting the ancient art used by Benjamin Franklin for whom liming the soil was a matter of fertilizing it with calcium (and sulfur) and not one of fighting soil acidity.

While we were fighting soil acidity we have failed to notice that most of the populations of the world are concentrated on the acid soils. They are not in the humid tropics where the soils are not acid. Nor are they on the arid soils that are alkaline, a reaction opposite to the acid. Soils that are not acid are not necessarily the supporters of many peoples. Yet in fighting soil acidity we labor under the belief that if a soil were limed to the point of driving out all the acidity, such a soil should be highly productive.

We now know that even while a soil may be holding considerable calcium or lime. To a small extent of its exchange capacity, it is also holding nutrients other than calcium. Among these are potassium, magnesium, manganese, and others. But these in total are held in much less quantity and by less force than are either the calcium or the hydrogen, the former a nutrient and the latter a non-nutrient. Should we put on lime or calcium enough to drive all the acidity out of the soil by putting calcium in place of the hydrogen, all the other nutrients would be more readily driven out than would this acid-giving element.

Liming the soil heavily, then, does not necessarily drive out only the acidity. Instead it would also drive out all other fertility. It might load the soil with calcium so completely that it could offer only calcium as plant nourishment. Plants would then starve for other nutrients even though on a neutral soil. Plants on such a non-acid but calcium-saturated soil would be starving for all the same nutrients, except calcium as they do on the acid soils. Making soils neutral by saturating them with calcium does not therefore make them productive. This is the situation of some of the semi-arid soils of our western states. In our struggle against soil acidity we need to remember that neutral soils are not the productive soils. Instead it is the acid by yet fertile ones that feed us and nourish the major portion of the other peoples of the world.

Calcium has been a good fertilizer for legumes on acid soils now for some years. It has been serving directly as a nutrient for the plants. But it has also served indirectly by helping other nutrients get into the plant roots more abundantly. It helps the nitrogen of the acid soil to get into the plant. It helps the phosphorus, the potassium, and other nourishing elements to be taken more readily by the crop. A plant grown for a short time on a lime-rich soil and transplanted to one low in calcium—that is, one that is acid—will take more nutrients from such a soil than will the plant that was starved in its early life for lime. It is because of this behavior of the calcium that a lime soil is soon in need of other nutrients besides the calcium.

We are discovering rapidly that there is need now for potassium on many recently limed but still acid soils. Other soils in similar condition show their serious needs for nitrogen. Lime, of course, may well be the first fertilizer needed. But when once this need is met on these soils that were highly leached long ago, the need for other nutrients may be quickly evident. Perhaps it is these fundamental soil facts that are bringing fertilizers into such prominence in the corn belt today, while only a few years ago limestone was the only soil treatment and the one starting then its extension into the widespread use it has today. Perhaps these are the facts behind the age-old rhyme that told us long ago that "lime and lime without manure, make father rich but son poor."

We now know that instead of saying that acidity has come into our soils we should say the soil fertility has gone out. Legumes which make good feed for milk producing animals must have fertile but yet acid soils from which to make the feed that will be good. Lime is one of the foremost fertilizers in making soils capable of supporting the protein producing crops. For this service to plants, phosphorus is also needed. These are taken out of the soil as the plant trades hydrogen as acid for them. Consequently the highly acid soil is simply one that has become deficient in fertility.

We can grow legume crops on acid soils if we will give them calcium and all the other fertilizers needed by the soil to grow them. Red clover was commonly said to be sensitive to acid soils. Yet liming the millions of acres has not restored this crop to those extensive areas. The high cost of its seed is sufficient testimony of the crop's scarcity today. This crop usually needs potassium, or phosphorus, or possibly other fertility elements on a soil deficient to the point of being naturally very acid. Then, too, when a soil is properly fertilized, red clover will grow even if the soil is highly acid. We now know that the soil acidity is not the problem in growing the legumes. The production of these protein producing crops is a matter of ample soil fertility among which the calcium is only one nutrient. If we provide this one by means of limestone and then add all the other necessary fertilizer nutrients for the soil in question, we can grow legumes of highly nutritious values as feed without removing all of the soil acidity. Growing legumes is a matter of feeding these crops, and not a matter of fighting soil acidity.

Soybeans came in as a "new" legume crop. They were reported to "grow on acid soils." But on such soils they were also reported to be "a hay crop and not a seed crop." We did not realize that if they were not building proteins and other complexes demanding soil fertility to make a seed crop and that consequently they could not be a nutritious hay in these respects. Soybeans need lime, too, if they are to give good feed. They are showing growth troubles when the soils are not well supplied with magnesium. They are also reporting the need for manganese on some soils. Soybeans can be grown on an acid soil that is fertile in more respects than in calcium only.

We need no longer hunt for "acid-tolerant" legumes. Any plant that is well nourished tolerates acidity. It causes the soil to become acid when it takes the fertility from it. The root itself is acid and makes the surrounding soil area acid by the carbonic acid it respires. It is this carbonic acid by which the plant carries on the business of taking calcium, potassium, magnesium, phosphorus, iron, and its whole array of nutrients from the soil. It trades hydrogen or acid for them. Acidity is therefore "natural" for any plant.

Growing legumes is not a problem of getting rid of the acidity of the soil. On the soils where we say acidity is a problem, the problem is one of putting in place of the acidity the list of plant nutrients lost excessively from the soil as it became acid. Legumes that make tons of vegetative mass on so-called "acid" soils do not make the nutrient values or quality of feeds made by those other legumes we say are "failing" on acid soils. We can grow some legumes on naturally acid soils but they will not be the equal in feed value of those on soils once naturally acid soils but given other fertility as well as some calcium in the belief that it was removing acidity. Good feed can be grown on acid soils provided that they are given the fertility required by the plant to manufacture it. Soil acidity is a problem because it means that so much fertility has gone out to let so much hydrogen come in.

DANGEROUS GRASS

Sick soils will not produce healthy plants. Sick plants will not nourish healthy animals. Sick animals will yield no income. What shall it profit us then, if our frantic search for a foolproof grass to grow on abused soil is successful?

Nationally we have become conservation conscious within recent years. We have come to recognize the threat to civilization from soil erosion. We have embraced the obvious solution, protective covering to heal the scars of wind and water, to hold the remaining surface and fertility.

But suppose we do succeed in getting the sick land back to grass? Suppose we find plants that will exist on it? They will hold the surface, which is desirable, but will they restore the land to useful production? Vegetation that will not support healthy animal life will not solve our problem.

Granting that a sod can be established, what kind will it be—sick or healthy? The query is not concerned with varieties, but with the nutritive content of herbage. Increasing cases of animal malnutrition, animal irregularities, animal diseases have been traced to feeds from the less fertile soils.

Cows sustained on the production of these soils may show symptoms suggesting milk fever in the late winter, even before calving, or before giving milk, and death may occur under similar symptoms much later in the year from an ailment called "grass tetany." Irregularities develop during summer in the gait, particularly of the hind legs, suggesting an attempt by the animal to walk on its toes. A slight rise in the middle of the back and other skeletal deformities may be noticed. Occurrence of these ailments is closely associated with those soil types that are commonly irregular in crop production and which have been leached and exhausted of their basic nutrient elements to such a low content as would misnomer their ailment by the less informative term of "high degree of soil acidity."

Chemical studies have been made of soil and of vegetation it produced that ailing animals consumed. When chemical findings are related to animal case histories, they designate the seat of the trouble as the low level in the soil of the nutrients essential for plants and required in larger amounts by animals. On the more "sour" soils where lime has been badly needed, but was not applied, and where nutrients other than calcium run closely parallel with it in deficiency degree, the pasture herbage has scarcely the equivalent of wheat straw in its content of calcium or lime and phosphorus.

Analyses of herbage which had defaulted in its support of a cow, and which came to the attention of a county agent as an emergency call in the absence of a veterinarian, showed a calcium content of but .27% and a phosphorus composition of only .08%. Ordinary wheat straw has .21% of the former and .12% of the latter.

The deficiency of either calcium or in phosphorus might be considered serious, according to these figures. In a certain section of Minnesota, according to the late Prof. C.H. Eckles and his colleagues, the cows showed what has been known as "phosphorus deficiencies" when the phosphorus content of alfalfa fed them dropped to .21%, and that of timothy hay to .11%, and that of prairie hay to .10%. The hay samples submitted by the county agent in Missouri would not prohibit this phosphorus irregularity, if we can believe the Minnesota figures to fit the case located farther south.

The calcium contents of the Minnesota hays provoking the deficiency disease were 1.81% for alfalfa, .39 for timothy hay, and .44 for prairie hay. The Missouri grass, even though it had a sprinkling of lespedeza plants, was lower in calcium than was either the prairie or timothy hay in Minnesota, when one recalls the preceding calcium figure of .27%. Feeding cattle herbage of such composition might well be classed as a case of gross deception. Giving them green pasturage but on a soil failing to stock it to the equivalent of even wheat straw in terms of the most dominant ash constituents needed by the cow, is like bringing on the spring season but feeding a winter ration. Too bad the animals can't prosecute under the law of mislabeled packages.

The animal's response to the "milk fever" treatment of calcium gluconate injected into the bloodstream gives major emphasis to the calcium deficiency. It shows that the soil has not been giving the animal enough calcium, or lime, in her feed to maintain body activities. Under such soil and feed conditions she has been compelled to give up lime, and possibly phosphorus from her own body store to the point of danger to her own life in order to build the bones of the foetus. We may not be sacrificing animals on altars because of religious devotion, but we seem to be sacrificing them to false gods of a false economy that refuses to restore an exhausted soil fertility. Backbones examined after such animals have given their lives to the cause of motherhood against the handicap of existing on the feeds from these base-deficient—particularly calcium-deficient—soils, suggest that these bones have been partially consumed periodically and then rebuilt into deformed shapes. Some have been rebuilt into solid rather than flexible spines in meeting the calcium shortage during pregnancy and rebuilding during non-pregnant or non-nursing times.

Cattle owners of long experience report increasing deficiency cases. An 80-year-old founder of a fine Hereford herd says, "They are coming to be all too common lately." His is a 49-year observation. They come now not as late in the annual breeding cycle as that period marked by the heavy milk flow just after calving. They are common, as early as two months before calf delivery. They come even in young, or growing, steers. The deficiencies in lime in the soil and their effects are so serious that fatalities among fine breeding animals and their offspring are making serious inroads into the animal sup ply of the country, to say nothing of the farmers' income.

Supplementing the ration with mineral forms, such as limestone and bonemeal, may seem adequate remedy when calcium gluconate is so effective in snatching the "milk fever" animal out of the last stages before death. Before pinning hopes on such supplements, it is well to remember that the very man who started the bonemeal feeding idea, von Gohren, pointed out as early as 1861 that some unfavorable effects might be associated with it.

Then, too, whenever soils are so seriously deficient in lime as to reflect it by deficiency diseases in the animals grazing on them, such soils may be expected to be deficient in other basic nutrients of which the shortage is not so simply detected. Crop removal and leaching are not confining their inroads on the soil's supply to that of calcium alone. These other seemingly more subtle deficiencies may still remain in the ration when the lime is supposedly supplied by the mineral supplement.

Sick soils mean sick plants. Sick plants make feed that may be expected to make sick animals. When the plant factory is running short of calcium, the lime content within the plant itself can be expected to be short. Likewise a good number of other items, such as possibly the vitamins, which are manufactured by the healthy plant, may be deficient. Fertilizing the soil is more than stuffing the plant with minerals. It is a case of balancing the plant diet for better results in the plant factory just as we try to balance the animal ration for better output by the meat or milk factory.

Plant rations are much simpler than animal rations. At most, a dozen to 14 elements are all that can be of concern even when plants are grown in water or without soil. Fortunately, our soils have not gotten so low in fertility that we are immediately concerned with this total number. Limestone and phosphorus treatments to soil are the first requisites in the light of plant and animal needs, because calcium is about 8 times as plentiful in plant ash and 40 times so in the animal body minerals as in the soil. For phosphorus, the corresponding figures are roughly 140 and 400, according to the United States Department of Agriculture. Other nutrients are not put into the plant or animal body in such large concentrations in contrast to that in the soil and the need for them is not serious. Remedying the plant ration by lime and phosphorus additions mainly to the soil will relieve us of remedying the animal ration in many cases, and will be much more simple than tinkering with animal physiology which is infinitely complex.

A simple soil treatment, like liming, can do much for the animal's sake in terms of higher content of minerals and protein in the forage part of the ration. Limestone applied to lespedeza has demonstrated its effects in many places. In one case it increased the lime content almost one-fifth. It was instrumental in helping the plant to rustle enough phosphorus out of the soil to increase the concentration of this nutrient element by one-fifth. It enabled the plant factory to pack more than one-fourth more protein into each pound of hay, to say nothing of the yield increase per acre in all of these items.

From the cow's standpoint her factory can be more efficient when her feeds are, roughly, one-fourth more concentrated in the items she needs. Other cases—not only of lespedeza—but of alfalfa and non-legumes tell of the same effects by even so simple a soil treatment as liming and suggest the soil as an opening to a simple attack on the animal deficiency problem. Certainly from the standpoint of the farmer, cures effected by soil treatment, through the plant, and to the animals, offer more hope than attempts to diagnose and prescribe for them after they become sick.

Mining our soils of their fertility is bringing us face to face with the simple fact that plant factories are not running as efficiently for feed production as they once did. That wasn't so very long ago. Our farm meat and milk factories are, consequently, also operating on less efficient levels—all our knowledge about better nutrition notwithstanding. Hope lies not so much in diagnostic surveys in the animal factory but more in the simpler approach to treating the animals to more nearly normal nutrition by way of normal feeds grown on fertile soils.

Humans, too, persons subject to hay fever, are vitally concerned in this matter of soil fertility if doubling of case numbers in the last 25 years is an indication. Prolific pollen-producing plants are the only survivors when declining soil fertility supports only widely scattered plants that must cross-pollinate over the greater distances between them. We can look for more pollen in the air and more hay fever as soil fertility goes down.

That sick soils will not make healthy animals is particularly significant at this time. We are thinking on a national scale of combating soil erosion by allowing much of the fertility depleted soil to go back to grass. In our desperate search for varieties of plants that will exist on such soils, perhaps we have given too little thought to whether the forage so grown would be put by the cow on her list of dietary delicacies. Perhaps we may well give ear to the voices of the many animals in their unattended deficiency ailments. They are seemingly shouting, "Don't let land merely 'go to grass.' Why don't you use sound methods of grass farming through soil-fertility restorative treatments requisite for good feed production and quicker and better soil cover?" Attention to the evidence of soil deficiencies as given by the dumb animals will react with profit both individually and nationally. Soil treatments also will serve the purposes of erosion control more effectively in the better cover developed more quickly.

PRESS RELEASE
SHOULD FARMERS RECEIVE TAX ALLOWANCE FOR SOIL-BUILDING

The 85% of this country's population living in urban areas do not yet feel any obligation to help maintain fertility resources coming to them gratis from people in rural areas, says W.A. Albrecht, chairman of the soils department at the University of Missouri. How soon will the country wake up to the obligation owed those who maintain reasonable levels of soil fertility so that the country may be well fed? Albrecht asks. Carefully lobbied legislation has set up laws, economics and taxation procedures so that this country's urban commercial businesses and industries have capital investments which are self-sustaining.

For example, the owner-investor of a limestone quarry may be allowed a depreciation figure as high as 15% of his income for rock taken from a quarry. And it may be a larger figure for the owner-investor of an oil well. Capital investment in these mineral businesses is soon recovered, Albrecht points out.

As yet, no economist or taxation authority has suggested the justice of a depletion allowance to the landowner for the maintenance of his soil fertility capital to replace mineral fertility taken from the soil and delivered as food to the urban population without charge. The landowner's investment in soil minerals for good production is gradually being liquidated under the economic thinking—or the lack of it—which contends that the farmer is thereby taking a profit. On the contrary, the landowner throws by installments his financial and the national security into the bargain every time he makes a sale of farm products, Albrecht says. Those on the urban receiving end of that transaction get those installments free and flush them into the sea.

Everyone is a party to the crime of soil fertility exploitation but yet are complaining against the rising costs of living. People are slow to see that such shortsightedness in economic, agricultural, and other policies toward the soil's fertility resources are seriously undermining national security. All this is more serious with a growing pressure on the soil's production potential by an increasing population, not to mention the rest of the world calling on this country to share that potential with them. Liming soils deserves consideration as an operation undergirding future food security—particularly foods of high protein content, Albrecht says. It has long been known that lime is needed for legumes. Again, people are slow to see that need as one for the production of protein, rather than the tonnage, yield of the crop. By the soil route, lime provides meat, milk, and eggs.

Viewed in this light, one cannot escape the question whether people dare expect the farmer to continue liquidating his fertility assets under the false idea of taking a profit and, at the same time, ask him to purchase large amounts of limestone to increase his liquidation rate all the more.

Isn't it about time that a basic agricultural policy, the required machinery of economics and taxation be designed to guarantee the self-perpetuation of the farmer's fertility capital which must feed everyone—both urban and rural? Albrecht asks.

Shouldn't soil fertility maintenance—and thereby of agricultural industry—be interpreted by the same views in economics and taxation as those prevailing in other industries? Albrecht continues to ask. This should be true now that fertility rebuilding by limestone and fertilizing the soil is moving itself into the category of soil chemistry for the nutrition of plants, animals, and people. Perhaps this country can bring about self-perpetuation of soil fertility capital under the agricultural business in the rural areas in the same manner as perpetuation prevails for monetary capital under all businesses in urban centers. If that situation is brought about, then rebuilding the fertility of the soil will become big business by meeting major soil needs.

• • •

CALCIUM-BEARING VERSUS NEUTRAL FERTILIZERS

Our increasing knowledge of nutrition has been compelling us periodically to list newly recognized requirements in the diets of plants, of animals, and of humans. If fertilizers are to be helpful in meeting these newer demands, then their composition must be shaped to improve the plant's synthetic performances and thus to initiate, by way of the soil the improvements in kind and quality of their products to be used for the better nutrition first of animals and finally of humans.

Our knowledge about plant nutrition was long content to list but ten requisite chemical elements, so ably arranged in a simplified memory picture around his own name by the late C.G. Hopkins. Today that list has been extended, at least by four. It may soon be further extended. For animal and human nutrition, the essentials were listed for a long time as proteins, carbohydrates, fats and minerals. Only lately accessories were added, referring not to a single item but to many as this all-inclusive term indicates. With the increasing number of vitamins now recognized under this category, our minds are prepared for an extension of this list, as in the work of H.H. Bunzell[9] of New York, when he finds that wheat germ gives effects on yeast growth beyond those of any, or all, of the vitamins yet listed.

Fertilizer thinking was long tied down to the three ingredient concept. Later it was adjusted to include the micro-nutrient necessities. This was a very easy adjustment when these were already passing into the goods mainly as unavoidable accompaniments or contaminants. Now the soil fertility has declined to the economic danger point, with resultant disturbances in animal and human nutrition manifesting themselves in many deficiency diseases some constructive thinking must be applied to revised fertilizer composition. This is especially important if fertilizer use as a soil treatment is to make crops yield not only more tonnage, but also feed of the quality and of the nutritional effectiveness it must eventually have. On the basis of better plant performance, the fertilizers and their functions may well be given critical examination in the light of (a) the various and the intricate soil processes, and

(b) the plant's complicated physiology, as science is rapidly elucidating them. It is from this viewpoint that the question of "acidity" of fertilizers deserves to be viewed. We need to raise the question whether this so called "acidity," is so simple as a mere matter of the physico-chemical condition relative to the hydrogen-ion concentration of the mixture itself, or of the ash resulting from its ignition.

The introduction of the hydrogen electrode as a laboratory tool, brought a greater refinement in measuring the degree of acidity than had previously been possible. But when scientists can see better, or farther, objectively, it does not necessarily follow that they can see more clearly subjectively. Soil scientists seized quickly upon the hydrogen electrode for more critical study of soil acidity. They found that when limestone was applied to the soil for improved legume growth, it also corrected soil acidity. From these observations they drew the conclusion that soil acidity was the enemy of the leguminous nitrogen-fixing, protein-rich forage crops. This conclusion that calcium carbonate can remove, or reduce, soil acidity was objectively correct. But to say that it is the correcting of the soil acidity by the limestone that improves growth of the legume crop, is subjectively incorrect. Such observation demonstrates that nature is consistent, but such reasoning illustrates that human logic may be decidedly inconsistent. Reliance on the effect of limestone as calcium carbonate, or as magnesium carbonate, on the acid soils for the neutralizing effects by the carbonate radical rather than for the plant nutrient significance of these two dibasic cations, calcium and magnesium, may be leading us astray in fertilizer thinking. It has been leading our soil thinking astray where it has been diverting our attention from the function of calcium as a fertilizer to that of its carbonate as an antidote for hydrogen presence.

That soil scientists and plant physiologists should have neglected the role of the element calcium and should have given the carbonate premier significance in soil improvement by liming for crops, seems strange. As early as the days of Benjamin Franklin a story of his experiences with gypsum, or land plaster, for clover improvement was widely told. That gypsum, as calcium sulfate, with no acid neutralizing power should benefit red clover points suggestively to the possible importance of the calcium. It emphasizes calcium all the more when chemical analysis of this crop tell of its lower sulfur but high calcium content, and when young animals demonstrate it as an excellent growth-promoting feed.

It was the observations by farmers that cast doubt on the accuracy of the deduction that liming is beneficial to the crop through acidity removal. Farmers using limestone to get clover on heavy soils with high buffering capacities found crop establishment and improvement where no change in degree of acidity could be shown. They showed that acid soils need calcium to get a clover crop even if the acidity is not corrected. Their suspicion of the inaccuracy of the belief that the degree of soil acidity was the disturbing factor provoked experimental tests to separate the effect of the calcium from that of the carbonate. For this purpose use was made of such compounds as calcium chloride in commercial Dow Flake, and of calcium silicate in the form of ordinary cement. Both of these gave beneficial results in legumes on lime-deficient soils. Here, then, the legume growth was improved by applications of calcium that carried no carbonate, and did not reduce the degree of acidity.

Similar confusion apparently prevails about fertilizer acidity and fertilizers are about to undergo universal acidity correction. Again, very fortunately, the economic aspect has come to our rescue unbeknown to us. The cheapest carbonates in the form of calcareous and dolomitic limestones are going to correct the fertilizer acidity. Unwittingly they are providing extra nutrients as calcium and magnesium to deliver the beneficial effects when in our confusion or misunderstanding of the facts, the acid neutralizing value of the carbonate is given the credit. If sodium carbonate were not more costly, and were more convenient, it might have gone in and given disastrous disturbances to our acid neutralizing belief. Its substitution of sodium for calcium would have revealed the wrong interpretation of the value of making fertilizers "neutral."

Up to the present time, fertilizer analyses have paid no attention to available calcium. This nutrient of a fertilizer deserves consideration since in the humid region the increasing calcium deficiency in the soil is roughly the reciprocal of the increasing soil acidity. That liming the soil is beneficial because it delivers calcium to make up this soil shortage rather than because it removes the hydrogen ions was clearly demonstrated by some research using carefully prepared clays of different degrees of acidity[?]. By mixing different amounts of clay with sand, the soybean plants could be given more or less calcium at any degree of acidity or pH. The plants grew better with less acidity. But they also grew better at any degree of acidity as they had access to more clay and to more calcium.

As a more accurate test, a series of clays with increasing amounts of calcium (representing increasing degrees of saturation of the clay by calcium) and accompanied either by decreasing amounts of hydrogen as acidity or of barium as neutrality were used to grow the same crop[?]. The amounts of clay for addition to the sand were chosen so as to deliver the same amount of available calcium in every case. Strange as it may seem, the crop growth followed the degree of calcium saturation. The crop content of calcium did likewise, regardless of whether hydrogen or the degree of acidity was decreasing, or whether all the soils were neutral.

Here the lime addition demonstrated clearly that its beneficial effect was not one of fighting the soil acidity by means of its carbonate addition as a neutralizer, but that it was one of supplying calcium as a plant nutrient. Viewing fertilizers in the same light, we may well raise the question whether it is the neutralizing of their acid that is significant, or whether it isn't the addition of the calcium as an extra nutrient, or possibly calcium as a mobilizer of other nutrients, that makes the so-called "neutral" fertilizers of more value as crop producers.

The increasing degree of calcium saturation of the soil makes the treatment more effective in delivering its avilable calcium to the crop. According to these studies, as the calcium was put on less clay to saturate it more completely, a larger percentage of the exchangeable calcium moved from the clay into the crop[3]. With the clay carrying 40% saturation, the crop used but 12.3% of the available supply. With 87.5% saturation of the clay the crop got 29.3% of the applied lime. The efficiency of use increased more than twice. The concentrations of calcium in the crop for these two degrees of calcium saturation of the soil were .50% and .76% respectively, or the crop was made about 50% richer in calcium concentrations by what corresponded to drilling the calcium into the soil. In relation to our need for calcium-bearing feeds, this improvement may be significant.

Drilling fertilizers with seedings may at times be detrimental to germination. This effect is reduced, and germination may be improved, by adding calcium chloride which is a salt that has no neutralizing value. This effect has been shown for such non-legume seeds as tomatoes and bluegrass. Whether this effect is one of lessening fungus injury to the seed or one of improved germinating physiology has not been determined[4]. Nevertheless, increased calcium offerings have been shown to lessen the fungus attack on soybean seedlings in what resembled the more common "damping off" troubles[6]. Even if the exact function of the calcium in the improved seed germination is not understood, its beneficial effect is recognized and its use becoming an adopted practice.

Such results point out that by putting the calcium, as has been done with the other nutrients, into the limited soil volume to saturate a part of it more completely, as is the practice by drilling, there is a much greater efficiency in getting the nutrients into the crop. This is the fundamental reason for drilling, rather than broadcasting, even limestone. Drilling makes the calcium carried by the fertilizer so much more effective than we have been wont to believe and brings calcium up for consideration as a significant nutrient within the fertilizer mixture.

For purposes of illustration let us imagine that the soybeans used in these studies were drilled with a 4-12-4 fertilizer at 200 pounds per acre. Let us suppose they made a ton of hay. According to their analysis they would contain the calcium equivalent of 40 pounds of calcium carbonate. With the gypsum of the fertilizer contributing the calcium equivalent of about 32 pounds of calcium carbonate, and with the neutralizer for the ammonium sulfate acidity adding about 60 pounds, then this drilled fertilizer would be delivering 92 pounds of carbonate. At a 30% efficiency figure found in the experimental studies, this fertilizer treatment would provide almost three-fourths of the calcium required for the ton of the soybean hay. Drilling the "neutral" fertilizers makes their calcium content effective. It suggests that when fertilizers are neutralized by limestone or dolomite, this is simply a case of supplementing the calcium already in the acid fertilizer in order to supply more nearly the amount of calcium badly needed by the crop. It is making for more effectiveness of the calcium, needed by the crop and hidden away in the fertilizer.

That calcium is of service in mobilizing other nutrients into the plant was suggested over 20 years ago by Professor True of Pennsylvania.[18] That it mobilizes soil nitrogen was shown by growing some soybean seedlings for ten days in sand only, and some in sand given calcium carbonate! These were removed, washed and transplanted into an acid soil in order to test the significance of the calcium they could get and take with them in consequence of contact with the carbonate for but ten days of their seedling life. The calcium so gotten carried over to influence their growth. Those plants with calcium made more growth by 50% in the first ten days after transplanting. They excelled in growth for the rest of the time. During this same initial period after transfer, and before they had nodules, they took 20% more nitrogen from the soil. The calcium that was carried within the plants served to mobilize the soil nitrogen into them.

Calcium serves also to mobilize phosphorus, according to studies with both leguminous and non-leguminous pasture crops. Phosphate used with limestone returned three times as much phosphorus in the crop as when phosphate was used singly.[7] A critical study of the data from the outlying fields of Kentucky points out that the crop increases from the use of lime and phosphorus in combination are greater, in general, than the sums of their separate effects.

Calcium is not only instrumental in mobilizing nitrogen and phosphorus into the crop, but it has been demonstrated for soybeans that as its supply in the soil becomes low, the nitrogen, phosphorus and potassium may even move from the plant to the soil.[5] Thus, the plant may contain less of these than was in the seed originally planted. Such movement in the reverse direction has not been shown for calcium. Apparently no growth occurs unless calcium moves into the seed and crop. Experimental results also give some suggestion that the same holds true for magnesium as for calcium and that

TABLE I

Diammonium phosphate as fertilizer in contrast to gypsum-bearing superphosphate and urea. (Results for bluegrass based on no treatment as 100).

	Forage yield	Nitrogen	Total in harvest Calcium	Phosphorus
No treatment	100	100	100	100
Superphosphate	100	96	86	97
Superphosphate + extra calcium	103	98	96	97
Superphosphate + urea	110	114	119	113
Superphosphate + urea + extra calcium	109	114	112	109
Diammonium phosphate	103	112	86	95
Diammonium phosphate + extra calcium	110	114	109	111

this element always moves into the crop if growth occurs.

With calcium mobilizing both nitrogen and phosphorus, and with all three of these nutrients associated with protein, which is the basis of growth, calcium may be more significant in growth promotion than direct measurement of calcium contents of crops might lead us to believe. It is some of these seemingly indirect effects that may be responsible for much that we believe is the benefit in making fertilizers neutral by means of calcareous or dolomitic carbonates.

That the calcium in the gypsum of the superphosphate is of fertilizer value has been shown by some work with bluegrass[11]. Superphosphate applied at the rate per acre of 200 pounds of 20 per goods served as the basis for using diammonium phosphate at equivalent rates. The same amount of nitrogen as was contained in this concentrated fertilizer was then applied as urea in combination with superphosphate of which the accompanying gypsom might exert its effects. These different treatments were used for bluegrass on a soil needing nitrogen, phosphorus and lime. Because of this latter requisite, extra calcium was used in amounts to equal that carried by gypsum. This was used in both the sulfate and carbonate forms. The results are given in table 1.

In terms of tonnage produced, the diammonium phosphate was no better than superphosphate coupled with a doubling of its own calcium content as gypsum, or about what one might expect from superphosphate on limed land. The nitrogen of the ammonia in the diammonium phosphate was not used by the plant to increase its growth as forage even though it moved into the crop. When, however, calcium equivalent to that in the gypsum of the superphosphate was added to the diammonium phosphate, then this nitrogen made plant growth, delivered nitrogen, and returned phosphorus in the crop on a par with that by urea in combination with superphosphate.

These facts indicate clearly that the calcium of the gypsum is serving to mobilize the nitrogen of the urea and the phosphorus of the superphosphate

TABLE 2
Increases in cotton from 5-8-5 fertilizer with different carriers of nitrogen (Louisiana data).

Nitrogen carrier	Increase by fertilizer Pounds seed cotton	Increase by "neutralization." Pounds seed cotton
Nitrate of soda	250	
16-20-0 Ammophos.	-109	
16-20-0 Ammonphos, neutral	-47	62
Cottonseed meal	116	
Cottonseed meal, neutral	196	80
Sulfate of ammonia	-81	
Sulfate of ammonia, neutral	1	82
Urea	23	
Urea, neutral	121	98
Calnitro	147	
Calcium nitrate	165	
Cyanamid	184	

into the bluegrass. This was not done when nitrogen and phosphorus in combination as diammonium phosphate were applied in the absence of the calcium. In the light of such effects, calcium will soon take on importance as an ingredient in fertilizer. These data suggest the possible danger in going to the more concentrated nutrient carriers that omit the calcium. They indicate that we may well think of using fertilizers in combination with lime or certainly in terms of the calcium they carry, more than whether they are neutral or acid in reaction.

The significance of calcium for the non-leguminous crop of cotton has been emphasized by the experiment stations of the South. Its service in mobilizing phosphorus was announced by F. L. Davis of Louisiana,[10] when, as a result of his studies on available phosphorus in connection with nitrogenous fertilizers, he said, "Calcium containing compounds apparently maintain soil phosphorus at the highest available levels." The data from that station reporting mean cotton yields for the three years 1938-40 in a test of different nitrogen sources in a 5-8-5 at 600 pounds per acre show some interesting effects from the fertilizers made "neutral."[13] The increases in seed cotton in consequence of "neutralization" are given in table 2.

If these small amounts of extra calcium used in neutralizing the fertilizers can give these increases, should not some significance be given to the calcium present in the fertilizer even before it was neutralized? The effects of fertilizer neutralization and those of the calcium-bearing nitrogenous compounds on the cotton, all suggest that emphasis on fertilizers should not go to their acidity but rather to their calcium-bearing aspect even for this crop. When Ammophos reduces the cotton yield in Louisiana, as the data show, this again brings the gypsum aspect to the superphosphate in the mixed fertilizers into importance.

Also, the Alabama Station[16] has called attention to the need for limestone to neutalize fertilizer acidity, which may be as much as 500 pounds of limestone per ton of 5-15-5 fertilizer. Applying 600 pounds of such a fertilizer after it has been neutralized would be equivalent to applying 150 pounds of limestone. Drilling limestone is not common practice for cotton, but drilled as a fertilizer neutralized it may be given benefits much as an application as light as 300 pounds of limestone does when it helps red clover in some soils of the cornbelt. Professor Tidmore points out[17] that "an application of limestone is the most practical method of correcting the acid condition of the soil and supplying calcium."

Much of the variation in cotton response to nitrogen from different sources in a mixed fertilizer may be connected with the variation in calcium content of that fertilizer, according to the suggestion of W. R. Paden of the South Carolina Station[14]. In speaking of their results he says "These data show clearly that no marked difference in yield would be expected from the various sources of nitrogen on limed soil. When the question of soil acidity has been taken care of, one might expect approximately the same yield from the various sources of nitrogen."

L. G. Willis[19] in a study of "the value of gypsum as a supplement to a concentrated fertilizer," particularly for cotton, suggests that the more concentrated fertilizers are deficient in some nutrient. He used limestone and extra gypsum in a search for this shortage. He hesitated to attribute significance to calcium since he says "freshly applied limestone did not correct the deficiency." But he follows with the report that "other observations, however, appear to indicate that exchangeable calcium in these soils is as suitable a corrective as are the neutral calcium salts."

Most of the southern soils need nitrogen, and phosphorus. They apparently fit into the category of the soil cited previously, within which the effects of the calcium were separated from those of the phosphate. The Louisiana soils show similar conditions for the concentrated Ammophos and poor crop yields. It is therefore most probable that much of the irregularity in the so-called acidity of the nitrogenous fertilizer is due to a shortage of calcium for the crop's most effective use of the nitrogen and phosphorus as well as for the crop's need of the element calcium itself. These conditions are aggravated more as the superphosphates are concentrated to reduce the accompanying calcium. Calcium deficiency is presenting itself more prominently because the long existent shortages are not being covered by heavier calcium dosages in the lower grade superphosphates.

Neutralizing a soil with calcium carbonate encourages manganese shortage in some crops. But as more limestone is put into a limited amount of surface soil to put more calcium into the plants, then more manganese is taken from the untreated lower soil. Accordingly, the limestone functioning as a carbonate plays a detrimental role, but functioning as a calcium contributor it has a beneficial role in the same crop[8].

Soils should not be neutral if the products grown thereon are to be rich in calcium in particular, according to research by R.A. Schroeder[15]. His recent work with spinach demonstrates that more calcium and more magnesium moved into this common, mineral-carrying, dietary component when the calcium content of the soil was increased and the soil kept acid at pH 5.2, than when the same calcium fertilization took place and the reaction was changed to nearly neutral, or pH 6.8. The calcium treatment was much more effective in giving calcium returns within the spinach, when grown on acid reaction. Three units of calcium applied on soil at pH 5.2 delivered more calcium in concentration and in total, in the spinach crop, than when 12 units were put on the soil at pH 6.8. It narrowed the potassium-calcium ratio and suggests a composition nearer the proteinaceous, mineral containing vegetation rather than that of vegetation that is mainly woody matter. According to this, a fertilizer can have less calcium and use it more effectively by having acidity present. Perhaps spinach will be more effective as a mineral contributor, or as an antirichitic factor, in our diet when we learn that the effects of calcium as a plant nutrient must be separated from the carbonate effects in acid neutralization, and that very probably even some hydrogen may be required in the soil to mobilize the calcium into the crop most efficiently.

Now that virgin soils are no longer available, we are more cognizant of the fact that we have been farming the organic matter of the soil. The seriousness of this is evident, especially in the South, where the farmer experience still maintains that much of the fertilizer should be in the organic form. These facts remind us that the fertility in the organic matter is tuned with the growing season for delivery of the nutrients at the rates of decay suited to the needs of the growing crop. The use of strictly mineral fertilizers with the seeding does not fit into the picture of plant needs so well. Consequently, the leaching loss from fertilizers is being appreciated. It suggests that fertilizers may be used on grass sods or crops growing heavily enough to take up the fertilizers quickly and to reduce the leaching loss. With more fertilizer used on seed crops, particularly those with legumes mixed through them, the fertilizers will be held back against loss in leaching. Such will be building fertilizer into the organic matter to extend the season of its nutrient delivery when the sod is plowed up and put to a tilled crop. This will spread the fertilizer effect over a longer time, and make it less of a hypodermic one. In fact, it will be a case of fertilizing the crops whose organic matter will have an additional fertilizing effect on other crops following.

Fertilizers have an opportunity for greater service as the plant functions and soil processes are more clearly understood. Their use will increase only as their service becomes greater. No fertilizer manufacturer would want his goods to render other than maximum possible benefit. Attention to other ingredients besides the nitrogen, phosphorus and potassium bids fair to improve fertilizer effects and to extend their service.

The present concern about improving the reaction of fertilizer is testimony that manufactures are eager to make their goods better. When these good intentions are supplemented by more fundamental information from research in plant physiology and soil science, fertilizer improvement will shift from this concern about neutrality to one of concern about calcium content. It may even aim to deliver hydrogen. It may add many other revisions that will be of greater value in making soils more serviceable for better plants, for better animals and better health to humans.

BUGABOO OF SOIL ACIDITY DISPELLED

Soil acidity is a "bugaboo that farmers for years have been uselessly fighting," according to Dr. W. A. Albrecht, chairman of the soils department of the University of Missouri. As a matter of fact, acidity may actually be beneficial instead of harmful if proper soil conservation measures are used.

"It is not the acidity in soils that is injurious," Dr. Albrecht explained, "but the shortage of nutrients that are replaced by acidity. Given the proper fertility, plants will turn in their customary or usual performance even in the presence of soil acidity. This acid condition is merely a case of increased shortage of plant food nutrients for which crops suffer."

Dr. Albrecht cited experiments with soybeans in which increased soil acidity made both calcium and phosphorus actually more effective than in more neutral soil, improved the feeding value of forage and kept the sand element lower.

"Our experiments indicate that it is no longer necessary to fight soil acidity," he declared. "On the contrary, acidity is beneficial if lime or calcium, phosphorus, potash and other plant foods are utilized to restore full fertility and if soils are helped to maintain their needed stores of organic matter by means of sod crops or corresponding recuperative rest periods.

"We can now say that 'acid tolerant' legumes have been discovered. But they tolerate acidity only when fertilizer materials are properly supplied in balanced amounts."

In this connection it was pointed out that the three vital plant foods on which crops depend most are: 1—nitrogen, which encourages early and abundant growth, builds protein and develops the fleshy portion of roots; 2—phosphorus, which hastens the ripening of seed and promotes early maturity; and 3—potash, which is the balance wheel, enabling a crop to make better use of the other plant foods, develop resistance to disease and maintain an improved quality.

LIME SOIL TO FEED CROPS—NOT TO REMOVE SOIL ACIDITY

Nodules on roots of clovers in acid soil far below streaks of limestone drilled with seedings show that legume bacteria do not require lime mixed throughout the soil, say William A. Abrecht, chairman, department of soils at the University of Missouri. Such observations suggest that limestone is needed to feed plants rather than to fight acidity. All acidity does not need to be removed from the entire soil layer in which roots are growing.

Measurements of soil acidity demonstrated that drilling limestone no deeper than a few inches did not change the degree of soil acidity very much. This was even true in soil near the limestone. Yet red clover had numerous nodules on roots at varying depths below streaks of limestone in the soil. Those evidences of action by nitrogen-fixing bacteria were in soil areas of decidely acid nature with pH values as low as 4.5. It can scarcely be believed that bacteria were dragged down there by advancing roots, Albrecht states. Very likely they were down there before-hand but went into action only when roots came along that had been properly nourished by contact with limestone calcium or magnesium in upper soil layers.

This nutrition served to make the symbiotic connection between roots and these particular bacteria possible. This evidence needs only to be seen to doubt the validity of the belief that soils must be neutral, or have all acidity removed before red and sweet clovers will grow, he continues.

In some other trials using sweet clover, a supposedly "acid-sensitive" legume, applications of mill-run, ten-mesh limestone at rates of 300 and 600 pounds per acre served to establish this legume better than the same application of pulverized or highly active limestone.

While none of the soil under these treatments showed measurable changes in degree of acidity, or pH, sweet clover roots were still getting enough calcium to nourish the crop from coarser particles that lasted longer in clay. According to Albrecht, roots were not so nourished where pulverized limestone was used. Speedy reaction and absorption of pulverized limestone made this soil fraction too much of a competitor to be matched by roots as a force taking up limestone calcium.

Apparently a few coarser limestone particles scattered through the soil to break down slowly and to feed the legume in those few focal points were all that was required. It was not necessary to drive out all soil acidity.

Much has been learned about clay and its capacity to adsorb and exchange calcium and magnesium. Also, it is known that plant roots have similar capacities taken by hydrogen—that is, acidity. From these facts it is known that legumes can grow on soils that are by no means neutral and free of acidity. Even when clay carries a set of nutrient ions well balanced for a particular crop, some heavier soils will still grow good legume crops when as much as 20% of the soil's exchange capacity is taken by acidity or hydrogen, Albrecht says.

The pH of the soil does not need to be brought up to 7.0. There is no need to get rid of all soil acidity for growing nitrogen-fixing, protein-producing, mineral-rich forages. Lime is required. But this serves to feed them by its contents of necessary calcium and magnesium, rather than to fight soil acidity by carbonates.

LIME-RICH SOILS GIVE SIZE AND VIGOR TO FRENCH STOCK

When anyone speaks about the agriculture of France, most of us think immediately of big horses and oxen with good muscles and heavy bones. Yet, when anyone speaks about French farm people, it is not uncommon for us to hear these farmers of a more mature agriculture and producers of fine livestock referred to with seeming reflection as "peasant" farmers.

Perhaps the man of the land over there may not have been formally educated in the science of farming; but, when it comes to understanding the art of agriculture, he surely must have long known the relation of his soils to the nutrition of his animals in order to have grown them to such size, style, vigor and vitality. This seems all the more true when we learn that he feeds them mainly on grasses and home-grown feeds. Apparently we must grant that even this "peasant" farmer knows live stock production "from the ground up."

That this older agriculture is built from the ground up in the fullest sense of those words was the belief that prompted my study of soils in France as an accompanying vocation while teaching soils to our soldiers at Biarritz American University. After a careful survey of the geology of France, there followed some travel over her main soil regions primarily in Army trucks and jeeps. The study, collection and analyses of soil samples in relation to crops were undertaken with the help of Captain C. E. Ferguson, originally with U. S. Soil Conservation Service. The net result was the conviction that, in assigning causes for the big live stock in this older country, one must give foremost place to fertility of the soil.

Here is a soil that serves in growing animals as well as—or possible better than—it does in fattening them. Here is an agricultural foundation, based upon generous stocks of lime and phosphorus, which builds bone from nutritious, mineral-rich forages and also produces proteinacious crops which builds muscle, possibly more than it provides big yields of starchy crops with fattening values.

Almost anywhere that one selects a soil in cultivation and puts a sample to chemical test, one is impressed with the soil's liberal supply of lime. In this calcareous nature of the soil one can see the reason why alfalfa (spoken of as a "lucerne"), clovers and other legumes are so common in their crop rotation schemes. One can also understand why most farmers answer no to a query as to whether limestone is used for crop improvement.

The geology of France helps explain the extensive areas of calcareous soils. Many of the broad stream valleys, with low or very gradual grades leading out from them—where most of the farm regions are located, are residual soils from limestone, from calcareous shales and from other secondary rocks with high contents of lime. Even geological erosion, and unobserved sheet erosion from top soil under cultivation are pushing the development of a new soil downward in the profile apparently fast enough to compensate for these losses. The farmer is seemingly making some new soil in the bottom of furrows just about as fast as he is wearing off the old soil at the top.

Then, too, this country is located fairly well north. It lies between the latitudes of about 42½°N and 51°N—equivalent to stretching out between Detroit and the tip of James Bay, or from Sioux City, Iowa, to Winnipeg, Canada, in our hemisphere. As a peninsular land, however, it does not have wide fluctuations in weather. It does not have very cold winters or very hot summers. It does not have short, alternating hot and cold or wet and dry spells. Instead, its seasonal changes are gradual. Its rains are drizzles rather than "gulley-washers." The water goes into the soil more that it runs off. Every rain has a high percentage of penetration and thereby a high potentiality in benefit to the growing crop. This is pronounced under the low evaporation at this northern latitude. So that, even though annual rainfall is not much more than 30 inches, it serves very efficiently especially for the shallower rooted crops such as grass.

France also has a distribution of rainfall and temperature which is known as "Mediterranean climate." These heavier rainfalls last during a very short season while the lighter rains are regular during the rest of the year. The soils, therefore, do not have enough water going through them to wash or leach out the lime excessively. Yet they are kept wet enough that cultivation breaks down soil minerals and rock fragments. Thus, the soils give up mineral fertility to balance the removal by growing crops, in keeping with the fertility-conserving kind of agriculture that is so common in these older countries.

Such combination of country and climate provide a good set of conditions, namely, plenty of mineral fertility and not so much rain. But when that rain comes it makes a grass which one can say—much as we do of our short grass country— that "every mouthful counts" in terms of animal growth. Here there are feeds for growth more than for fattening, since the plants have the fertility to compel them to do more than just catch fresh air, water and sunshine to give a starchy product and fattening values. It has the contributions from the soil that are needed to build bone and brawn in big animals.

Where lime has not been leached out, then other elements of soil fertility also remain. It is well to remember that calcium serves to mobilize other nutrients into the crop. Even though these others are, at times, not so plentifully present, yet they serve efficiently because they are associated with the lime.

Fortunately for France, many of her limestones are rich in fossils. These skeletons of animal life in the ancient seas represent considerable phosphorus. In testing what would be considered almost a sandy or even a gravelly soil one is often surprised to find it high both in lime and phosphate. This is the fertility combination which represents nearly complete chemical constituents of the skeletons of farm animals—a combination that is so essential for growing leguminous feeds that produce young animals so efficiently.

The farmer of France has for years practiced feeding his animals on homegrown feeds. Because these crops from fertile soil are highly nutritive, he does not have to search for supplements to bolster bulky roughage feeds. For generations he has clung to the principles of the old art of agriculture for which science has only recently given us a better understanding. We have gained a fuller appreciation from such experiments as those carried out, for example, by the work of Professor Weaver at University of Missouri.

Professor Weaver pastured different lots of hogs, each on a different crop. It was significant to note that alfalfa, regularly admitted as needing a fertile soil, made 592 pounds of pork per acre. Soybeans, claimed by some to be a crop which can be grown on a lime-deficient soil where alfalfa fails, produced only 175 pounds of pork per acre. Likewise, for each bushel of grain supplements fed while the hogs were on pastures, the alfalfa has a pork-producing value of 192 pounds while that from soybeans dropped as low as 67 pounds.

In short, only about one-third as much pork was obtained from the crop which is said to grow on soils of much lower fertility than that required for alfalfa. It means that, after all it is fertile soil which makes live stock. The farmer of France has long been growing good animals largely because of the fertility of his soil, which has been well maintained in terms of lime and phosphate. Although there naturally, fertility has been carefully conserved by the wise and consistent use of manure.

It may be that the farmers in these older countries have been not so much the leaders as they were the followers in this whole matter. It may be that allowed the animal's choice to take the agriculture to the more fertile and more lasting soils. In these older agricultures, originally nomadic, it is quite possible that the flocks and herds, more than their owners, led the way to particular soils where the plow came later to bring a permanent agriculture. It may have been the choice of good natural herbages by the animals, or the biochemical assay of the soil fertility by live stock, that led pasturing animals initially and arable agriculture later to the fertile soils and kept them off those not so productive.

Regardless of factors leading to the initial selection of agricultural lands, whether by man or by flocks and herds, the lime rich and relatively phosphatic soils have contributed much to the agriculture of France. It will be well, too for France if that fact is not forgotten as she comes out of the present political turmoil and economic shake-up in Europe and begins to make plans for her future. There are many suggestions that in the days to come she may be depending upon her lime-rich soils in a still larger way for feeding not, only live stock but her people as well.

LIME YOUR SOILS FOR BETTER CROPS

The science of the soil has done much for our better understanding of how the soil and the plant roots interact to make the crops grow. From better understanding, some principles have resulted for better guidance of our farm practices.

Liming the soil is one of those practices improved through science. We formerly encouraged liming as a struggle against soil acidity. It is now practiced to put calcium into the soil for nutritional service to the crops. It helps them in their synthesis of proteins and other complex compounds of higher food values to man and beast.

Calcium plays its role as a small part of the material of construction . It is recognized more readily in the ash. In animals and man, calcium is recognized easily as bone. In all life it is far more important than merely a part of the final structure. It serves as the tool in many life processes. It is a necessary tool for fashioning the different proteins that only plants can fabricate from the elements. It seems to be associated with the processes by which livestock assembles these plant proteins into choice animal products of great nutritional value. We have long been liming for legumes and we have connected livestock with legumes. But we have been late in recognizing this basic principle of the interaction between the calcium of the soil and the roots of the crops. As a matter of fact it is the working principle of this food creation assembly line.

Calcium serves, in the growh of plants, to mobilize other essential chemical elements into the plant more speedily. It puts a higher content of the ash elements into the forage. It is always associated with the crops that we say are better feed for young animals. It is associated more with feeds for growth and reproduction than with those for fattening only. It is associated with the soil's microbial processes that build up soil nitrogen. It is also effective in making green manure and other organic matter decay more rapidly and release their fertility for crop production. All life, from the lowly microbe to man himself, is dependent on a good supply of available calcium in the soil.

Liming the soil is one of the contributions to the better nourishment of all that grows on our farms. This soil treatment must, however, be judiciously connected with other treatments. It must not, therefore, be used excessively. If wisely used, this farm practice—as it is now undergirded by the science of the soil—will bring about better understanding and use of the other necessary soil treatments. This better knowledge should conserve not only the body of the soil, but also its fertility or internal strength by which all life must be fed.

7

MAGNESIUM

BALANCE IN SOIL, PLANTS AND BODIES

To a plant physiologist it may seem like a hackneyed statement to say that the balances among the several mineral fertility elements available or exchangeable in the soil will influence the balances of the "ash" elements in the crops grown on it. It is by no means such a hackneyed idea that the soil fertility which determines the composition of crops also determines the nutrient values to animals fed on them. Even if the farmer-layman's empiricism has taught him that animal health is a reflection of the fertility of the soil, it may be helpful to see essential chemical elements playing their various roles in nutrition, from the soil up through microbes, plants, animals and man. Such facts are presented in recent scientific reports, apt to remain hidden too long. This knowledge may be helpful even to persons appointed to authoritative positions, when they contend that variations in the productivity of the soil have nothing to do with variable nutritional values of what it grows.[1,2]

Hidden in reports of late research is increasing information matching the inorganic composition of the soil against the biochemical behaviors of the plants grown thereon. Animal feeders are now using not only the animals' discriminating choices of the same crop on different soil treatments, but also are matching the biochemical values of forages grown on chemically catalogued soils against the animals' physiology as refined as balances of the soil-borne elements in the bloodstream. Not only are these latter balances considered as pairs of the nutrient elements, but students of animal feeding are including attempts to catalogue the natural balances of elements in the soil, in the feed and in the healthy animals in triples, quadruples, and more, of those soil-borne. Imbalances or balances in the forages, attributed to those in the soil, are demonstrated by uncanny discrimination—complete refusal or ready acceptance—on the part of animals used in test assays. The wisdom of their choices has been verified through chemical and biochemical measures.

Hidden in the literature are many reports telling us that disastrous irregularities in animal health, due to soil deficiencies, are so similar to those occurring in man that the same name can now be used for the problem in both man and animal. It is educationally comforting to note that we are adopting a more fundamental approach in considering the role of natural laws in the degeneration of human health. Perhaps we will eventually view our own nutrition from the ground up and study the effects of balances and imbalances as determined by synthesis of dietary compounds by plants supporting both animals and man. Individually we may accept the adages, "To be properly fed is to be healthy," and "We are what we eat."

Of the essential nutrient elements in the soil, magnesium is an excellent one to discuss here picturing the concept of balanced forces of creation, which start with the soil as foundation. Magnesium is a close associate in natural chemodynamics with calcium. The latter is the major inorganic element in the human body. The properties of calcium and magnesium classify them as the "alkaline earths." Calcium is usually present in much larger quantities than magnesium. In the human body we have 1.6% calcium and 0.05% magnesium—a ratio of 32:1. But while calcium acts as *parts of construction, magnesium acts more as tools in the biochemical performances* in the body.

Calcium and magnesium, naturally precipitated together from seawater, form our limestones. These do not often occur as only magnesium carbonate, but more often as pure calcium carbonate, and then as combinations of the two with increased amounts of magnesium carbonate until they are chemically equivalent in dolomite limestone.

We have been tolerating confusion when we merely say "limestone," or even "lime," without distinguishing as to their application to soil or use in industry. Unwittingly, we have often used magnesium. This mineral is coming into prominence on its own, now that we are applying the other elements separately, but still we are prone to neglect it. Magnesium is more important in a greater number of body processes than is calcium.

During its movement in drainage waters from the prehistoric lands to the seas, magnesium was precipitated along with calcium as limestones. These substances were not always deposited in a fixed ratio, consequently, we have limestone either as nearly pure calcium carbonate, or with added magnesium carbonate in amounts varying from none to the equal molecular ratio occurring in dolomite. This mineral contains one element of calcium and one of magnesium in ratios, by weight, of 21.73% and 13.8% respectively. Their carbonate compounds are in ratios of 54.26% calcium to 45.74% magnesium. In the dolomite deposits which are less pure, or contaminated more by clay inwash to the seas, these percentage figures are smaller. The impurities of the original limestone, such as the silicates or clays, are left to develop into soil from the weathering of rocks.

In the course of this natural process, the carbonate compounds are removed completely. But the calcium moves out into drainage and back to the sea more readily than the magnesium. Consequently, the resulting clay fraction is relatively richer in magnesium during weathering. Erosion of such clay from uplands, and its deposition in lowlands, has been a means of distributing magnesium more widely and favorably than we appreciate. It was very probably by such a natural process that much of the high-magnesium soil of the lowlands of southeastern Missouri was inwashed by the Ohio River from the weathered dolomitic limestones in its drainage basin, and not from the Mississippi River. Very probably these Missouri lowlands are not the work of the latter river, which brings its erosion load from soil areas suggesting more highly calcareous materials, including readily erodable strata of such substances in the soil profile.

Thus, soils developed highly from limestones under higher rainfalls would be mainly the impurities left from the original rocks. Since these impurities had survived a cycle of weathering from rock to more insoluble residues in the depths of the sea, they would not suggest their rapid weathering into available plant nutrients from their uplifted limestones and from their repeat of such a traverse. This is a natural fact contradicting the oft-heard remark that "soils from limestones are usually productive soils." That idea must consider the degree to which the limestone soils have been developed in the particular setting.

In the development of soils from rocks containing sodium and potassium as well as calcium and magnesium in their original silicates, the first two are broken out and removed more readily than the second pair. Thus, the semi-humid soils may be rich in calcium and also in magnesium. With the higher degree of development of the soil from more rainfall, the calcium for crop nutrition becomes deficient before magnesium does. For these reasons soils of our mid-continent have not shown impending deficiencies of magnesium in crops so widely. Also, when calcium is deficient and limestones are applied to the soil, they usually carry magnesium and unwittingly cover the magnesium needs amply. No attention is paid to the fact that the limestones so used as fertilizers add both calcium and magnesium, the foremost plant nutrients, in balanced amounts. Moderately weathered virgin soils usually were found relatively well stocked with calcium in available forms adsorbed on the clay and humus. But where no dolomitic limestones contributed to soil development, the magnesium was not ample for extended years of soil exploitation. These are facts now coming more clearly into focus when, in the springtime, animals turned out to start grazing the lush early growth suddenly die of what is called "grass tetany."

In the early 1930s, research at the Missouri Experiment Station, using standardized colloidal clays, suggested that, as the minimum for the heavier agricultural soils, at least half of their adsorption, or exchange capacity, should be taken up by calcium. Later studies of magnesium suggested that this companion divalent element, in favorable balance with the calcium, should be adsorbed on the clay in amounts of about one-seventh to one-tenth of the calcium equivalents. Thus, when for many legumes calcium at 65% of adsorptive capacity was found more nearly optimum, the corresponding requisite for magnesium was 10%. Variation in the soil's active organic matter is a significant factor buffering these percentages when differing from these values.

Calcium and magnesium represent 75% of the soils' available essential cations. This places these two elements at the top of the list of soil fertility elements and in rather specific ratios in the plant offered by the soils. Yet these are not listed on the fertilizer bag in connection with legal inspections of this product of extensive and vital commerce. When potassium on the clay-humus colloid of soils is ample at 2% or, at most, 5%, of the soils' capacity, the situation just suggested is even more grotesque.

Considering the ratios of calcium to magnesium—less than 2 to 1 in dolomite and 7-10 to 1 as available nutrients in the soil—it is surprising that in the chemical composition of plants, in general, the ratios between calcium and magnesium are so much narrower at values of 1.6 to 1.0; while in warm-blooded bodies they are so much wider at values of 32.0 to 1.0. All this seems to emphasize the importance of magnesium when its deficiencies range from what would seem but a minor amount in the warm-blooded body to a major amount in vegetable matter. Yet so little is said about magnesium itself, much less about its balance with other nutrient elements.

That the quality shortages in food and feed bring on failing nutritional support as serious as functional degeneration—and its self-announcement—is a new concept. This is especially significant when the shortage of one single element of soil fertility, such as the alkaline earth, magnesium, in the food should provoke in man the same disorder which has long been known as "grass tetany" in ruminant animals. This same ailment, due to a magnesium deficiency with its consequent degeneration in nerve function, can now be listed simply as "tetany," and is by no means limited to cases where grass is the main food.

We now know, also, that this is a degeneration in humans which is not transmitted to them by animals, or vice versa.[1] There is a common cause for the separate cases of the same ailment or degeneration, *viz:* the shortage of an essential inorganic element which must come from the soil via quality food and feed. It is the failure of nutrition to be fully supported by the requisite fertility of the soil expected to grow nutritious foods and feeds.

The baffling nature of tetany has kept hidden the real cause of the sudden death of apparently healthy cattle or sheep when they are shifted from dry feed under housing to luscious growth of young herbage. Postmortems reveal no recognizable anatomical pathology. The preceding convulsions suggest nervous irregularities and point to disturbed magnesium-calcium interrelationships, when these two soil-borne elements can exercise either contrary or similar effects on neuromuscular transmissions. When "deficiency of the magnesium ions and excess of calcium ions increases the release of acetylcholine[2] which excites the muscle," and when "deficiency of either will prolong the effect of acetylcholine" one can understand why the diagnoses have not been able to pinpoint one particular factor of only these two as the cause.

The interrelations of such small amounts as may bring nerve excitation are still too intricate for us to separate even two factors like the amounts of calcium and magnesium in the fluid which bathes the nerves. "The increase in acetylcholine and the extended prolongation of its effects can give rise to neuromuscular upsets."[3] It is essential to note that Dr. Andre Voisin, of France speaks of the "ions" of the inorganic magnesium and calcium. "Ions" are the most active forms of these minerals when their salts are in water. He is not speaking of the chelations with, or combinations into, the larger organic molecules whereby they are not so highly active, do not pass so readily through membranes, nor modify the physicochemical condition of their medium, transmit electricity so freely, disturb water relations in tissues, etc. So combined into the larger organic molecules, they behave in plant tissues in what we call "a buffered state."

This means that their physicochemical characteristics are not readily shifted or quickly changed. Should these be modified a bit, they move back readily to their former state. Their elemental inclusion into much larger organic molecules makes this steady chemical state which characterizes the several living substances. It is part of their "power to survive." It is the "shock-absorbing capacity" of healthy living tissues. These living substances do not have a high salt, or ionic content, save as any salt may be separated from even the cell's protein by confinement within the cell's vacuole; by extracellular restriction or by movement within the excretory system enroute to elimination. Living tissues and processes are highly "buffered" because they are highly organo-molecular and not "salty" or "ionic." It is by the "ionic" states of magnesium and calcium that the troubles, called tetany are brought about.

It is a very significant material fact that calcium and magnesium are a part of the cell walls of plants, among the several larger organic molecules of cellulose, hemicellulose and others. Composing the cell walls, "the microfibrils are embedded in a matrix of substances containing a preponderance of sugars other than glucose—which are amorphous or, more probably, paracrystalline. Among these, linear or branched polymers of xylose, mannose, and other sugars are known as hemicelluloses. "The other major group of substances in the matrix is the polyuronides; one such is pectic acid, which occurs in the form of methylated derivatives and often as the calcium and magnesium salt. The molecular chains of pectic acid are said to be linked both to the hemicelluloses and to the cellulose through calcium and magnesium bridges and through phosphate groups."[4]

Cells of root hairs as membranous tissue constructed of cellulosic fibers tied together by calcium (and magnesium), should suggest our thinking of the danger of a disturbance in the structure of that membrane from losing these two inorganic cations to the colloidal clay of the soil in contact with them, when the latter has a low degree of calcium saturation with its reciprocally high degrees of hydrogen saturation, or of soil acidity. Studies at the Missouri Experiment Station have shown such troubles in the root membranes unless they are in contact with clays of saturation by calcium above 50% of capacity. The root membranes with their necessary calcium determine whether nutrients move from the soil into the root in proper amount and balance to bring about plant composition which is nutritious as animal foods; or whether even the seed-given nutrients may not flow in reverse from plant to soil to give vegetative bulk of less nutrient content (nitrogen, phosphorus, potassium) than those originally present in the planted seeds. As parts of the construction material, no more extensive than the cellulosic walls of plant cells, calcium and its relation to magnesium point to their role in moving—or failing to move (see accompanying graph)—not only themselves but also other nutrient elements from the soil into forages to determine the nutritional services in fitness or failure for animals and man.

ITS RELATION TO CALCIUM IN BODY TISSUES

In a previous discussion, we considered the disturbed interrelations of magnesium and calcium in the fluid around the nerves as a causal agent in the nerve breakdown called "tetany." This deduction seems to be a logical one when membranes, or cell walls, of plant roots undergo changes disrupting the plant's nutrition because their contact with the soil's moist clay is exchanging to the erratic amounts of calcium and magnesium. This is a plant's deviation from its normal physiology. It duplicates what is considered a parallel case of the nerve disturbance (tetany) in a warm-blooded body. Experiments with varied degrees of saturation by magnesium and calcium on the clay have shown corresponding variations in nutrition and healthy functions of legume plants. The intake of cations gave normal, protein-rich growth, and generous nitrogen fixation. The absence of the latter produced an erratic, mainly carbonaceous plant growth, during which there was a reverse movement of the inorganic nutrients from the plant to the soil.

This latter indicates clearly a serious disruption in the structural properties and physicochemical functions of the root's cell walls, not only of the root hairs, but also of the successive cell layers from these hairs to the root interior. It suggests a breakdown in the unique function of the layers of root cells when, as normal, interface membranes—in contact and exchange with adsorbed nutrient elements on the clay—they control the intake and outgo of essentials for the healthy growth of plants. Apparently the aforesaid breakdown occurs because of either insufficient calcium or excess of magnesium and other cations replacing the calcium in the cell walls where their microfibrillar structure of cellulose is cross-tied by calcium.[1] The clay as a colloid, matched against the root colloid, has been shown an able competitor for holding cations against the latter's taking or removing them and vice versa.[2] Hence, we might expect the disturbance of the calcium in the cell wall to be causally related to the latter's control when we say "the 'semipermeable' membrane of the root determines the exchanges through it."

Irregularities in the plant because of irregularities in exchanges of calcium and magnesium with the clay colloid seem very similar to the upsets of nerves due to similar deficiencies and imbalances of those cations in the fluids bathing these bits of impulse-transmitting body tissue. Since the degeneration of health can be traced to the disruption of the physicochemical functions in the walls and other parts of cells, and since performances of these minute body portions are biochemically so similar, regardless of whether they be cells of plants or of warm-blooded bodies, it will be of interest here to give attention to calcium and magnesium in relation to at least one membrane of the human body.

For theoretical consideration, there are the suggested modifications in the intestinal wall—closely similar to those in the walls of the plant root—when magnesium sulfate is used as a purgative. Shall we not envision this excessive magnesium as displacing the calcium in the cellular wall structure of the intestines to disrupt their power of controlling intake and outgo? Should we not expect, then, their allowing the larger amounts of water and other liquids or substances from the bloodstream to be the flushing agency? Then, should we not expect the duration of the purge to be no longer than the time required for the bloodstream to absorb the magnesium from the cells of the intestinal wall and replace it with calcium to restore the normal physicochemical control against excessive losses of liquids and other matters from the blood to the intestinal canal? The sudden drain on the blood's low supply of calcium, which prevails in certain kinds of arthritis, may be so dangerous that one dare not consider Epsom salts as a purge in such cases. An extended purge by dripping magnesium salts, used for dehydration in preparation for brain surgery, may put excessive magnesium into the bloodstream to threaten the patient with coma. In view of these facts it is evident that the intestinal wall must be undergoing a change in its membranous structure with consequent breakdown where calcium is replaced by magnesium, and then vice versa for recovery.

We are slow in coming to appreciate the significance of "deficiencies" and "imbalances" in the soil-borne inorganic elements which may cause irregularities in our bodies, as they do in the soil, in its microbes and in the plants. All these struggle to be healthy and to maintain self-protection; but their biochemistry can manage only what is possible within the limits their environment provides. Numerous degenerations of body functions suggest similarity in cellular principles which are common not only to man and his animals, but also to life strata still lower, namely, plants and microbes. Using the soil as in a mining operation, rather than managing it as nutrition for microbes and plants dependent on organic matter as well as minerals for their foods will finally bring us to recognize degenerations based on the failing creative capacity, that is the fertility, of our soils.

It may sound like silly arithmetic to tell the beginning student of biological sciences that the cells of living tissues multiply by dividing. But we must also tell him that each part of the equal division of the cell must enlarge by growth of itself before it can divide again in the continuing growth process. This kind of multiplication by cell division holds true whether it be in the simplest, lower life strata (microbes or plants), in the cold-blooded, intermediate forms (insects and reptiles) or in the warm-blooded, most complex bodies at the apex of the biotic pyramid (animals and man). Growth through cell division follows a universal basic pattern, common to every life form, whether we view it in a single cell under the microscope or in the multicelled individuals of any species of larger bodies. This self-duplicating process is always carried on through nutrition according as the growth potential of the soil in its geoclimatic setting allows. There is self-duplication in function, as well as in form, to maintain similarity of offspring to parent in both these categories.

The biochemistry of the cells is also a duplication when growth from the start resides in the (presently considered two) nucleic acids, simpler units of proteins, so named because they are always found in the cell's nucleus, where duplication by division begins. These nucleic acids are the warp and weft, as it were, weaving the growth according to the characteristic pattern of the various species. The expenditure of energy by which the body struggles to do the work required for its existence and growth is also similarly patterned in the biochemistry of the many species. The conversion of stored energy from carbohydrates in food follows the same pattern of chemical reactions, that is, it is a duplicated process within the cells of the many life forms. Nutrition, whether it is serving to give energy or to bring about growth of any body, calls for the specific diet of "go" foods and "grow" foods in quality and quantity commensurate with the degree of complexity of the life form.

When healthy living units are so highly similar in the processes of growth and of provision of their required energy at the levels as basic as the very cells themselves; and when the activity of every living unit as a whole is the summation of the activity of the separate cells, must we not view the decadence of health as resulting from deficiencies in nutrition which bring degeneration—or weakening form and function—from within, rather than from some overpowering external agencies? The preceding concepts are undergirded in their logic, now that health irregularities in man and animals are exhibiting more and more similarities in symptoms. Under superficial knowledge only of the intricate body functions, we are apt to blame the animals for giving diseases to man (brucellosis), or vice versa.

With more basic knowledge from continuing research bringing us into fuller comprehension of the cellular biochemistry duplicated in both, the same health irregularity must be suspected as occurring in both from the same deficiency in the same physiological setting. This has now been illustrated for *The Magnesium Deficiency Tetany Syndrome in Man,*[1] once considered to be grass tetany,[2] and limited to herbivorous feeders. It is significant that this deficiency is connected with the soil-borne element magnesium or its imbalances with other soil-borne essential inorganic nutrients given our attention in this present series of discussions. Consideration of magnesium in its relations to potassium may suggest imbalances occurring more commonly when we remind ourselves that potassium is a monovalent, and magnesium a divalent, chemical element, and also that they are, respectively, an alkali in contrast to an alkaline earth. Accepted tests show that for healthier plant growth, the supply of exchangeable potassium of the soil needs be but 3%, while two or three times that amount of magnesium is required. It is also common knowledge that potassium is taken from soil and accumulated by plants much more rapidly and to a much greater degree than are bivalent ions, such as calcium and magnesium. This tells us what many studies have shown, namely, that the plant's content of potassium increases considerably and suddenly following the application of potassium, thus creating or accentuating various mineral imbalances.

This ready entrance of potassium into the plant lowers its content of sodium (another monovalent ion) until the sodium may be but one-third of the potassium in chemical equivalent. The ratio of potassium to calcium and magnesium combined may be nearly doubled, or approach the suggested upper limit (1.84) in forage, threatening dangerous disturbance to livestock. The potassium may be pushing the magnesium content of the forage so low that it brings down the magnesium in the blood serum of the animal consuming it, causing the animal to develop tetany and die. Studies of potassium fertilization of forage in relation to the depression of magnesium levels in the blood serum serve as limits by which tetany may be invoked or avoided.

Advance in our basic knowledge of biology as a whole shows that degeneration of our health—too often called "disease"—is the result of deficiencies and imbalances of essential mineral nutrient elements coming into the nutrition of both man and his food animals via the soil.

ITS EXCESS, ACCORDING TO PLANT SPECIES

We know that the essential positively-charged nutrient elements, or cations—calcium, magnesium, potassium, sodium, manganese, zinc, copper and others—are taken out of solution and adsorbed by colloidal clays and humus of the soil, but are, nevertheless, exchangeable to plant roots offering the nonnutrient hydrogen in trade. We need to consider just what part of that adsorption-exchange capacity by each nutrient element will offer a balanced diet for the healthy growth and multiplication of each desired plant species.

A contribution to the answer to this question was made in Scotland by a study of what increasing amounts of magnesium do to rhododendron plants. This species is erroneously believed to require acid soil; it really requires one of low calcium content. It does well on a high-magnesium soil, and consequently served well to study what, for most commonly cultivated crops, would be an excess of magnesium.

For testing the growth of the rhododendron, the researchers used a very acid soil (pH 5.0) in which three stages of acidity reduction (above pH 5.0, above 7.0 and near 8.0) were brought about by increments of magnesium carbonate. The reduction of the soil acidity from roughly pH 5.0 to 8.0 caused the plants to grow better. This fact tells us that this species does not grow well on soil with an acid or hydrogen-saturated clay humus. Instead, it requires a soil with the exchange capacity of that fraction of the soil highly loaded with magnesium. The rhododendron is a magnesiphile and a calciphobe; that is, it is magnesium-loving and calcium-hating. In experiments, it grew best when magnesium carbonate (not calcium carbonate) had increased the pH roughly from 5.0 to near 8.0. Just what this high degree of magnesium saturation did to the plant's chemical composition is shown most simply in the accompanying graph, in which the concentrations of nitrogen (N), calcium (CaO), potassium (K_2O) and magnesium (MgO) are shown on the scale on the left as percent of dry matter; the phosphorus (P_2O_5) is shown similarly by the scale at lower right; and the manganese is given as parts per million in the scale at the upper right.

The significant results show: (1) the adverse effects of high magnesium in the soil on the movement of calcium, potassium and manganese into the plant; (2) the favorable effects on the movement of nitrogen and phosphorus into the plant as a result of saturating the soil with magnesium; and (3) the very large increase in the concentration of the magnesium in the plants when the magnesium in the soil was increased. The "antagonistic" effect by the magnesium on the calcium is an almost directly inverse one. The graph shows that the line for the concentrations of calcium goes downward at an angle about equal to that of the line showing rising concentrations of magnesium. This has been a well-known fact for many years. Similarly, there is the antagonistic reduction of potassium in the plant by the increased magnesium in the plant due to that in the soil, when, at the same time, its carbonate reduced the degree of soil acidity. Also, there was a very significant reduction in the concentration of the manganese in the plant. Relatively speaking, this latter was one of the largest reductions in the elements for which analysis was made. Perhaps the most surprising result was the increase in the amount of phosphorus taken into the plants when magnesium in the soil was increased. In the quantitative determination of phosphorus in the laboratory, it is common practice to precipitate it as magnesium phosphate, a most insoluble compound. Yet, contrariwise, putting more magnesium into the soil mobilized more of the soil's phosphorus into the rhododendron plants. This tells us that chemical analysis of the soil gives by no means the same values we get when the values are determined by the biochemistry by root contact in the soil. Increase in the nitrogen of the plants was as expected, since it is the constituent of protein, the chemical compound carrying life, and its increase goes with increase of growth and the factors bringing it about.

All this clarifies the interrelations (all too poorly comprehended) between the nutrient elements in the soil and the different crops created by these elements' quantitatively different roles. It explains the variations in the chemical compositions of any single crop as the result of its diet varying according to the exchange capacity of the colloidal clay and the soil organic matter.

INDIRECT MODIFICATIONS VIA MIXED FLORA

From observing the general pattern of distribution of plants on the earth, that is, according to the science of ecology, we are coming to realize that the fertility of the soil is a prominent factor in control of it. Accordingly, the nutrient mineral balances of the soil influence these balances in the growth of the plant. This fact has been established by extensive works of soil science and of plant physiology. The soil studies point first to the three inorganic nutrient elements, calcium, magnesium and potassium, which occupy, respectively, 60% to 70%, 10% to 20% and 2% to 5% of the adsorptive-exchange capacity of the clay-humus colloid. Then some 5% is given to essential trace elements and approximately 10% to the nonnutrient cation *(positively charged ion)*, hydrogen, or acidity. Secondly, these studies point to three, also inorganic, but anionic *(characterized by surface active negatively charged ions)* elements associated with the soil's organic matter, namely, nitrogen, sulfur and phosphorus. The phosphorus may well be so categorized, since it is commonly in the oxidized, or phosphate, form just as are nitrogen in nitrates and sulfur in sulfates, all connected with organic matter.

Knowledge of the association of phosphorus with energy changes in the metabolism of organic compounds within the cell is comparatively recent. It was very recently that Melvin Calvin, in his Nobel Prize paper, connected phosphorus with photosynthesis. He reported that, in its first stage, this process yields a compound of three carbons and one phosphorus, of which two unite, via the dropout of the phosphorus, to give the six-carbon sugar, glucose. In these current discussions of magnesium along with calcium and potassium, the other major adsorbed cations on the clay-humus complex, we have concerned ourselves with variations in their amounts and the resultant balance and imbalance in vegetation. We have discussed how these imbalances represent similar situations in nutrition of animals in relation to the ailment called tetany, connected more specifically with the irregularities in the nervous systems of both animals and man.

Studies using colloidal clay titrated to differing degrees of saturation by the nutrient cations, calcium, magnesium and potassium, as well as by trace elements and the non-nutrient cation of hydrogen, have suggested that for good growth of legume crops and their significant fixation of atmospheric nitrogen into their proteins, the percentage saturations cited previously for the soil colloid represent balanced availabilities of those cations. Mathematically, then, with so little of the highly active monovalent (*capable of binding one complement only*), potassium, we can consider its ratio to calcium and magnesium combined more plentiful and less active divalent *(capable of combining with two complements)* cations, in the fractional arrangement,

POTASSIUM

CALCIUM + MAGNESIUM.

each as percentage parts of the total exchange capacity and in milligram equivalents per 100 grams of soil. Accordingly, the numerator varies over but small number values when doubling or trebling. But the much larger number values for the denominator—calcium and magnesium—need much wider additions as numbers before they disturb the ratio significantly. Discussions so far have considered direct relations as chemical elements. It is aimed to point out some indirect relations mitigating the dangers of magnesium deficiencies.

Modifying the flora of the grazing animal is an indirect means of controlling the nutrient balance of cations when the balance in the soil may not be modified. The introduction of white clover into a combination of grasses is a case in point. While extra potassium favors the development of white clover, this is a legume crop with liberal concentrations in itself of calcium and magnesium. Thus, it works against magnesium deficiencies related to high potassium in the grass-legume diet which the animal consumes. Without changing the fertility on the soil colloid, the threateningly high potassium gives more white clover in the mixed flora diet and encourages the animal to choose, by protein values, the legume providing more magnesium as protection against tetany. Commercial nitrogen fertilizers contradict and offset, indirectly, the above beneficial effects via magnesium uplift in the flora, since nitrogen depresses the white clover, which, in turn, reduces the animal intake of magnesium as protection against the shortages of magnesium in the grasses, thus inviting the danger of tetany.

The two monovalents, potassium and ammonium, considered in their play against the divalents calcium and magnesium, serve well, both directly and indirectly, to emphasize the importance of so-called "balance" and "imbalance" even if concerned only with the nutrients held on the clay-humus complex and commonly measured by soil tests. This balance becomes all the more important in relation to other matters of indirect relations via soil organic matter, varieties of crops and other factors. When plant nutrition from the soil is not so simple, certainly the animal nutrition from the forages becomes no more simple, relative to balanced diets for healthy growth by plants, animals and man.

IMBALANCES AMONG COMPANION ELEMENTS

Hidden in a 20 page pamphlet is evidence than man suffers *The Magnesium Deficiency Syndrome*[1] which has been a baffling and disastrous ailment among livestock for many years. It has been called "grass tetany" because it occurs in the spring when animals are put out to graze after a winter on dry feed. During recent years veterinarians have connected grass tetany with a deficiency of magnesium in the soil, resulting in disturbed nerve transmissions and irregularities associated with the characteristic convulsions and sudden death. No advance warning of the impending disaster is given.

Andre Voison,[2] a capable physiologist as well as a veterinarian, in his translation of *Grass Tetany* from the French, has brought together the essential facts reported in some 340 research references. He pictures this ailment, common to both livestock and man, as a reflection of deficiency not in the parts of a compound ration for the animals, but in the vegetation as the soil grows it. The pasture is often the scene of the disaster. The significant factor is not always the specific minimum amount of magnesium alone, nor is it one to be revealed by soil tests. It is not a case of such specificity. Rather, it concerns itself with improper nutrition of the plant, possibly due to a whole set of imbalances in the quantities of the four cationic (positively charged) elements, namely, calcium, magnesium, potassium and sodium, in terms of which a deficient concentration of magnesium results in herbage and health troubles.

Calcium and magnesium are less soluble alkaline earths, each carrying two electrical charges. Potassium and sodium are highly soluble alkalis, each with one electrical charge, and of widely differing behavior in the soil. For example, through the ages, sodium has been readily carried to the sea, making the water more salty. But potassium, although equally soluble, has been held back much more by the clay in the soil and provides a higher ash constituency of plants. Calcium and magnesium also differ widely as essentials in living matter. Calcium is the foremost ash element in warm-blooded life forms, where magnesium is almost a trace element. (The percentages are 1.5 and 0.05, respectively.) These four elements, when weathered out of the rock minerals, occupy most of the exchange capacity of the clay of our soils, save for some hydrogen held there also, but as a non-nutrient for plants.

The behavior of magnesium as it moves into the plant is not simply a matter of the exchangeable amount on the clay. Its movement into the plant depends on the amount necessary to balance the concentrations of potassium, sodium and calcium and on the withdrawals made by the species of herbage. These withdrawals vary with the plant's synthesis of carbohydrates or proteins. Extensive literature dealing with tetany has resulted in a consideration of the balance of the four nutrient elements in herbage for livestock. Certain minimum percentages of these elements in the dry feed have been suggested as inviting tetany. Similarly, percentages of the elements required for prevention of the disease have been suggested. The work by Naumann[3] affords an excellent review of the mineral imbalances occurring in herbage of tetany pastures as revealed by a large number of chemical analyses of soils and pasture grasses in the area of the Lower Rhine River, where the incidence of grass tetany is high.

He cites the characteristics of tetanigenic herbage by listing its percentage of six essential nutrient elements in relation to animal requirements. Of the two soluble alkalis, sodium and potassium, the latter was high (3.88%) in the dry matter; the former was very low (0.13%). The magnesium was low (0.17%), relatively three-quarters of the requirement. Consequently, the potassium was far out of balance in relation to the magnesium and the sodium.

The magnesium content at a mean of 99 ppm was more than sufficient, while copper was 8.3 ppm, which is approximately the lower limit of safety, or about 70% of the requirement. The concentration of the phosphorus element in the dry matter was 0.41%, barely covering the requirement. According to these results, tetany may be anticipated when the single element magnesium is low in the feed and food, but its amount as related to imbalances with respect to other elements seems to be the baffling aspect of the ailment. Consequently, the intercationic balance of the nutrient elements adsorbed on the clay becomes the basic matter of concern.

Since tetany is a human problem, also, perhaps the balanced nutrition of the plant via the soil will become significant in human nutrition as well as in feeds for animals.

BIOCHEMICALLY, SO LITTLE IS SO IMPORTANT

Now that untimely degenerations of the parts and processes of the human body have led to the collection of voluntary contributions for research studies, and we have learned more details of physiology with its underlying biochemistry, we are discovering that more and more of the basic functions of human and other warm-blooded bodies show close similarities in the behaviors maintaining health. In spite of these facts, we are slow to believe that experimental studies of details in animal bodies allow us to envision applicable suggestions for requisites of health in the human body.

We have long known that cattle have tuberculosis with the secondary symptoms of infection by the same tubercle bacillus found in human tuberculosis. Since this disease indicates that deficiencies in essential nutrient chemical elements and compounds invite microbial invasion, and since proper nutrition and reduced activity will arrest this degeneration, we should move speedily to the practice of prevention of degenerations of many kinds by individual study of the requisites for maintaining health. While relief of the afflicted is a worthy humanitarian practice, it is far more rewarding for each individual to guard his own abstinences and practices, and thereby arrive at a national health, rather than to hope for that result to come via taxation and direction from federal officials.

Doctors Wacker and Vallee have reported on *The Magnesium Deficiency Tetany Syndrome in Man.* Tetany is another example of the same affliction affecting both man and beast. But it is not a microbial infection. Rather, it is due to the deficiency of magnesium, an inorganic or mineral nutrient element in the soil growing feed and food. Acceptance of the fact that man suffers this same affliction in common with cattle seems to meet bold resistance, even by bureaucratic appointees who are supposedly concerned with human health. We do not seem ready to view disease in the negative, that is, as a deficiency within the body. We view it mainly in the positive, and search for an agency attacking from without.

"Magnesium," Doctors Wacker and Vallee tell us in their documented report, "is an essential nutrient for animals and plants, suggesting that a dietary inadequacy of this might readily result in a deficiency disease. Indeed, such deficiency states have been induced in animals. Tetany and convulsions, subsequent to experimental magnesium deficiency, were first shown to occur in rats in 1932, and later in other animal species. Spontaneous magnesium deficiency tetany has been observed and well characterized in cattle . . . The varieties of neuromuscular aberrations credited to magnesium deficiency are so numerous that they do not add specificity to knowledge of the metabolic functions of this element."

"This is a problem which has been overcome recently by the development of the flame photometer. Almost as a direct consequence of these circumstances, a new specific clinical entity, *human* magnesium deficiency tetany, has been described. The syndrome is virtually identical to that of hypocalcemic tetany, from which it can be differentiated only by chemical means. Its manifestations correspond almost exactly to those seen in magnesium-deficient animals. In each of the patients in whom the disease has been observed, the parenteral administration of magnesium sulfate promptly and completely reversed the symptoms, signs and chemical changes of the syndrome. An appreciation of the clinical consequences of magnesium deficiency resulting in tetany requires an understanding of the biochemical and physiological actions of this [nutrient] ion."

"The biochemical fact that only lately has magnesium been found in laboratory tests to be an activator of many enzymes explains why the cause of tetany as a deficiency of an inorganic, soil-borne nutrient element has been so baffling so long. We need to remind ourselves that the photosynthesis of sugars in every green leaf depends on magnesium as the inorganic core of chlorophyll. There it is the 24 parts (as the final ash, portion of a large organic molecule and not as an ion) in a total of either 900 or 925 parts of which all the rest is organic substance. A host of enzymes has been found to be activated by magnesium. Unfortunately it has not been possible to tranlate these in vitro [in the laboratory] effects with absolute certainty directly to physiologic events in the living animal. Most of the studies have been performed on isolated enzyme systems where magnesium ions were simply added to a given enzyme under observation, and the . . . resulting increase in activity was measured . . . Thus it has not been possible to prove an absolute requirement for magnesium. On this basis, a definite physiologic role for magnesium in these systems cannot be assigned."

Because the soil-borne element, magnesium, is so small a part of so many enzymes, which are doing so much in spite of their being present in such small amounts, and since they are absent in the resulting products which they catalyze, it has been difficult to ascribe sudden disasters such as convulsions and death to a deficiency of magnesium in the soil, especially since it operates in no closer chemical contact than in the liquid bathing the nerves. Nevertheless, it makes the part of the soil in nutrition more significant, in giving ecological order for man as well as animals, to tell us that "we are what we are, because of where we are" in relation to the degree of development of soil from the rock according to the climatic forces.

RELATION OF SOIL TEST TO CROP ANALYSES

Improved technical aids in the laboratory have helped increase our knowledge of the soil's supply of nutrient elements and its relation to the plant's content of these factors. This has given us a clearer vision of what we can consider a balanced diet as measured by soil tests. Some experimental studies made in Scotland since 1949 have concentrated attention on magnesium in soils and crops.[1] The effects of magnesian and calcic limestones on the magnesium contents of herbage and other crops were measured. Whether crops grown on soils relatively low in readily soluble (available) magnesium respond to its application was considered. Attention went to the effectiveness of the use of different materials which contain this element on the growth of the crop and on its chemical composition.

The relation of potassium to magnesium was also studied, since potassium can modify the assimilation of magnesium by the plant. In addition, the plan allowed measurement of the relations of different rates of applied nitrogen and phosphorus on successive cuttings of grass during the growing season. There were two main reasons for these experiments. First was the increased incidence of animal disorders (tetany) associated with deficiencies of magnesium. Second, there was the possibility of a deficiency restricting crop yields, especially with the application of large amounts of fertilizers with no magnesium.

Investigators used freely-drained soils from glacial drifts of varying origins, with pH ranges 5.2 to 6.5; ignition losses, 2% to 13% as indices of organic matter; and clay contents of 8% to 19%, save two soils with but 4% to 5%. The contents of magnesium, soluble in acetic acid and ammonium acetate, ranged from 1.5 mg. to 18.4 mg. per 100 gm of soil and 1.3 mg. to 21.5 mg. per 100 gm of soil. All but three soils contained less than six milligrams-percent of magnesium. This last soil-test value is a suggestive one, since in a significant area of northern Scotland about half of the agricultural land seems to contain less than 6.1 milligrams per 100 grams of soil; and nearly one-fifth has less than 3.1 milligrams. Ten magnesium materials were used to add this element to soils. There were mainly natural minerals, or those burnt, and supplying magnesium, calcium and sulfur.

Since the emphasis in the study was on herbage for grazing as related to the threat of tetany, a danger from magnesium deficiencies in pastures, the mixed grasses and clover were the major crops used. There were also oats, barley, yellow turnips *(swedes)* and potatoes. The differences in the uptake of magnesium by the various crops stand out decidedly. The differing physiology of crops largely determines their ability to obtain inorganic nutrient elements from the soil in order to prevent deficiencies in the ration or diet. Of course, if the soil is too low in supply, no plant can deliver the element in question.

The experimental results for potatoes and swedes on soils with magnesium no higher than 6 milligrams per 100 grams—120 pounds per 2,000,000 of soil, or per acre plowed seven inches deep—but given increments of calcined magnesium sulfate and of kieserite, a slightly soluble hydrous magnesium sulfate, tell us that the treatments had no effect on the yields. But they did increase the percentages of magnesium in both crops. Without applied magnesium, the mean percentages in the fresh tubers and roots were 0.0156% and 0.0087% magnesium, respectively; while the corresponding values with the 36-pound magnesium treatment were 0.0164% and 0.0102%. These represent increases by 5% and 17% respectively. When the soils for these two food crops were liberally treated with nitrogen, phosphorus and potassium, "the nitrogen and phosphorus had no large or constant effect on the magnesium contents of the tubers and roots; the mean percentages of magnesium for 10 experiments on potatoes and 16 on swedes being 0.0173% and 0.0089% respectively. The potassium had no influence on the magnesium content of swede roots, but tended to increase the percentage in potato tubers. Healthy crops grown in the northern half of Scotland have contained as little as 0.008% and 0.006% of magnesium in tubers and roots, respectively. Differences between crops are much greater than the variations produced by normal dressings on NPK fertilizers."[1]

This report tells us that applied magnesium is not much of a direct factor in modifying crop yields, thus explaining why so little attention has gone to it as commercial fertilizer. The report does not refute the possibility of indirect effects of magnesium on other elements via enzymatic activities, or others, as has been suggested.[2] It tells us that crops measure the magnesium of the soils biochemically in greater detail than we measure it chemically to categorize it according to the nutritional quality of the crops it produces. In the grass crop, the uplift of magnesium content of the hay and the herbage was accomplished by mixing clover—a legume crop—with the grasses. The effect stands out prominently. Magnesium treatments, coupled with different amounts of applied potassium, were tested by analyses of the mixed herbage, and of the rye grass, the orchard grass and the clover, the last three separated from the mixture. There were three cuttings per year.

"The magnesium treatment applied in March did not increase the yield, and had practically no effect on the amount of herbage . . . The percentage of magnesium in the clover was only slightly greater at the second and third cutting than at the first. These results illustrate the well-known fact that clovers generally contain more magnesium than do the grasses."[1] The average magnesium concentrations for magnesian soil treatments, coupled with the highest treatment by potassium, were as follows: rye grass—0.15%; orchard grass—0.23%; mixed herbage—0.24%; and clover—0.46%. These results demonstrate that the roots of legumes have a greater ability than non-legumes to take exchangeable cationic nutrients from the soil.[3] Also, it shows that the uplift effect as soil-borne elements in mixed herbages and hays results because a higher concentration of the soil's several cationic elements in legumes supports their creation of more protein-rich forages.

In these experiments the added clover made the difference in higher magnesium concentration as possible prevention of tetany. But the amount of magnesium in clover is only about one-tenth of its calcium content. The quantitative ratios among these basic elements in the plant are reflected in similar ratios of supplies adsorbed on the clay of the soil growing the legumes. But legumes, like these clovers, cannot grow successfully unless the soils are relatively well supplied with the basic, or cationic, nutrient elements: namely, calcium, magnesium and potassium. Even then, in a more specifically balanced lot, or diet, the needs of specific plants and crops have not yet been fully established. Chemical contents of the soils are slowly being precisely measured and related to their value as nutrition to the crops produced. This knowledge serves to emphasize the connection between "the handful of dust" and the creations therefrom.

REQUISITE FOR NUTRITIONAL QUALITY OF CROPS

Research here in soil and nutrition has placed major emphasis on the balance (as a plant diet) of the positively-charged nutrient elements (cations) exchangeable from the soil's clay-humus colloid to the plant roots. The criterion for establishing that balance among calcium, magnesium, potassium, sodium and the non-nutrient hydrogen (as so far considered) has been the effective symbiotic relations between the legume plants and their specific nitrogen-fixing bacteria. Through these the legumes supplement their soil-nitrogen supply with that from the atmosphere to become protein-rich, mineral-rich feeds and foods. These several nutrient cations can be supplied from soil reserves of pulverized rock particles of sizes commonly carried by water and wind.

Under such criteria of matching the managed fertility support of the soil against the crop's needs for cationic nutrients, the study of soils and their microbes demonstrated that these are the two foundation strata of the entire biotic pyramid. They have been the biochemical support of all the other life strata. Natural grinding and mixing of rock-minerals from the earth's surface by climatic forces has built soils matched to crop needs—under the above criteria.

But while the ratios between the nearly half-dozen cationic nutrient elements on the soil's clay-humus colloid have been established, we have not yet worked out a balance of the soil's negatively charged elements. These include the anions, nitrogen, phosphorus, sulfur, and some of the trace elements. Among the latter are some which can function as either positively or negatively charged. These are said to be "amphoteric."

These anions are held in the soil and are more available to microbes and plants through the soil's active organic matter which connects them with the higher energy reserve supplies of carbon for microbial action. They are active and available to plants in the "living" soil. Of these elements, phosphorus has too long been considered only in the group of inorganics, or rock minerals. But since this anionic nutrient has been recognized as so important in biochemical energy changes—even in the first step of photosynthesis of sugars and possibly of lignin compounds—we need to connect phosphorus closely with the soil organic matter in plant nutrition.

Theoretical consideration may well be given to such a one of the anionic nutrients aiding the effectiveness with which mycorrhizal symbiosis of fungi and non-legume plant roots increases plant nutritional values. This would be similar to the case of legume-bacterial symbiosis where the cationic element, calcium, is such an essential. Unfortunately, the anionic sector of the group of requisite fertility elements, as well as the many organic nutrient compounds, is still much unknown in plant functions through which soil management can give uplift to the nutritional quality of food crops.

Our early separation of the functions of nutrient cations in plants from those of the anions in the soil seems to be a natural consequence of educational sequence. First, we become familiar with inorganic chemistry before any interest in the organic arises. Second, for geological studies in mineral decomposition and soil formation, the cationic activities and losses to the sea exceed those of the anionic. The former consists of many elements with which we become familiar early in the study of chemistry. The latter is mainly the colloidal silica of clays, pushed aside in early chemistry to await the day later in the educational program when newer technologies elucidate colloidal chemistry, mineral structures and reactions of the residue of rocks weathered into soils.

Then also, the comprehension of the intricate roles played in plant nutrition by the anions, nitrogen sulfur and phosphorus is delayed still more when within the plants they are combined into large organic molecules as reduced elements. But they are readily oxidized into forms of increased solubility and release considerable energy to the responsible microbes. Combination of anions with carbon in organic matter magnifies this dynamic energy aspect. It marks nitrogen release from its combination with carbon.

In the role of soil fertility in plant nutrition, the complicated molecular biochemical connections of the anions are not clear; nor is the union of either inorganic cations or anions with larger organic molecules by what is called "chelation."

That soil microbes, acting as wrecking crews and salvaging agents of plant residues, should conserve and mobilize many large organic molecules in close root contact for uptake as nutrition is still an embryonic concept. That their action affects the flavor and quality of vegetables still awaits scientific cataloging, though it is widely proclaimed by empiricism.

The fact that organic matter in the soil is essential for growing quality foods is emphasized when one of the larger producers of frozen vegetables uses the practice of "fertilizing the fertilizing green manure crop" and grows its vegetables only in the second year, after heavier fertilizer and green manure treatments of the soil. Organic matter and the microbes struggling for energy therefrom give crops the ability to survive and grow in spite of soil doctors.

Now that the limited knowledge of balancing the fertility cations absorbed on the soil's colloidal complex has shown itself as such a prominent control factor of crop quality, we are forcefully reminded that (1) we have not yet given "balance" to the fertility anions in the soil under like criteria, (2) nor has the "balance" of soil organic matter per se, or against cations and anions, been divided into specific ratios or relations as manageable matters. Our ignorance of soil management for growing quality crops exceeds our knowledge of the subject. This fact is emphasized in fertilizer sales literature reporting research. Many ideas are still hidden in nature's unopened books.

MAGNESIUM IN THE SOILS OF THE UNITED STATES

In the foregoing discussion no attention was given to the broader pattern of magnesium of the soils of the United States as a whole. Yet for its companion cationic element, calcium, our country divides itself, soilwise, naturally into an East and a West. The 98th meridian of longitude marks the division closely. The division by soils runs roughly south from the northwestern edge of Minnesota to the southern tip of Texas. Those to the west are called "pedocals"—"pedo", for soils and "cals" for calcium, with free carbonate of it in horizons or concretions in the soil profile. Those soils of the East are called "pedalfers"—again soils with aluminum "al" and iron "fe" prominent in the profile under conditions implying the shortage of any calcium as active there in its carbonate.

In the development of a soil from various rock minerals, the movement of magnesium down through the profile has not been given as much prominence as calcium. Yet in the drainage waters, as an average, from the country in its entirety, the mineral residues on evaporation of those waters—more often appreciated as the so-called "lime" clogging the coils in the water-heater—contain one-fourth as much magnesium as calcium, by weight. Calcium carbonate makes up nearly half of that residue from the waters, to make "lime in the tea-kettle," a common observation in Western United States.

The United States Geological Survey has done extensive chemical analyses of drainage waters. In its Professional Paper No. 135, 1924, Dr. F.W. Clarke gave an extensive collection of data. From those Mr. S.B. Detweiler, now retired from federal services, gave us the generalized magnesium map for the country, shown here.

These data suggest their relation to the varied degrees of soil development under the climatic forces, especially the rainfall as it is in inches per year in excess of the evaporation from a free water surface, also in inches per year. The former may also be given as percentage of the latter. Consequently, we would expect low magnesium in our soil waters in the southeastern states. Accordingly, in the states northeast and east of Ohio and east and south of the Mississippi and Ohio Rivers, the "very low" and the "low" magnesium, namely 1-3 ppm and 4-9 ppm, respectively, are expected as the map reports. Then, in the high rainfall of Washington and Oregon, where the extremes of rainfall occur, magnesium is also "low," or 4-9 ppm. In the rest of the area and a much larger one, magnesium is reported as "medium" and "high," at 10-19 ppm and over 20 ppm. The Dakotas, Minnesota, Iowa, Illinois and Indiana with increasing annual rainfalls in that order from less than 20 to 40 inches per annum all show high magnesium. That fact serves to point out that the geological factor and not only the rainfall must come in for consideration. We, therefore, speak of the geo-climatic setting as determining the development of the soil.

The "low" supply of magnesium in the soil as a deficiency in crop production came into prominence some years ago[1] in the citrus groves of Florida, when attention first turned to the so-called "trace" elements. Emphasis had gone to the Marsh seedless grapefruit, which was giving larger yields as boxes of fruit than were the "seedy" ones. But when fertility elements, not common in commercial fertilizers, were applied separately on highly calcareous, sandy soils, it was the magnesium that increased the yields of the "seedy" fruits far above those of the seedless. But also, the flavor and taste were so much improved that there was not much premium on the seedless for the customer looking for quality along with quantity.

Magnesium demonstrated its biochemistry connected with the better survival of the species through healthy reproduction. But with that there came also the other products giving the quality as taste, possibly also assets in the reproduction of the species in passing over dormancy from the season of seed production to the planting of that, as it occurs in Nature. With our concern for the production of big bulk per acre, we are apt to forget that quality as fruit may be in the many compounds unknown, but coming along as aids in species survival. Magnesium is associated with many enzymes, and that element, like the enzymes, is a case where so little can do so much, without being necessarily spent in the service.

While magnesium, as mapped "very low" and "low" may be a deficiency in highly developed soils, the converse, or excess of magnesium, may be the case in the less-developed soils in areas of lower annual rainfalls and mapped as "high" in magnesium. Early botanical literature says much about the required calcium-magnesium ratio. Irrigators suggest caution of magnesium-potassium ratios and calcium in relation thereto in the applied waters.[2] More recently with our appreciation of the adsorption-exchange activities by calcium, magnesium, potassium and sodium on the soils, colloidal complex and their suggestions as to what ratios of these cations on it are a balanced diet for legumes and other more nutritious plants, there comes the ecological suggestion that areas "high" in magnesium on the map may be disturbing to fuller plant nutrition and crop growths. Excess magnesium may be equivalent to calcium deficiency, if not also of potassium.

Calcium plays a role as a fertilizer defined as an element entering into the plant's growth of its tissues for larger yields. But it also serves as a "soil amendment," whereby the root hairs are maintained as highly calcerous, so called "semi-permeable" membranes. In that state, they are prohibiting the outgo of nutrients from plants back to the soil. Simultaneously they are fostering the ingo of nutrients—including nitrogen, phosphorus and potassium— from the soil to the plant. If magnesium in excess on the clay will saturate the root membrane by replacing the calcium there, should we not interpret that as a need to saturate the immediate seedling zone with calcium? Such is the suggestion coming from many farmers in the areas on the map where magnesium is labeled as "high" in the drainage water.

Agricultural crops as well as citrus are telling us that magnesium is coming into more concern with our soil exploitation of both the organic and inorganic aspects of fertility. The larger look at this element includes the soils of the country as a whole, and the testing of soil for magnesium makes this the fourth, even for labeling of commercial fertilizer bags, though commonly connected with calcium under the term "lime."

RHODODENDRONS . . . A PROBLEM OF SOIL FERTILITY, NOT ACIDITY

Rhododendrons, azaleas and other shrubs belonging to that same family, are considered "hard to grow" on soils containing much lime or calcium. It is commonly said, "They require an acid soil." So far as earlier publications report, it was not known whether poor growth on calcerous soils by these plants is due to the soil alkalinity—that is, the high pH; or whether it is due to injurious effects by the calcium itself; or by some other factor induced by the soil's surplus of this element.

This same confusion prevailed—and still persists—in connection with legumes of which the opposite is said, "They require a calcareous or non-acid soil." Legumes have been shown to fail on acid soils, not because there is present so much of the element hydrogen—which gives them a low pH or makes them acid in chemical reaction—but because from a soil naturally developed so highly that much hydrogen has come in, there has gone out the calcium, magnesium, potassium, and other nutrient elements, displaced by the hydrogen or acidity, to starve these protein-producing forages. It is not the chemical soil condition which we call "an acid reaction" that is injurious. Instead it is the absence of what gives complete nutrition for the plants. Legumes grow well on an "acid" soil if they can be properly nourished there.

The confusion about the growth of rhododendrons and its requirement of acid soils, or its failure to grow on alkaline or neutral soils, has recently been shown to be another case where it is not the soil reaction but the failing nutrition of this flowering shrub that is the disturbing factor. It has long been known that rhododendrons showing a yellowing of foliage and failing to grow when transplanted to high-lime soils are restored to normal growth by soil treatments in some cases using magnesium sulfate, and in some by aluminum sulfate. This suggests that these plants cannot tolerate much calcium in their fertility diet from the soil, but will tolerate the magnesium.

Using this observation as his postulate, Dr. Tod of the Edinburgh and East of Scotland College of Agriculture reported (Miscellaneous Publishing Number 164) his separation of the effects by soil alkalinity from those by excess of soil calcium. He used an acid soil, growing rhododendrons normally, and made additional pots of it increasingly alkaline in reaction by adding two increments of magnesium carbonate in place of calcium carbonate, or ordinary limestone. This left the soil low in calcium (0.25 to 0.38 milligrams equivalents per 100 grams soil), but gave initial pH values of 4.7, 6.8, and 8.4 in his several three-pot series. The phosphorus in the soil was "very low," while the supply of potassium was "medium."

The seedling growth was slow and the color of the foliage was a normal green with no signs of the well-known yellowing on neutral or alkaline soils of high pH. There was little difference between the plants grown on these different treatments. They flowered for the first time after five years, with the earliest date of that shown by the soil treatment with the highest magnesium.

Chemical analyses of the plants (see figure 1) showed that the concentrations of the inorganic, or mineral, elements were what are probably within normal limits. Phosphate in the plants was high. The manganese there was low, but evidently not of deficiency level since no evidence was ever shown previously by leaf symptoms. The magnesium in the plants was pushed up decidedly by this soil treatment. But, while along with this there were increased concentrations of the plant's nitrogen and phosphorus also, it reduced the concentrations of manganese, potassium, and calcium in the plants. These results give suggestions as to what the highly developed soil for rhododendrons representing plant nutrition must offer as natural diet rather than a certain pH or degree of acidity as a soil "condition" in terms of chemical reaction.

We need to see "soil acidity" as an index of the degree of natural development of the soil in going from rock to the sea. Thereby we can get nature's suggestion as to what is left of the rock making soil in terms of plant nutrition. Plants are not sensitive to degrees of acidity. But they are very sensitive to deficiencies in the required diet of soil fertility.

LAND BULLETIN

This late work brings together research reports in some 340 references and the life experiences of an able scientist-veterinarian about what is "the disastrous meeting of animal and grass." It considers the question, "Can tetany be due to incorrect application of mineral and organic fertilizers combined with certain methods of intensive grazing?"

The author with many years directing a school of veterinary, managing grazing land in northwestern France and paying close study to pasture productivity as measured by healthy and highly productive livestock, gives us this work as the latest one of his series connecting soil with vegetation and thereby with warm-blooded bodies. The book is more than prescriptions for treating sick animals (it has that for the practitioner). It is a commendable contribution to the biochemical processes undergirding the health of all that composes the biotic pyramid resting on a fertile soil. It is an excellent partner to his *Soil, Grass and Cancer*. It is similarly fundamental for any studious reader concerned with life processes whereby food is nutrition for microbes, plants, animals and man. Like his preceding works, all originally in French, this one too will find importance in other languages.

The dilemma of so many sudden deaths of animals turned on luscious growths of grass has long been accepted. It has not been analyzed physiologically for its prevention. As a biochemist with honors in veterinary science and long experienced in managed grazing, Dr. Voisin brings together theories, facts and many remaining questions pointed toward this all-too-common disaster (not considered a disease by research). He puts the best of deductions into focus to challenge the reader's hope for prevention through management of the soil, the forage and the animal according as all are biochemically integrated into a chain of synthetic services in creation. His analytical thinking works "from the ground up."

Dr. Voisin considers the oft-observed correlation of tetany with irregularities in the mobility and supply of magnesium in the soil, the forage, and the blood. He shows also that the magnesium does not stand alone as a possible causative factor. He discusses the balance and antagonistic behaviors of this nutrient element in relation to several others in soil, grass, serum and urine. They are considered as possible therapeutic agents. He includes calcium, potassium, sodium, phosphorus, nitrogen and sulfur, not only as pairs in ions and compounds, but also as possible imbalances of triples and quadruples as fertilizers on the soil, "ash" constituents in the feed, as parts of organic molecules built into tissue or body functions and in metabolites or secretions, all connnected with observable symptoms of irregular health. With all these related to form practices of "manuring" the soil, this book of over two hundred pages will be challenging reading to any one whose concern connects itself with healthy agricultural production by which all of us must be fed.

8

DIFFERENT SOILS, DIFFERENT PLANTS

SOIL FERTILITY: ITS CLIMATIC PATTERN

Our North and South are divided much in terms of soil conditions as the East and the West. So that one can realize that as we have more rainfall starting with none of it in western United States and coming east there is an increase in the soil fertility until we reach the midcontinent. On going farther east, there is a decrease of it. However in that area we still have the clay content of the soil going upwards. The soil also shows increase in the saturation capacity in the northeastern area. But more rain removes the nutrients from that saturation capacity. The exchangeable essentials for plants go down. The acidity of the soil begins to come in beyond about 25 inches of annual rainfall. In the United States at 25 and 30 inches of precipitation we have the highest point of soil construction with a minimum of destruction. More climatic soil destruction comes in as one goes further east.

Viewed as a simple process in diagrammatic form, we start with the rock and build soils with more rainfall. We build more clay in the soil until about 30 inches of rainfall. With more annual rainfall we start washing nutrients off that clay. As a consequence soil acidity comes into the soil. More weathering of the rock to make soil up to a certain limit is good. But more weathering beyond that is bad. It merely washes the fertility out and we don't have the producing power for protein though we might have the producing power for wood or carbohydrates.

If we superimpose that diagrammatic concept on the soil map, you have the climatic pattern of the soil development and all that depends on the soil. The corn belt is part of it. In the middle of the United States there are the deep, black soils toward which our forefathers were moving. Coming westward to that deeper soil built American independence. Our westward movement, however, is overshooting that point now to the extent of losing some of our independence. We are asking the question whether democracy will survive. Unfortunately time prohibits elucidation of that philosophy. But it is well to realize that as long as we could come west and find food, security, we could remain independent. We were not compelled to live with our social troubles. Democracy was built on the fact that each individual controlled enough of the resources he needed to let him feel independent rather than constantly be dependent on, and thereby subject to, someone else.

The pattern of the virgin vegetation, wildlife, domestic animals, our crops and ourselves in the United States as dependent on the soil, the great resource which feeds all of us, is more significant than we are bent to believe. According to the high degree of soil weathering you can see why there are forests in the eastern United States. In terms of rocks as undeveloped soil you can see why the coniferous forests are in the western mountains. The pines are in the southeast. The spruce forests are in the north and in the high mountains. That's where either nature hasn't made soil yet, like in the Rocky Mountains, or where the soil was washed out so badly that there is little or nothing of nutrients left. Wood is all that will grow under deficient soil fertility. Carbon, hydrogen, oxygen, air, water, sunshine fabricated into nothing more than wood represent the soil's productivity. Those and other elements are not synthesized into proteins that can reproduce themselves. Instead they are synthesized possibly into the starches that can serve to hang fat on an old animal if you can produce and reproduce the animal somewhere else. It is only in the mid-continent where we have the grass agriculture.

Much has been made about grass and grass agriculture. But what, after all, is grass? Grass is a crop that can stop growing in the summer when the dry spell demands it and then pick up growth again when the rain comes. Trees can't do that. But what is more significant grass is on a soil which is not washed out as a result of the low rainfall in total connected with the dry spells. It is that extra fertility left in the low rainfall soil that makes the grass nutritious. It is not the variety or the pedigree of the grass. Just at this moment we are on the verge of national propaganda about a grass agriculture. That propaganda would have us move grass from out of the west and put it over the east. It would do nothing about feeding the grass transplanted to the east on the same soil fertility level that it originally fed on in the west.

It was the fertility of the soil and not the variety of the grass that made the buffalo. The buffalo came only a limited distance toward the east. Where did he survive? He survived and was winter meat for the Indians in Kentucky where thay have the fast horses and the fine women today. These buffaloes were also in some of the valleys of Pennsylvania. They were in the same valleys where today the German farmers, farming so well, are located. The buffalo also stayed out west where today we grow the "hard" or high-protein wheat and the Hereford cattle. Is it a nonsense matter that the buffalo voted with the Hereford cattle . . . or that the Hereford cattle voted with the buffalo? Is it mere coincidence that the race horses of Kentucky or that the best farmers of Pennsylvania vote with the buffalo for a certain soil area? We don't think it is.

There is the basic soil fertility by which the buffalo could survive and reproduce. There is the basic soil fertility by which we build the stamina and capacity of the race horses. There is likewise the good fertility that makes possible the thrifty German farmers. So when we say "grass agriculture" we need to take a look at it as we need to do for other things done in the United States lest they be done under propaganda rather than under the compulsions of the basic facts and sound logic.

If we consider the native vegetation across Kansas with its 17 inches of rainfall in the West and 37 in the East, it is clear that with more rain in the East there is more crop. But there is also the disappearance of lime from that soil and the disappearance of other fertility in Eastern Kansas also. Shall we wonder why the buffalo did not come east to the tall Kansas grass or big blue stem? He gave his name, not to that tall grass, but to the short grass where the hard wheat grows today. Does not that grass-soil-buffalo pattern help us see the soil in control?

The map of the protein in the wheat of Kansas of 1940 shows that the concentration of protein varied in that grain from a low of 10 to a high of 18%. That was nicely illustrated in the lower tier of countries where in 1940 there was a gradual increase of wheat protein on going westward. Wheat is harder in the western part of Kansas some folks believe because it is a drier climate and has less rainfall. That is scarcely the correct explanation. It depends on what the soil is and does more than on the rainfall. Protein in Kansas wheat is falling with time because they are mining the nitrogen, the humus and the other essential nutrients out of the soil. In 1949, the protein in the Kansas wheat varied from 9 to 15%. Nine years before, it varied from 10 to 19%. Such are the reductions, if those data are representative. While the protein was going down Kansas was growing more bushels. But it doesn't take much soil fertility to pile up starch and to make many bushels. It takes soil fertility, however, in balanced and ample supplies to make protein in the wheat.

This difference in crop quality according to soil development in Kansas may well be a pattern for more extensive areas. If we take the chemical composition of the crops in the western United States, or if we start with them grown on those soils which are only slightly developed in the West and analyze them for their potash, their lime and their phosphorus, the percentages of these added together amount to roughly 5%. As we come eastward to the midcontinent where the soils are more developed under more rainfall to be more washed out, the total of these three elements drops to nearly 4%. Then if the same is done for crops in the East and in the South, the total amounts of 2%. Accordingly as the soil fertility is being weathered or washed out, we are making crops that are made out of air, water and sunshine and less out of the fertility of the soil. Now by virtue of that declining fertility, whether by different soils or with lime in the same soil, we are therefore substituting carbohydrate delivery in our crops for the protein and nutritional values that should be in them.

Crop substitutions and crop juggling are no substitution for soil fertility. But when we can't grow red clover we search the world over in the attempt to find a substitute. Nature does what might appear to be the same thing in the way of substitutions. She could grow grass as we would call it by pedigree or variety in the West. She couldn't grow that grass in the East. She found a substitute but that substitute was trees which make only wood. In addition, she didn't attempt to grow very many animals in alpine or other coniferous forests. It is only in the hard-wood forests that you find some squirrels. You don't find squirrels in a coniferous forest. Even a squirrel knows that one will not find any nuts there unless some hunter should be found in there. We are concerned that you see the fertility in the soil as the determiner of the kind of life that is anywhere, or in the ecological pattern in general. Because we have technologies to bring foods, feeds, different plants and different animals from one place to another. This covers and blots out the picture too commonly.

If we make a map of the beef cattle of the United States then the beef cow, which is mainly protein, finds herself in greatest numbers west of the Mississippi River on the soils that still contain ample fertility. They are under only moderate rainfalls and not under high rainfalls and where the fertility is washed out. It is nothing unusual that the beef cows are in the same region where we had last year's champion basketball teams. It was Baylor University that had the college team champions in Texas. Oklahoma had the University champions, and the Phillips Oilers of Bartlesville, Oklahoma were the professional champions. If you will look at your All-American football selections and find where they came from, is it a coincidence that they come from the same region as the beef cows come from with their protein-introducing services? Growing basketball champions is a nutritional problem much as is the growing of beef. Champions are at the rule and T-bone steaks are high priced because we don't realize that only the more fertile soil produces beef. Beef steaks are high priced because the fertility of the soil in its synthetic capacities can build up the basic essentials that can be made into protein is slipping out from under us.

If as dealers in cattle we merely want to hang on fat, or want the pig which is an animal that we must nourish for only six months before we can escape the responsibilities of good feeding by passing it to the butcher, then we can operate east of the Mississippi River. There we have carbohydrate aplenty. But with feeds grown there we are even having trouble keeping the hog living long enough with the help of protein supplements to hang on the fat. We are even marketing them with less fat than we once did. We say the housewife doesn't like the fat. It would be more correct to say that we can't keep them living long enough to take the risk. Such are the problems because we are not nutritionists informed enough to know that the soil has a part in the ecological pattern of even our domestic animals.

We have tried to give you this picture hastily because it will be helpful for you to realize that you can go anywhere in the world and find that this pattern stands out if you can apply these basic principles of soil production in terms of the rock and the climatic forces. The nutrition of man as the two-legged animal is no different in fundamentals than the nutrition of the four-legged ones. Unfortunately for us, however, the four-legged animal has nutritionally helpful instincts to guide it. Man seemingly has thrown these instincts away which once guided him in feeding himself well. Unfortunately he hasn't developed enough of a knowledge and understanding of nutrition to make his good judgment an equivalent of the animal instinct. Consequently, he has put himself into regions wherein the deficiencies of the soil are severe enough to undermine his stamina and particularly when by technology he has reduced his body's struggle requiring and developing stamina. And so he can go on limping along in terms of his ability. Seemingly he is limping along in terms of some of his mental capacities. Undergirded by so many technologies he apparently doesn't know how weak he is.

Man has fought the microbes—and unfortunately so in our opinion—as enemies of his health. He has fought them long enough to convince us that the microbe is not the cause of much that is considered disease. Degeneration of his own body through failure of proper nourishment is really the problem which we ought to approach now that degenerative diseases more than those with microbes as symptoms are killing us off. Perhaps I would not be entirely out of place to predict for the 20th century that it will probably be the time when, in terms of better understanding of ourselves and our health problems, we shall emphasize nutrition. In the 17th century, we studied anatomy. In the 18th, we learned about physiology. In the 19th, we investigated bacteriology. Now probably we can piece all those sciences together until the 20th century will emphasize the fundamental knowledge on how to feed ourselves, so that we shall not degenerate, even in the absence of microbes as our enemies. As we cease to fight the microbes and turn to nutrition there is hope that we shall eventually come to understand how to feed ourselves. The climatic pattern of the soil fertility considered in a large way will give us suggestions by which we can see these seemingly subtle forces at work. As we fill out in the details of that pattern we shall get still other suggestions by which we can very probably nourish ourselves in reality from the ground up.

TOO MUCH NITROGEN OR NOT ENOUGH ELSE?

That plants may go on a "nitrogen jag" has long been pointed out by the grazing cow when she lets the rich green spots of grass grow taller while she grazes the short grass all around them even shorter. These spots mark the liberal doses of nitrogen in her droppings that result in a luscious, massive growth. But the cow says, "No, thanks, I don't care for it." Those tall, deep-green spots, fertilized by much nitrogen applied through her droppings, do not appeal to her as a balanced diet, perhaps, and so she bypasses them. At any rate, her body physiology directs her appetite to balance her ration if she can. The excess of nitrogen represents an unbalance to her, and she says so by refusal.

"Too much is too much" only in relation to something else. If too much nitrogen is used in relation to the supply of phosphate, potash, calcium or other growth factors, the unbalanced situation causes trouble. It is the lack of balance in plant nutrition that is disturbing. This is merely saying that there is too much of some nutrients or not enough of others. That is the way it must be said when the absolute amount of each nutrient needed for each particular function is not yet known. We do know, however, that when an adequate amount of nitrogen is available, and other necessary factors are adequate, then growth and yield can be truly spectacular. That animals do instinctively select food which provides a balanced ration was suggested by some work by Dr. George E. Smith of the Missouri Agricultural Experiment Station. In this test, rabbits were fed grasses grown on soil that had been treated only with nitrogen. This work was a part of the studies leading to the bio-assay of soil fertility by using the animal to measure the value of soil treatments, rather than a mere increase of yield in bulk or by measuring the total nitrogen to multiply by 6.25 and calling the result "protein."

Nitrogen fertilizer on the grass, it was true, made a large and luscious green growth that would seem a great tempter—if only the human eye judged it. It appeared equally significant as a means of growing of more grass per acre—if just the growing of more grass were the most valuable part of our efforts to improve pasture production. But the rabbits, when fed the grasses from areas with different soil treatments, had their own criteria for judging the resulting food values. The seemly beautiful green, nicely cured grass hay from the plots where nitrogen alone was used was not taken eagerly. It was consumed only as a partial defense against starvation, and it did not keep the rabbits from getting dangerously close to that before their death was prevented by shifting the ration. Other rabbits given grass hay from plots that had no soil treatment maintained themselves, consuming the ration more completely. In dealing with a ration of fertility elements for plants, we too commonly consider the plant's ration as merely the sum of the separate items. We think of calcium, plus nitrogen, plus phosphorus, plus each of all the others necessary. These are taken into the plant and eventually delivered through it to the manger and thereby to the animal for its use. Through chemical analysis of plants—after we have burned off the carbon, hydrogen, oxygen and other contributions of weather origin—we believe that soil fertility is a collection of some 10 or more elements taken from the soil for the use of animal and human bodies.

This concept suggests that, if that is all we need to do, we might just as well use a shovel and truck to haul calcium and magnesium as limestone from the crusher to the mineral box. As a curative help to an animal already in disaster this may have some value. It illustrates the widespread failure to appreciate the fact that plant nutrition is not as simple as limestone, plus phosphate, plus potash, plus any other thing in any amount merely dumped on the soil to produce crops to haul to the feeding rack. An important matter in plant nutrition is the fact that plants must eat where they are. Unlike the cow, they can't pass up readily the place where there is too much nitrogen or, rather in the converse, where there is not enough of nutrient elements of distinctly mineral origin to better balance the nitrogen in their ration. Consequently, they run their manufacturing business of synthesizing the fertility of the soil into organic combinations by means of air and water the best they can. As a result, plants must naturally vary widely in their chemical composition, even if folks in regulatory services contend that they do not. If there is much nitrogen, they weave this into chemical combinations with carbon, hydrogen, etc. that build a lot of green vegetable bulk which may not keep the plant from lodging and may not result in seed to keep the species multiplying. Plants must weave as the woof and warp permit. But the plant is doing as the soil conditions demand, whether we call it too much of some or not enough of others.

"GROW" FOODS OR ONLY "GO" FOODS, ACCORDING TO THE SOIL

That the soil and its *internal supplies of essential plant nutrients* should be involved in this sudden appearance of the problem of a food shortage may seem far-fetched. This internal situation of the soil has not been a change as an explosive disaster. It has been coming on gradually. Absorbed in reshuffling economic and social situations involving peoples and votes, the fertility of the soil as the foundation of agricultural production was being exported or lost to the rivers and the sea, without our notice or appreciation of it. Hidden away, as many of us may heedlessly believe ourselves to be in the midst of our extensive continent, we have been content with its liberal stores of fertility; not so much of it in the soils of the East, but more in the deposits of glacial drifts as ground and well-mixed rock materials to provide plant nutrients generously in the central states; and then still more in the chernozems or the fertile black prairie soils along the shelter belt where bisons once roamed but where now wheat and Hereford cattle thrive. We have had little occasion to believe that the soil and its capacity to provide mineral rich "grow" foods rather than only the woody "go" foods are of profound significance in the present world war. We are coming, in an international way, to appreciate the truth of the Russian proverb which says "An empty stomach knows no laws."

The soil is the ultimate foundation of all life. It supplies the basic dozen (possibly more) chemical elements that are the nutrients coming from there as ash. The soil contributes those to serve in our vegetation as the means of fabricating the carbon required. Our animals, their health and rates of reproduction have reflected this disposition on our part to look to the crop and to disregard the soil. We have been unable to grow our animals to greater maturity. We have been marketing them younger. We have been changing our breed types and searching for other breed types as the exhaustion of the fertility of our soil has been going on without our heed of it.

Increasing animal "diseases" have likewise been telling us that the store of fertility in our soil is declining. New kinds of "diseases," for which the physiological bases are still unknown, are on the increase. Eye troubles, acetonomia, rickets, milk fever in cattle, and pregnancy diseases in sheep are illustrations of what has been coming into prominence as animal manifestations labelled "disease," when very probably such ought to be traced back to a deficient nutrition coming by way of declining soil fertility. Certainly our national health picture as it is coming into clearer view from the data collected in assembling our armed forces will give us a clear conviction that our health is determined according to the soil. This view should likewise bring into focus the international picture as it rests on the different soils. Regardless of the multiplicity of colors that may be involved, the picture should have but a single caption as a forceful reminder of what has been said in part before, namely, our national health, as well as "our national wealth, lies in our soils."

BOTH SOIL AND PLANTS ARE RESPONSIBLE

Only slowly are we coming around to realize that the variable fertility of the soil brings about variation in the chemical composition of the vegetation grown on it. The name of the species, and even the variety of the plant, seem to have set up an implicit faith in the minds of many that they determine the plant's chemical make-up. That faith, or belief, is so completely accepted that even the section of federal controls concerned with proper labeling of foods and drugs, contends in print—and in court—that the soil does not influence the chemical composition of the crop it grows. But when our animals, both wild and domestic, demonstrate their discrimination within the same plant species and variety which they will take from one field and soil but not from another; or when the cow refuses to eat the grass growing taller and greener where there are fecal or urinary droppings, while she eats the short grass around it shorter, there is clear-cut evidence that different soils, or the same soil given different fertility treatments, cause different chemical compositions of the same kind of plant growing on them.

The Department of Soils of the University of Missouri cooperated with the section in the Horticultural Department concerned with vegetable gardening in measuring some of the variations in chemical composition of Swiss chard. This was done according to some controlled variations in the soil fertility. Those soil variations were managed by means of the colloidal-clay technique, or by the adsorption of the cationic elements on the clay, and by some of the anionic elements held by some of those cations. The series of elements under carefully controlled applications to the soil included: calcium, magnesium, potassium, nitrogen, phosphorus, and sulfur. The amounts of clay mixed into some quartz sand could be varied, and served to control the total amounts of the nutrient elements available to the plants. The degree of saturation of the clay by each element was the means of varying the ratios of the amounts of one element to another.

The nitrogen and the calcium were the two elements of concern in one of the many tests. Either one varied through the four amounts, namely, 5, 10, 20, and 40 milligram equivalents, (ME) while the other was held constant at one of those corresponding amounts. In one series, the calcium was held at 40 ME and combined with 5, 10, 20, and 40 ME of nitrogen respectively, in triplicates. Then this latter series of amounts of nitrogen was combined with

20 ME of calcium; then another nitrogen series with 10 ME of calcium; and finally still another nitrogen series with 5 ME of calcium. Then there was another complete set of series similar to the one above. The amounts of calcium varied through the four values of 5, 10, 20, and 40 ME. Each of these was used in combination with constants as 40, 20, 10, and 5 ME of nitrogen to give another group of four series.

It was by means of these combinations in the variations of nitrogen and calcium, both connected with protein synthesis by the plant, while the phosphorus, potassium, magnesium, and sulfur were constant at controlled values, that the plants were grown and put under chemical analyses for their concentrations, as percentages of their dry weight, of oxalate, total nitrogen, calcium, magnesium, and phosphorus. Variations in the nitrogen as 5, 10, 20, and 40 ME in combination with high calcium at 40 ME gave concentrations of calcium in the Swiss chard varying from 0.748 to 1.032%, respectively, in the increasing order with increasing nitrogen additions to the soil. The highest concentration of calcium in the chard was an increase of 38% over the lowest one. The mean of the four was 0.889% of calcium in the chard.

With the 20 ME of calcium as the constant soil treatment in combination with the varied nitrogen, there resulted the variation in concentrations of calcium from a low of 0.676 to a high of 0.784%. This was an increase by the latter over the former of 16%, but not in any order in relation to the increase in nitrogen applied. The mean was 0.739%. Then with 10 ME of calcium, the varied nitrogen gave concentrations of calcium in the chard varying from 0.600 to 0.824. This was an increase of 37%, while the mean of the lot was 0.737%. Then with 10 ME of calcium, the varied nitrogen gave concentrations of calcium in the chard varying from 0.600 to 0.824. This was an increase of 37%, while the mean of the lot was 0.737%.

But when the calcium was held at a constant in the soil with 5 ME per plant and combined with the four variations in nitrogen, the concentrations of calcium in this vegetable's "greens" spread from a low of 0.488 to a high of 0.820, an increase of 68% and a mean of the lot at 0.630%. In these four series the concentrations of only calcium varied as much as 16, 37, 38 and 68 %. Can one say there are no differences in the chemical composition due to changes in the soil fertility?

This illustrates the variations of the calcium concentrations in this vegetable because (1) the amount of calcium offered in the soil varied, and (2) another nutrient like nitrogen in the soil was varied in each series even though the amount of calcium there was constant.

According as the supply of calcium in the soil went lower, the mean concentration of it in the Swiss chard also went lower. But the effects of the individual combinations in calcium with nitrogen as soil treatments were not consistent in the order at which the concentration of calcium in this plant decreased. The four mean values of calcium concentrations in the plant for the four amounts of it in the soil (40,20, 10, 5 ME) were 0.889, 0.739, 0.737, and 0.630. These serve to point out that with the highest and the lowest offering of calcium in the soil, the concentrations in the plant were decidedly the highest and decidedly the lowest. But for the two intermediate offerings in the soil namely, 20 and 10 ME, the means of concentrations in the plants were 0.739 and 0.732%. There was no wide spread. These suggest by the more uniform concentrations in the crop what the more favorable concentrations in the soil for it are.

In this test it was clearly demonstrated that calcium, which is the inorganic element required from the soil for our bodies in larger amounts than is any other element, varies in its concentration in the Swiss chard. This variation is not only according to the variable amount of calcium active in the soil, but also according to the company it keeps with varied amounts of nitrogen there. Now that nitrogen in its various chemical forms is applied to the soil so extensively and so generously, there are decided variations in the concentrations of other elements in the vegetable greens consumed by both man and animals. The concentrations in the Swiss chard of the magnesium, coming from a constant supply in the soil, varied with the different levels of calcium there. The mean values for the concentrations of magnesium in the plants were 0.437, 0.705, 0.520, and 0.425 for the accompanying 40, 20, 10, and five ME of calcium. Between the highest and lowest, the former was an increase of 65 percent over the latter. This tells us that the metabolic functions within the plant are also factors, or determiners, of the amounts of fertility elements taken from the soil.

The plant's performance in building concentrations of elements within itself are functions not entirely of amounts offered as soil fertility. Only at certain amounts of each element in its relation to each of the others as their combination represents a "balance," or suitable integration of their separate nutritional effects, are there the maximum effects of each expressed in the plant growth in what would seem to be most efficient growth and higher values of it as feed and food. The imbalance of the fertility in the soil seems to reflect itself in the oxalic acid which the chard synthesizes, as an organic compound that combines with the calcium and magnesium that makes insoluble and indigestible oxalates of them. It puts them out of chemical action in the plant. These interrelations are best shown in the bar graphs in figure 1.

By increasing the nitrogen as the variable in the soil, while the calcium and other elements were constant, each increase put (1) higher concentrations of calcium into the plant, save for the highest application of nitrogen, (2) more magnesium there in the same order, and (3) pushed up the concentration of oxalate tremendously. By increasing the calcium as the variable while nitrogen and other elements were constant, each increase put (1) more calcium into the plant, (2) more magnesium there, save for the highest offering of calcium, and most significantly, (3) almost the same amounts of oxalate as its means of reducing the excesses of those two elements by making insoluble and also indigestible when eaten.

Nature demonstrates everywhere this simple fact that the plant, per se, does not determine its final chemical composition as nutritional values to man and beast. The fertility of the soil is the main determiner of that. The plant as a species has limits within which it operates. Those operations are limited also by the fertility of the soil.

For quality as nutrition in our vegetables we must (1) choose the species and (2) manage the fertility of the soil growing them. Then, if as our animals do, we take them raw and fresh "right off the stump," we shall demonstrate our eating as one for health's sake just as our wild animals demonstrate how they use their food and not drugs and medicines to keep themselves healthy.

PHOSPHORUS IN CROP VARIES WITH NITROGEN APPLIED

In the preceding article, the concentrations of calcium and magnesium were rereported for Swiss Chard, pointing out how widely these properties varied when the amount of nitrogen applied to the soil was varied. Those chemical examinations of this vegetable demonstrated clearly that *fertilization with the nitrogen salt, ammonium nitrate, (1) decreased the concentrations of the ash—or inorganic—elements, calcium and magnesium in the chard; (2) increased its concentration of nitrogen, and, (3) increased the crop yield as "greens."* It is significant that the first effect listed above was a decrease and the last two were increases—all brought about only by increasing applications of this one fertilizer salt. Those data point out clearly the error in the common belief and contention that soil fertility treatments, giving increases in crop yields, bring no changes in the concentrations of the essential elements, and no changes in the nutritional values of such vegetable crops. *Yet there was a decrease of the bone-building element, calcium, within each unit weight of the chard when its yield was increased.* More yield from heavier fertilization gave less nutrition as calcium per unit of this food.

Then, to make still larger the mistake in disregarding such changes in the concentrations of the elements caused by changes in the soil fertility, there occurred a higher concentration of the oxalate synthesized by the crops according as the soil treatment with nitrogen was increased. Oxalate is the organic substance which makes both the calcium and magnesium insoluble as compounds with it and thereby indigestible. All this suggested itself as really a case of "adding insult to injury" in terms of food quality or nutritional values of the crop. First there was "injury" in the lowered concentrations of the calcium and magnesium. Then, second, there was "insult" in the increased oxalate made by the plant to make even those lowered concentrations insoluble and indigestible.

Since calcium plays its major role in the building of our bones, with almost its total in our skeletons; and since it is in combination mainly with phosphorus there, though also in other body parts, like the blood, it is significant to note how the concentration of phosphorus in the vegetable, Swiss Chard, was modified by the fertilization of the soil with the nitrogen salt. Here again, the chemical data pointed out that the concentrations of phosphorus in the chard decreased as more nitrogen was applied to the soil. This property of these "greens," as single determinations, varied from a low of 0.85% to a high of 2.67% in the dry matter. This makes the plant look like a decided deceiver when it plays the phosphorus it gives us per mouthful over a range as wide as 300% difference. This happened when the phosphorus offered by the soil was constant. Such deception in the bone-building element, phosphorus, which plays important enzymic roles also in giving the body energy, was brought about because the company it kept with the nitrogen was the disturber of its behavior.

Phosphorus was measured only in its total amounts, and not in its different possible combinations with calcium as different solubilities. In nature, the element phosphorus is almost universally coupled with four units of oxygen per one of itself. This makes the phosphate anion, two of which with three of calcium ions to give tricalcium phosphate. This is a rather insoluble compound. But the two phosphate radicals may also make their combination with only two calcium and two hydrogen ions, as dicalcium phosphate. This is an acid phosphate of a bit higher solubility. Then, again, the two phosphate anions may also combine with only one calcium—coupled with four hydrogen ions—to give their most soluble and acid compound, monocalcium phosphate. Variation in the amount as total phosphorus does not tell us how it varied in these different combinations with calcium serving in the plant's or other body processes as different degrees of acidity, and different activities of both the phosphorus and the calcium in nutrition.

These facts make the combination of phosphorus and calcium a more unique one of these soil-borne elements in the warmblooded bodies than is generally appreciated. They connect such bodies more directly and strongly with the soil fertility than we are apt to believe in speaking of "soil and nutrition."

IMPORTANCE OF PHOSPHORUS IN SOIL IS
SHOWN IN COLLEGE EXPERIMENT
A PRESS RELEASE

It is commonly believed, says William A. Albrecht, head of the soils department, University of Missouri, that soil phosphorus is mainly useful to insure a good "set" of seed, to increase grain yields and promote sturdy root growth. But its value is not limited to these benefits. In annual plants like the grasses, an increase in root development (size) due to phosphorus has not been clearly demonstrated. However, since phosphorus is essential for cell reproduction, it should also play an important part in the production of new growth, as when grasses are cut frequently or grazed closely.

In greenhouse experiments at the Missouri Agricultural Experiment Station, it was found that frequent cuttings of a young crop of grass provide a good clue to the amount of available phosphorus in the soil. For rapid and repeated growth recovery, the grasses require an ample supply of active soil phosphorus. This is clearly demonstrated in the accompanying illustration, which shows the results of a test using oats.

This experiment suggests that repeated cuttings of a young, growing grass crop provide a better test of how well the soil fertility is balanced than does the measurement of total yield in the mature crop. The failure of young oats to put on new growth quickly after a number of cuttings indicates a shortage of one or more of the important soil nutrients. Differences due to a poor supply of soil phosphorus show up in the early stages of plant growth. It is equally clear that phosphorus is needed as a help for quick recovery of grass after cutting or grazing. This indicates the importance of the statewide system of soil testing laboratories in Missouri's campaign for pasture-livestock farming. The first step on any farm is to take stock of the soil fertility as related to the pasture crops to be grown.

We must remember that phosphorus is not so effective when used only in surface applications, cautions Albrecht. It must be put down into the soil, since it does not move downward readily.

Phosphorus, like all other elements of fertility, must be built down into the soil as much as possible at the outset of the establishment of a more permanent pasture. The surface applications can be added later. Pasture shortages due to summer droughts may be more or less serious—depending on the lack or abundance of phosphorus in the soil. Sometimes the losses attributed to drought may in reality be due to starvation for phosphorus, the fertility element that its help in keeping young grasses is generally not appreciated for active in their vegetative reproduction.

Grasses can recover each cutting (or grazing) only when they are well fed by the soil.

SOIL NITROGEN AND VITAMIN C IN PLANTS

The variable fertility of the soil causes the plant to vary in its chemical composition. This includes not only the concentrations of chemical elements it takes up from the soil, but also the compounds it creates, whether these serve as materials of construction of the plant's body or as tools in the energy-releasing and tissue-building processes. Nitrogen, applied now so extensively and generously as a fertilizer salt when by no means a large share of the applications is taken by the crop, is disturbing even the concentration of the vitamin C synthesized by spinach (Bloomsdale long-standing) for example, for the high concentration of which vitamin this garden "greens" is commonly recommended. In some studies by the Missouri Agricultural Experiment Station, the nitrogen of the soil was varied through a range of 5, 10, 20 and 40 milligram-equivalents (ME) per two plants, with each amount in combination with one amount (in replicates of 10) of that same series of allotments of calcium. This study demonstrated what such soil treatments—used particularly to modify the protein production by legume crops—would do in modifying the production of vitamin C in this garden vegetable, considered a good dietary source for this vitamin.

Vitamin C is not similar to proteins in either chemical composition or molecular structure. In fact, it is more nearly like a carbohydrate, or like glucose. It contains six carbon atoms, and six of oxygen, just as glucose does. But where the latter has 12 of hydrogen, this vitamin has but eight, and by no means in similar molecular arrangements. These atomic and molecular properties make it resemble the sugars and not the proteins. It is very likely a modification, by the plant's metabolic processes, of the sugars of photosynthetic origin. The variations in the amount of the nitrogen applied to the soil gave decided variation in the amount of this preventor of scurvy in relation to the yield of the crop. These facts are graphically shown in figure 1.

With the increased applications of nitrogen, the first three of those gave increased yields, one over the other, but the fourth and highest application did not extend the increase. Instead it reduced the yield. The concentration of the vitamin C in the plants was highest in the smallest crop. Here, then, the concentration of the vitamin shows an inverse relation to the vegetative bulk produced. As there is more growth, that extra production seems to carry on without requiring such high concentrations of the vitamin C, which is a catalyst or tool and not part of the construction of the tissue. This suggests that vitamin C serves as a stimulator of the speed of the chemical processes within the plant, much as the rider's whip serves in case of the race horse. Seemingly, when the fertility elements in the soil are out of balance, with even only one element like the nitrogen in this case responsible as either a deficiency or an excess, then the plant increases the concentration of the catalyst. Seemingly, it "whips" the chemical processes more to bring about the growth of the plants.

Some striking correlations of the ascorbic acid, or vitamin C with the inorganic composition of the spinach were evident. When the concentrations of this vitamin were high in the spinach, those of magnesium and nitrogen were low. Neither potassium nor magnesium suggested any connection of themselves with ascorbic acid. Of added interest was the fact that the concentrations of calcium and phosphorus—usually associated more prominently with anabolic than with katobolic or respiratory processes—were parallel to those of this vitamin. These facts exhibited by the spinach suggest that within the plant, like within our bodies, there are variations in the processes of metabolism to make adjustments for the variation in the nutrients which the soil offers to feed the plant. Unfortunately for the plant, it is fixed in location and limited in the volume of soil which its root zone can encompass. It cannot break out, like some hogs, and help itself to the better feed of its choice from the neighbor's lot. Perhaps we shall be appreciating more the need to consider the nutritional quality, rather than only the yield, of the vegetables as they represent nutrition for us.

VARIED SOIL POTASSIUM MEANS VARIED ORGANIC VALUES

In the preceding reports it was shown how the variation in the supply of nitrogen in the soil brings about wide differences in the inorganic compositions of vegetable crops, especially in the concentrations of the calcium, the magnesium and the phosphorus. Then it brings also wide variations in concentration of the vitamin C, an organic compound of nutritional value; and also of the oxalate, another organic compound created by the plant. But the oxalate prohibits the calcium and magnesium from serving in their functions as soluble and active nutrient elements. It is well, therefore, that attention be given to another soluble inorganic element commonly added to the soil in fertilizers and also leached from the soil—namely, potassium—to see how the variation of it causes varied plant compositions.

In studies at the Missouri Agricultural Experiment Station, soybeans were grown on soil which was varied only in the amount of "available" or exchangeable potassium in it. All other elements were at fixed values at the outset. Since the soybean crop is a legume, and can therefore take nitrogen from the atmosphere for its synthesis of protein—if it has the legume bacteria for root-nodule production—the first crop was grown on the soil which was kept sterile or free of those necessary bacteria. Since the bacteria may be accidentally introduced, the second and third crops, grown on these soils to test the effects of the exhaustion of the soil fertility on the plant composition, were not kept sterile. They had nodules and took or "fixed" nitrogen from the atmosphere because of the bacterial inoculation introduced on planting the second crop to serve also for the third crop. Here, then, we could see the effects of varied potassium on the chemical composition of the soybean plants when this same plant species was behaving physiologically as a non-legume in the first crop, then as a legume in the second and third crops. We could also observe the effects of exhausting the soil of its fertility, since three successive crops of soybeans from the same "mother-source" of seed were grown and carefully removed—roots and all—from the soil for analysis of each crop. No additions of fertility were made after the initial soil treatments. The largest crop yields when growing as the non-legume, first crop; the lowest yields as the legume, second crop; then the intermediate yield as another legume crop under more soil fertility depletion are shown in figure 1.

While many extensive chemical analyses were made, it is significant to note—at this time—the effects of the varied supply of potassium in the soil on only the sugar and starch in the plant tissue as the concentrations of them are related to the yields of the crop. You are doubtless familiar with the differences in sweetness of peas, if you have observed different varieties of them for this quality. There are differences in sweetness also according to the different soils on which the same variety is grown. Perhaps your "sweet-tooth" is not sensitive to sugar in "greens" but even the cow has a "sweet-tooth" when by spraying saccharin (a sweet, non-sugar chemical) on crops, one can tempt her to take plants she would otherwise not eat.

The sugar represents the form in which the plant produces its combination of carbon, hydrogen, and oxygen as carbohydrates, the plant's own energy foods and ours also, from sunshine power. Starch, also a carbohydrate but of different molecular arrangement, is the plant's storage or reserve form of its energy food supply. Four levels of potassium were used, namely 0, 5, 10 and 15 milligram equivalents (ME) per 50 plants, as the varied additions to the soil. The crops were harvested before the blossoms formed, and analyzed as vegetable matter and not as seed harvests. The differences in the concentrations of the sugar and the starch in the soybeans grown in triplicates for each of the three successive crops at the four levels of potassium in the soil, or the twelve conditions, are shown graphically in the two figures. They show the impressive revelations of what varied compositions and nutritional values are brought about in the vegetation when only one nutritive element, potassium in the soil, is varied.

The figure 1 reveals also how the crop which is a legume by pedigree, but behaving as a non-legume in the absence of nodule bacteria, grows more vegetative yield when it may be losing nitrogen from the plants to the soil, or may have less nitrogen in the crop (roots and tops) than there was in the planted seed. Then, behaving as a legume in cooperation with nodule-bacteria, how it may be taking nitrogen from the air and building itself higher in concentration of protein by that means, but may be giving smaller vegetative yields. The first crop behaving as a non-legume contained less nitrogen than the 318 mgms. of the planted seeds by 26.0, 23.8, 17.9 and

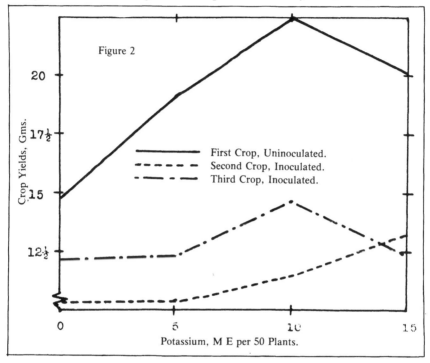

Figure 2

First Crop, Uninoculated.
Second Crop, Inoculated.
Third Crop, Inoculated.

Crop Yields, Gms.

Potassium, M E per 50 Plants.

23.6%, respectively. The behavior of this crop vacillated between that of a non-legume and a legume.

As the fertility of the soil was lowered by successive crop removals, the soy-beans moved to store much starch and to fix less nitrogen from the at-mosphere. They became a crop to fatten more than to grow animals so far as the nutritional services they offered are concerned. When the non-legume behaviors represented but crop bulk of lower sugar and higher starch accord-ing as there was increasing potassium fertilization (figure 2) while the legume behaviors represented high sugars and low starch in the second crop and before the soils were more highly exhausted by successive cropping, can any one in truth and in honesty contend that the fertility of the soil is no factor of significance in controlling the chemical composition of the crop growing on the soil?

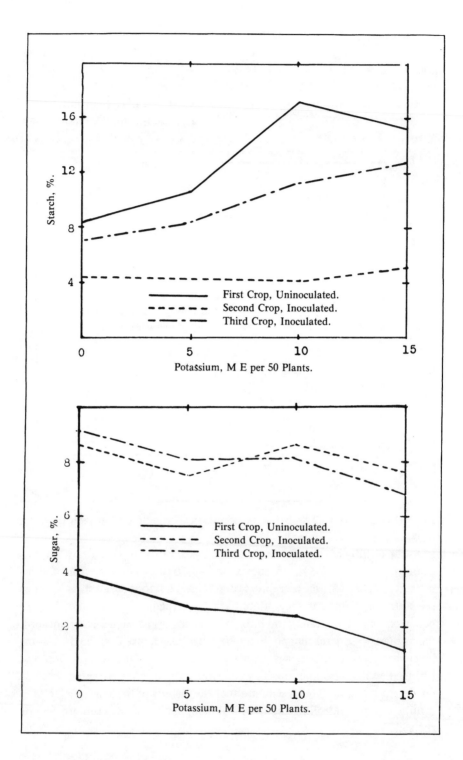

First Crop, Uninoculated.
Second Crop, Inoculated.
Third Crop, Inoculated.

Potassium, M E per 50 Plants.

First Crop, Uninoculated.
Second Crop, Inoculated.
Third Crop, Inoculated.

Potassium, M E per 50 Plants.

Only slowly will we realize that it is the soil that creates and sustains us, with wide differences in quality thereof as the fertility of the soil varies. Here is a clear cut exhibition of the much neglected fact that the soil determines the chemical compositions, both inorganic and organic of the crops we grow.

"BALANCED" SOIL FERTILITY REQUIRES HIGH PHOSPHOROUS

The essential nutrient element, phosphorus, represented an unusually large part of the earlier kinds of commercial fertilizers. They carried then, and still carry, nitrogen, phosphorus and potassium as their fertility contents for legal and labelling purposes under the common N-P-K symbols. There was originally a wide ratio between the phosphorus and each of the other two constituents of the fertilizers when the mixtures were labelled 2-10-2 and 2-12-2, with the three elements present in the 1-5-1 and 1-6-1 ratios respectively. Now that the nitrogen (N) and the potassium (K) have more recently been increased in the mixtures to give a 1-1-1 ratio like the 12-12-12, for example, which is emphasized for the economic advantages in handling the more concentrated material, this ratio may be nutritionally disturbing if not even detrimental to the growth of the plants. This "pushing up" of these companion elements of the phosphorus has been shown to lessen the amounts and concentrations of the phosphorus going into the vegetable matter grown for consumption as human and animal foods. This says nothing of the synthesizing processes within the crops which may be disturbed to give us less of the organic compounds the plants create for our nutritional benefits not yet cataloged.

More recently human food supplements, carrying organic phosphorus compounds of higher concentrations, have come into extensive use to the dismay and counter campaigns by some organized groups of folks. But since the consumers are recognizing the improvements in health resulting from the use of such supplements of organic phosphorus, it might be of broader health service if we should reconsider the phosphorus problem in the soil for crops. We need to remind ourselves, first, that in cases of the humid soils, where the most abundant agriculture is located, those soils have always been low in their phosphorus supply. They havè shown their responses to applied phosphorus by better crops most extensively through animal choice of forage and better nutrition of both animals and man. The legumes in both their forages and seeds have been the commercial supplements to home-grown feeds to the point of having become big business. Those legumes render better service as nutritional supplements in the humid region when grown on soils treated with both calcium and phosphorus. All of these facts suggest that perhaps phosphorus deficiencies may be the cause of "hidden hungers" more often and more seriously than we realize and recognize only under clinical symptoms; and then not unless we find such manifestations of health troubles occurring repeatedly in the same body part. Animals indicate their phosphorus deficiencies by depraved appetites. Shall we not entertain the thought that extensive shortages of phosphorus in the soil for our protein-producing crops might mean deficiencies of organic phosphorus compounds for humans?

If then some food supplements, like organic phosphorus compounds are used with satisfaction to better health by a few individuals, it would seem well to consider health on a national scale or pattern, and to study the services by such supplements to human foods in their relation to the climatic pattern of soil development. Would it not be well to investigate whether phosphorus deficiencies in human nutrition are as extensive and serious as they are in plant nutrition in a given soil area? This would seem wise when phosphorus shortage in the soil has made phosphatic compounds big fertilizer business—for healthier crops and healthier animals. Then when the nitrogen and potassium are pushed up in their fertilizer ratio to phosphorus, which as an imbalance in the plant's diet is apt to cut down the concentrations of the latter in the crops, may we not be undermining the health of plants, animals and man by bringing on phosphorus deficiencies as hidden hungers? It would seem wise to test that question by feeding ourselves organic phosphorus supplements to learn if better health does not result. If it does, such results would tell us that the food supplement would not be necessary if we would study the soil and provide "balanced" fertility in relation to the composition of the plants for their better nutritional values. Health from the ground up would be preferred by all to any health patched up by antidotes and hypodermic needles.

BACTERIA HELP LEGUME ROOTS MOBILIZE FERTILITY

When the hotel menu sets the price of the dinner according to the meat, fish or eggs you choose, one is reminded that we, like all forms of life, are constantly faced with a struggle for the necessary proteins. In feeding livestock, the protein concentrates are, as supplements to the carbohydrate crops we grow on many soils so widely, a serious economic problem. Whether we are growing the garden or the field crops, enough of nitrogen, and also calcium phosphorus, magnesium, potassium and all else of the inorganic elements that must accompany the nitrogen, represent the plants' struggle to make its protein.

Since it is the protein which carries life in its compounds in any living body or tissue, the struggle for proteins is simply the struggle to survive. If the living tissue of the microbes, plants, animals and man cannot add protein unto itself, it cannot grow, protect itself or reproduce its kind. Plants may survive at low concentrations of proteins in their tissue by requiring less from the soil. But then what they are has less food value for animals consuming them. Legume plants, which require—as we well know—much fertility from the soil, will use not only such to build more protein for higher nutritional services to livestock eating them, but they will also use the microbes in their nodules on the roots to make those parts of the plant more efficient producers of the plant's parts above the ground. Legumes can create and contain so much higher concentrations of proteins than the non-legume plants because their nodule bacteria make the roots more efficient in taking fertility from the soil via the extra nitrogen taken from the soil atmosphere.

Because legume plants contain higher concentrations of protein in relation to their concentrations of carbohydrates than non-legumes do, the former as forages are used as protein supplements to the latter to give the animal more nearly a balanced ration for efficient nutrition. Just as there is a problem of balancing the ration for the animal, so there is the problem of balancing the fertility for the plant in order to have protein of biosynthetic origin in the plant tissue to balance the carbohydrates of photosynthetic origin.

Calcium (and phosphorus) are associated with the plant's production of the proteins, especially so in the legumes. Potassium is associated with the plant's production of the carbohydrates. Consequently the ratio of the calcium to the potassium in the soil growing the crop must be considered in balancing the nutrition of it to make proteins rather than mainly carbohydrates. Balancing the diet of the plant—regardless of the kind of plant—must be planned as a way of managing the crop's nutritional quality rather than only its quantity as yields. On the humid soils of eastern United States, limestone as addition of calcium (and magnesium) to the soil is our major fertilizer. As a pulverized natural rock, it is the chemical means of encouraging the plant's synthesis of proteins. Such is the case for both legumes and non-legumes.

But for the higher concentrations of proteins in the legumes, the bacteria-producing nodules on the legume roots must also be active on the soil as well as the higher fertility. These microbes, bringing nitrogen from the atmosphere to give higher concentration of protein in the roots, make those subterranean parts of the leguminous plants more efficient feeders of themselves, to grow the entire plants more efficiently. In an experimental attempt to demonstrate the truth of the above hypothesis, the clay separated out of the soil was electrodialyzed and given different treatments to let it carry calcium—in amounts of 10 and 20 milligram equivalents (ME) per soil unit. Then with each of these amounts of calcium on the clay, there were combined 5, 10, and 15 ME of potassium as the soil units for growing soybean plants. Then sets of each of these series were given inoculations of the nodule-producing bacteria, while corresponding sets of the series were kept sterile of those bacteria.

The plants of the inoculated series used nitrogen from the soil air, to be added to the plant's nitrogen from the seed. Those series produced plants of high concentrations of protein. The sterile series of plants were limited to the nitrogen supply originally in the seed. The former behaved physiologically like legumes do naturally. The latter plants, though classified as legumes by their pedigrees, were compelled to behave physiologically like non-legumes because of the absence of nodule-forming bacteria.

It would not commonly be granted that even for plant yields, we can apply the old adage which says, "More precious things come in smaller packages." Nevertheless, such was the case of the inoculated crops grown in these tests. As normal legumes taking nitrogen from the air to be higher in concentration of protein, they had smaller yields than the sterile, non-legume crops of soybeans (figure 1). This was true whether the increased offerings of calcium ($Ca = 10$, $Ca = 20$ ME) by the soil gave increased yields, or whether the increased offerings of potassium (5, 10, and 15 ME) gave similar effects.

These results tell us forcefully that by using only crop bulk as the measure of what a legume crop is doing in response to soil treatments, we may be decidedly mistaken about the soil as it is modifying the nutritional quality of the crop as forage feed. It is the fertility of the soil and not the plant's pedigree which determines the nutritional value of what we grow.

MICROBES GIVE LEGUMES THEIR PROTEIN POWER

In the previous discussion there were cited (a) the lowered vegetative yields of soybean plants, and (b) the higher ratio of plant tops to roots, when the nodule-producing bacteria for this legume were applied to the seed and thus introduced into the soil. The yields varied as more potassium and calcium were absorbed on the clay to be "available" for exchange to the plant roots and yet not be in solution in water for dangerous "salt" effects or for loss in drainage. Those differences in but two elements—the inorganic fertility of the soil and the organic living differences in the microbes present as another and lower form of life accompanying the soybean plants—served to alter both the mass and the anatomy of them. The organic part of the soil as cause of change in the plant compositions has not been appreciated or widely recognized. Some folks, even in national offices of food authority, still insist that even the inorganic fertility of the soil cannot change the chemical composition of the crop, much less its nutritional values as feed and food. The differences in plant composition due to inoculation by microbes serve readily to expose the ignorance of such insistence.

The soybeans were grown as two series, with and without inoculation provided, representing two levels of calcium (10 and 20 ME) of which each was in combination with three levels (5, 10, and 15 ME) of potassium in the soil. The plants were grown and then chemically analyzed for their concentrations of the three cations exchangeable from the clay—namely potassium, calcium and magnesium. They were analyzed also for two anions—phosphorus and silicon. It is sufficient at this time to cite the variations in the concentrations of only the three cations. As the soils were inorganically different—in either calcium or potassium—it is more significant to cite them due to a difference as small as the presence of one single species of microbe, the *root-nodule bacteria*.

The story of the chemical composition differences of the crops is told most simply by the accompanying graphs. The left half shows the concentrations of potassium as lines A and B; of calcium, as lines C and D; and of magnesium, as lines E and F, according to the varied potassium applied in combination with 10 ME of calcium on the soil. The first of each of those pairs of lines, namely A, C and E, represents the concentration of the particular cation in the inoculated plants. The second line of the pair, namely B, D and F, represents the concentrations of the cations in the plants grown on soils (or plants) not inoculated, or sterile of the legume bacteria.

The right half of the figure is a similar presentation of the effects on plant composition by these same varied levels of potassium in the soil combined with 20 ME of calcium when both are adsorbed on the clay. The scale of concentrations of potassium is shown on the left side of the figure since it is a higher one than the single scale on the right of the figure suitable for the concentrations of either calcium or magnesium, normally within closely similar ranges of concentrations. The different kinds of lines were used by pairs to represent each of the separate cations for plants inoculated and not inoculated, as shown in the legend. The most significant fact exhibited by the graphical picture is the fact that, because of the introduction of legume bacteria into the soil, the soybean plants put higher concentrations of the three cations into themselves. This is clearly shown when the potassium line A (inoculated) is higher on the scale than line B (not inoculated). Similarly the calcium line C is higher on the scale than line D; and the magnesium line E is higher there than line F, regardless of whether the calcium level was 10 ME or 20 ME. These are decided increases in the capacity of the plants to concentrate more of each of these three inorganic essentials into each unit of vegetation, for example, merely because some particular microbes were present in the soil. Unfortunately, we have not studied the differences which might occur in foods because of other kinds of microbes, present or absent, in soil.

It is also important to note that the concentration of calcium in the inoculated soybean plants was not depressed much by the higher amounts of potassium in the soil, but it was depressed decidedly in the plants not inoculated. The concentration of magnesium in the plants was depressed decidedly by increases in the potassium of the soil, but much more so in the not-inoculated plants than in those inoculated. In examining the results of this study, we need to remind ourselves that the non-nodulated roots of greater mass per plant had the same amount of clay with which to make contact for plant nutrition as the nodulated roots did. Nevertheless, the concentrations of the potassium, calcium and magnesium were higher in the nodulated plants with less masses of roots per plant, because of cooperative help from the bacteria. Here there were decided differences in the chemical compositions of the plants as the result of a small organic difference—namely, the bacteria in the soil. There were also differences in the concentrations of the calcium and the magnesium in the plants because of differences in the potassium in the soil. Can one say with truth, then, that the fertility of the soil does not cause the chemical compositions and nutritive values of a crop to vary?

FERTILITY EFFECTS SHOW EARLY IN PLANTS

The study of non-leguminous plants fails to reveal the force of the soil fertility in bringing about chemical composition differences of plants, which one appreciates more by studying the *legumes* as producers of higher concentrations of proteins and inorganic essential elements. The variation in nitrogen metabolism of the latter may serve as an index of the nutrition elements' irregularities, other than nitrogen. In past articles, the fluctuation in the nitrogen metabolism—measurable by differences in plant growth, degree of nodule production, nitrogen concentration and content, and nitrogen fixation—has been demonstrated *influences* of other elements such as calcium, phosphorus, magnesium, potassium, etc. on the plants' behavior in accordance with the soil treatments by such and others.

Since legumes do not grow well on the highly developed soils of eastern United States unless limestone is applied to them—since that treatment is effective not so much because its carbonate reduces the degree of soil acidity, but because its calcium (and magnesium) nourish the plant so much better than is possible on the untreated soil—it seemed wise to learn how early in the life of soybeans (a legume) and limestone would be effective.

Soybean seeds, sterilized to destroy possible nodule-producing bacteria, were planted into calcium-deficient sand. Similar seeds were planted into the same kind of sand given pulverized limestone at the rate of five tons per two million pounds, simulating a heavy application of limestone. After a 10 day germinating and growth period, these plants were taken up, washed carefully and transplanted as two separate sections into an acid soil (pH 5.5) which had been growing well-inoculated soybeans in the field.

From both halves, harvesting of 50 seedlings each were taken (roots and tops) at 10-day intervals. These were measured for (a) plant height, (b) dry weight, and for (c) nitrogen content from which concentrations could be calculated. The data for these three criteria of the limestone's effect on the plants' lives, when in contact with the limestone during only the first 10 days of its life, are graphically shown in the accompanying chart. The data include only the time the plants were in the soil. The plant age is 10 days more than the figures used and includes the 10 days germination and growth in the sand. It is interesting to note that calcium increased the height of the plants, even if it did not increase their weight. Also the nodules, not graphically reported, increased in numbers earlier as the result of the contact with calcium at the beginning of the plants' life. The nitrogen increase in the plant started earlier as the result of the calcium nutrition in those early days of growth.

It is quite unusual that the calcium-fed plants increased their nitrogen by 18.4% over the calcium-starved plants during the first 10-day period of growth in the soil, even before they had produced nodules. Then calcium in the roots made them more effective in taking nitrogen from the soil's supply. During the second 10 day period and the advent of nodules, the calcium-fed plants again increased their nitrogen content faster than the calcium-starved ones. The nitrogen increase in the plants fed calcium for the first 10 days of their life over those not so treated amounted to an average of 17% plus for the five 10 day periods measured. These increases in nitrogen content occurred through increased growth rather than increased concentration within the dry matter. This latter was constantly higher in the initially calcium-starved seedlings. Both treatments at the outset in the sand, followed by the in-soil growth, demonstrated the lowering concentrations of nitrogen in the dry matter during these 50 days of plant growth in the soil.

Here was a clear-cut demonstration that there was (a) lengthening of the plant stems, (b) increased metabolism of nitrogen, (c) production of more chlorophyll resulting in greener color, (d) more nitrogen fixation and other increased physiological changes—all modifying the chemical composition as a result of soil treatment (calcium only) of no more time length than the first 10 days of the seed's life and the seedling taking off to make the plant. Surely there is not much constancy in the chemical composition of plants, when contact with limestone for but 10 days makes such differences for the next 50 days of the plant's life!

BIG YIELDS OF BULK—LOW PHOSPHORUS CONCENTRATION

Phosphorus is commonly deficient in the humid soils for their production of feed and food crops. Some 20 years ago, an agronomist, J.G. Hutton, reported, "Phosphorus, when applied alone for 30 years, has increased the yield of all crops."[1] Total chemical analyses of the soil were cited then, and earlier, as indication of the shortage there of this less soluble nutrient for all that grows. Phosphates came into use as fertilizers early in the form of bone meal. Later, basic slag from the steel-smelting furnaces, and rock phosphate from the mines, were additional sources to meet the demand for fertilizer phosphates.

Treatment of bones with sulfuric acid brought the bone phosphorus into more soluble form as "acid phosphate" and helped us to appreciate how rapidly that soluble mono-calcium phosphate reverted to the insoluble tri-calcium phosphate form in soils calcareous enough to grow protein-rich legumes better in consequence of fertilization with phosphorus. As a negatively charged ion, or anion, phosphorus unites with the divalent calcium, a cation, to be insoluble. It unites with the trivalent elements iron and aluminum to become extremely insoluble. As a consequence, the weak carbonic acid of the plant root is not able to activate those forms of phosphate significantly for plant use. The natural mineral phosphate, *apatite*, is also very insoluble. Consequently, with natural mineral phosphates of the soil so insoluble, or so unavailable to the plant roots—and with the total supply of phosphorus in any form in the soil so low—it is readily evident that most crops are growing under a deficiency of this nutrient element.

Since phosphorus is an anion, we cannot expect it to be adsorbed on and exchangeable from the negatively charged colloidal clay molecule, as is the case for the cations—calcium, magnesium, potassium, and others. Consequently, we do not have as clear a picture of its behavior in the soil as we do for the cations. Nevertheless, it behaves according to its anionic properties. In the studies of inoculated soybeans, able to use atmospheric nitrogen—as such legumes can to make themselves mineral rich and protein rich in contrast to uninoculated soybeans behaving like non-legumes and limited to soil or seed nitrogen—it was shown clearly that the phosphorus—like the cations—was taken from the soil to give higher concentrates of it in the plants behaving as legumes. There was also a negative correlation between the vegetative yield and the concentration of phosphorus in it. Also significant is the fact that as the potassium in the soil was increased, the phosphorus concentration in the crop was decreased. (See figure 1).

Thus, with our emphasis on bigger yields of vegetative bulk of soybean

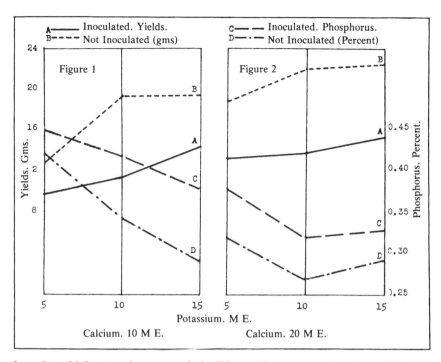

Figure 1

Figure 2

A———— Inoculated. Yields.
B— — — Not Inoculated (gms)

C— — Inoculated. Phosphorus.
D— · — Not Inoculated (Percent)

hay, for which potassium was a help (Figure 1), we are not apt to realize that we are also practicing a deception on the animals expected to feed on it. But such is the case, which may be more of a deception of ourselves in the final analyses. With the increased treatment of the soil with potassium, the concentration of the phosphorus in the forage feed went lower. Silicon—another anion not yet considered an essential element for man and animals though found in hair, hoofs, and nails—was also lowered in its concentrations in the soybean plants, according as the potassium in the soil was higher. (See figure 2). Also, silicon went lower in its concentration very pronouncedly in the plants when the calcium adsorbed on the soil was increased from 10 to 20 milligram equivalents. (Figure 2). Silicon, which is the abundant anion in the soil as remnant of decomposing original rock to give the clay colloid, behaves similarly; as do all the other ions, under the "balanced" effect of the whole group in their respective movements into the plant root to make up its part of the inorganic constituents or ash.

Phosphorus and silicon, may be included in the list of the many other essential elements as variables in the chemical composition of the crop when the soil is variable even though the plant species (and all else) is constant. Phosphorus varied from a low, taken as one, to a high of one and two-thirds (0.27 to 0.45%). The silicon varied from a low, taken as one, to a high of more than three (0.81 to 2.54%). Since phosphorus is generally low in most any food or feed crops we grow, its variation there brings the serious danger of its being a deficiency in nutrition so much more quickly. Can we believe, then, that the soil does not cause differences in the chemical compositions of plants, and has no possible nutritional effects via the foods we eat? Shall we censure those who would supplement their own diets by organic phosphorus concentrates available in the food stores? Surely one's own nutrition for one's own health is still one of our freedoms.

BORON INTERRELATED WITH POTASSIUM

In the preceding several sections, the interrelations of one fertility element to others in the soil as they modify the chemical composition of the crops grown have been discussed. But only the major, inorganic elements have been considered. It is well, then, to look into the balanced diet of the plant so far as the trace elements in balance with the major ones are concerned. As a case in illustration: boron in relation to potassium may be of interest.

Deficiency of boron in the soil, and thereby in the crops, has recently been given much attention. The symptoms of its shortage have included heart-rot of some root crops; high sugar in the leaves but low sugar storage in the sugar beet; and high starch in the leaves of the potato plant but small tubers and poor starch storage in them. While such symptoms represent ample carbohydrate production, there is a failure—probably of its conversion into protein, as one might theorize from the failure of alfalfa, a high-protein forage—to develop its tips of the plants or the areas of growth where protein would seem to be failing. When the trace elements seem to play their roles in the enzymes as protein-like substances, those are more plentiful in connection with growth processes involving regular proteins than they are in carbohydrate synthesis and storage.

The closer connection of boron with the synthesis and functions of proteins is suggested by the recently presented evidence of boron's essentiality for warm-bodied life, namely animals and man. The skin irregularities connected by boron in the diet suggest that this enormous excretory organ outside of the body is not functioning as it should when eczema and mange in animals and acne in humans are remedied if boron is taken by mouth in solutions of borax. Professor C.M. Woodruff of the Soils Department of the University of Missouri, with the help of H. Sinha of India, demonstrated the necessity of having boron in the soil, if higher applications of potassium were not to be damaging to the growth of the soybean plants. In the absence of boron, the potassium at but 2% saturation of the soil's exchange capacity was the limit of beneficial effect by this monovalent cation. Larger amounts reduced the growths of the plants. But when but one pound (or two) of the element boron were used per plowed acre of two million pounds of soil (1 ppm), the increased applications of potassium, up to saturation of 20% of the soil's exchange capacity, were without detriment of notice. Thus the plant's ration was given an increase of potassium by 10 times and yet that plant ration was "in balance" to all appearances with other major elements when the trace element boron was present in the ratio as small as one part to 2800 of potassium. In the absence of boron, 280 pounds of potassium per acre were the upper limit of the plant's use of this element with good effects on vegetative growth. This imbalance in boron absence disturbed also the plant's uptakes of calcium and magnesium, usually considered requirements in the soil at 75% and 7.5% saturations, respectively, of the exchange capacity when in balance with potassium at not more than 3% saturation.

Nature has a large number of elements going into the plant from the soil. Yet, seemingly, when all are plentifully present along with much organic matter, each may vary over a wide range of apparent excess without noticeable disturbance in the plant's growth. Their "team-work" seems to be excellent. But when one single element is not carrying its full share in plant nutrition, or is in deficiency, then other elements also seem so much more severely out of balance as excess, or as deficiency, when among the major elements. Dr. Woodruff and his understudies point out that while imbalances in the major fertility elements of the soil disturb plant growth and cause the plant's chemical composition to vary widely, we dare not forget that imbalances between the trace elements and the major ones may even be more disturbing to crop growth and its nutritional values, not only according to chemical analyses of the ash, but also according to tests via nutrition of the warm-blooded animals and man.

BORON IMPROVES ALFALFA QUALITY

Plants, like alfalfa, which make higher nutritional values for feeding young livestock, require higher fertility levels in the soil. The trace elements are included in the requirements as suggested by the crop improvement, left, from boron application.

Yellowing of top leaves preceded by insufficient delivery of boron by the dwarfed stem growth suggests that dwarfed stem growth stands may be in trouble.

Upper leaves often red before the typical "yellow top" shows up. The internodes of the terminal shoots become shortened, forming a rosette. Death of the terminal shoots become shortened, forming a rosette. Death of the terminal bud follows. Boron troubles appear most strikingly in the late summer—especially during prolonged dry periods. At such times, plant roots must obtain water and nutrients at depths below surface soil layers. Frequently this moist zone is beneath the level of the soil organic matter from which most of the boron seems to come. Testing the soil for available boron is complicated because in the spring when surface soil is moist, the soil usually supplies boron. Alfalfa can make a vigorous normal growth. Later in the summer the characteristic "yellow top" appears.

Under boron deficiencies, nitrogen-fixing nodules fail to form on alfalfa roots. Galls sometimes develop there but these become black, shriveled masses before the plant matures. Such abnormal legumes do not take nitrogen from the air. Compared with healthy plants, they appear lighter in color, ripen at an earlier date, give lower yields and are of poor quality as feed. Under severe conditions, the plants may die from boron-induced nitrogen deficiency. This trace element, boron, is needed so that the plant can take on nitrogen-fixing microbes. According to Sheldon, boron is needed for other plant processes, too. The transport of materials within the plant has frequently been associated with this element. Tests at the Missouri Agriculture Experiment Station show that concentrations of tryptophane—a part of plant proteins often deficient—may be increased by as much as 54 percent in alfalfa hay by applying boron to Putnam Silt Loam.

When studied under greenhouse conditions, the amounts of this compound, as parts per thousand of dry matter, dropped from 2.8 for full soil treatment to 1.1 where only boron was withheld. Similar results were found with soybean hays. Usual methods of nitrogen analysis for protein were too crude to reveal boron effects on the quality of alfalfa hay. While further research is necessary in order to discover functions of boron in life processes of alfalfa and in the soil, there is evidence that boron, a trace element, improves the nutritional quality of alfalfa as hay. Many Missouri farmers are cooperating with the department of soils in an effort to further evaluate the effects of added boron on maintenance and improvement of alfalfa stands.

BORON HELPS MAINTAIN POTASSIUM BALANCE

An illustration of the intereffects among the amounts of the fertility elements in the soil, on their respective concentrations within the plants grown on the soil, was recently demonstrated at the Missouri Agricultural Experiment Station. This demonstration included the interrelations among four essential elements: namely, the three major exchangeable cations—calcium, magnesium, and potassium, and the single anion, the trace element—boron. The boron seemed to maintain the balance among them in their going into the soybean plants. The study serving in this demonstration revealed the important, but not widely appreciated, depressive effects of the increasing saturation of the soil's exchange capacity by potassium on the uptake of calcium and magnesium by the legume crop of soybeans, when the last two essential elements were of constant exchangeable supplies in the soil. The lowering of the calcium concentration in the soybeans according to the exchangeable potassium increase in the soil is shown in figure 1 by the graph line labeled "Calcium minus Boron." In the same figure, there is shown the increasing concentration of potassium in the leaves of the soybean plants according as there was increase of exchangeable potassium in the soil, by the graph line labeled "Potassium minus Boron."

It is significant to note, however, that while the increase in potassium concentration in the soybean plants showed up as nearly a straight line function in the first part of the graph, the corresponding decreasing concentration of calcium did not follow the same pattern in its early portion of the graph: namely, an equal calcium decrease per unit of increase in potassium added to the soil, or per unit of increased potassium concentration in the plants. Instead, the major depressing effects on calcium by added potassium were brought about by the first potassium increments: namely, those less than 4% saturation of the soil's exchange capacity. This agrees with the usual consideration of 3% of saturation by potassium of that exchange capacity as a recommended soil saturation degree by this monovalent and highly soluble cation. The above were the facts demonstrated when no boron was added to the soil. The buffeting effect of the trace element boron against this depressing effect by increasing potassium was the most startling part of the demonstration—when two pounds or less of the element boron were applied per two million pounds of soil. That the presence of the boron in the soil reduced the depressive effects by the potassium on the calcium going into the plants is shown also in figure 1, by the graph line labeled "Calcium plus Boron." Boron served similarly to lessen the depressive effects by the potassium on the magnesium concentration in the soybean leaves.

When calcium is a major ash element in the warm-blooded animals, and when it is so highly essential to legumes for their greater activities in fixing nitrogen, the boron—as an aid in moving high concentrations of calcium into forage feeds—maybe indirectly a very important fertility element. It may be some such similar indirect effects by which we have recently found evidence that boron is itself an essential element for warm-blooded bodies and have cited earlier the inter-effects among boron and calcium in the better growth of the duckweed (Lemna minor) common on ponds. It is also significant that boron acts indirectly with similar importance by way of magnesium. This role of the trace element boron in prohibiting the imbalances between the three major cations, calcium, magnesium and potassium, gives this extremely small amount of an essential element a significance within the soil—plant—root area which we certainly have not yet appreciated. When so little of one trace element as a pound or two per acre balances four essential elements so much more favorably for better growth of the high-protein crop like soybeans, this fact indicates how much of a problem lies ahead before we can feel confident that we can balance the applications of all the essential elements, major and trace, to insure plant compositions which will result as truly nutritious feeds for healthy animals and humans.

SOIL EXHAUSTION

Depletion of the soil fertility is a serious factor bringing about lowered nutritional quality in the succession of crops on the same soil. This simple fact is not yet widely recognized. It is even denied by some who contend, "There is no scientific basis for the theory that crops grown on poor soil . . . are nutritionally inferior in any way . . ."[1] Chemical studies of soybean plants, reported nearly 20 years ago in the Missouri Agricultural Experiment Station research bulletin No. 330, show how widely three successive crops varied in concentration of (a) their organic compounds—namely sugar, starch and nitrogen (protein); and (b) their inorganic elements—namely calcium, phosphorus, magnesium and potassium. All soil treatments were the same, except (a)—the amounts of exchangeable potassium on the colloidal clay, and (b)—the absence of nodule-producing bacteria from the soil in the first crop, but their presence in the second and third.

TABLE I

Yields Gms. (1)			Potassium ME/culture	
	0	5	10	15
one (2)	14.70	19.32	22.51	20.22
two (2)	10.48	10.38	11.37	13.60
three (2)	11.94	12.36	14.50	12.42
Nitrogen % (1)(2)				
one	1.57	1.24	1.16	1.18
two	3.31	3.34	3.33	3.18
three	2.56	2.68	2.21	2.70
Sugar %				
one	3.89	2.68	2.42	1.31
two	8.68	7.46	8.60	7.69
three	9.08	8.08	8.20	6.86
Starch %				
one	8.39	10.62	17.35	15.52
two	4.21	4.11	4.09	5.19
three	7.16	8.38	11.21	12.84

(1) Gms. represents the grams of dry matter; / represents the per cent in the dry matter.
(2) Crop one was given no nodule-producing bacteria, but crop two was; hency they were present and active in the soil for crop three.
(3) The seeds for all plantings were from a common lot genetically similar mother plants.

TABLE II

| | Potassium ME/culture | | | |
	0	5	10	15
Calcium %				
one	0.44	0.41	0.41	0.43
two	0.64	0.54	0.53	0.57
three	0.39	0.41	0.27	0.30
Phosphorus %				
one	0.19	0.19	0.20	0.21
two	0.27	0.27	0.29	0.26
three	0.23	0.23	0.20	0.25
Magnesium %				
one	0.34	0.28	0.25	0.23
two	0.20	0.19	0.19	0.22
three	0.15	0.18	0.14	0.16
Potassium %				
one	0.73	1.32	1.68	2.18
two	0.87	1.02	1.38	1.44
three	1.12	1.30	1.05	1.50

TABLE III
Nitrogen — Mgms.(1) + .Losses — Potassium ME/culture

	0	5	10	15
one	−82.6	−76.1	−57.0	−74.9
two	+28	+28	+60	+115
three	−13	+13	+2	+12

(1) The total nitrogen in the seeds planted in each pot was 318 mgms.

The yields of the soybean crops, including the entire plants as both roots and tops, and their organic compositions of nitrogen, sugar and starch as percentages of dry matter are given in Table 1. The data are arranged in their order according to the increments of exchangeable potassium added to the soil, and to the three successive crops. The inorganic compositions of calcium, phosphorus, magnesium and potassium, each as percentage of the dry matter, are given similarly in Table 2. The gains or losses in total nitrogen in the crop (both roots and tops) relative to that initially present in the planted seed are given in Table 3.

As regards the yield data, the following facts stand out clearly:

(a) The largest vegetative yields resulted from the first crop when the plants without nodule bacteria were behaving physiologically as non-legume plants and not as legumes, their proper classification according to their pedigrees.

(b) The first crop of the three had less nitrogen in the dry matter than there was in the planted seed. Nitrogen was lost from that initially present in the seed and by the amounts shown in Table 3. Those losses ranged from 14.7% to 26.1% of that initially planted.

(c) The yields of the second crop (the first inoculated crop, behaving as a legume) were the lowest, in total, of all three crops. Yet this crop used atmospheric nitrogen for its growth, in amounts ranging from 8.8% to 36.1% increases over what was initially planted in the seed. In terms of crude protein, it was the most nutritious forage.

(d) The third crop—inspite of the fertility depletion of the soil by two previous crops—was still taking atmospheric nitrogen for its nutrition of the inoculated legume plants, save for the one case where no exchangeable potassium was added to the colloidal clay. (table 3)

According to these data, the fertility and the bacteria of the soil—not the plant pedigree—determined whether the plants behaved as legumes with reference to their use of atmospheric nitrogen and their delivery of varied concentrations of protein as quality in nutritional values. Relative to the changing organic compositions of the crops in succession and with depletion of the soil fertility, it is well to note the following facts:

(a) The low concentrations of sugar, but the high concentrations of the starch in the first crop suggest a non-legume physiology in which the carbohydrates of photosynthesis are quickly converted from active forms as sugar into inactive storage forms as starch.

(b) Conversely, the second and nodulated crop suggests its physiology as a legume by its high concentration of sugar but low concentration of starch—with the former awaiting biosynthesis into protein through extra nitrogen fixed from the atmosphere which is suggested by the data in table 3 and by the concentrations of nitrogen (average 3.29% in the dry matter) in table 1—representing nearly the double of that in the first crop (average 1.28%) behaving as a non-legume.

(c) The third crop also had a high concentration of sugar, but a higher concentration of starch—with the latter suggesting the failure of conversion of the sugar into proteins as a sequel of the depletion of the fertility. The failing nitrogen fixation is suggested by the one negative and three small, but positive, figures for the increases of total nitrogen in the third crop over that in the seed.

Relative to the changing inorganic compositions of the successive crops, it is significant to note that:

(a) The calcium concentration in the second crop behaving as a legume was about a third higher than that in the first, a non-legume in behavior. The calcium in the third crop, also acting as a legume, was lower than that in the first crop, indicating depletion of the soil of calcium, the element required generously by legumes active in nitrogen fixation.

(b) The phosphorus concentration in the soybean plants was increased by the inoculation or by leguminious physiology, to carry this effect to the third crop, as a more nutritious feed in terms of concentration of this element.

(c) The magnesium concentrations in the crops declined as the soil was given more exchangeable potassium, and with the succession of crops.

(d) There was a decline also in the mean concentrations of potassium with the successive cropping.

According to these data of chemical compositions of the soybean crops—both organic and inorganic—there is certainly some "scientific basis for the theory that crops grown on poor soil . . . are nutritionally inferior . . ." in terms of the important food compounds they synthesize and of the concentrations of essential elements which they supply. There is also evidence that successive cropping of the soil depletes its fertility in terms of the elements supporting protein production by the crop.

THE FEEDING POWER OF THEIR ROOTS

The service given inorganic elements by organic compounds of the soil, called *chelation*, is a prominent factor in plant nutrition. The inorganic ion becomes inactive by combining with an organic compound of protein-like properties. By that combination into the large molecular complex moving into the plant root, there is more of the inorganic elements moved into the plant than when the soil offers that in its smaller, ionically active unit to the plant root. This service is especially unique in that the inorganic element and the chelator compound need not necessarily have been combined before they enter the root. It has been demonstrated, by means of the divided root system of the plant with the two parts in separate containers, that by offering the organic chelator in one container (or one part of the soil) and the inorganic ions in the other, the former is taken into the plant and serves to move more of the latter into the plant roots from the other container than when the plant grows without the added organic substance serving as the chelator.

Laboratory compounds with this chelating property contain nitrogen in amino combinations of it, much as is found in proteins. It is suggested that the chelating, or non-ionizing, effect on the inorganic element results because of its combination with that amino, or protein part. Thus, the increase in the plant's content of the inorganic element occurs simultaneously with the increasing concentration of the plant's amino, or protein-like, nitrogen. This results in plants of higher nutritional values as forages for animal feeds. By their higher concentrations of crude proteins, the plants increase their power of feeding on the essential inorganic nutrient elements adsorbed on the clay. The roots of higher protein contents have an increased capacity to remove the adsorbed inorganic elements off the clay of the soils, or to take these off to a higher percentage of the total supply. This is a case of the plants being nourished by the soil organic matter as a means of feeding themselves more effectively on the inorganic, rather than vice versa as we commonly believe. This fact was established experimentally at the Missouri Experiment Station through the research by Dr. Hampton, now of Texas. It was illustrated, also, in the Australian observation that sheep will exhibit the symptoms of cobalt and copper deficiencies when feeding on a pure stand of a non-legumenous grass (Phalaris tuberosa) grown on the Ninety-mile Plains. But if the protein rich legume—namely, subterranean clover—is seeded and grown with that grass to only a small percentage in the feed, the sheep will be provided with enough of the trace elements in question to keep them healthy.

These facts tell us that the soils are not necessarily deficient entirely in the inorganic trace elements. We are merely growing crops too low in protein and protein-like compounds to give them feeding power enough in their roots to take those essential inorganic elements from the soil. Also there is not enough of the protein-like organic matter maintained in the soil to serve as a chelating agent to move both the inorganic element and the chelating nitrogen into the crop. In either case, there is the emphasis on the importance of the quality of the soil organic matter by which the higher nutritional value of the crop as feed results at the same time that the crop's power of feeding itself on the inorganic fertility of the soil becomes greater. These facts suggest that the soil organic matter improves the chemical composition of the plants and increases the feeding powers of their roots.

VEGETABLE QUALITY REVEALS ITS CONNECTION
WITH SOIL ORGANIC MATTER

It has become a greenhouse practice to replace the soils in the benches after a few years of use. Yet, in nature, we view the soil's service in growing crops as a nearly perpetual one. Much has been said about maintaining our soils in a permanent fertility. In greenhouses without benches, where the earth floor is cultivated, the troubles—because of lowered productivity—also arise in a decade or two. Where the more perennial crops are grown under glass, like the large purple grapes in Europe, the lifetime service of the soil is extended by planting the vines just inside the outer walls. The houses are small and narrow. The successful grape growers tell us, "The roots of the vines must get out of doors."

When such soils under glass begin to fail in their productivity, moving of the house corrects the problem in a moderately humid climate. Closer study of the trouble proved that it was caused by the soils in glasshouses becoming salt-laden under (a) the limited watering (less than annual rainfall rates); (b) the higher temperatures; and (c) the generous applications of commercial salt fertilizers. Nature did not accumulate the disturbing salts of sodium, potassium, magnesium, aluminum, sulfates, nitrates, bicarbonates and others to prohibit crop growth on virgin soils in a moderately humid climate. Soil troubles in glasshouses in that climatic setting come earlier, as more soluble fertilizers are used. They come later as more organic manures are used in the fertility treatments. Dangers from soluble fertilizers applied in the fields with the seeding—which dangers are lessened by special fertilizer placement—increase as the soil's content of organic matter declines.

Scientific studies are now beginning to uncover what suggests itself as the secret of the natural protection which the soil organic matter and the dense microbial population give to our crops against soil salts. Those crops of large yield and high quality are taking so much of available inorganic fertility elements from the soil that, if they were water soluble in the immediate root zone, they would suggest salt injury to the plants. It is slowly dawning on us in agricultural practice that while we make (and recommend the use of) salt fertilizers—which are particularly high (1) in water solubility; (b) in ionization; and (c) in chemical activities—yet when those inorganic elements move into the first cell inside the root they are no longer in true solution, nor behaving as single ions. They have been united into the living, organic compounds to be no longer strictly inorganic and separated in their action as we have them in our thinking.

In that fact there lies part of the secret of high quality of vegetables. We do not take to very much of any kind of salt readily. Even for the wild animals, the "salt-lick" is an act of desperation and not the law of nature when wildlife takes its medicine by choice of plant species or the same species chosen according to soil fertility growing it, and not by going to the drug shelf. For truly high quality in our vegetables, we must shift our concept away from the inorganic fertility as water soluble ions, and also away from them as an ash complex within the plant. We need to view those inorganic elements as the potential creators of life, moving into the plant cells to become only a small part within a large organic complex.

The highly ionized elements we have outside the plant roots are not the rule within the cells. There may be some ionized potassium in solution around, or outside of, the plant cell. In those large non-ionized complexes, the organic portion bears a ratio to the inorganic much the same as the combustible dry matter of the plant bears to its ash, namely 19 or 20 to 1. That makes the plant's ash compose but 5%. Only a small ash, or salt, content is required with all the inorganic elements in proper balance for quality in good plant growth and yields.

This concept of the use of the inorganic elements within the larger organo-complexes, as part of the living processes, suggests itself as also a prevailing function of the inorganic fertility in the microbial processes of the soil. It has been demonstrated as a means of moving more inorganic fertility and of the less soluble from the soil into the roots. It is a way by which the so-called insoluble fertility becomes available to microbes and plants. This has long been a natural process that seems to be revealing itself as a secret of nature, now that we have discovered a similar behavior in the laboratory which we call "chelation." Only slowly are we putting science under nature's secrets of growing better vegetation, when she is returning more of the organic matter back to the soil.

CHELATION

When someone says, "I don't believe it!", it may be a confession of ignorance and not necessarily a denial of the fact.

That same contradictory remark, directed against the importance of the soil organic matter for growing vegetables of better quality, comes often from those who have never enjoyed, *gastronomically, the doubted fact demonstrated by nature as an established truth.* It comes even from some scientists and agronomists, who remind us that vegetables can be grown in water solutions of nothing but the simple inorganic elements commonly and naturally breaking out of rock minerals which give us our soils. They present that demonstration as if it were proof that organic matter (and clay) without water-soluble elements could not be helpful in growing crops. This is like saying that the fact that one can be nourished and live as a vegetarian denies the possibility of being nourished and living as an eater of meat—demonstrated by the polar explorer, Vilhjalmur Stefansson.

A recent discovery in the chemical laboratory, spoken of as "chelation," suggests the secret of nature's chemistry using the organic combined with the inorganic matters in growing better crops, by emphasis on the former. This revelation should be helpful to those who do not like to accept practices of an art in nature without first comprehending the science under-girding or explanation. Chelation views the processes in the soil and in the plant for its growth without separating them into the inorganic and the organic kinds of chemistry, as we did in formulating our earlier concepts of soil fertility and plant nutrition. It gives a clearer concept of the small, highly active, inorganic elements in combination with organic molecules, many times larger, for the better nutritional services by the former as well as by the latter. This concept had long been suggested in the many observations coming from those practicing the organic art, but which the science had not yet formulated satisfactorily for itself.

It is a widely recognized fact that phosphates, insoluble and soluble—and particularly the latter—are more effective in growing better crops when mixed with barnyard manure. Also, the combined soil treatments of ammonium salts and soluble phosphates mobilize more of the latter into the plants for better growth than when soluble phosphates only are applied. Sodium nitrate in the combination does not increase the mobilization. Calcium nitrate even reduces it.

The element nitrogen—the common symbol of the living compound, protein—is prominent in bringing about the chelation of calcium, iron, cobalt and many other elements, as examples. The nitrogen serves to connect the inorganic with the larger organic part of the final inorganic-organic complex that results from the chelation. This robs the chelated inorganic elements of their common property and chemical activity which we usually emphasize for them—namely, their solubility in water and their ionization, respectively. This concept of chelation helps us to visualize the services by the soil microbes in their "take-up" of the salt-shock when ammonium phosphate, for example, is added to the compost heap; when those soluble, inorganic, nutrient elements are put into insoluble but much larger organic complexes; and when thereby both parts of that complex are made more available as nutrition to the plant roots.

The laboratory-synthesized chelator, *ethylene-di-amine-tetraacetic-acid (E.D.T.A.)*—put into a soil of no iron content containing one-half of the root system and the other half in soil given iron in the presence of phosphates, thus making both less available according to solubilities—demonstrated that this chelator (E.D.T.A.) was taken by the roots from the first half of the soil. It served to mobilize the iron from the other half. It corrected the chlorosis which occurred under similar conditions, save that there was omitted the application of the special chelator. The use of water leachings from highly organic soils as substitute for the synthetic chelator (E.D.T.A.) served for effective iron mobilization just as the special compound did. Such facts suggest that very probably microbes and soil organic matter have been natural chelators at work for better plant growth during the past ages.

Such views of soil organic matter should not stretch our mental capacities too much when chlorophyl is a case of chelated magnesium. That complex is made up of one part of this inorganic matter in 40 parts total organic and performing the marvels of photosynthesis by plants. The magnesium is not ionized, but can be taken out by acids. Also the hemaglobin in our blood is a chelated complex that has but one part of inorganic iron in 55 parts of organic items. In addition, vitamin B-12 has cobalt chelated in a corresponding wide ration. Yet this vitamin was discovered in the cow's droppings by chickens long before the chemist did, and long before he had the concept of chelation. Perhaps in due time we shall appreciate nature's use of soil organic matter for growing higher quality into our vegetable foods. Let us hope that we can accept more widely the natural art of organic fertilization without the pressure from so-called "educational helps" in sales literature.

NATURAL LAWS REGARDING SOILS AND PLANT COMPOSITIONS

Knowledge about the human body and its many functions has been accumulating very slowly. The additions have awaited the coming of each new science and the contributions in its particular field, at the rate of about one per century. The professions, like those of dentistry and medicine, have quickly accepted any knowledge or practice applicable in the alleviation of human suffering. Only in the latter part of the 20th century will we probably be credited more with the addition of the science of nutrition to better health by building the body's self-protection than to the economics of the home.

We seem to forget that more than a century ago,"the survival of the fittest" kinds of living things, each in a particular climatic setting, gave us the concept of evolution of the species. We have been slow to see that the different life forms fit, each into a certain place in the climatic pattern. Such fitness comes not because of comfort according to how cold, warm, wet or dry. Rather, it comes according to the climatic forces as they develop the soil and its fertility array from the original rocks. The soil must serve in growing plants with ample contents of proteins. Only those compounds will sustain and reproduce life. In plants, like in animals and humans, proteins must be in balance with the carbohydrates, which give calories and energy, or serve as "starter" compounds for the synthesis of proteins from them—if the balanced fertility serves accordingly. This century may be the one when the threatening degenerations (diseases) will bring us to recognize the natural laws concerning the chemical composition, or nutritional value, of what we grow for services in keeping us healthy through natural prevention of degeneration, for which we have been hoping in vain for scientific cures.

The first law tells us that with the increase in the climatic forces of rainfall and temperature which are weathering the original rock, there is, first, the construction and then, second, the destruction of the soil, so far as survival of more complex life forms is concerned. In the United States this may be illustrated by going east from near-zero rainfall in the west—to give increasing soil construction in those more productive soils until one reaches the midcontinental area. Then, with more annual rainfall on going further east, there comes excessive soil development, or soil destruction, in terms of its fertility for growing both quantity and quality of proteins.

The second law tells us that, at the maximum of soil construction, there is a wide ratio of the exchangeable (available) calcium to the exchangeable potassium. This is illustrated by the soils along the 98th meridian of longitude running from the western edge of Minnesota to the tip of Texas. This natural law of the soil composition is cause for the corresponding rations of these two essential inorganic elements in the natural vegetation and farm crops grown on those soils. Thus it is a natural law that there is a variable chemical composition of the vegetation according to the variable fertility of the soil, determined by the degree of soil development the climate gives it. Accordingly, the potential nutritional support of plants, animals and man goes back to the climate via the fertility of the soil that grows the foods and feeds.

The third natural law tells us that calcium is associated with the chemical synthesis of the proteins by plants (and microbes), while potassium is associated with the synthesis of their carbohydrates. The latter process, commonly spoken of as "photosynthesis," may well be considered a supra-soil performance. Such classification seems fitting since photosynthesis is a compounding of carbon, hydrogen and oxygen—all weather-given elements taken from air and water—into carbohydrates by sunshine energy. The synthesis of proteins is a biosynthetic process: that is, one by the life processes of the plants. It seems to be a case in which some of the carbohydrates serve as the raw materials out of which proteins are made. This is brought about by combining with those carbohydrates some nitrogen, some phosphorus and some sulfur, all coming from the soil. Simultaneously, some calcium, some magnesium and several other soil-borne nutrient elements are required, while more of the carbohydrates are consumed as energy materials for this conversion process.

The fourth law, concerning the fertility of the soil in relation to plant composition, tells us that on soils under construction by the limited climatic forces or with a wide calcium-potassium ratio, the mineral rich, proteinaceous crops or foods, as well as the carbonaceous ones, are possible. But on the soils under destruction by excessive climatic forces or those with a narrow calcium-potassium ratio, protein production is not so common—while production mainly of carbohydrates by the crops is almost universal. In the climatic setting of the former soils, nature grows healthy animals; in that of the latter soils, she fattens less healthy ones.

Out of these simple natural laws (given us by combining the climatic, pedological and physiological facts) comes the principle of concern to all of the namely, the homely fact that it is the proper nutrition of our bodies—more particularly through ample proteins of complete quality and ample inorganic elements commonly associated with the natural growth of them—that creates healthy conditions for growth, self-protection and normal reproduction.

Nature's laws, not those made by man, connect plant compositions and their nutritional services in animal and human health with the fertility of the soil according to the pattern of climatic forces developing it from the rocks.

DEPLETED SOILS—SPECIES EXTINCTION

When nature puts her virgin climax crops of different plant species in different places, she is exhibiting the different chemical compositions of plants and their different qualities as food for any higher forms of life, according to the fertility differences in the soils growing them. Nature's crops represent each as "the survival of the fittest" by way of what the soil provides as plant nutrition to guarantee that result. That was a fact Sir Charles Darwin emphasized a century ago. It is surprising that these natural laws seem to be unknown to those appointed to positions of national authority for legal enforcement of matters of human health. That there are soil differences under the different nutritional values of the crops grown on them is indicated every time a cow breaks through the fence to get out of the pasture. She is prompted by more deep-seated causes than a mere desire to get on the other side, or to escape confinement. Careful observation of that condemned misbehavior reveals that she is usually going from the exploited, time-worn soils on the inside, to the virgin, unharvested ones on the highway or the railroad right-of-way on the outside. Little has been written concerning the cow's wisdom about the fertility of the soil growing the higher nutrition quality in the feed she prefers, and which, if offered to her satisfaction inside the fence, would eliminate the need of any fence to confine her to it.

An unwarranted faith in the plant's pedigree seems to be responsible for the erroneous contention that the nutritional value and measurable chemical composition of the crop are constants, regardless of differences in the fertility of the soil growing it. Along with that contention goes the belief that the differences in the soils give differences only in the crop yields as volume and weight. Such beliefs suggest that all the basic facts of ecology, and all organized knowledge added since the thinking of Darwin, or during the last 100 years, have remained in the darkness for many of whom those should be basic facts for passing judgment on matters in their areas of responsibility.

Among those who till the soil there are many who remind us that it is the soil that determines the nutritional values, while the genetic factor of the seed merely sets limits to the range of variations which the soil factors can demonstrate. To say that the soil fertility is of no significance in modifying the quality of the crop may be taken as a confession of misinformation, but it dare not be taken as negation of the basic facts of nature as we learn them from ecology, plant physiology, and from animal behaviors. Experimental rabbits demonstrated the fact that body growth, physiology and sexual vigor varied according to the differences in the fertility of the soil growing a single plant species of forage as feed.

Equal weights of the hay from four separately treated plots were offered along with a constant amount of corn. Repeated trials with lots of five rabbits (two males and three females) gave repetitions of the animals' clear-cut choices of decreasing amounts of hay consumed per day, according as the hay was grown on the same soil given increasing amounts of chemical nitrogen as fertilizer treatment. The maximum consumption of hay occurred always from the check plot of no nitrogen treatment on the soil. As a sequel to the above trial, the same hay species from each separate plot and the same corn were fed in order to measure the body growth as gains in weight per single amount of nitrogen fertilization. It was also used to note the development or destruction of male sexual vigor.

The results showed decreasing gains in body weights as more nitrogen served as fertilizer for growing the hay. There were also decreasing amounts of hay consumed by the animal lots as more nitrogen was applied to the soil, but that was associated with increasing amounts of corn chosen rather than the hay. These data all indicate the struggle by these animals against poor nutrition for body growth which could do little more than let the animal take more of the corn as fattening feed rather than of the supposed protein supplement in the form of high concentration of nitrogen in the hay, but not that as quality protein of choice by the animal.

Since the young males had demonstrated a delayed arrival at sexual maturity, their ration was shifted to a highly complete one for growth, including many choices of feeds, so they were brought into sexual vigor. That was readily recognized by the fighting of the males if left as pairs in the pens with the young females. The positive sexual interest was tested with females in oestrus, and then each lot was put back on the hay-corn ration by which their slow growth rate had just been demonstrated. Within the brief period of one week of feeding on the test series of hays grown on soils given the larger amounts of nitrogen as fertilizer, the loss of sexual vigor inhibited the males from mating with females in oestrus. Accordingly, one week of feeding on those hays of lowest quality for body growth was long enough to rob the males of their mating instinct; or to bring about, thereby, the extinction of the species.

Such simple facts are observable in nature by anyone who will study them. Unfortunately for agriculture, it is being viewed at long distance as if it were only an industrial manipulation of dead materials with emphasis on technologies for mainly economic advantages. Sight seems to be lost of agriculture as a biological demonstration by the forces of nature of which man is more of a spectator than manager in complete control. It is regrettable that agriculture is so smothered under views of it as but economics, that even the appointees to high office will contend that the soil no longer represents the power of variable creation for all that lives, moves, and has its being on the face of the earth.

SOIL ORGANIC MATTER MOBILIZES THE PHOSPHORUS FOR PLANTS

Scientific studies are uncovering what seems like a natural protection against excessive salts in the soil, via the soil organic matter and the living soil's microbial population. Nature uses the inorganic elements mainly as inclusions within larger organic-complexes. This has demonstrated itself as a means of moving more inorganic fertility of the less soluble nature from the soil into the plant and about within it. This emphasizes *the availability of the insoluble.* Now we have discovered in the laboratory the process which we call

Chelation[1]—whereby, an inorganic ion is stably fixed within a larger organic molecule so that both are taken into the plants for their better nutritional service there. We now comprehend what has been nature's way by which the insoluble fertility of the soil has become the available to the microbes and the plants during the past ages. But only slowly are we putting science under nature's secrets by which she grows better crops by returning more organic matter back to the soil. Chelation is the term that interprets what observations in agricultural practice have often suggested. It is a widely recognized fact, for example, that both the soluble and the insoluble phosphates (particularly the former) are more effective for improving the crop when first mixed with barnyard manure. Also, the simultaneous applications to the soil of ammonium salts and soluble phosphates will mobilize more phosphorus into the plants for better crop growth. Sodium nitrate applied in combination with the latter does not. Calcium nitrate in place of the sodium even reduces the mobilized phosphates, as compared with what occurs when soluble phosphates are applied alone. The element nitrogen, the common symbol of our only living compounds, i.e., the proteins, is prominent in bringing about the chelation of calcium, magnesium, iron, cobalt and a list of other elements, as examples. It is the nitrogen, in particular, that serves to connect the inorganic elements more stably into the large organic unit of the final complex that results from chelation. It suggests the proteins, and other forms much like them, as the major means of chelation which robs the inorganic elements of their common property and chemical activity which we usually emphasize about them—namely, their solubility and their ionization, respectively.

This concept of chelation should not stretch our vision beyond its elastic limits when chlorophyl, the green coloring matter in every leaf, is an age-old illustration of nature's use of chelated magnesium. In its chemical composition, this photosynthetic agent represents about one part of the inorganic in about 40 of total organic for building sugar from water and carbon dioxide under the sunshine's energy. Magnesium is similarly chelated in a long list of other enzymes of both plants and animals. Hemoglobin in our blood is a case of chelated iron with about one part of it in 50 parts of organic matter. This is the means for taking up oxygen from the air in the lungs to be carried by the blood stream and given up to the tissues while the iron is not ionic.

Then cobalt is also chelated into vitamin B_{12} in a similarly wide ration of the inorganic part of the complex. The importance of this chelation compound was discovered by chickens taking to the cow's droppings, long before we as chemists had any vision of it. Natural chelation under the dynamics of organic matter and microbes, may be expected to illustrate itself more widely now that much research work is studying it, and to increase our appreciation of this one of nature's secrets, now that the chemistry has given foundation and pattern for our visions of the chemical aspects a bit more fully.

Natural chelation, under the dynamics of organic matter and microbes, may be expected to illustrate itself more widely now. (Chelation is the process by which an inorganic ion is stably fixed with a larger molecule, so that both are taken into plants for their better nutritional service there.) Much research work is studying it. To increase our appreciation of this one of nature's secrets, chemistry has given foundation and pattern for our visions of the chemical aspects a bit more fully. The commercially available chelator, *ethylene-diamine-tetraacetic-acid (EDTA)*, was put into soil of no-iron content along with one half of the plant's roots. The other half was in similar soil given iron as well as ample phosphates, to make both less available according to their solubilities. Yet this commercial chelator was taken by the plant roots from the one half of the soil. It served to mobilize the iron from the other half into the plant roots and to correct the chlorosis of the plants which occurred under similar soil conditions omitting the applications of this special chelator.[2]

More significant, however, was the additional demonstration which added water-leachings from a highly organic soil, as a substitute for the manufactured chelator, EDTA, only to find that this natural substitute served in iron mobilization for the cure of chlorosis just as the EDTA did.

Such facts help us to visualize the services by the soil microbes in their absorption of the "salt shock" when ammonium phosphate is added to the compost heap; when its soluble inorganic nutrient elements are taken into insoluble, much larger organic complexes; and when, thereby, both parts are made more available as nutrition entering the roots of the crop plants. We are gradually visualizing that, *within the soil, the organic fertility as chelating is dominant over the inorganic in about the same ratio as the combustible organic part of the plants is dominant over the incombustible, the inorganic, part there.* That such ratios prevail—relative to the advantage of making the insoluble become the available, via the soil organic matter—was recently demonstrated by some research using barley as green manure for feeding radioactive phosphorus into a crop of soybeans, according to the unpublished data from the research studies by Vernon Renner of the Missouri Experiment Station.

Barley plants were grown on sand cultures with a controlled nutrient medium containing radioactive phosphorus. They were harvested, dried, pulverized, sampled for chemical analyses, and then that pulverized organic matter was mixed thoroughly into the soil—in the ratio of one part of the former to 500 of the latter. This represented the common field rate of two tons of this dried green manure per two million pounds of soil per acre per plowed depth. The soybeans were harvested after a growth period of 60 days. Chemical analyses were made to determine their contents of total phosphorus and of the radioactive phosphorus. This would, via radioactivity, determine the phosphorus contributed to the soybean roots by the green manure applied to the soil. The total phosphorus, minus the radioactive part, would determine the phosphorus coming from the soil, which was a mass 500 times as large as the applied organic matter in the barley as the green manure. This separation of the phosphorus given by the organic matter of the soil from that given by the larger—originally more inorganic part of the soil—showed that one part of the phosphorus taken into the soybeans was radioactive, therefore, taken from the green manure turned under. Five parts of the phosphorus taken into those soybean plants were not radioactive, hence were taken from the original soil. Thus, it is established very clearly: when the phosphorus coming from the barley as organic matter which was only part, while the soil was correspondingly 500 parts, yet phosphorus from those two sources respectively went into the plant in the ratio of one to five; the phosphorus from the soil organic matter was just 100 times as effective in feeding the insoluble but-yet-available phosphorus to the soybean plants as the soil was when its soil test (by the extracting chemical reagent) reported the soil "high" in its available phosphorus.

Some of our pioneer agronomists, as able chemists and scholars, may have had a vision of nature's unique phenomena of the chelation of inorganic fertility of the soil by the organic matter, and the microbial processes connected with it, in what they considered "the living and creative soil." Nearly a half century ago, Prof. A.W. Blair of New Jersey said, "It is well known that by judicious use of lime and vegetable matter on the soil, reserve of locked-up mineral plant food may be made available."[3]

Others spoke about maintaining the soil fertility and a permanent agriculture, by returning organic matter to the soil in combination with natural rock fertilizers.[4] Those pioneers did not visualize productive permanence in soils treated with water-soluble salts. They were pointing to the importance of the organic matter for soil productivity in the years ahead.

DEPLETED SOILS CHANGE SUGAR, STARCH, PROTEINS AND YIELDS

Those who contend that a given plant does as well on any soil on which it grows as it would on another soil (except for the volume or weight of crop produced) have a wrong understanding of the nature of plant inheritance. In one experiment, potassium (potash), recognized as an essential factor for the *plant's production of carbohydrate and needed often for increased yield of plant material, was added in various amounts to all but one of four plots of soil which were otherwise alike.* Seeds from the same mother plant were used to give a constant genetic background. Of three crops, the first was not given legume bacteria for nodule production, while the seeds for the other two were treated with bacteria which established prominent root nodules (See A, B, C graph illustration.) In terms of crop yields, the first crop was a bountiful one, varying in quantity with the amount of applied potash. Nevertheless, in terms of total nitrogen, it gave back no more in the total crop (both tops and roots) than what was in the seed originally planted.

The second crop took nitrogen from the atmosphere to increase nitrogen in the plants over the total in the planted seed. However, the third crop did not give more nitrogen than was present in its seeds because removal of the preceding crops of plant tops and roots had depleted the soil to such an extent that even with the root nodules, the third crop was not able to utilize atmospheric nitrogen. The third crop gave larger dry matter yields (plant material with moisture removed) than the second. Although the seeds planted for the second and third crops were identical in every way, *nutritional properties of the crops were quite different because of differing soil characteristics.* In the same experiment, measurements were also made of the sugar and starch amounts in the various crops. The results (see graph illustration) show that within each identical and identically treated seed group, soil characteristics had an important effect on the sugar and starch proportions in the crops. (In the diagram, "B" and "C" indicate the seeds that were inoculated with nodule-forming bacteria; the "A" seeds were not so treated.)

These observations show the serious error of those who argue that soil is of no importance in determining the nutritional value of the crops grown on it. It is the soil which determines nutritional value. The genetic factor present in the seed and transmitted to the growing plant merely sets limits to the variation ranges the soil factors can produce. To argue, as have government officials, that the soil—however deficient in natural fertility—is of no significance in determining the crop quality is a confession of misinformation, not of scientific knowledge. Experimental work with rabbits has shown that body growth and body physiology, even the maintenance of sexual vigor, varied according to differences in the soil fertility on which their feed crops were grown.

Tests were made with hay grown on soil with no nitrogen, and other hay grown on companion lots, otherwise the same, which were treated with various sized doses of commercial fertilizer nitrogen. In repeated trials with lots of five rabbits (two males and three females), the animals were offered equal amounts of four different hays along with constant quantities of corn. The rabbits chose mostly the check plot hay which had no nitrogen treatment, and consumed decreasing quantities of hay crops grown with larger amounts of chemical nitrogen used as fertilizer. Thus the rabbits demonstrated an ability to recognize differences in the nutritive values of the same plant species in the several crops grown on a differently fertilized soil.

Naturally the animals which chose to eat less hay showed smaller gains in weight than the others. Thus the properties of the soil samples and the forage grown on them had an indirect but definite effect on the characteristics of the animals. The data indicated that the animals were struggling with poor nutrition and body growth. They avoided the supposed protein supplement in the artificial, high-nitrogen content from hay, which, though it was nitrogen, did not correspond to the high quality protein which they needed.

The unbalanced nutritional feed quality obtained by some of the rabbits even produced sexual infertility, which was not present when the animals were on a diet known to be complete for growth.

The facts that have been outlined will be observed in nature by those who do not have preconceived ideas about plant growth. Unfortunately the professional agriculturalist often views the effects of soils on the plant's growth with a distant outlook, as if the only problems were those of industrial manipulation of dead materials, with emphasis on the various technologies for economic advantages only. People who approach agricultural research in this way have lost sight of agriculture as a biological demonstration by the forces of nature, where man is more spectator than manager in complete control of soil and produce. Such unrealistic views of agriculture have led to expressions and views by high government officials that soil is but a chemical and physical agent for the production of larger quantities of crops. They seem unaware that the soil of our planet is a complex material developed through many centuries, having the power of creation, not only for plants, but for everything that lives, moves and has its being upon the earth.

"DEEP-ROOTING"

When we speak of "deep-rooting" crops we are apt to give a wrong impression. By that description, we are leading folks to believe that it is the characteristic behavior of the crop that sends its roots down deeply anywhere. After all, roots are not being sent. They go only on invitation; and that invitation must include refreshments, namely, something to drink, i.e. water, and something to eat, namely, fertility in the soil.

Roots don't grow in nor go into a dry soil. As the season advances and the sun's drying effects penetrate more deeply into the surface soil, the roots of a corn plant, for example, are also going down deeper. By this, the plant escapes the danger that its water supply may fail. Its roots are taking water out of the soil. They exert an additional drying effect on the soil behind their advancing front, as they bore down into soil that is more moist. But while roots are growing downward within the fertile surface soil they are big, thick roots. They are nourishing themselves from the soil, as roots do, in addition to getting nourishment from the plant tops. The fertile surface soil layer helps the roots to attain massive growth. While they are growing in such soil, the tops of the corn plants are also growing well too.

However, if the crop is on a shallow surface soil overlying an acid, heavy clay subsoil—the high acidity indicating its low fertility—then when the roots grow down out of the drying surface soil to enter the subsoil, they become very thin. They are then merely going. They are barely growing. That they are finding plenty of water is shown by the fact that the growing top of the corn plant does not wilt. But they find too little nitrogen in the humus-

Sweet Clover grows thick, deeper-reaching roots to make more tops, not as the soil is only plowed deeper (A); but as the surface soil is fertilized (B); and as the fertilizer is plowed down 6 inches, (C); and still deeper, 12 inches, by subsoiling (D). Photo by the Missouri Agricultural Experiment Station.

deficient, and thereby nitrogen-deficient, subsoil for the continued luscious growth of the corn. Consequently, the plant transfers nitrogen from the lower, older leaves to the upper, younger ones. Then the lower leaves turn yellow and look burned.

All too often this so-called "fired" corn is said to be suffering from drought or water shortage. If that were true, then the tops would be wilted rather than the lower leaves changed from a green to a yellow color. Plant roots may be going into the subsoil and getting water, but unless it is a fertile subsoil, they are very thin roots. They deliver too little fertility to help the plant much, because they can't help themselves. Root appearances tell us the story of subsoil fertility. Thick portions of roots record the more fertile soil horizons; thin portions, the less fertile ones. Plowing has long been a practice to help plants take more fertility out of the soil. Now as its fertility is dwindling, more folks are plowing to put fertilizers into it. Erosion is also shaving down the fertile surface layer thinner and thinner, so it is becoming necessary to plow deeper while putting fertility down into the subsoil. We are beginning to see the wisdom of building up the surface soil by building fertility down into the subsoil.

The crop roots must be nourished into big ones by fertile soils if they are to give big crops. Merely plowing deep to turn up the infertile subsoil is no help. In fact it may be the opposite. It may mean near disaster to a crop. Putting fertilizer into the surface soil—dried during much of the growing season—is not the equal of putting it down deeper, but yet within root reach. Plowing is a means of putting heavier applications of fertilizers down into the soil. Subsoilers are even more efficient in putting some soil treatments farther down. Roots reaching down to attain thick, massive growth serve to put organic matter deep down, where little was before. This modifies the soil structure. It invites the roots of the following crops to go still deeper. Instead of letting the surface soil become shallower, it helps to deepen it. It is a case of making the fertile soil deeper so the crops will be deep rooting—not merely planting what is said to be a "deep-rooting" crop and expecting it to make the soil deeper. It is a case of inviting big, thick roots down for nourishment rather than sending a few thin ones there without it. It is, in reality, a help toward building up the soil by building down, and at the same time building bigger returns by means of bigger crops.

MOBILIZING THE NATURAL SOIL POTASSIUM

Students of zoology learn that the life history of the individual's development is an epitome of the history of the species. In the development of our knowledge, we seem to follow a similar pattern when our education is apparently the repeated experiences of our predecessors. None of us can start learning fully equipped with the total knowledge accumulated before we came. Each must repeat and relearn. Early recognition of that necessity should make us cautious. It should help us to learn by less costly methods and high-priced experiences. Help in just that respect is the aim of education. Reports are in print and volumes in libraries are available. A study of them lets us learn through the costly experiences of others, by paying no higher price than reading about and comprehending the "how" and "why" of them.

Man has been growing crops for ages. Records of those behaviors of nature are extensive. But for too many of us those facts are hidden ideas because they remain buried in unopened books. The nutritional qualities of what we grow, the variation in the chemical composition of vegetable or field crops, and other factors that make up the quality of food, were shown to vary with the fertility of the soil in a series of preceding articles. Yet there are many who contradict those facts (but do not refute them with evidence).

It is appropriate to unearth from their burial some of the above principles of variation in the chemical composition of crops according to the soil and its fertilizer treatments. They have lain forgotten since 1914 in Bulletin 170 of the New Hampshire Agricultural Experiment Station. At that date, Messrs. B.E. Curry and T.O. Smith reported their studies of the hay crops, demonstrating the wide variation in their concentrations of potassium according to the varied fertility of the soil. These men did not take kindly to the idea of using commercial fertilizers to add potassium to those granitic soils, when those with clay contained, in total, the equivalent of 2 and 3% of potassium oxide per acre per foot of depth. "Some very sandy soils have been found which contain as much as 1% of potassium oxide (equivalent). Such soils carry a considerable amount of minerals in connection with the same," they reported. They conducted experiments on about a dozen soils, using hay crops for test plants. They measured (a) the yields as pounds per acre; (b) the concentrations of potassium (as potassium oxide) in the dry matter; and (c) the total potassium removed by the crops when the soils were given (1) no fertilizer treatment, (2) Chili saltpeter or sodium nitrate, (3) saltpeter and potassium sulfate, (4) saltpeter and acid phosphate, and (5) saltpeter, acid phosphate and potassium sulfate.

Using the average values of their data from that many soils, their records presented by graphs in the accompanying chart set out these facts:

1. No proportional relation could be established between the yields and the percentages of potash in the crops.

2. The amount of potassium removed shows clearly that as the yields increased the potassium taken increased.

And (3) The other nutrient elements applied as fertilizers to the soil served to lower the hay crop's concentration of potassium in some cases, and to increase it in others, even though each element added served to increase the crop yields. Nitrogen added singly served most to lower the concentration of potassium in the crop. Phosphorus used alone reduced the concentration some below that of no treatment; sulfate of potash also reduced it but less than the preceding two treatments. It brought little change in the yields. That fact tells us that the potassium was available from the natural pulverized rock supply in the soil. It was not the factor limiting the yields. But when all three, viz.: nitrogen, phosphorus and potassium, were added to the soil, the yields, the concentration of potassium in the crop and the amount of it taken from the soil were highest. This tells us that some other fertility or soil factors needed to be corrected to gain still higher yields.

Research is repeating just such studies today, when it would be less costly to search out of the literature just such knowledge established nearly a half century ago. Little attention is now going to the natural delivery to the crop of potash from the tremendous supply in the natural minerals of most any soil. Little recognition is given to the imbalancing effects on plant composition by adding—for example—soluble nitrogen, of which but a low portion is taken by the crop. Even as early as 1914, the addition of the three elements, nitrogen, phosphorus and potassium, suggested that other fertility elements not in the commercial fertilizer bag need to be considered for higher yields and possibly uniform quality, as animal nutrition. At that early date the owners of livery stables observed that Chile saltpeter on their hay ground made their horses unable to stand up under the road work expected of them. Buried in the unopened publications there is the evidence which tells us that the manuring of the hay meadows was mobilizing the natural mineral potash from the soil into the crops; that mobilization was high enough to give larger total amounts in good yields; and it resulted in wide variation of the concentration of the potassium in the forage when separate elements such as salts were applied to the soil. At that early date the animal health responded according to the soil growing the feed under commercial fertilizer treatment. Mere contradiction of the facts in these buried and unopened reports isn't a refutation of their truth about nature's behaviors. To say "I don't believe it," is not necessarily a negation of the report. It may be merely a confession of a lack of knowledge of it.

TRACE ELEMENTS AND AGRICULTURAL PRODUCTION

We are slowly realizing that the essential chemical elements contributed by the soil in only "trace" amounts—for the support of microbes, plants, animals, and man—are no less essential than those taken from the soil in larger amounts. It seems most logical to view the "trace" elements, not as parts or constituents of the masses grown, but rather as tools in the process of growing them. "Trace" elements are possibly rendering repeated or recurring services. They are very probably entering into a reaction to bring it about, then coming out to repeat the reaction on another mass, just as we envision the help by catalysts modifying immense masses but themselves never consumed by or retained in them.

Such functions of copper, for example, in the body will not be measured by an ash analysis of the young and then the older life form. Nor is quantity a variable when a contribution of this element relieves a symptom, and then that symptom cannot be re-established for a long time by withholding copper. The contributed copper does not escape from the organism. Instead it protects that body for a long time without extra copper being required. In the plant's production of carbohydrates or the animal's laying on of fat and other equally gross and common manifestations, then, one would scarcely expect "trace" elements like boron, manganese, copper, zinc, molybdenum, iodine, and others to demonstrate much effect. If one hammer and one saw are the essential tools for constructing a dog kennel, the conclusion does not follow logically that there will be a correlated increase in the number of hammers and saws in constructing 100 kennels or dog houses 100 times as large. Nor would an inventory of these kennels and dog houses find a single hammer or a single saw necessarily within them at the close of the constructing performances.

"Trace" elements must be viewed as tools, or as enzymes which do not conform to common correlation thinking where large masses are concerned, and are connected with large causes controlling their behaviors. In our research, therefore, we have looked to the high protein-producing crops—namely, the legumes and more especially those of highest feed value in growing young animals and in aiding their reproduction.

In the field trials, several trace elements (and also the neglected elements—magnesium, sulfur, sodium, etc.) were used as a multiple rather than single application. After such multiple treatments register their effects, then trials with the separate elements can well be undertaken. That the synthesis of the separate components of the proteins—namely, the different amino acids—might be related to the "trace" elements, was the hypothesis under test with alfalfa, for example, in Missouri. Grown in Colorado and imported into Missouri, alfalfa, as a dried feed, is an excellent protein supplement to corn. But grown on Missouri soils—even on those treated with the major nutrient elements—it is not of such high value in this respect. When corn protein is deficient, especially in the amino acids tryptophane, lysine, and even methionine, it seemed well to treat alfalfa growing in Missouri with the trace elements—some used separately and several in combination—to learn whether these protein components are shifted in their concentrations in the alfalfa by "trace" element fertilization.

It was interesting to note that boron was effective for increasing tryptophane decidedly and lysine almost as much. It is significant to note also that the major influences by the "trace" element fertilization registered themselves in increased concentrations of those amino acids most grossly deficient in corn; and likewise of lowest concentration in the alfalfa grown on the Missouri soils without "trace" element fertilization. While boron alone containing no sulfur did not increase the concentration of methionine in the alfalfa, the other "trace" elements carrying sulfates did. This was verified by other work and demonstrates the suggestion that soil deficiency in the neglected element, sulfur, (and possibly other neglected elements) may be responsible for the proteins which are incomplete in methionine, the sulfur-containing amino acid. In the bio-assay of the effects on the plants by "trace" elements as soil treatment, it is highly probable that the animal has been registering the incompleteness vs. the completeness in the required amino acids of the proteins. We have been too easily satisfied when we measure these as "crude" proteins by determining the total nitrogen of which almost half may be in chemical combination other than the amino or readily usable form. When by means of "trace" elements via the soil, the amino acid nitrogen in the plants can be increased without increasing the total nitrogen, there is the suggestion that the "trace" elements may be more fully understood only when we study the plant parts and processes in which the "trace" elements probably play their major roles, namely, the synthesis of the proteins, the enzymes, and the other phases in cell multiplication or cell reproduction.

THE FIFTH SEMINAR, OR TRACE ELEMENT CLINIC 1949

This clinic-seminar was the fifth one in a series of demonstrations and discussions to help us look to the soil in our nutrition; to get us to think a little deeper. On the farm, when we really think through its agriculture, all our thinking will lead to consider the soil fertility. That is the foundation of agricultural creation. When we think our troubles through, we shall see the soil as the possible origin of nutritional deficiencies, not commonly traced that far. If we do trace them to the soil, the prevention of the troubles will be simple through ministrations to the soil with fertility elements or simple compounds and not to the animals and humans with medicines. We must learn to look to the soil for our health; we must get that three times a day, off the dinner plate with a knife and fork. This clinic-seminar had the testimony of people and of dairy cattle to tell us that the soil is the means of proving the old saying that "To be properly fed is to be healthy."

Some 20 patients, being fed trace elements, volunteered to tell their case histories to the doctors around the consulting table. There were five doctors, including one in dentistry. Records of the blood tests of nineteen, afflicted with Brucellosis, were presented, showing them originally positive reactors to the agglutination test for Brucella infection, but now completely negative after trace element therapy. The time period required to bring that change about varied from six to twenty-five months, apparently, required to arrive at the negative reaction, built by the body mechanisms needed to resist the virus or the microbe. The ages of these recovering folks varied from seventeen to 65 years, with the majority of them in their forties.

As for the dairy cows and their testimony about trace element deficiencies coming as failing health by way of the soil, two farms are under observation and tests. More farms are added to the list for study. On one, the cows are still being given trace elements as supplements in their feed. Others are treated via trace elements applied to the soils and coming via the crops. The results in the improved health of the cows, the restored high milk output, the higher rate of conception and delivery of calves are already telling us that trace element deficiencies in the soil must be considered as cause of the poor health, and offer the possibilities of remedy by the trace elements fed via the soil as the required therapy to eliminate what is called "disease". On another farm, the soil treatments, including all the essential fertility elements that soil-testing and even suspicion suggest as considered deficiencies, have been applied, namely, calcium, magnesium, potassium, manganese, copper, cobalt, zinc, nitrogen, phosphorus, and others, as contaminants, have been applied to the soil. There the better health of the cows is again the testimony. There is no more foot-rot, almost no milk-fever, the hair and skin are clean, glossy and softly pliable, and regular conception results with no more than two services by the bull or artificial insemination. The calf crop is of one-hundred percent, or with no abortions, and above all more milk regularly with the farmer-owner rather than the veterinarian looking after those cows for what they can't look after themselves, are the interesting features about the farm. In the minds of the Nichalsons, several generations put together, the dairy business in southwestern Missouri is not yet going to the dogs. It is carrying those several families forward with optimism.

CONSIDER THE SOIL—NOT ONLY TECHNOLOGIES!

Because we turned away from much of the art of agriculture, we have serious confusion. Let us comprehend the fact that soil fertility, properly coupled with plant nutrition, is a form of creation—a form of outdoor biology—and is not a matter merely of scientific technology. We seem to have lost sight of the fact that the creative business of agriculture has always started in the soil. In terms of wise fertilizer use the most shocking confusion prevails when we talk about soluble fertilizers—considering water as the agency for solution—and then we make laws requiring that fertilizers must be water soluble and thereby so-called "available."

In fact and in nature, these soluble fertilizers are never taken out of the soil, because the plant takes them into itself along with the water that it takes from the soil. The use of the major amount of water by the plant is that of keeping the respiring leaf tissues moist for the exchange of gases—carbon dioxide and oxygen. That escape of water from the leaf is called "transpira-tion." It is in that service that most of the absorbed water goes from the soil into the atmosphere. The use of soil water is controlled by the meteorological situation, which invites water to evaporate from the leaves of the plants against the forces holding the water in the soil. The plant is an innocent con-nection between those two opposing forces that act on the water. Does the moisture in your breath move nutrients from your bloodstream into the tissues, or from your stomach into your bloodstream? Yet we take to the con-cept that the transpiration by the plant has something to do with the move-ment of nutrients from the clay of the soil into the roots.

The transpiration stream of water from the soil, through the plant, and in-to the atmosphere is independent of the nutrient stream from the soil into the roots. the water uptake by the roots is the result of atmospheric conditions favoring evaporation from the leaves with a set of dynamics which are more than a match against the forces holding the water on the surfaces within the soil. Nutrient intake by crops is a function of three colloids, or possibly four, in contact. First of all, there are the nutrients on the clay colloid, or on the organic colloid of the soil. The soil colloid is in contact with the root membrane, which is another colloid. That root membrane is in contact with the contents of a cell on the inside—namely, the protoplasm (or cytoplasm.) In turn, that cell is in contact with another cell. In that you have the combination of three or four colloids in contact. The movement of the nutrient ions from the clay into the root membrane and into the cells follows the chemical laws controlling their traverse there because of the differences in activities, adsorption capacities, interfering ions and other factors along that line.

Movement of nutrients into the root is independent of the transpiration of water. We have demonstrated transpiration going forward regularly—water moving from the soil through the plant to the atmosphere—when the nutrient ions were moving in the reverse directions—namely, going from the plant back to the soil. We have demonstrated the ions going into the plants regularly when there was no transpiration. You can demonstrate this when you put a bell jar with atmosphere saturated with CO_2 and with water over the plant. You can stop the transpiration but you don't stop the ionic movement into the plant. Some recent work at the California Technological Institute shows that the desert plants put water back into the soil while they are growing, therefore the water can be going back into the soil while the nutrients are going in the opposite direction. We must get rid of this water-soluble fertilizer bugaboo, in considering soil fertility and plant nutrition, because transpiration runs independently of our control. And we need to concentrate our efforts on keeping the stream of fertility flowing more regularly into the plants.

Let us not cover either our ignorance or our responsibility in maintaining soil fertility by trying to blame the water situation in the soil and the rainfall. The idea that the "drought" is responsible for the failure of plant nutrition still persists. But what is commonly called "drought" isn't trouble in terms of water only. It is apt to be due to the fact that the upper layer of the soil—where the fertility is—dries and the roots must go down through a tight clay layer, which has almost no fertility. Then, because of crop failure in the absence of plant nutrition in that soil layer of stored water, we try to blame the drought or the bad weather. Our confused thinking about drink for plants emphasizes the water acts as an alibi for our ignorance of plant nutrition and the soil fertility factor, where the emphasis properly belongs. During drought we don't use water to the best of our ability. We neglect to remind ourselves that the plant is about 95% air, water, and sunshine—and only about 5% fertility. We are too indifferent to that fact to consider carefully how we can use that 5% as the requirement to produce the other 95% of plant growth.

We blame the water. We blame the weather. The water of transpiration from the plants is like water going over the millwheel—only a part coming down the millstream. The amount of grist that one grinds in the mill is determined not so much by the amount of water that goes over the millwheel—the amount of which is fixed or limited—as by the diligence with which wheat is kept going into the millstones for 24 hours a day at full capacity. We haven't been keeping the soil fertility well and properly supplied to the crop plant, we are therefore in error when, for disturbed yields, we blame the drought.

THE SOIL AS A FARM COMMODITY OR A FACTORY

It was only a few hundred years ago when the nomadic pastoral existence of peoples shifted to a stationary agriculture and brought with it territorial claims in the name of the individual who tills the soil. That period gave us land ownership with full land and mineral rights, and complete freedom as to land use. It gave birth to the commodity concept of the land, with privilege of barter or sale of the land area in question. Viewing the soil as if it were a common agricultural commodity that we might sell, or save, we have brought ourselves face to face with the need for its conservation, not only in territorial area and body mass, but in terms of the producing capacity inherent in its chemical composition as plant producing value. Now that land has been bartered and traded for years, not only its space dimensions have been carefully and legally defined, but its productivity is undergoing refined definition. Under that attention land has become soil, as a distinct object of study and classification. Values formerly unknown are being attached to it and magnified. Emphasis on these values of the soil is doing much to move land out of the commodity picture or concept, and, as in older countries, to take it off the list of items for simple exchange and sale. We shall be moving rapidly toward a higher appreciation of the soil as it represents our future security and less and less as it is to be considered a commodity.

When carefully examined for its services and functions, the soil plays a dual role. In the first place it is a stock of raw materials. In the second place, it is a factory. As the former, it must contain and retain in stable form against loss by weathering, those items necessary for annual plant growths over an extended time period. As the latter, it must convert the more resistant plant nutrient elements into such forms as are taken by the plants and at such rates as will produce significant plant bulk for an economical crop. We can therefore not view the soil as if it were so many pounds of commodity to be sold like we sell butter, beef, or grains at so much a pound. Rather the soil is the locality where under sunshine power, the contribution of but 5-10 percent of mineral or ash materials by the soil starts their assemblage with the other 95 to 90 percent as inflow of air and water to give us that mystical performance we call crop growth, or agricultural production, and the greatest creation of wealth for human good. Considering the matter from that viewpoint no one would deny the need for soil conservation. Who would destroy the very tool of the earth by which the sun and the skies may be brought to clothe her and to feed and shelter her people?

Because of a limited understanding of the functions of the soil, we have not had a clear concept of handling it even as a commodity. We have not known, or reminded ourselves, what part of it is plant nutrient, much less how much of each nutrient supply we are selling annually. We have not translated our stock of goods on the shelves in the soil store into monetary units which can be added or substracted, or can take in part an inventory. Each deal, or sale, has not made the fertility cash register ring up the removals so as to give us totals at the end of the day or year. We have not translated soil organic matter, phosphorus content, calcium deficiency, or soil acidity, into units of human effort and deeper concern, by which values are most permanently fixed and appreciations most effectively generated in our minds. Given to us by nature for the grabbing (still the method of territorial procurement by many nations), we are yet to develop the appreciation for them, and seemingly only after their exhaustion. As a partial help toward understanding the soil's contribution to plant growth and the magnitude of the performances involved in making a crop, let us first turn to a picture of the composition of vegetation in general for the soil's part in it. The soil contributes but 50 pounds per 1,000 pounds dry matter. But unless these are delivered promptly, the remaining 950 pounds will not be captured from the air and water, and the sunshine power will remain unused.

Conservation of the soil in the fullest sense does not call for the hoarding of the plant nutrients in the soil, but for their wisest use with fullest preservation within the soil. Using more familiar cropping systems, or specific rather than general vegetation as given, we may well examine our business of selling the soil to learn how long we can continue marketing it as a commodity. Much better, let us try to learn how we can run it as a factory without selling off annually much of its essential equipment. Commercial fertilizers have come to give us a monetary value of plant nutrient items. It will be helpful to determine what the annual cash register report would be, should it ring up the fertility removal in terms of the respective nutrients, at fertilizer prices for their return. It may bring appreciation of the fact that the annual fertility turnover is an unrecognized "big business." In that turnover there are hidden some secret costs and some bookkeeping that is deceptive to degrees more challenging than many accounts submitted to congressional investigating committees.

As a simple case, let us assume a two hundred acre farm on virgin Marshall silt loam divided into five 40-acre units, bearing corn, oats, wheat, clover, and grass. With a subsoil laden with storage water and with liberal yields per acre, no larger than 50 bushels of corn, 35 bushels of oats, 20 bushels of wheat, 2 tons of clover hay, and 1½ tons of grass hay equivalent, a five year round on an acre would remove the following in the annual rotation and with the following monetary values.

	Five Year Total Pounds	Annual Pounds	Value
Nitrogen	191	38.2	$3.82
Phosphorus	43.5	8.7	1.30
Potassium	187.6	37.5	1.87
Calcium	106.3	21.2	0.02
Magnesium	39.7	7.9	1.12
Sulfur	9.5	1.9	0.02
Iron	6.3	1.2	---.---
Sodium	6.3	1.2	---.---
Silicon	106.0	21.2	---.---
Annual total value per acre			$8.15

Perhaps it will be no mistake if we disregard the values of the iron which is required in such small amounts as contrasted to the supply in the soil; or if we assign no value and no detriment to the sodium and the silicon, respectively, both considered non-essentials for plant growth. Before dismissing the significance of sodium too light-heartedly, however, it may be well to remind ourselves that it was only about one hundred years ago that the sodium and chlorine delivery by crops dropped to the low level that made agricultural discussion common then as to whether it would be good practice to feed animals ordinary salt or sodium chloride. Then too, our declining soil fertility is reflecting an increasing share of the plant ash as silicon as we go from the better legumes of higher feeding value through the plant series to non-legumes and lower nutritional significance. The significant item in the table is the high value of the fertility taken from the soil annually, given as the figure, $8.15 per acre. Have you ever imagined that on a two hundred acre farm the fertility equivalent of $1,630 is taken out of the soil annually? We do not appreciate the possibility for economic and soil fertility leaks that this unrecognized capital turnover involves. In this capital turnover and its leaks, there are well smothered most of the economic disturbances for which the numerous remedies in the form of changing gold standards and other panaceas are so freely offered in our thinking which stays at no small distance above the surface of the soil. This $8.15 an acre represents an annual production of 3,824 pounds of organic output at the cost of 200 pounds of the soil commodity. One pound of the soil is expended per 19 pounds of produce grown. In terms of the fertilizer prices for the soil expended, the organic matter produce is costing more than 20 cents per hundred weight.

Have we granted that every ton of produce coming from the field is liquidating $4.00 per acre of the assets we initially purchased in the form of a farm? Have we thought that a rent of $4.00 per acre would cover only one-half of the fertility coming out of the soil? Who has been willing to grant that in our economic arrangements we have failed to charge against the produce going off the land this cost to replace to the soil the removed fertility, even if we handle our soil only as a commodity? We have been selling our soil without appreciating its cost, and then find ourselves at a loss to understand our economic troubles. We haven't even understood the material we are selling as a commodity. Should we view the soil more as a factory and less as a commodity, we would return more of the stuffs taken from the soil store and would market more of that portion of the produce captured from air and water. Let us examine the idea of passing the vegetative produce through the animal machine to learn how much the animal will carry away and how much can be returned to the soil.

The working or fattening animal excretes, as an average, 85% of the fertility ingested. Then if the $1,630 worth of fertility capital all goes through such animals they would excrete $1,385. Should they be milking or growing animals, a 65% recovery would excrete but $1,060 of fertility that might go back to the soil. Even with animal use of much from the soil and with no manure loss, one must still be prepared to write off an annual inventory loss of soil fertility on this farm amounting to $245 and $570 annually in these two cases. Such figures take into account no loss of the fertility in the manure before getting it back to the land and are only the losses going off "on the hoof." Additional losses must still be proportionate to the difficulty or the carelessness in manure handling or getting its fertility back to that part of the farm where crops can use it again. Should this manure loss be held to the minimum of about 25%, then this would permit the animal fattener to return $1,222 or 65%, and the dairy farmer $795 or 50 %, of the $1,630 of the rotating fertility capital. Should they permit one-third loss of the manure, which still represents good manure management, then $923 and $706 or approximately 45% and 55%, respectively, of the fertility capital are taken away from the soil.

Should any grain or forage be sold rather than be fed, then by just these percentages of that item's fertility content would the rotating capital suffer additional loss, and the soil be that much more nearly in the commodity sale category rather than in that of the factory. It might seem that fruit farming, where so much of the bulk of output is water, should be more conservative of soil fertility. Let us take an apple orchard of larger tree size with 30 trees per acre, forty feet apart. In terms of only the three major plant nutrients, the total, annual rotating fertility capital would be represented by $2.74 per acre. This, for the apple grower, is much less than the $8.15, which was the amount for the general farmer. But again the loss is 55% of this amount. Though smaller in the absolute, it still represents a loss of more than one-half of the offerings by the soil.

For the peach grower with smaller trees, at 100 per acre, the balance sheet would show a total annual rotating capital of $1,306 per acre. In his case the removal is greater in absolute than for the apple grower or for the general farmer and again 45% of the rotating capital goes off the soil. Thus fruit farming in apples is lower, and in peaches higher in rotating capital annually per acre. The fruit farming does not lessen the responsibility to the soil, only perchance as the seasonal risk is greater and the fruit farmer does not so nearly duplicate the figures annually.

It is conceivable that there may be methods of producing farm products of such nature, and of marketing the parts of such chemical composition so that little more than carbon, hydrogen, and oxygen originating in the air and water is moved off the farm. Should only butter go off, for example, it would sell no soil fertility save that in the casein and in solution in the water in the butter. Sugar cane juice is seemingly mainly carbohydrate, but yet even it carries fertility along with the sugar in solution, reflecting in the juice the fertility of the soil growing it. Escape from the problem of returning fertility is not an easy one. It may be more simple to accept the fact that most any system of farming brings with it the responsibility of knowing how much fertility is leaking out of the rotating supply and how much must be regularly restored.

Should we take the simple calculation that about 50 percent of the rotating fertility is being removed annually, it is still necessary to recognize how this is related to the entire stock in the soil. Using Marshall silt loam with 3,800 pounds nitrogen per acre in virgin surface soil producing the crops previously listed with yields not above 50 bushels of corn or other crop equivalents, with the loss—not covered by clover return—amounting to 19.1 pounds per acre per year, this would be just one-half of one percent of the original supply. Using phosphorus at 1,200 pounds in the virgin soil with only 33 1/3 percent loss, or 2.9 pounds annually, this is more than one-fifth of one percent of the total. Should these annual rates of loss continue, then the Marshall silt loam would be exhausted of its nitrogen store in 200 years. Using the soil as a commodity it would be "sold out" in that time. More complicated calculations are needed to express the declining curve accurately, but yet these results are sufficient to bring us to the conviction that our soils can not be taken as commodities—and still serve as the basis of a permanent agriculture. If our farming is to be permanent and profitable, our soil must be a factory to which we bring regularly or restore promptly the calcium, phosphorus, nitrogen, and other fertility elements escaping from the stock of rotating capital, and in which we maintain these at high operating level. We cannot have permanent agriculture that sells out its soil as a commodity, nor can a national economy of permanence be built on an agriculture operating blindly on such a policy toward its soil.

THE HEALTH OF MAN AND THE SOIL . . .

Man is as healthy as the soil he lives on. Plants must take from the soil those properties which, as herd feed, produce the kind of animals that give good milk and produce healthy calves. Man's best proteins, as in milk, eggs, and lean meat, must be brought from the soil through this vital life line. To be well fed is to be healthy, but to be filled up does not mean to be well-fed.

Carbohydrates have been at the head of the foods list, with proteins second, but proteins and the mineral elements have not been commonly considered together in their close association. They have been classified as those compounds containing nitrogen in total to the extent of about 16%. It is this lack of complete understanding of the protein compounds, of their functions in our bodies, and of the services by the inorganic elements connected with them that much of the irregularity in being well-fed arises. Feeding for health calls for foods and feeds that are more than mere bulk for filling purposes. It demands the appreciation of some physiology, and some comprehension of body functions. Rather than rebuild the fertility of the soil to nourish the tired crop, we have researched the corners of the world for another crop to take its place. By this procedure we have introduced more crops that are making vegetative bulk, and are producing less of real nourishnment for animals. They have been called "hay crops, but not seed crops."

Carbohydrates, composed mainly of air, water, and sunshine, are amply produced for fattening services, but proteins are becoming scarcer in the feeds, which means increasing troubles in the health and reproduction of the animals consuming them. While failing to see the declining fertility of the soil responsible for less milk, less meat, and poorer reproduction, we are calling for more artificial insemination and other procedures looking more toward improved breeding than improved feeding. Legume plants have long been the cow's choice among forages, probably because of the higher concentrations of proteins and inorganic elements in these nitrogen-fixing feeds. Is it possible that the instinct of the animals is directing them to recognize these better proteins when they break from the fertility exhausted soils to graze the grass on the still fertile soil of the highway? It is only when our soils are better in terms of all the essential elements, that they can grow the complete proteins. They should be complete as regards all the eight or ten different amino acids recognized as required for survival.

Instead of turning to drugs and vitamins to meet our health problems it may be more advantageous to find out how best to feed the soil. Soils are the basic resource not only for feeding cows, but also for feeding humans as well. Perhaps there are still enough humans in close contact with the soil, and perhaps enough thinking folks, to carry the responsibility of leading us to undertake the conservation of it and to manage its food potential wisely. If so, then our population may be balanced against its chance for all to be well-fed—and thereby healthy!

9

THE PROTEIN STRUGGLE

PROTEINS ARE BECOMING SCARCER AS SOIL FERTILITY GOES LOWER

Eventually, we shall learn that meat prices are going higher because proteins are becoming scarcer. All this is happening because the soil fertility supplies are going lower. Only the renewal of the fertility and the restoration of the creative capacity of the soil can maintain the production of proteins, feed us along with our animals, and keep the stream of life flowing. Cattle don't create our beef proteins from the elements. They only collect them via the components of the proteins which the consumed plants and the microbes created from these simpler sources. As a consequence, our more complete food proteins in red meat, for example, depend on the higher fertility in the soil by which the forages and the other feed plants are grown. Only very slowly are we coming to see that protein production—which is the very continuation of life itself—depends on the synthesis of these compounds by the plants. Still more slowly are we realizing that the plant's processes for creating proteins are, in turn, premised on the regular and generous fertility delivery by the chemical and biochemical activities within the soil.

Primitive man was highly dependent on his herds and flocks for protein. This scarce item constituted a problem in his, as well as of our, food supply. He was more dependent on them as he migrated farther inland or away from the sea and its fish proteins. Foods from that marine source represent the maximum of fertility in terms of the many essential chemical elements. Man's late entrance into the drama, enacted by all the hungry life forms, suggests that the sea was then already well stocked with all the different creative elements that could be washed there. It contained those elements washed in from the rocks in the course of the development of the soil and under the climatic forces. With his evolution linked closely to the sea water, we may well expect the physiology of man's body to be highly complex. We may expect his body processes to demand complex combination, not only of the major fertility elements, but of the "trace" elements as well.

Primitive man on the move, like cattle on the range, covered extensive fertile soil areas for more protein security. When man lived largely by means of his herds and flocks, it was they, more than he, that looked after the soil fertility for both of them. Already at this early age, he might have been looking after the kinds of crops grown. Man has commonly observed the different kinds of plants he can use. But he has much less commonly observed the fertility of the soils under them. Little of his concern went to the soil's creative power through which the weather can produce them. Consequently, man and his herds moved from crop to crop. Fortunately for him, however, in that shift, the herds led the way. After the animals had grazed out an area, he moved his tents in the direction which the animals determined. They had gone ahead to assay the nutritional quality of the forage according to its value for body growth and repair more than for fattening values.

In the Old World, then, with man on his slow move westward along the northern Mediterranean shore under his limited technologies, it was this fortunate assay of the soils by the herds and flocks which guided agriculture into the more fertile European valleys. It is in these same valleys today where the lucerne (alfalfa) still grows. It is this and other legumes, fixing the atmospheric nitrogen to build up the soil in respect to this element, that determines the size of the manure pile (usually seen in the front yard) and thereby the size of the farming business and the degree of prosperity of the family. Under the legumes and under the surface soils, however, there are also the weathering phosphatic limestones interbedded with potassium-bearing shales. While the soils are but slowly developed from these rocks under the Mediterranean climate, one can understand why the older soil is not worn out or is only slowly eroded at the surface, while the newer soil to replace it is developed by the weathering forces pushing their effects deeper into the fertility-rich subsoil and parent materials. It was this soil depth that has been the fount from which the protein potential has been flowing these many years.

In the New World, man's early agriculture and westward moves were helped much, like his travels across the sea and land, by many technologies. The plow, as one of those, went ahead of the cow over here, even for her misfortune is some cases in relation to protein-rich forage grown by ample soil fertility. Often she had no choice. She was expected to support herself even where the low-protein crop of corn demanded fish protein under each hill for it to make the protein it required to guarantee its own survival. Cleared pine forests were not the cow's choice of territory. When the Creator Himself could make no more than wood on those highly weathered soils—and then only by returning to the soil all of the vegetation He created there—the cow would naturally be expected to put up a cry for imported protein supplements as in the case of the corn plant. She was compelled to call for feeds more concentrated in this nutritional component, as well as all the extra elements required when utilizing crops that give proteins in the supplementary amounts required for fodder and even corn grain. The cow requires more proteins if she is growing, reproducing her kind, protecting her body by herself against invading microbes or foreign proteins, than if she is merely making fat.

Our westward move was in rather rapid order. Our increasing technologies helped to extend the life lines from less fertile, back to more fertile soils, and to bring protein-rich byproducts from the milling, brewing, packing and other industries. All these served to reduce and to keep hidden many of the fertility deficiencies for protein production in the highly weathered soils we crossed in going west. On such soils, which originally produced wood and now under the plow, there is the belief that by crop selection, according to certain plant pedigrees, their products would necessarily be high quality feeds for growing animals. The protein problem finally showed up and all the more serious. While we were marching westward, the economic situations did much to keep protein feed concentrates moving in the opposite direction. We were thus unwittingly solving the problem of protein deficiencies in the East. The plow went much in advance with expanding crop acreages. It was keeping far ahead of the herds which followed slowly. But before long, the herds had come west, too. They moved to the deeper soils with lime-laden exchange capacities, and with unweathered mineral reserves that were windblown from flood deposits hauled in by rivers from the mountainous West. Moved as they were to soils which represent fertility mixtures as complete as possible, these animals found their bonanza in the midcontinent and on the plains. When they came west to rustle for themselves and to copy the soil area which the American Bison had mapped out for himself, the cow herds reached their zenith as reproducers of their own kind and climaxed man's claim for making them.

While the cattlemen deserve much credit for what they have done for the success of that phase of agriculture that gives us one of our finest food proteins, namely, beef, let us not forget that the cow deserves credit too. Viewing the cattle business carefully, even the cattlemen confess that credit must go to the cow in combination with the soil fertility which she has chosen wisely more often than have her owners. It was an experienced cattleman of the plains country who said, "We really don't raise them. We only count them." Since that remark was made during the depression days, it was appropriate repartee to reply, "If you don't, the banker will."

Now that our westward livestock expansion has about expended itself and we are settling down to feed our animals on what grows right where we and they are, we are more conscious of the fact that proteins are becoming relatively scarcer and their costs are therefore going higher. Tempted, as some may be, to hope for economic adjustments suggesting manipulations, or for legislative enactments for price control, those of longer experience in any kind of agricultural production are turning to consideration of the possibility of creating better feeds through more and better plant proteins. They agree, that if we are to feed rather than only fatten our livestock, we must treat the soils with extra fertility.

Soil conservation is becoming less and less a matter of fighting running water which has always been running down hill. Conservation of the soil has now been recognized as a matter of rebuilding the fertility strength of a weak and broken soil body. It has become a matter of growing more proteins in more crops to keep the soil covered, and also, for that soil cover to serve as animal nourishment. These crop proteins are more scarce than we realize because the fertility of the soil, which is required to produce them, was going without our notice of its departure until much of the soil itself was going, too. When our pioneer leaders were talking about the benefactor to agriculture being one who could make two blades of grass grow where but one grew before, they were not expecting him to bring in substitute grass crops of which each blade had less than half the nutritive value of the one blade that was displaced. They were asking not merely for two blades, but for doubled feed value from the same soil area. Doubled feed value called for double proteins along with doubled carbohydrates; this called for doubling the soil fertility per plant. Can we call him a benefactor who is giving us two blades of grass by doubling the carbohydrates but gives us no increase in proteins, vitamins, inorganics, etc., beyond those in the original one blade? Shall we call him a benefactor who will fool us with fillers and fatteners when we need body growers and body protectors like the proteins?

The past decline in soil fertility was kept hidden from us (but not from our livestock) by bigger crop quantity of lowered nutritional quality. It is true that we have found substitute legume crops. For example, let's take the Red Clover, once common in the midcontinent. Red Clover failed because it was starving for nutritional help from the soil. Once plentiful, these nutritional elements were soon mined out after many Red Clover and other high-protein crops were taken off. The substitutes spread rapidly because we were satisfied with their yields as bulk. We forgot to call in the cow and submit the crop for her approval under her criterion demanding, not one that merely fattens a castrated, mature male, but one that makes calves become cows and cows come with calves. Her criterion does not approve "new" crops making merely more carbohydrates to dilute their proteins. The cow brute approves, as "grow" feeds, only those feeds with a nutritive ratio narrower than most of our highly-heralded forage substitutes. She disapproves substitute crops delivering more bulk without extra fertility to hold up the nutritional values of those crops. She turns thumbs down on what is only a substitute, making bulk where the predecessor failed because the declining fertility prohibited it from making of itself the higher nutritive values in that same bulk. In spite of our many "new" legumes, we doubt whether the pioneer farmer, who used Red Clover as supplement to corn, would grant that we have yet produced another legume forage to supplement corn grain equally as well as Red Clover supplemented the corn when both were grown about a half century ago.

Considering limited acreage, scarcity and high price of seed, plus our campaigns to "Lime the Soil for Clover and Prosperity" few of us would grant that we have done much for medium Red Clover. We are compelled to believe that all our delicate measurements of pH of the soil, our fight on soil acidity on a national scale, and the millions of tons of carbonates put on the land by financial helps suggesting political porkbarrel procedures have been in vain for keeping this good protein-producing legume from going out when corn, the carbohydrate producer, remained. Are we not ready to look to the nutritional demands which red clover (or any other nutritious forage) makes on the soil that grows it? Can we as crop men not treat the soil to feed the plants properly, just as the livestock man knows the feed demands his animals make in order to satisfy them? Is the certification of the seed and of the variety name any guarantee that it can create a crop from any soil merely because we scatter that seed of noble pedigree anywhere under blue sky, ample rain, and generous sunshine? May we not need more than lime and reduced acidity there? May we not need lime to feed this forage some magnesium and some calcium? Is the introduction of phosphate rock enough? The increasing use of potassium is helping to hold Red Clover on some soils, but on others, this soil treatment has not sufficed. Quite contrary to the opinion of many, a little nitrogen fertilizer along with the clover seeding has done much to establish this crop on some soils. Didn't the pioneer use it on the black soils of the prairies showing by chemical analysis from four to six thousand pounds of nitrogen per acre plowed layer?

When the sulfur-containing part of our required proteins, namely the amino acid, methionine, has now become almost the major deficiency in our feed crops, and to the degree that invites its commercial chemical synthesis on a large scale, it is significant to note that Red Clover has lasted longer on the experimental plot where both rock phosphate and the sulfur containing superphosphate were used than where rock phosphate was applied alone. Then, too, when Red Clover is still growing nicely on the old, very acid, Jordon plots at Penn State College where only manure has been used these many years, there comes the suggestion that possibly not only the elements: Sulfur, magnesium, potassium, the trace elements and others, but also some organic compounds in cycle from the plant back to the soil and into the plant again, may be the soil deficiencies bringing failures in our protein-producing legumes of such high feed values as Red Clover. In spite of all our faith in legume seed pedigrees, the plant's lifetime nourishment is not provided in that way. We cannot expect a clover crop (or any other protein-producing crop) merely because we turn the seed out to rustle for itself. The soil must be fertile in all the requirements for feeding the plant so it can create its proteins. Raising protein-rich crops is no different than raising cattle on the range where they rustle for themselves. In both cases, the soil is the source of what they make. Protein production by the plants and in turn by the animals is therefore determined by the soil fertility. We are slowly realizing that failures of our choice protein-producing crops register the failing soil fertility, and, already hidden too long to connect with soil failure as the cause, the mounting animal failures.

Making a calf crop doesn't give much credit to the herdsman. That accomplishment must be credited mainly to the cow. The herdsman is largely an observer. With the fact cows once made calves entirely without our help, it raises the question whether our management of the cow is really a help or a hindrance in her calf-making performance. One must suspect the latter on noting the high percentage of sterile cows, or so called "shy-breeders," continually hampering the profit aspect of the cattle business. Cow failures are following in the wake of soil fertility neglect. Under artificial procedures, the numerous matings required for conception which usually succeed eventually in case of natural insemination, cause us to give up and turn the shy-breeder over for slaughter; this should provoke some serious thinking. Such observations ought to raise the question whether the larger dose of semen repeatedly served by the male, in the former practice, is not a kind of successive hormone administration to bring about better ovulation and eventual conception. This may not be the case under the limited semen supply used in the latter practice.

The physiological load of reproduction carried by the female is larger than that of the male. Also this fact is not commonly appreciated when we contend that "The bull is half of the herd." Neglect of the nutrition of the cow, especially the generous use of proteins and all that comes along with their production by crops on fertile soil, suggests itself as the major cause of the trouble when we want to carry our cows through the winter cheaply. In that saving of feed, we are "penny wise and pound foolish" when we suffer the loss of the cow's breeding service for at least a year and consequently have a low percentage calf crop. The feeds of low protein content may keep the cows in enough fat to resemble a "good condition" but that is not "breeding condition" or reproducing ability. When considering that the protein of corn grain has fallen from 10.3% to an average of 8.3% in some thirty years, to say nothing about what may have happened to the quality or nutritional completeness of that protein from mining rather than managing our soil fertility, this fact seems too far removed from shy-breeding cows to make us see any possible causal connection between the former and the latter. Cow failures are the sequel to soil fertility failures.

Under declining soil fertility and corresponding decline in feed values, the load of reproduction is becoming too heavy to be carried successfully during the period of gestation. If the increasing abortions and the mounting percentages of so-called "midget" calves are not studied more critically in terms of nutrition, rather than dodged by putting the blame on some aspect offering more mental escape, these losses may occur astoundingly often. Only recently, a herd was reported as having 25% of calf crop defective as "midgets." For last year, the figure was 18% of the crop. Abortions in some parts of Missouri bring about figures equally as appalling. In this latter case, the fight on some microbes—which may be only a symptom and not the cause—stimulates the search for serums from similar microbes under laboratory culture which gives an escape via what suggests a kind of blind alley. This so-called "disease" is now having the cows killed to eliminate the "disease" while it is eliminating our cows too. It is following a line of reasoning like burning down the house to get rid of bed bugs. But in the case of the "midgets," even the belief that it is a breeding problem is of no consolation. It is not limited to any one breed in either of these groups.

Any struggle to escape via some hopeful aspect of genetics suggests itself as only a delay of the day when the cause will be located. Reduced body size may well suggest reduced nutrition to the geneticist when the genes, the chromosomes, and the nuclei, as the very centers of genetic performances, are the most specific in their types of proteins for life-carrying activities. Whenever a chromosome is divided, each half must grow back to size again if it is to permit the next regular division of each of the two new cells. If the dividing process is not to play itself out of that very possibility, it must do that growing of protein by protein nutrition. Of all the growth behaviors, those under genetics must certainly find their physiological foundation in the proteins. That foundation certainly is not to be found in the fats and the carbohydrates. If our failing soil fertility is still supporting the plants as producers of carbohydrates, but is letting them down as producers of proteins, is it too much of a stretch of the imagination to see the cow being let down in calf production to the "midget" level during gestation by that low level of feeds pulled down by the deficiencies in the soil?

When the means by which body characters are transmitted from generation to generation seem so mystical to many folks, genetics as a new science is seized in hope of an explanation, especially when so much is still unknown and yet Nature has done so much. The plant breeder has been hoping to breed legume forages which will "tolerate" soil acidity. He has had hopes of breeding cereals that will "tolerate" low winter temperatures, the smuts, the rusts, and hosts of other troubles suggesting themselves as manifestations of the plants' physiological inequality to the soil's limited offerings. Other aspects of the setting which involves the plant is the struggle to create the proteins by which it grows and protects itself from invasions by foreign proteins. If the hopes for this procedure of breeding unusual "tolerations" into the species were to be successful, should it be beyond the breeder's hopes—if we followed that line of reasoning to its limit—to breed animals to tolerate starvation and save all the feed? An experiment set up with that hope would go forward for only one generation, in fact, no farther than one hoping to breed a race of bachelors. Shall we look to the breeder to uncover the changed genetics responsible for the "midgets" or shall we search out the changed, disturbed or destroyed physiology in the calf because of malnutrition of the mother and of the calf in the foetal stage? A few studies of the blood chemistry of the "midgets" have found such low levels, and near absences, of some of the soil-borne essential elements to suggest the source of the trouble in some nutritional deficiencies in the cow's feed, or troubles going back to the soil for their origin. Even then, the soil-borne essential elements must do more then hitchhike from the soil through the crop, through the cow to the foetal calf. The creation of the "midget" calf suggests its irregularities traceable to irregularities in the fertility of the soil and the feed grown on it. It is leaning toward a waning faith in breeding but a waxing hope in feeding.

The cow is one of the higher forms of life and just below man in the biotic pyramid. Consequently, like him, she lives under greater hazards of threatening nutritional deficiencies because of her lofty position giving higher chemical complexity. Unfortunately, her nutrition is too completely controlled by man prohibiting her to care for herself in that activity by her own instincts, however she struggles to demonstrate those for her own good. Man, who follows no instincts of his own for his better nourishment, prohibits the cow from following hers. Instead, he labors under the delusion of sufficiency of his wisdom for wise guidance of the nutrition of both himself and her.

Lessons may well be taken from nature. Careful observation of the ecological pattern of wildlife, and of its struggle to get its proteins, has much that is significant help in our efforts to feed our livestock. It will point to the proteins as the problem, not in terms of business transaction trading them from one place or person to another, but in terms of the fertility of the soil to create them. Agriculture is first and always a matter of creation and then, later, one of speculation. One doesn't do any horse trading without a horse. Neither does one do any creation of life without some soil as the basis of it. Now that we have connected the essential element, nitrogen, in the soil with more protein in the crop and with more crop, a major lesson from Nature has developed. Cells multiply to increase the total yield when they get more nitrogen and other elements from the soil to make more protein. More protein means more cell multiplication. Since we have been building up the soil in calcium, phosphorus and potassium beyond what legumes were using in getting nitrogen from the air, the increased chemical nitrogen now used as fertilizer is demonstrating some miraculous effects in the way of bigger crops.

Nature responds quickly when we strengthen the weakest link as we do in providing fertilizer nitrogen, which is the weakest fertility link in the soil for protein production.

High protein crops, however, make such good feed for growing young animals. This is true not just because these feeds contain much nitrogen as proven by burning the crop in sulfuric acid, but they are good feeds as growth promoters and health promoters because in making such complete life-carrying substances, they must be taking a long list of many things from the soil. Along on that list, they have been taking the trace elements. Also they are taking compounds as well as elements. Because the high-protein crops do so much in their creative ways, experiments have shown their roots must be equipped to exhaust the fertility supplies of the soil to a lower level. Crops making more protein for good nutrition for us are making it first for nutrition for themselves; therefore they must also take more from the soil for these special accomplishments. Now that chemical nitrogen suddenly comes in to do so much, we dare not forget that all the other elements in our soils are being exhausted all the more rapidly. Our legume crops were and are bringing about the same situation. On test plots where legumes were used in crop rotations for 60 years on Sanborn Field of the Missouri Experiment Station, the soil fertility, outside of nitrogen, is lowest. More and better protein can be had only as we learn to put into the soil all the fertility elements and compounds required to create it, first, in the microbes and the plants, and then in our animals. The natural seasonal birth pattern of our grazing animals brings the parturition in the spring of the year. One might believe that this is due to the shift from lower to higher temperature giving a favorable matter in terms of comfort relative to cold and heat rather than the nutritional comfort, or the "inner" comfort. It is the warming soil that starts plants growing. The result of the higher soil temperature speeds up the fertlity delivery to feed the plant roots. The growing spring plants are high in protein since the shorter days have not pushed up the plant's photosynthesis to the point of making carbohydrate production and cellulose bulk delivery their main activity. Protein production, and a high concentration of it with the accompanying compounds to carry on this process within the early spring growth of grass, is the reason young grass is good grazing for the mother which has suddenly taken on the increased physiological load of giving milk for the young. Nature has synchronized the biochemical performances of the animals and the plants to fit those chemicals and biochemicals of the soil.

The grazing wild sheep move upward higher into the mountains with the advance of the spring season. The later advent of the first grass growth at higher altitudes is the reason, but it is also the means of giving these wild animals their supply of protein concentrates in the herbage. They don't purchase protein supplements on the market. The Swiss dairyman, who also cannot import protein supplements, follows the same principle by moving his cows to higher altitudes for grasses. These grasses in their early protein-rich stages of growth, are dependent on freshly weathered rocks for their fertility supply. Nature's lessons through wildlife and the habits of even our livestock tell us that proteins are the problems for our plants. Consequently they are then the problems for our animals and ourselves, too, since we only collect them. The struggle to live through the winter presents a problem for plants, too. This problem is solved by nature because the shortening days of the autumn reduce the plant's rate of piling up carbohydrates, and allow the plant's conversion of those into proteins by means of soil fertility to dominate. This process may well be called "hardening off" the plants to prevent, what some would call, "winter killing." Winter wheat and barley are often said to have "winter killed." It would be more logical in most of those cases to forget "winter killing" and consider it "winter starvation" for proteins. High protein contents in the autumn help plants to go through the winter. All of this tells us that increased winter killing is due to declining soil fertility, and that it is capable of prevention by more nitrogen and all else that goes with it to make the complete proteins the plant needs by which to live.

Critical studies of nutrition, whether of microbes, plants, animals or man, point to the proteins in quantity and in quality as the problem. Natural phenomena all about us suggest the growing scarcity of these compounds, and grown to the present degree of shortage in no small measure because we have not refined our concepts of the proteins, their functions in physiology, and the soil fertility by which they in their more complete array of amino acids are created in agricultural production. In dealing with living things, the many factors involved make the picture in its entirety a rather large and complex one. We cannot comprehend the whole. We do well to see only the parts. We have not yet learned what good health of our animals, or of ourselves, really is. We do not study animal good health. We study mainly animal "bad" or "failing" health. Working backward from the carcass and the cadaver by post-mortems, we call in the pathologist to explain, and to put on a label, if not even a quarantine. But this usually lets physiology—an explanation and understanding of the real cause—remain unknown. We have been using the label "X-disease," for example, which means that the "X" is unknown. Too long has "disease" been an unknown, too. But slowly we see body degeneration compelling us to believe that much that we call "disease" should be considered malnutrition, and should send us to growing better feeds of more total and more complete proteins.

"To be well-fed is to be healthy," but that calls for plenty of complete proteins possible only on fertile soils. Our failure to feed completely is not the only contributor to troubles in growing our livestock. We must also look to the possibility that we are subjecting our animals to slowly reacting poisons. The "X-disease" may be only one case of our poisoning our animals—and ourselves—now that we are using such deadly poisons that serve as insecticides and herbicides. They may be hom(o)(i)cides too. These are all chemically complex compounds, built out of the so-called chemical ring carbon structures. The human body cannot break these down. It may only rework them and possibly with disastrous effects. The ring compounds the body uses are most powerful in the smallest amounts. The "X-disease" is now connected with chlorinated naphthalene or a double ring compound. This fact points to the many other ring compounds taken out of the soil by plants and appearing, for example, in the bean seeds, the potatoes and in the fruits.

We may thus be delivering poisons for one form of life, and for one supposedly beneficial effect, while unwittingly dealing a slow death to our livestock if not ourselves. We must protect our animals from excessive drugs and slow poisons as well as prevent malnutrition by means of good feeding. Only as we see feed proteins in their complete array of the quantities of amino acids balanced for body growth, for reproduction, and for protection against the invasion of foreign proteins like viruses and microbes; only as we learn more about how the cow would feed herself for offspring production rather than how we would carry her cheaply through the winter or fatten her; only as we discover the details of plant physiology by which we can know the crops which in combination will give us the complete proteins as feed; and finally, only as we know more about the soil fertility management that will undergird the plants' struggle in making proteins from the required chemical elements, can we expect to start the assembly line of the creation of livestock so that it will run in high order and without mishaps at all stages along that line. Only as we build up the soil can we escape the fact that our proteins that minister to better health to man and his animals are becoming scarcer because the soil fertility for the soil's power of creation is going lower.

MANAGING NITROGEN TO INCREASE PROTEIN IN GRAINS

Water supply and weather conditions have too long been offered in explanation of much that in reality is soil fertility and plant physiology. This becomes increasingly evident as we better understand the chemical and biochemical dynamics in the soil and the biosynthetic services within the plant creating feed and food compounds for us. Variations in the protein content of wheat and corn are not attributable primarily to plant variety or to the conditions under which the plant is grown. They correspond, in large measure, to variations in the fertility of the soil itself. The tendency toward higher protein content or "hardness" in wheat as one moves westward through Missouri and Kansas has long been associated with the rainfall factor. Careful study, however, reveals that the fertility of the soil and not the weather's vagaries or the specific variety is responsible for the concentration of protein in the grain. A high concentration results when a generous supply of nitrogen is delivered by the roots just before the heading of the wheat takes place. Accordingly then for high protein or hard, horny grains, the roots must have access to adequate supplies of available nitrogen at that stage of the plant's development. If not already there, they can be provided by applications of soluble nitrogen.

That this hypothesis is correct was established by Dr. R.L. Lovvorn, now of the U.S. Department of Agriculture, and Professor M.F. Miller at the University of Missouri. They demonstrated wide variations in the "hardness" or in the concentrations of crude protein in the grains of a single variety of wheat. This was accomplished by successive applications of nitrate fertilizers at intervals of two weeks from April 4 to May 29 on a series of plots in a field of Putnam silt loam. On this soil, with its shallow surface layer overlying an acid, tight-clay subsoil, the successive applications of soluble nitrogen gave increasingly higher concentrations of crude protein in the wheat. The kernels were less and less yellow in color and more nearly translucent. They were harder. The percentage of protein stepped up from a minimum of 8.92 from the early applications to a maximum of 17.00 from the later applications. This was an increase of 8.08% in the absolute. It was a relative increase of almost 90% in the higher over the lower concentration.

Here then on acid soil, developed under conditions of heavy rainfall, the variation in the stage of plant growth at which nitrogen was made available to the crop produced as wide a range in the concentration of protein as has been recorded for the entire wheat crop from Missouri to western Kansas. Thus in Missouri, which is regarded as a "soft" wheat state, apparently we can have any kind of wheat and any kind of flour, from the "soft" (biscuit) to the "hard" (light bread) variety, depending upon the fertility of the soil rather than upon the weather or the variety of wheat. The time of applying nitrogen affects not only the concentration of crude protein in the grain but also the total yield of grain and of protein. Although the late application increased the concentration of protein in the grain, it reduced the yield of both grain and of protein. The yields of grain dropped from a maximum of 24.2 to a minimum of 11.7 bushels per acre. Yields of total protein fell from 160 to 91 pounds per acre. These data were for single plots and for different dates of nitrogen application.

Here is the suggestion, then, that for good vegetative growth and large yields of grain, the nitrogen must be available early in the growing season. For a high concentration of protein in the grain, extra nitrogen must be available shortly before heading time. By correlating the nitrogen application to the physiology of the plant so as to determine whether the nitrogen is employed in making vegetative mass or in synthesizing protein in the grain, it should be possible to produce both a large yield of bushels per acre and a high concentration or percent of protein in the grain. If a strain of wheat grown in Missouri and Kansas showed such variations in concentration of protein in the grain, should they not be attributed to the variation in the stages in the plant's development at which the roots encounter large amounts of available nitrogen in the soil? If so, then it is logical to believe that the higher concentration of protein in the wheat grain as we travel west from Missouri across Kansas, is to be explained on the ground that the roots find soil strata with more available nitrogen at successively later dates in the plant's growth period. If that is so, it follows that the delay in making contact with the nitrogen supply would depend upon the depth of the strata in the profile. Making this contact near heading time means a hard, horny, or high-protein grain.

This reasoning is validated by the studies of Professor J.C. Russell of Nebraska, who found that the smaller amount of soil moisture required for the production of nitrates in contrast to the quantity needed for plant growth permits the nitrates to be made and to move downward in the soil faster than the roots can follow. It should not strain the imagination to visualize the nitrates in the downward movement through this underdevoloped, mineral rich, near-Chernozem soil, being overtaken by the wheat roots just about "heading time." This would naturally mean lower yields in bushels per acre and higher concentrations of protein in the grain. Soils of the more humid region that do not have generous nitrate delivery from the reserve organic matter in a narrow carbon-nitrogen ratio nor the higher inorganic fertility mobilizing it, cannot be expected to have either high-grain yield or high concentrations of proteins in the grain. They do not provide the microbial performances associated with, and required for, such a specific timing of natural delivery of nitrate as occurs in the semi-humid soils farther west.

If the results of three surveys made in the last 10 or 11 years may be accepted as conclusive, there has been a decline in the protein concentration in Kansas wheat equal in significance to the relationship between the timing of extra supplies of available nitrogen and the protein content of the wheat grain. A survey of the percentage protein of Kansas grain made in 1940 showed a range of 10 to almost 19%. In a similar survey ten years later, in 1949, protein concentration was found to range from 9 to less than 15%. During this ten year period, Kansas produced seven record-breaking wheat crops. One of them was nearly 300 million bushels. Annual removal of so much nitrogen from the soil without adequate replacement suggests the possibility that the supply of nitrogen in the soil may have been reduced to a level at which it is no longer capable of maintaining the high concentration of proteins in the grain of which that state once boasted. If so, attention must be given to the use of commercial nitrogen fertilizer on the wheat crop near heading time if production of the high-protein grain of the past is to be continued.

We do not know of any report of studies of the concentration of crude protein in the corn grain as related to the application of nitrogen as specific periods in the plant's growth. It is significant, however, that the concentration of protein in the corn grain dropped from 9.5 to 8.5% during a 10 year period in which there were substantial increases in the yields of grain. It is interesting to note the reduction in the protein content of corn as reported in successive editions of a standard handbook of feeds and feeding. In the

Eleventh Edition, published 40 years ago, the only figure quoted for crude protein of dent corn was 10.3%. In the Twenty-First Edition, 1950, five grades of corn were cited, for which the protein figures ranged from 8.8 to 7.9, with a mean of nearly 8.4%. During the interval of 40 years between the two editions, crude protein in corn dropped from 10.3 to 8.4, a reduction of 22%. Thus, it is strongly indicated that the high rate at which nitrogen is being removed from the soil without compensating replacement is adversely affecting the concentration of protein in corn, as well as in wheat.

In view of the declining concentration of crude protein in both the corn and wheat grains, the question arises whether the array of amino acids which compose it is now as complete in terms of the nutritional requirements of animals and man as it was at the higher concentrations of proteins in these feed and food grains. It is logical to expect that nitrogen which is available early in the plant's growth period will be more completely metabolized into the complex proteins composing the germ. Whether this extra metabolism guarantees the conversion of the nitrogen into the more complete list of essential amino acids remains to be established. Nitrogen delivered later in the plant's growing period shows up as protein in the endosperm and distributed as simpler amino acids through the starchy reserve portion of the grain. This suggests the use of the nitrogen almost wholly for making the simpler, more common amino acid, leucine. In its chemical structure, leucine is similar to starch or to the simpler carbohydrate structure with its six carbon atoms. Thus, one might be inclined to accept the late delivery of nitrogen as the reason for its quick attachment to this common carbon chain by some simple amination process rather than by successive biosynthetic elaborations resulting in a less common amino acid like tryptophane, for example. Compared to other amino acids, leucine is relatively simple in structure. It is widely distributed and is found in the starch rather than in the embryo portion of the seed. It makes up about 25% of zein, the incomplete corn protein which lends itself like cellulose to artificial fiber synthesis. For these reasons, this "late" protein in the plant's biosynthetic processes seems decidedly "crude" as far as its nutritional service to animals is concerned. Leucine is regarded as a conversion of nitrogen into protein but it hardly rates the high nutritional evaluation of the truly complete proteins.

We are experiencing a world shortage of proteins but are slow to recognize the lack of soil fertility adequate for biosynthesis of complete proteins as responsible for it. Instead, our complacency in larger production of "crude" protein, according to ash analysis, by soil treatments, and our dependence on commercial nitrogen for higher yields per acre, are apt to lull us into indifference about the fundamental use of nitrogen via the crop's biosynthetic services and the soil in relation to other aspects of fertility if we are to be well fed. The time of root contact with nitrogen in the soil by the growing crop, has significance for the quality as well as the quantity of the final food product.

DOUBLES PROTEIN YIELD

A way to double the yield of protein from an acre of lespedeza has been found. It involves two common treatments, liming and phosphating. The discovery was made when Missouri research workers began to combine different fertilizer treatments after having determined their effects when applied singly. On the level prairie type of Putnam silt loam, superphosphate was used both alone and in conjunction with limestone. The clearly visible differences in lespedeza growth and the extent to which grasses and other foreign plants were smothered prompted not only careful measure of the crop stand and yield, but also a chemical study of the crop.

Where no treatment was applied the hay was only 762 pounds an acre. Phosphate alone gave 889 pounds, or 16% increase, but when limestone and phosphate were combined the hay yield mounted to 1394 pounds, an increase of 83%, and almost five times the weight increase from phosphate. Yield figures alone fail to tell the complete story. Phosphorus in the lespedeza given phosphate was 24% larger than that in the untreated crop. Combination treatment increased the phosphorus content by 76%. Lime gave the crop capacity to take more than three times as much of this essential element. Such results suggest that if the phosphate investment is to be returned with profit in form of increased phosphorus taken into a crop like lespedeza, we may well look to the limestone level of the soil.

That the phosphate investment was supported by the limestone may be reasoned from the greater protein harvest. We can't grow protein for livestock without the phosphorus that is an essential constituent of it. More protein from each acre demands more phosphorus from the soil. This protein can't be manufactured, seemingly, by the plant unless it has access to limestone, or calcium, along with the phosphorus. While the protein in the harvest mounted, the calcium content in the crop also moved upward. Where phosphate was used there was an increase of 23% of calcium in the crop over that from the untreated soil; but addition of limestone, the carrier of calcium, increased this element in the hay by 85%.

That calcium is concerned with protein production within the legume and that it has some significance in making phosphate applications more effective is supported by the fact that protein production per acre mounted at a rate which paralleled phosphorus consumption by the crop. But when limestone supplemented phosphate, the protein harvested rose much faster than the phosphorus taken from the soil. This indicates forcibly that the use of limestone made the phosphorus go farther in protein production. For example, that phosphate treatment which increased calcium content by 23% and the total phosphorus by 24%, resulted in 31% greater protein harvest. Thus the rise in protein was similar to the greater phosphorus intake.

On the other hand, the combined treatment, which accounted for that

85% increase in calcium and 76% of phosphorus, boosted the protein harvest 146%. In this case protein production was proportionately greater than the phosphorus intake. Use of lime to make phosphate more effective is illustrated in another way. Hay from the phosphated soil contained 11.3% protein and 8.8 pounds of it were required to yield a pound of protein, or only 1/10 pound less than from untreated soil. Lime jumped the protein content to 13% and reduced the hay required to supply a pound of protein to 7.6 pounds.

Putting this kind of hay thru the cow would mean a greater and more effective delivery of protein from her physiological machine. Efficiency of limestone with reference to the phosphorus utilization by lespedeza reflects itself in greater efficiency in the cow's utilization of the hay. Whether she will put a higher ash content and more vitamins into her milk from feed of such better composition only later tests can determine. It seems logical to expect that cows fed on hay rich in phosphorus and calcium should not break down with milk fever on calving; because they will have built up a calcium reserve in their body instead of depleting it to the danger point in foetus development.

Not only legumes, but the corn crop as well, fits into this general idea of better use of fertilizer treatment of the soil when supplemented by limestone. Last summer, analyses were made of the total corn plants as fodder when in the tassel and presilk stage during July to learn further of this interaction of lime and fertilizers. Here, as with legume, this same relation held; but with greater significance, since total draft on the soil for phosphorus by corn is much higher than by lespedeza. Yields also were increased much more by the addition of lime to the fertilizers. Lime was effective in making the crop take more phosphorus, more nitrogen and more of the other nutrients.

Building fertility is a slow process and many of us are reluctant to put money back into the soil in the form of fertilizers. This reluctance may have come in part from applications of only one ingredient when there was a multiple deficiency. Under such conditions, returns may be only moderate. In most soils more than one fertilizer nutrient is needed, and usually lime should go along with the more costly ones. Its value as a fertilizer and particularly as a supplementary agent in making other plant nutrients more effective should be widely recognized. The small additional investment will guarantee greater returns from all treatments. Limestone may be considered individual crop insurance. When we appreciate more fully the need by soils for some of these elements so fundamental as lime, phosphorus and others, and when we apply them not singly, but jointly, we shall support the legume sod crops in the fertility restoration and conservation service which we expect them to perform.

MORE AND BETTER PROTEINS

Unlike carbohydrates and fats, but more like vitamins and minerals, proteins are required in the nutrition of man and animals as specific chemical structures. None of these will substitute for any of the others. As for proteins, the body demands them as certain very specific chemical arrangements of the constituent elements. While the list of vitamins—still growing as a set of specific chemical structures—is a recent matter of the last 20 years, the known 22 amino acids composing the proteins represent evolutionary knowledge extending over a half century. Ten of these are specifically required for the survival of the white laboratory rat. Eight are absolutely essential for man if he is to live. It is the provision of these specific parts of the proteins—more than of mere compounds carrying nitrogen—that has probably become the major part in our struggle for good nutrition.

Proteins have become a problem of creation in agricultural production. Proteins can be popped up either in quantity, or in quality, only by soils more fertile in terms of both the inorganic and the organic respects—many known and possibly unknown. It is this significant fact connected with the soil that the declining protein production by our crops ought to be calling our attention more universally. Just how plants make proteins is still one of nature's mysteries. We have given little thought to the possibility that plants are struggling to make their necessary proteins, just as animals are ranging far and wide to collect theirs. Nor have we thought that healthy man must be highly omnivorous and that all of these are efforts to make certain that each form of life is getting the complete list of the required amino acids. Only recently have we become concerned about feeding our crops in place of merely turning them out at seeding time to rustle for themselves until "rounded up" at harvest time.

Unfortunately, for ourselves, in connection with the protein foods and the protein-supplementing foods, we have already too long called anything protein when it contains nitrogen in some organic combination. To date we have made sharp distinctions about the quality—for our nutrition—of the nitrogen in our organic compounds, when little more than half of the organic nitrogen we feed, or eat, is really in the amino combination for which we emphasize the amino acids. We must become more specific in our thinking about proteins, by considering them a balanced combination of their component amino acids as the human or animal body requires them.

Alfalfa grows well with little added fertility on soils blown by the wind from out of the Missouri River bottoms. It grows well on such soils representing deposits of soil materials brought from much farther west. But alfalfa is in trouble on some of the western volcanic soils of such recent deposit that they are deficient in sulfur because of volcanic ignition. While we are slowly recognizing the declining concentrations of proteins in our corn and in our wheat, the seriousness of that decline is not yet realized widely enough for much to be done about it. In the case of wheat, pre-harvest protein surveys—taken by counties over the State of Kansas by the Crop Reporting Service of the U.S. Department of Agriculture in 1940 and 1949-1951—tell of the declining concentration of the protein in this food grain.

When our corn and our wheat crops are slipping lower in their creation of proteins in total; when these food essentials are already known to be incomplete in the essential amino acid, tryptophane, for example, in corn, and lysine in the case of wheat; and when those originally more fertile soils produced higher concentrations of proteins in these same grains once upon a time, isn't it high time for us to look at our national protein problem? Shall we not view it as one of soil-fertility exhaustion under two of our most extensively grown grasses, which corn and wheat are? Shall we view our meat problem and our milk problem as merely matters of economics? Shall we not recognize the great natural forces which are responsible for the bad economics?

Shall we believe that a different kind of agriculture, called grass agriculture, will solve the problem? It ought soon to become clear that the human's struggle for meat—the choice food protein—is merely part and parcel of the struggle by all life for its proteins. There will be no escape from that struggle by asking our animals to eat grass grown on any soil and to give us the relief from that struggle by their solution of the problem. It is not solved when our farm animals ask the plants on less fertile soil to provide them with protein. The abundance of this nutritional necessity in our crops, in our larger numbers of domestic meat animals, and in the markets for ourselves will become possible, not because we juggle crops or systems of agriculture and economics, but only because we prop up the whole biotic pyramid consisting of microbes, plants, animals, and man by means of the most completely fertile soils as the foundation of it.

PROTEINS AND REPRODUCTION

The question I am asked is the probable relationship between the protein supply of the land and the birth rate of the people there. We are, of course, only at the beginning of knowledge about such matters. But a high intake of proteins seems to me—in the light of a whole chain of living evidence—to increase both fecundity and longevity. Let us start in the soil and examine the evidence logically—and ecologically—from the ground up.

Protein shortages are intricately connected with the behavior of animals, plants, and microbes—all of which are successive parts in the biotic pyramid that has man as its apex, and the soil as the foundation of the whole structure. The soil's pattern of fertility elements for various countries was possibly the determiner of man's migrations on the face of the earth. The soil's pattern may be more subtle, but it is more uncompromising than any politics. For it is the soil that determines the proteins by which we get protection and by which we have reproduction.

The provision of proteins in any area does more to delineate the different life patterns than almost any other ecological factor. It is these protein compounds that alone can keep life flowing. They build the body tissue. The fattening of our beef cattle in the eastern half of the United States (grown largely farther west), and the growing of pigs in that eastern part as animals mainly fat—may seem an arrangement in accord with natural economic controls, but it goes deeper. Underneath the control by economic forces there is in reality the specific control by a deficiency, of proteins, going back to the soil. This controlling deficiency is more often the shortage within the feed and food supply of some of the protein's constituent parts, namely, the amino acids. Eight or possibly 10 of the amino acids are considered absolutely essential (and required regularly) for the survival of the experimental white rat—and inferentially for the human species. Man and the animals must be given these amino acids. These creatures cannot create their proteins from the simpler chemical elements (except to limited extent by microbial helps in the intestinal tract). Only plants and microbes are equal to this accomplishment. These lower life forms struggle for their required proteins too. But they can grow and reproduce by means of a more limited list of the amino acids. Consequently, the mere growth of plants is no assurance of their serving as a feed which will guarantee growth of the animals consuming them.

The soil fertility pattern as it expresses itself in the pattern of protein potential is, then, a significant determiner in any ecology. The areas favorable to man and the food animals supporting him are those where the soil processes under the particular climatic forces are breaking down the rocks and minerals to provide the flow of all the essential chemical elements to the plant roots. These must come in such amounts and ratios as will support those plants synthesizing the complete proteins. The favorable place, then, for our protein rich plants in the climate-soil-ecological pattern is on the moderately weathered soils. Those plants include not only the legumes, but also the protein rich herbage that puts our protein-producing beef cattle (lean meat) and sheep (lean meat and wool) on these same soils under range conditions. As man pushes himself off these protein-producing soils on the "fringe" soils, he must extend his life lines from the latter back to the former—except as he can tolerate increasing degrees of malnutrition and partial starvation. Now that we have overrun the earth by means of technologies, have exploited our soils by them, and have extended our life lines to the point of fishing the Antarctic for proteins in whale meat, we are seeing those life lines shortened gradually if not already breaking and often severed.

Much land remains as acres, but the serious shortages in the soil as source of complete proteins offers provocation for a revival of remarks once made by Malthus. There are qualitative deficiencies, and while many phases of man's behavior are subjects of debate, no one to date has come up to take the negative side of the proposition that "Man must eat—and particularly of the proteins."

Our use of antibiotics is acceptance of the synthetic services for our protection by the lowly microbes. From next to the soil, at the bottom of the biotic pyramid, these chemical services are passed up to us at the top for our protection against other but dangerous microbes. Plants, too, offer protection in their many compounds simulating proteins, when they give us vitamins, hormones, via catalytic and stimulating effects still unknown. Proteins are still the major protection against disease and degeneration. Our bodies may often suffer from insufficient ability to corral and to create antibiotic, protein-like substances for protection against invasions by foreign, death-dealing microbial proteins. Yet with a little help from proteins brought to us by the microbes, the plants, and the animals, we carry or create sufficient proteins for protection.

Plants also protect themselves by means of proteins. Experimental trials demonstrate that by increasing fertility elements in the soil—which serve for increasing proteins in the young plants—there was provided increased protection against attack by fungus. In another experiment, more nitrogen and calcium offered vegetable plants for higher concentrations of proteins in food crops, gave more protection against attack on the plants by leaf-eating-insects. Here is suggested this: that the increasing fungus of our crops and the increased insect attacks on them seem to be premised on deficiencies of protective proteins in the plant; and these, in turn, on the deficiencies of the fertility in the soil. Seemingly, our wild animals gather their own "medicines" by instinctive selections, not only among different plants but also among the same species according to differences in the fertility of the soils growing it. Our domestic animals manifest similar selections within the limits permitted by our enclosure of them within fences, barns, etc. While proteins are the major nutritional "cure" for tuberculosis, we are still unmindful of the many other diseases against which complete proteins may possibly be a protection.

Some experiments using sheep and rabbits, under carefully controlled procedures, demonstrated that soils and proteins can control reproduction possibilities. Ewe lambs were fed on legume hays grown on a less productive soil given (a) no treatment, (b) phosphate, and (c) both lime and phosphate. Their body weights increased in the proportion of eight, 14 and 18 pounds per animal for the above treatments, respectively. Equal amounts of hay per head per day were consumed. The wool from lambs fed hay grown with more complete treatment, was the only one among three lots which could be scoured and carded without the destruction of the fibers.

As an additional test of the possible casual connection between soils, proteins, and reproduction, two hays—grown on varying soil treatments-were fed to two lots of male rabbits. Marked changes in reproductive potentials resulted. When the feeding program was modified, by merely interchanging the hays for the lots of rabbits, only three weeks elapsed when the lot of originally impotent animals was restored to sexual vigor. In the same short period of three weeks those on hay grown with limited soil treatment had fallen to the same low level of the other lot before the hays were interchanged. When, in these tests, the soil treatments for improved production of protein by legumes, as measured in terms of increased nitrogen in their hays, were the only variables responsible for shifting the sexual vigor from impotence to potence and vice versa, one can scarcely refute the casual connection between soils, proteins, protection, and reproduction.

When plants get their proteins in varying degrees of completeness—when herbivorous animals must depend on the plants for their proteins as a collection of all the required amino acids—when protection against invasion of our own bodies by death-dealing agencies is given us by proteins—and when the stream of reproduction of any life can be kept flowing only by means of proteins, shall we envision man as capable of sidestepping this pattern of controls? Man's extension over the earth was according to the protein-producing capacities delineated by the reliable animal instincts. But man's extension of his kind under his own technologies pushed him away from the fertile soils that were guaranteeing proteins, protection, and reproduction of himself and his species.

It pushed him on to the "fringe" soils in these respects, but at the hazard and necessity of using his technologies to reach back to, and keep connected with, those same fertile soils—which brought him protein foods, and all that comes with them, for supplementing his hazardous location. These lifelines may soon become tangled with lines of economics and politics. They may be shortened or cut off, and such fringe soils supporting only mono-cultures of crops then demonstrate man's nutritional insecurity. They generate hungers apt to be interpreted in most any other way, except that they are the result of a protein shortage going back to fertility shortages in the soil. Man is a social animal when well fed, but if put under starvation he even becomes cannibalistic, or gets his proteins at the price of murder. When the pre-death struggle of the protein-starved man to save himself as an individual rises to the desperate height of cannibalism, is this not akin to the immediate pre-death struggle of the processes of our bodies manifested by increased rate of heartbeat, increased blood pressure, and temperature rise as fever? If then a segment of the human species under protein-starvation makes a desperate survival effort in the form of increased reproduction, when other efforts for that have appeared in vain, would this not seem to aggravate the hazards for survival all the more? Would not such a manifestation seem of more logical interpretation when considered mainly as the pre-death struggle by the species?

Naturally, there are possibilities for wide variances between our individual conceptual schemes for man's behavior under severe hunger. But when in his fundamental physiologies man is viewed as another animal, he can scarcely set himself outside of the natural forces which seem so completely in control.

If the complete proteins determine body protection and reproduction of our animals; if the life forms just below man depend on plants for these essential foods still non-synthesizable by either science or industry, and if plant proteins are determined by the soil, then the soil fertility as it controls the animals in their reproductive potential would seem to be also the logical power in control of man's reproduction too.

BETTER PROTEINS

Meat proteins have always been considered a major and essential part of our nourishment. It is true that the proteins as body-building and body-repairing necessities are not fully understood in their functions in the body chemistry, in their protection of us against disease, and in all they do for us. But when we "cure" tuberculosis we give the patient rest. We feed him all the proteins such as meat, milk, and eggs he will take. In the hospitals, the best defense against shock and the favored means of sponsoring quick recovery, is the regular administration into the bloodstream of protein hydrolysates.

Proteins are being more widely appreciated because nutrition, as a growing science, is discovering how essential they are. They can give us calories as well as build body tissue and blood. They multiply the cells to give us growth, or life. When once upon a time nutrition emphasized mainly calories coming from carbohydrates and fats, it is now looking for more than these fuel foods. It is looking to reproduction, growth, and maintenance of the body in which those fuels are burned. The stove first, and the coal second, goes the pathway of concern. It is only the proteins that multiply themselves; only they can carry life.

Late knowledge of plant physiology suggests that carbohydrates give off their fuel values only by burning themselves in what appears like the flame of the proteins. Proteins have always been the problem. They are coming now to be decidedly more so. They are telling us that the solution calls for attention to the soil under the animals, and not just a dependence on more animals. We must assay what we eat for its separate amino acid contents if we are to judge the food value properly. In like manner, we may well assay the forages and the grains we give our animals for the ratios of the respective amino acids as a fitting ration out of which the steer is to make beef proteins, the dairy cow is to make casein in her milk, or any other animal is to reproduce itself and carry on all that precedes, accompanies, or follows that process.

We feel proud when nitrogen fertilizer on wheat makes the grain more horny or "harder." We pay a premium in many cases on such "hard" wheat. But this extra of crude protein is not necessarily better protein because it may not really contain more of those amino acids commonly deficient. It may consist of more of those already plentifully present. It may unbalance the nutrition still more in respect to the proper array of these essentials. By merely dumping nitrogen on the soil, we may not be making better proteins even if it is making more of them per acre. It is not the quantity or the yield, but the quality in terms of proteins more complete in the required amino acids that deserve attention in the use of soil treatments with nitrogen so commonly considered symbolic of protein.

Magnesium is one of the fertility elements deserving attention in connection with better proteins when it has been found influential in connection with the concentration of the particular amino acid, tryptophane, in forage. Liming with pure calcium stone may not be enough when dolomite, or the magnesium-calcium stone, might help the delivery of more tryptophane in the grasses and various legumes to give better proteins. Sulfur, the distinguishing feature of the commonly deficient amino acid, methionine, has never had much attention in fertilizer, except that it has been carried along unwittingly in superphosphate because we used sulfuric acid to react with the rock phosphate in making it, or in ammonium sulfate from this acid used there to collect the ammonia. But when the experimental use of sulfur pushed up the concentration of methionine in forages, and when this long-neglected element has shown its effect on the yields of grasses on some field trials in parts of Missouri, we may see the deficiencies in the better proteins going back to the deficiencies in the sulfur as an element in the fertility of the soil.

Perhaps the trace elements, too, that is, the copper, zinc, boron, manganese, molybdenum, and others in the soil will be credited with having a hand in helping our crop plants make better proteins. Research with these used as soil treatments in connection with the resulting amino acid array in alfalfa, suggests that trace elements are much more influential in pushing up the concentration of these commonly deficient amino acids, methionine, and tryptophane than in giving higher concentrations of the already abundant supply of leucine, for example. Here is the suggestion that if better proteins are produced, the soil must be fertile in the trace elements as well as in the major three, nitrogen, phosphorus, and potassium, so common in the fertilizer formulae of the past.

It is a dangerous belief that grass can give better proteins merely because it is grass. Grass made its reputation as a producer of better proteins to build the brawny body of the American bison, because of the fertile soil on which it was growing and not because it was known as buffalo grass, little blue stem, or by any other choice species name. Transplanting the grass species will not guarantee the better proteins for better feed unless the corresponding better fertility is provided along with the transplanting. More grass and more livestock are not enough without attention to the soil that must feed the grass so it can make its own better proteins of the complete array of amino acids, and so that they in turn can help the animals make better proteins.

Our meat problem, or our milk problem, is not one of more attention to monetary economics and exchanges between sections of the country. It is one of fertility economics of soil restoration and maintenance with the costs of production over the country as a whole. Offering prices at all time peaks, or rolling them back are activities that will not grow more proteins. Only more of the fertility in the soil in sufficient completeness of all essentials will grow them. When the beef supply per person is below 60 pounds per year in contrast to the 75 of some 50 years ago, perhaps it will dawn on us that making better proteins is not a simple manufacturing procedure depending on ample technologies assembled, but a matter of creation which according to our best knowledge—still like that of a few thousand years ago—starts with the soil.

Better proteins can be had only by making better soils to grow them.

SOIL FERTILITY FOR PROTEINS

The very mention of the word "protein" calls to one's mind the problem of providing this essential part of foods and feeds. In the kitchen, the lean meat is the first protein the housewife thinks about in her efforts to supply a diet for her family that is not deficient in this respect. On the farm, the word "protein" connotes bloodmeal, tankage, and other animal offal; or the many "meals" which include cottonseed, soybean, gluten, bran, shorts, and other milling byproducts. Whether it is a matter of feeding people or of feeding livestock, the provision of plenty of protein is the first desire, but one not so simply nor so cheaply accomplished. Supplying protein is a decidedly difficult problem in contrast to the ease of producing plenty of carbohydrate. Carbohydrates are readily and widely grown. But when it comes to the proteins they are so much less common that we first think of them as purchased supplements.

In the distant past the pioneers grew them. In the recent past their ample supply on the market has permitted ready purchase. But very recently compelling economic conditions are apparently bringing us more and more to think about growing our own supplies. This is necessary in order to balance the carbohydrates and get extra margins of profit in having both as home-grown products. It brings into clearer focus the necessity of putting fertility treatments on the soil of your garden. Fortunately, such rebuilding and conservation of the soil for the future not only provides protein more cheaply now, but also looks forward to make one highly independent of any market for his supply of it. We need more folks among the producers of milk and meat growers—which are our best protein foods—who will think more about providing most of their needed protein by building up the soil, with its resulting conservation as an added profit.

Growing one's own protein, however, is not so simple a matter. The vegetable proteins we purchase are mainly seed parts. Making protein is a part of the plant's struggle to reproduce itself. Even for the plant, this is not a simple task. Legume forages, and the seeds of those like peas, peanuts, and beans are relatively rich in this requisite food constituent. But the high concentration of protein in the seed demands its having been first synthesized and put up in the forage part of the plant before it is localized and concentrated in the seed of the crop. Legumes do not grow well nor do they manufacture much protein, unless the soil supplies them generously with calcium, phosphorus, potassium, and the others of the soil-borne essential mineral elements that serve not only in the physiology of the plant but also in the life processes of animals and man as well.

All plants manufacture carbohydrates in fairly generous amounts. These are the basic compounds building up the plant body. The very growth of the plant spells carbohydrate construction. This process takes its necessary raw materials from the air as carbon dioxide which it combines with water through the power of the sunshine. Some few contributions and in some small amounts, including potassium, magnesium, and iron are needed from the soil. But these serve only as helpers or catalysts in the construction process. They do not occur in the final or resulting carbohydrate compounds like sugar, starch, cellulose and others. This is the process of photosynthesis operating almost wholly on air and water as the raw materials that bring themselves to the plant and hence represent very little of a struggle by it. It is they that build the plant factory and serve as its fuel supply. Proteins, in contrast, are not so simple in chemical composition, nor are they so abundantly synthesized by the plant. Carbohydrates seem to be the starting point for their construction. This conversion is brought about not by sunshine power but rather by the "life" processes of the plants. Proteins vary widely in their chemical composition. They are still a kind of mystical chemical compound as to their particular structural make-up. There are infinite kinds of them, too. We know they are combinations of complex compounds called "amino acids," which are the simple building stones or structural parts of all proteins.

Unfortunately, these amino acids cannot be synthesized either by the animal or the human body processes. We and higher animals below us all depend on plants to synthesize these for us from the simpler elements. The plant in turn, is highly dependent on the soil fertility, that is, calcium, phosphorus, nitrogen, and other nutrients for help in synthesizing them. These amino acids are the components of its own proteins within which alone the life processes of cell multiplication or growth can be carried forward.

SOIL AND NUTRITION

We are gradually coming to believe that the soil—in terms of food it grows—is a controlling factor in agricultural creation. By subscribing to the production criteria of more tons and more bushels, we have watched the crops but have forgotten the soils that grow them. Accordingly, we have introduced new crops which readily pile up carbohydrates and caloric bulk. When dwindling fertility makes protein-producing, mineral-providing crops "hard to grow," we fail to undergird them with soil treatment for their higher nutritional values in growing young animals. Soil fertility—as help toward more protein within the body, as protection against microbial and other invasions—has not impressed itself yet.

Instead, we have taken to the therapeutic services of protective products generated by animals, and even microbes, in our bloodstream as disease fighters. The life of the soil is not attractive. The death of it is no recognized disaster. Hence, it may seem farfetched to any one but a student of both the soil and nutrition to relate the nutritive quality of feeds and foods to the soil. The provision of proteins is our major food problem. Carbohydrates are easily grown. For the output of these energy foods very little soil fertility is required in terms of either the number of chemical elements or the amounts of each. But in order for the plant to convert its carbohydrates into proteins by its life processes and not by the sunshine power, calcium, nitrogen, phosphorus, and a long list, including the trace elements, are required.

Plants and microbes—even those in the cow's gut—synthesize the amino acids that make up the proteins. Animals cannot fabricate these amino acids. They only collect them from the plants and assemble them into their proteins of milk, meat, eggs, and other body-building foods. We recognize about two dozen different amino acids as components of the proteins. We know that life is impossible without providing the complete collection of at least eight of them. When even the trace elements—manganese and boron—applied to the soil at rates of but a few pounds per acre for alfalfa increase the concentration of these essential amino acids in this crop—especially those amino acids deficient in corn—there is evidence that the nutritive quality of this forage is connected with the fertility of the soil. In believing that we need "minerals" according to such analyses of our bodies and our foods for their inorganic contents, we consider the soil as the supply of these and the plants as conveyors of them. We conclude therefrom that limestone fed to the cow in the mineral box is the equivalent in nutritional service to lime used as soil treatment coming through the plant. Crops that do little more than pile up carbohydrates, as was demonstrated with soybeans, make big yields of bulk. To be content with the above simple faith is to be agronomically gullible.

Our reluctance to credit the soil with some relation to the nutritive quality of our feeds and foods is well illustrated by the belief persistent during the last quarter of a century: that acidity of soil is injurious and that the benefit from liming lies in fighting this acidity. In truth, it lies in its nourishment of the plants with calcium and its activities in their synthesis of proteins and other food essentials.

As yet we do not appreciate the pattern of soil fertility in the United States, that in pre-colonial days allowed only wood crops, or forests, on the soils in the eastern half. It grew protein as meat in the bison on the buffalo grass in mid-continent, and in some scattered areas farther east like particular valleys of Pennsylvania or the present race horse area of Kentucky. It permitted corn in the forested New England when each hill was fertilized with a fish. Corn on the eastern prairies grew well without such stimulation.

We may well ask whether the soil in its fertility pattern is of no import relative to nutritive quality of what it produces when—(1) we grow cattle and make beef protein more effectively today in the former bison area; (2) when that area is now growing the high protein wheat; (3) when we fatten cattle farther east on the more weathered soils and combine this speculative venture with pork production that puts emphasis on fat output by carbohydrates and the lessened hazard by marketing these smaller animals nearer their birthday; (4) when soil fertility exhaustion has pushed soft wheat westward; (5) when the protein in corn has dropped, because of soil exploitation, from an average figure of 9.5 to 8.5%; and (6) when the pattern of the caries of the teeth of Navy inductees during World War II reflects the climatic pattern of soil fertility. Such items related to the national pattern of soil fertility suggest than many of our agricultural sucesses(or escapes from disaster) have been good fortunes through chance location with respect to the fertility of the soil when we have too readily, perhaps, credited them to our embryo agricultural science.

When a crop begins to fail we search far and accept others if they make bulk where the predecessor didn't. The grazing animals have been selecting areas according to better soils. All these are animal demonstrations that the nutritive quality of feeds is related to the soil that grows it. But to date, the animals rather than their masters, have appreciated this fact most. Shall we keep our eyes closed to the soil's creative power via proteins, organo-inorganic compounds, and all the complexes of constructive and catalytic services in nutrition?

When the health and functions of our plants, our animals and ourselves indicate the need, isn't it a call for agricultural research to gear production into delivery of nutritional values related to the fertility of the soil, rather than only those premised on bulk and the ability to fill? "To be well fed is to be healthy." Good nutrition must be built from the ground up.

PLANTS STRUGGLE FOR THEIR PROTEINS, TOO

Man and other warmblooded animals are always hungry for proteins. Man is ever craving meat, fish, eggs, cheese and other foods of animal origin. These compose the item on the menu that sets the price of the entire meal. He is hungry for what was another animal body, or the body products creating and feeding another young and growing body. He needs what is more nearly "living" foods if he is to keep his own body living. It is the proteins in our food by which our body, (a) grows; (b) protects itself from its own degeneration and its disruption by invading foreign, living proteins; and (c) reproduces its own kind. Domestic animals, breaking through the fence to feed on the grass of the virgin soil of the highway, or on the railroad right-of-way, are telling us that they are struggling to get out for more protein per mouthful of the grazing there—than from the grazing of crops where the fertility of the soil has been depleted by estensive cropping and little maintenance of the soil fertility. Wild animals marauding our cultivated fields—even our gardens—risk their lives in the open to get feed they recognize as more nutritious—because its growth on more fertile soil makes it of higher conecntration of nitrogen and all else that distinguishes the protein from the carbohydrates and fats.

Students of wildlife tell us that a few small areas of forest cleared, and grown to protein rich crops by soil treatments, will increase the fawn crop of deer not only by more births but also by more twins as well. The struggle by wildlife, like that by our farm animals and ourselves, is for more protein, too. Nitrogen is the one element, going from the soil fertility supply into the plant, by which we distinguish proteins from carbohydrates and fats in making chemical analyses. But in order to grow proteins and their nutritional quality into plants, rather than just carbohydrates and fuel food values there, all the other nutrient elements for plants must also be offered them by the soil. When a plant makes proteins, it does more than attach the element nitrogen to the carbon chain in carbohydrates or fats. That synthesis is a biochemical reaction carried out only by life processes. It is not even considered a process as simple as carbohydrate production by photosynthesis, using the energy from sunlight. Plants are struggling to get soil fertility completely enough to build up their proteins just as animals and man are searching to find foods offering this essential to them. Plants naturally differ widely in their concentration of proteins (nitrogen x 6.25) in their total bulk, that is, in the percentage of nitrogen in their dry substance (D.S.). Nature has given us protein rich plants, but they do not deliver much tonnage of vegetative growth.

When plants are naturally low in their concentration of protein, or of nitrogen (N), they make much vegetative growth per acre. This simple natural fact, or natural law, namely, that large yields of vegetative bulk by a crop should suggest lower concentration of protein within it, and lower feed and food values in terms of body growth, health and fecundity.

The curve does not go high enough beyond sugar cane to include forest trees where the living protein part is limited to the cambium layer under the bark. Much bulk or dry substance (D.S.) does not guarantee much protein (nitrogen x 6.25) or necessarily much food value. We need to know food value of the crop, that is, the protein values, and that in relation to the fertility of the soil, rather than only the bulk produced per acre. We need to realize that a large amount of vegetative growth suggests a small concentration of protein and other growth values in it.

TO PRODUCE PROTEIN

You can have plants jam-packed with nitrogen without having that converted into the amino acids that make up protein. The nitrogen must be in the form of NH_2 to produce the amino acids. It is all too often in plants in such forms as NH_3, NH, NO_2 or NO_3. Look what happened in this state during our dry summer of 1954 when we had one case after another of nitrate poisoning because the nitrogen in the plants was never converted to the NH_2 form.

But that is the whole story of our present-day agriculture. It is easy to produce bulk, to grow great tonnages of carbohydrates and fats—crystallized sugar, cornstarch, butterfat—which are essentially only air, water and sunshine. Or take the broiler chickens the way we are turning them out today. They are mainly hydration; mostly water and a little bulk, but there's little protein-rich meat on them.

To produce protein, though, is a different matter. We still have much to learn about achieving the fertility balance in the soil to make protein in our plants. Remember, on soils where there is less and less fertility, nature grows wood, and wood is cellulose. There is no protein there. That's the way it is with much of our hay. We have gone to the extreme of pelleting the stuff, in part to try to get animals to accept it and eat it.

DO WE OVERLOOK PROTEIN QUALITY?

Our struggle to get the inert nitrogen from the air and to compound it into our diet began even before agriculture itself came into being. About four-fifths of every breath of air we take is nitrogen. Yet we cannot use this nitrogen in our bodies. Nor can we salt our food with nitrogen fertilizer to get what we need, for that too is in the wrong form. We must rely on the work of microbes, plants, and animals. They only can build inorganic nitrogen into the organic forms we call proteins and which we can use as food. The microbes in this trio are no longer as essential as they once were. It is now possible to manufacture synthetic nitrogen in factories. But as simple as this conversion may sound, we must still pay for it. It costs about 10 cents a pound to convert nitrogen into fertilizers.

From this point onward, the creative aspects of plants and animals become more significant. Our effort to eat resolves itself into a problem of obtaining nitrogen as protein. We like to have it come to us as meat, milk, or eggs. We like to get our nitrogen in beefsteak. We do not fully appreciate the fact that such animal proteins are products originally built by plants. Animals only assemble proteins. They must find the nitrogen in the vegetable or plant proteins they consume. Plants can absorb nitrogen from the soil in simpler forms. Once they have taken it up, they unite it chemically with carbon compounds. The resulting nitrogen compounds are called amino acids, and there are 20 of these known to us. These amino acids in turn are used to build protein. Amino acids have certain features in common. However, they differ in one main characteristic. This is in the nature of a group of carbon and other atoms which is attached at one point to the main amino-acid molecule. This group is the so-called "side chain." The complex side chains are built only by plants—not by animals. It is these different side chains which decide whether an amino acid is one which animals, and man, must have to live. How the plant marshals these widely varied mixtures of amino acids into the huge protein molecule is still an unexplained mystery. Each living plant species has proteins with its own specific pattern. The structural difficulties encountered in making each of these proteins are complex.

We cannot distinguish the creation of protein from the process of growth. We must reason, then, that protein manufacture takes place where growth is taking place. Protein manufacture cannot be a simple adding together of the amino acids. It is a complete integration of them into the specific protein of the plant species. We can separate a protein back into its amino acids—and we can again separate these acids into even simpler chemical elements. But even though we can do this, it gives us no clue regarding the processes by which the amino acids were put together in the first place. In our digestive tract, the food proteins are broken down by enzymes such as pepsin and trypsin. If we do this chemically, in the test tube, we find a portion with the nitrogen in the amino form, holding the amino acids together. This particular form does not account for all the nitrogen in the protein. Some nitrogen is also stored away in another form, the amide, and still more is stored away in complex ring compounds.

The soil regulates the balance between these different nitrogen compounds inside the protein. It supplies the nitrogen which goes into the protein, and it also supplies the other substances which convert the nitrogen into protein. One of these other substances is potassium. The way in which this element affects the conversion of nitrogen has been shown in experiments with alfalfa, grown on a sand medium. When the potassium content of the sand was increased, the alfalfa responded by converting more nitrogen into the complex ring structures mentioned above. Likewise, as the potassium increased, less of the total nitrogen went into the simpler forms. These ring structures are not an exact measure of better protein; they are evidence that it is of higher quality. They do indicate that more of the kinds of protein needed by animals are present. Sulfur, like potassium, is also needed in the manufacture of proteins. Analyses of over 250 plant samples which were grown on a wide variety of soils and nutrient solutions have given evidence of the effect of sulfur in this process.

The simpler—and we think, the less useful—forms of nitrogen make up, on the average, about 50% of the total nitrogen in the forage, according to these analyses. Yet, in alfalfa, which was decidedly deficient in sulfur, this value jumped to over 80%. When more sulfur was offered to the plant, the relative amount of the simpler nitrogen compounds dropped back to normal. Amide nitrogen in the protein is manufactured from the simple nitrogen compounds, ammonia. It, too, has an agent which must be present before the manufacturing process can go on. Without adequate manganese, plants cannot produce this compound of nitrogen. The 20 amino acids are the end-points into which these other nitrogen compounds are assembled. Plants create amino acids as the products of a manufacturing process within the living plant tissue. This is their struggle to produce their proteins in order to make their growth. These life processes require the soilborne elements more than we yet appreciate. Much more is required for amino acid synthesis than the mere combination of nitrogen and sulfur from the soil with carbohydrates. For these synthetic processes, plants need at least calcium, potassium, magnesium, boron, manganese, copper, and zinc. Should we not, then, expect a greater variety and a larger amount of amino acids in plants growing on soils which are well supplied with all of these nutrient elements?

Part of the answer to this question has been provided by a group of five Missouri soils. Each of these soils was treated to deliver differing quantities of the elements listed. Lespedeza was grown on these five soils, and we experienced wide differences in the array of amino acids within the lespedeza from each soil. A very minor difference in any of the substances mentioned above made a difference in the makeup of the lespedeza protein.

Similarly, a single soil was treated with varying amounts of the trace elements manganese and boron. Again, this time with alfalfa, it gave a marked diversity of the amino-acid pattern. Animals consuming these forages need amino acids which they cannot make within their bodies. They need an assortment of the different kinds, and in turn, many elements of soil fertility will be needed before these various kinds of amino acids can be built.

We are talking about going back to an agriculture which emphasized forages and grasses. We need to know more about the proteins in these forages. Are the soils which grow them capable of producing proteins which contain the many kinds of amino acids needed by animals? Among these amino acids, a typical one is tryptophane. It particularly demonstrates the complexity of those that are essential for human or animal nutrition. Here we find nitrogen bound with carbon to make a closed chain—what the chemist calls an "indole" ring. Tryptophane is one of the complex amino acids which humans and animals must have to live. In addition to being required in the diet, it is also important because it can replace the B-vitamin, nicotinic acid, in the relief of the deficiency pellagra. Yet, in corn, one of our most common feeds, the supply of this amino acid is so meager that its lack must be taken into account when corn is used in mixed feeds. If some other feed is not added to the mixture to make up for the lack, the mixed feed will fail to produce the results expected for it.

The soil can help in building tryptophane, and this fact is of more than a little importance. We have found, at the Missouri Experiment Station, that soybeans getting low amounts of zinc, manganese, boron, magnesium, calcium, and phosphorus were always lower in tryptophane. As more of the zinc and the other inorganic elements were made available, more tryptophane appeared per pound of forage. The same soybeans continued to show about the same amount of total protein, regardless of whether zinc and the other elements were provided. The total protein showed little if any relation to the amount of this essential amino acid, tryptophane. So, by all our usual standards, we had a soybean plant high in protein. But we hadn't answered the question of whether this was good protein, and we don't know if it was high in tryptophane. We dare not overlook this assistance of the soil in the build-up of nitrogen compounds. We must look to the end-product, the kind and quality of protein coming out of the soil, not the quantity.

Life chemistry is carried on by means of the compounds known as enzymes. These complex substances start and accelerate the chemical reactions in the plant. Their directing influences depend upon their three structural parts:

1. A large, specific protein particle.

2. A non-proteinaceous organic molecule, which when identified has often been found to be a vitamin.

3. An inorganic activator.

The manner in which these three are linked together remains obscure, yet each demands equal consideration. For when one of them is absent, the other two cannot function. Herein lies the life-giving function of the soil. As the different soils deliver divergent quantities of the inorganic elements (activators)—calcium, zinc, and the like—so the enzymes in plants enable them to build better and more protein. Biochemists as basic scientists may well busy themselves with studies of vitamins and proteins. But they dare not neglect the contribution made by the inorganic elements, or activators, from the soil. These substances serve in enzymatic roles, and if agriculture and medicine are to sustain or improve our health, then the two sciences must discover and interpret this enzymatic performance. As the structural pattern of proteins presents more and varied amino acids, their values as food improve. In doing so, they make for what we call differences in quality. Improved quality of protein means improved health. The nitrogen supplied by the soil can be a measure of protein only when we consider it in the array of specific organic nitrogen compounds. We dare not be content to count nutritional values of nitrogen only by crude protein. Plants serve in the cycle of nutrition not as mere haulers of ash, but as bio-synthetic creators of life with protein "not too crude" according to the more fertile soil.

USE EXTRA SOIL FERTILITY TO PROVIDE PROTEIN

The very mention of the word "protein" calls to one's mind the problem of providing this essential part of foods and feeds. In the kitchen, the lean meat is the first protein the housewife thinks about in her efforts to supply for her family a diet that is not deficient in this respect. On the farm, the word "protein" connotes bloodmeal, tankage, and other animal offal, or the many "meals," including cottonseed, soybean, gluten, bran, shorts, and other milling byproducts. Whether it is a matter of feeding people or feeding live stock, the provision of plenty of protein is the first desire, but one not so simply nor so cheaply accomplished. Supplying protein is a decidedly difficult problem in contrast to the ease of producing plenty of carbohydrate. Carbohydrates are readily and widely grown. But when it comes to the proteins they are so much less common that we think first of them as purchased supplements. In the distant past the pioneer grew them. In the recent past their ample supply on the market has permitted ready purchase. But very recently compelling economic conditions are apparently bringing us more and more to think about growing our own supplies. This is necessary in order to balance the carbohydrates and get extra margins of profit in having both as home-grown products. Such will, of course, solve the problem of buying proteins but at the same time it will bring into clearer focus the necessity of putting fertility treatments on the soil. Fortunately, such rebuilding and conservation of the soil for the future not only provides protein now more cheaply, but also looks forward to make one highly independent of any market for his supply of it. We need more folks among the producers of milk and the growers of meat—which are our best protein foods—who will think more about providing most of their needed protein by building up the soil with its resulting conservation as an added profit.

Growing one's own protein, however, is not so simple a matter. The vegetable proteins we purchase are mainly seed parts. The yields of these per acre are determined by the fertility level of the soil. Making protein is a part of the plant's struggle to reproduce itself. Even for the plant, this is not a simple task. Legume forages, and the seeds of those like peas, peanuts, and beans are relatively rich in this requisite food constituent. But the high concentration of protein in the seed demands its having been first synthesized and put up in the forage part of the plant before it is localized and concentrated in the seed of the crop. Hence, the forages and hays of legumes, too, are rich in protein. It is this property that makes them good feed for the young or growing animals. However, legumes do not grow well nor do they manufacture much protein per acre, unless the soil supplies them generously with calcium, phosphorus, potassium, and the others of the soil-borne essential mineral elements that serve not only in the physiology of the plant but also in the life processes of animals and man as well. All plants manufacture carbohydrates in fairly generous amounts. These are the basic compounds building up the plant body. The very growth of the plant spells carbohydrate construction. This process takes its necessary raw materials from the air as carbon dioxide which is combined with water through the power of the sunshine. Some few contributions and in small amounts, including potassium, magnesium, and iron are needed from the soil. But these serve only as helpers or catalysts in the construction process. They do not occur in the final or resulting carbohydrate compounds like sugar, starch, cellulose and others. This is the process of photosynthesis operating almost wholly on air and water as the raw materials that bring themselves to the plant and hence represent very little of a struggle by it. It is they that build the plant factory and serve as its fuel supply.

Proteins, in contrast, are not so simple in chemical composition, nor are they so abundantly synthesized by the plant. Carbohydrates seem to be the starting point for their construction. This conversion is brought about not by sunshine power but rather by the "life" processes of the plants. Proteins vary widely in their chemical composition. They are still a kind of mystical chemical compound as to their particular structural make-up. There are infinite kinds of them, too. We know they are combinations of complex compounds called "amino acids," which are the simple building stones or structural parts of all proteins. Unfortunately, these amino acids cannot be synthesized either by the animal or the human body processes. We and higher animals below us all depend on plants to synthesize these for us from the simpler elements. The plant, in turn, is highly dependent on the soil fertility, that is, calcium, phosphorus, nitrogen, and other nutrients, for help in synthesizing them. These amino acids are the components of its own proteins within which alone the life processes of cell multiplication or growth can be carried forward.

For carbohydrate production the soil must provide the plant mainly with potassium. For protein production more than this rather common element of soil fertility is needed since the plant's construction of sugars, through the help of potassium as the forerunner. Seemingly these sugars are both the raw materials and the energy source from which amino acids and their combinations as proteins are build up by the plant. But this is possible only when many additional soil-borne minerals are also provided. The chemical structure of amino acids suggests that they might have initially been sugar-like compounds into which some nitrogen, some phosphorus, and some sulfur are connected. But this protein compounding process—unlike sugar production—does not proceed under just sunshine power. It goes forward in the dark. It is powered through combustion of some carbohydrates or through a process that may well be called biosynthesis or "life" synthesis rather than photo- or "light" synthesis as is the case with carbohydrates.

Even though calcium is not a chemical part of the resulting protein compounds, it plays its important roles in their synthesis. We must have calcium or lime present for—and connect it with—protein production by plants much as potassium is connected with carbohydrate production by them. So when we need to lime the soil for legumes we now know that we are not fighting soil acidity, but rather we are fertilizing or supplying some soil fertility by which we grow more protein more effectively along with the production of carbohydrates. More fertility in the soil is the means by which plants do more than make energy feed values in their carbohydrates. It is this means, contributed by the soil rather than the weather, that makes proteins synthesis possible. Growing our own protein means less attention to the weather and more concern about treating the soil with manures. Unfortunately, we have not appreciated how important soil fertility converted into protein is in the process of multiplication of cells or in any of the processes of reproduction and growth. Protein is also protection against disease in the body's resistance. Better soils for better feeds to give better bearing of young, better milk production and better health has not been our thought so much as have more feeds for increasing the body weight through laying on of fat. Likewise in thinking about fertilizers and other soil treatments for crops, our measure of their efficiencies has been the increase in plant bulk. We have not looked to the better food quality in the crop that was given lime or other fertilizers on the soil growing it. Instead we have been satisfied with more quantity or more tons. In milk production, too, the value of protein supplements has been measured mainly in more gallons (mainly water) of milk, or more pounds of butter fat, which is an energy food. We still don't measure their effects in the pounds of protein output in the milk as brought about by the protein input of the feed. Quality of forage feeds in terms of better body growth, better reproduction, better meat or better milk in solids-other-than-fat, has not yet become the main reason for our closer attention to growing more and better proteins rather than buying them. Such qualities have not yet been appreciated as the more deeply significant reason for building up our soils to a higher level of fertility.

Protein-producing power per acre should be the newer criterion for evaluating land. Not gallons of milk per acre, but rather pounds of cheese-protein per acre would be a good measure of efficient dairy farming. Agriculture originally was primarily a food-producing effort. Fundamentally it is still the sustainer of life. In the recent past, however, it has attempted to swing itself into the industrial class, but shortages of foods push one back quickly to agriculture for the production and consumption of them rather than their sale as even Victory gardens testify. Conservation of soil may well measure its own efficiency, not by reporting how little soil is eroding, but how much protein per acre we are producing by use of the land without loss of it.

Such is the philosophy of some of the trials being carried out on the Missouri Soil Conservation Service Farm operating under the cooperative efforts of the Soil Conservation Service Research and the Missouri Experiment Station. Pounds of beef per acre from grass-cover intended to prevent erosion testify forcefully that merely keeping the water from running off may not help much toward more and better grass. In fact, contour furrows in the pasture may even hold so much water as to make bluegrass a poor feed during a period of high rainfall. In these trials, pastures only contour-furrowed caused loss in animal weight on this area of heavy clay subsoil under a shallow surface soil.

Three pasture areas were under test as separate areas fenced out of a large uniform bluegrass pasture in 1942. One was given no treatment; one was given furrows on the contour for water conservation; the third was renovated by some surface tillage and fertilizer applications. During the four years of the records the pounds of beef produced per acre were, (a) 115, with no soil treatment, (b) 103, with contour furrows, and (c) 151, with renovation through fertilizers. These results point out clearly that merely holding back water was of no help as more feed value. Rather it was even of detriment. They point out positively that the soil treatments with extra fertility made more protein per acre. This was the report by the cattle, as they measured it, when the human eye could scarcely distinguish differences in forage yields. More protein per acre goes back to more fertility in the soil, when animal physiology is testifying.

When the plant is building protein it, too, does this with varying degree but according to the nutrients it gets. Quite contrary to expectations, more bulk of forage per acre is not necessarily proof of higher concentration of protein in the forage or hay. Experimental studies have shown that it is not necessarily the large tonnage per acre that makes the most protein per acre. Rather it is the combination of nutrient mineral elements in the soil, or the fertility ration we feed the plant that encourages its internal activity in protein production rather than mere storage of carbohydrates. Plant diets from the soil must conform to certain ratios of the nutrient elements to each other much as economic animal feeding demands certain nutritive ratios. These nutrient ratios for plants are suggested by the different degrees of soil development, for example, in the United States. On the highly developed or leached soils of northeastern, eastern, and southern United States, which originally grew only forests and where the ratio of calcium to potassium is low or narrow, we may well expect carbonaceous or woody crops today. In the midlands of the United States which originally grew grass with many natural legumes on less leached, calcareous soils—and also grew buffalo without purchased protein supplements—the crops were originally proteinaceous. Here the soil fertility suggests a high or wide ratio of calcium to potassium. This concept in terms of the calcium-potassium ratio gives us the natural principle by which we can visualize the synthetic activities of the plant as either those of making mainly carbohydrates, or making proteins as well. Plants making mainly carbohydrates build much bulk readily through sunshine power. But when plants build proteins, they burn much of these carbohydrates in converting them into proteins. As a consequence, this gives less bulk per acre. We can, therefore, not be certain that much crop means much protein, nor that even the crop, whose pedigree says it is a legume, is rich in protein.

Experimental trials have demonstrated the truth of this principle. The soybean hay crop was much larger when potassium was liberally used in contrast to calcium or lime to nourish the crop. But when calcium was higher in relation to the potassium (with phosphorus amply supplied), the crop was only four-fifths as large. But this lesser bulk contained more total protein than the crop that was 25% larger. Coincidentally the phosphorus in the smaller crop was almost twice as concentrated and the calcium almost three times as in the larger crop. It may seem difficult to believe that we can have less yields as bulk or tonnage per acre and yet have greater yield in the form of nutrition as protein and minerals when the plants are properly fed through the soil. But this less bulk can be offset by using extra potassium also. We need not hold down the tonnage yield. Instead we can use potassium for that increase and then also extra nitrogen, calcium, and phosphorus to get a higher concentration of protein along with it.

NITROGEN, PROTEINS AND PEOPLE

The use of anhydrous ammonia has encouraged our wider recognition of the fact that only through nutrition of plants can the inorganic fertility elements of the soil direct the biosynthesis of the elements, carbon, hydrogen, and oxygen coming from the air and water, into the required organic constituents, i.e. the amino acids, of living proteins. It is the green plants, in the ultimate, that must supply animals and man with their required proteins. As the soil acreage per person becomes less and less, the human species becomes more vegetarian and less carnivorous in its food habits. But we need to remind ourselves that the soil can be either good or bad—even disastrous—nutrition for animals and man. That fact was forcefully demonstrated by the drought and excessivly high temperatures in Missouri during the summer of 1954 by which much of the nitrogen in the corn crop was not nutrition as protein, but was poison as nitrate and possibly nitrite. That season introduced us to a new human ailment designated as "Silo Filler Disease" by those habitually given to the use of the term "disease" for most any irregularity in health. That season also helped arrive at the explanation of a much older animal affliction connected with the feeding of silage of certain seasons, and the grazing of stalks after corn picking, which had been described as "forage poisoning" or "corn-stalk disease."

During the drought of June-September 1954 and the maximum temperature during the first week in July at 112 F., the enzymes active in the area of the corn leaf usually outlined as yellow by nitrogen deficiency, were inactivated to give a white area there instead. Serious doubt as to whether the corn plants would recover under future rains, and the usual shortage of green feed by that time, compelled some farmers to turn their livestock into the corn fields which were pastured with no disturbances to the health of the animals at that date. Doubt about the possibility of a grain crop was reason for many to hope for one in allowing the crop to stand while the white, scalded leaf areas turned brown, and the upper, shortened portions of the stalks with their leaves almost telescoped into each other, made little if any farther growth even after a two-inch rain during the first week in August.

Since that moisture restored more active microbial nitrification in the soil—as drying and rewetting usually do—it also mobilized more nitrate nitrogen into the plants to concentrate there since the enzymes in the leaf ends carrying on its metabolism had been destroyed. According to Dr. Went of Missouri Botanical Gardens, higher temperatures cause tomato plants to be higher in nitrates than those grown in lower temperature. Chemical analyses of the stalks showed that there were increasing concentrations of that kind of oxidized nitrogen in the internodal sections of the stalks from their top to bottom by the middle of September. By that date the hope for a crop of corn grain had been abandoned. The small crop of the fodder began to go into silos. One day's filling of that storage with the night following was time enough for the anaerobic respiratory processes of the ensiled plant tissues to set free considerable nitrous oxide, which was deadly for the silo filler on going down into it for the next day's work of continuing that operation. Postmortems showed the oxides of nitrogen responsible through inhalation into the lungs and reaction with the hemoglobin of the blood to disturb its normal carriage of oxygen to the various tissues of the body. Such experiences coined the term "Silo Filler Disease."

At about the same time in the season, some farmers needed cattle feed sorely. Having seen their neighbors pasture their scorched corn fields in July, they decided to pasture their own in September. There were many cases in which this late date of grazing the stunted corn plants meant a quick death of the cattle. These disasters were then associated with similar ones of many years earlier when cattle and horses were "diseased" by ensilage and by grazing the dry cornstalk well into the winter as the gleaning operation long after the grain harvest had been gathered. Those earlier disasters had not been well explained as to their cause. They had given us the term "corn stalk disease" which now may well be taken out of the category of "disease" and listed as nitrite an nitrate poisoning, to which there has unfortunately been added the extra terms "from too much fertilizer nitrogen."

This latter terminology, implying a correct explanation, is unfortunate in that it may not be the whole truth. Careful reading of the history of the cases studied by the University of Illinois in 1918 suggests that they too were due to high nitrates in corn stalks. Those occurred before nitrogenous fertilizers were heavily applied. The evidence of the unfairness of this implication that applied nitrogen was deadly rests on two significant facts. The corn stalk disease in Illinois occurred on the soils of late glaciations with high content of readily nitrifiable organic matter, and second, the attacks came late enough in the season to suggest that the trouble reached its climax only after the animals were taking the lower parts of the stalks where the higher nitrates (and nitrites) were accumulated which tests in the winter of 1954-1955 showed them for Missouri as deadly concentrations.

In placing the blame on the application of fertilizer nitrogen for such disasters, one forgets these similar ones reported in Illinois as far back as 1918 before such fertilizing was practiced. One disregards also the seasonal factors of (1) temperatures high enough to concentrate nitrates and to kill the leaf enzymes normally digesting the nitrogen there, and (2) the timing of the August rainfall to give the highest concentrations of nitrate produced by the soil and accumulated in the stunted plants by mid-September which would not occur during a season as favorable as 1958 was. In mid-Kansas in March 1948, also before heavy applications of nitrogen were made, a dry autumn and winter followed by thawing snows with rainfall in March moved enough nitrates into shallow wells to make their waters deadly for babies given artificial feeding formula made therefrom. Hasty conclusions about applied nitrogen being responsible in such cases seem to classify them as erroneous ones. Those problems and disasters remind us of the need to gain more knowledge about soil fertility and plant nutrition so as to diagnose the natural biological factors responsible in case of unusual climatic conditions provoking such disasters, rather than conduct post-mortems under hysteria from the economic loss and the veterinarian's limited knowledge before we conclude that the fertilizers were responsible. Distinction between the crude proteins, which include the nitrate nitrogen, and the complete proteins in terms of the amino acids would make us more cautious about falling into such serious errors in placing the blame.

One needs to be cautious about using the word proteins when there is so much about those living substances that we don't know. The fact that in feeding corn grain, even to a fattening animal, we must add to the diet some "protein supplements," reminds us that this non-legume plant species does not synthesize all the amino acids required to be complete protein for nutrition of even castrated males. It may be failing in part because of the way we fertilize the crop. But corn protein is deficient in two or possibly three required amino acids. By that shortage, even others it offers are not fully efficient as protein in feeding the animal. Hence, we put our faith blindly into breeding rather than feeding the future hog to make more lean and less fat. Whether any non-legumes can give the complete proteins which we need for our hopes in growing more animal proteins seems doubtful. If that is the fact, then in fertilizing non-legume forages with nitrogen in their dry matter, one dare not believe that the plant's higher concentration of nitrogen resulting from fertilization can be all protein and in the correct array of the required amino acids representing better animal feed. Synthesis of protein of these higher nutritional values is not a matter of only the balance of the fertility of the soil as we know it, but also one of the particular species of plants, like the legumes, high enough in the evolution of the many complex physiological processes by which all those creative processes of protein synthesis are a natural part of the plant tissues. If our declining soil fertility has brought into use successively lower evolutionary species, as we know from the lowered feed values of the introductions as new forage plants, the uplift of the inorganic fertility only can scarcely be the equivalent of sudden evolutionary transformation of the common forage crops into higher plant species. We dare not accept the false premise that fertilizing non-legumes can make them the equal of properly fertilized legumes in supplying quality proteins for animal nutrition.

If we observe closely any ecological plant climax demonstrated by nature, we are reminded that plant diseases are reduced if not eliminated, weeds are excluded, and high seed production is the result. All this occurs where there is no crop rotation but where only the same crop appears year after year, and the entire production of its own kind of organic matter there is returned to the soil as the larger part of the nutrition of the crop next year. There is no burning to get rid of disease and insects harbored by the preceding crop. These facts point out how with little mineral, or inorganic, decomposition in soils of the arid regions, but with mainly decomposition of organic matter, remarkable crops are grown naturally. Such facts suggest that we are expecting climax crops from the return to the soil of much inorganic fertility, but of little or no return of organic fertility. When the high organic matter of the soil is protection against salt injury by heavy fertilization in contact with the crop seeding; and when also high soil organic matter is protection for soil life against complete destruction by pesticides. We need to consider our neglect of maintaining the organic matter of the soil by which the life there survives, not because of us but rather in spite of us. In connection with the synthesis of proteins by plants, there comes up for theoretical consideration the suggestion from the services by urea in the cow's paunch as a protein substitute, that if we could get urea fertilizer into the plant before that compound is so quickly decomposed, urea should be a remarkably better help in the plant's synthesis of proteins than other nitrogen carriers.

Urea has its nitrogen not only already in the amino or NH form, but that common form of protein nitrogen is already connected directly with a carbon atom, another characteristic of protein—nitrogen. Since urea in the waste from the animal body results from only partial decomposition of ingested proteins, it ought to simplify the plant's struggle to make protein if the plant could take and use urea as the starting compound in that synthesis rather than be compelled to use the simplified elements, or even ammonia. Such theoretical thinking raises some questions. Can the use of similar organic substances by the plants in the natural ecological climax growing on their own accumulated residues be the secret of the absence of competing plant species or of weeds? Can possibly their proteins synthesized by them in the climax be more complete in the many amino acids and thereby be their protection against diseases and insect pests? Can such naturally good health and survival of the plants be due to their synthesis of a more complex chemical composition in the evolutionary scale, and that in turn be the higher nutritional values when wild or domestic animals graze such climaxes of natural vegetation?

The answers to such questions and the solutions of such theories must await the research efforts of the future. When diseases of domestic animals are multiplying and when plant diseases and insects of our crops are becoming more disastrous, shall we not consider the possibility that these life forms are becoming victims because of deficiencies of the proteins by which they once protected themselves as plants do in an ecological climax or animals do in the wild? Shall we not believe that the declining soil fertility, or its imbalance, is moving each higher form of life downward in its physiological capacities or is reversing the course of evolution by the extension of species above? Can man survive merely by more and more powerful poisons to eliminate the lower forms competing with him for nothing more than crude proteins by which they can but he cannot live? Are we not falling into plights of our own creation because we are forgetting that people, too, are part of the great biotic pyramid and for survival are dependent on nitrogen for proteins coming via the soil as the foundation of all kinds of life?

Our national agricultural problem is erroneously considered as only a matter of economics and technologies. It is forcefully demonstrating itself as one that will not classify itself in either of those categories. View simply, in our humble opinion, what we call the agricultural problem is one that needs to let agriculture concern itself with the handful of dust into which the climatic forces blow the warm air and moisture as the breath of creation. More study and appreciation of that mundane, but biologically active part through which agriculture builds its new values annually will be required before agriculture will cease to be considered a problem. More study is needed also before inorganic nitrogen, blown under its own pressure into that handful of dust can play its fullest role (under man's management) in the various phases and to the highest potential in agricultural production. The challenge presents itself clearly and forcibly.

SOIL AND PROTEINS

Raindrops of the same size and shape are falling today, with the same impacts and foot-pounds of energy for work, in breaking down soil granules as they always have. But the chemical composition and other properties within the soil are significantly altered. A major, but unappreciated, change has been the decrease in the stability of the soil granules or in the stability of the soil structure. Soils that once retained well their loamy condition and plow-turned forms all through the winter, and through many rains after tillage, are now soon beaten down by only a few of them.

As a result, much of the subsequent rainwater runs off and does not enter the soil. We do less fall plowing. Our soils must be spring plowed, if they are to remain granular and well aerated as a good seedbed through a significant part of the crop season. This decreasing stability of the soil's granular structure is only another way of saying that the incidence of a weakened, if not a "sick," soil body should be taken as the major change in our soil; and thereby the basic cause of the increase in erosion. Here is the big reason why water has not been going into our soil, but running off. It has been increasingly destroying the means by which food is created and agriculture is maintained.

Acid soils that are highsaturated with hydrogen, which is not a plant nutrient and therefore desaturated of calcium, magnesium, and all the other nutrients, do not granulate readily. Nor do they grow the nitrogenous crops to give calcium rich, nitrogenous humus in the soil that brings about the stable granulation. Soils deficient in fertility are of weakened soil body. They are subject to severe erosion. When surface soils lose their fertility, to become similar to subsoils in this respect, they—of necessity—erode as badly and as rapidly as subsoils. Barren soils erode because they are not fertile enough to feed the crop we grow on them. In other words, our soils cannot take the impact of the rainfall because their fertility has declined too far to permit a stable soil structure to grow cover quickly enough for prevention of excessive runoff and erosion, and to add organic matter.

To emphasize the decline of fertility in our soils may seem to be a mistake. Nevertheless, it is a fact that while the bushels per acre of both wheat and corn have been going upward, the concentration of the protein within each of these grains has been going downward. While our crops have been yielding bushels per acre bountifully, those bushels have consisted mainly of the photosynthetic product, starch. Implied, then, in our conservation of the soil, is our struggle for food protein in order that we may survive. It is the fertility pattern of the soil according to the climatic pattern that determines whether we have largely calories in carbohydrates or whether we have also proteins, minerals, vitamins and all the other essentials of good nutrition for man and his animals.

In attempting to conserve the surface layer of the earth's crust, one dare not disregard or run afoul of the climatic forces in control of the development of the soil. They are in control of the assembly lines of agricultural production and in all creation originating in the soil minerals and soil organic matter. Either they supply us—or they deny us—the nutrients serving as the foundation of the entire biotic pyramid, with man at the top.

Soil conservation is not the application, on a national scale, of any single practice. It is the use of many practices according to the conditions of the soils. Conservation calls not only for prevention of erosion, but also for efforts in building up the soil in its fertility supply by building downward.

SOURCES

CHAPTER 1. FUNDAMENTAL ALBRECHTISMS

CHAPTER 2. BIOLOGICAL PROCESSES

CHAPTER 3.   ASPECTS OF SOIL FERTILITY

CHAPTER 4.   SOIL ORGANIC MATTER

130   2. Lichtenstein, E. P., DDT Accumulation in Midwestern Orchard and Crop
          Soils Treated Since 1945, *Journal of Economic Entomology*, 50:545-547,
          1957.
132   Man-Made Organic Supplements, *Let's Live*, May 1959.
135   European Composts Really "Make" Manure, *Let's Live*, March 1950.
138   Organic Matter Makes "Healthy" Soils, *Let's Live*, June 1963.
140   Organic Matter–Under Time and Treatment, *Let's Live*, July 1963.
142   Changes in Quality of Soil Organic Matter, *Let's Live*, August 1963.
144   Soil Humus . . . Chelator of Inorganic Elements, *Let's Live*, September 1963.
146   Humus . . . Soil Microbial Product, *Let's Live*, October 1963.
148   The Value of Organic Matter, *The Rural New Yorker*, May 3, 1952.
152   Organic Matter Balances Soil Fertility, *Natural Food and Farming*, February 1963.
152   Young Soils Soon Get Old (Sanborn Field Testifies), Fertility Feature (signed
          by William A. Albrecht), source unknown.
153   Nutrition and the Climate Pattern of Soil Development, Abstract of a paper pre-
          sented by William A. Albrecht, University of Missouri, at the Centennial
          Celebration of the American Association for the Advancement of Science on
          September 16, 1948, in Washington, DC, *Science* 108:599 (November 26), 1948.
          abstract published in the *Journal of the American Dietetic Association*, February
          1949.

CHAPTER 5. MYCORRHIZA

158   Mobilizers of Organic Plant Nutrition, *Let's Live,* November 1963.
161   Misconceptions Persist, *Let's Live*, December 1963 and January 1964.
          1. Presented in private correspondence to the author.
          2. Liebig, Justus von, 1846, *Die Chemie* in *An Wendung aus Agriculture und
             Physiologie*.
162   3. This term means "building their own nutritive substances by photo and
             chemosynthesis."
          4. McCarrison, H., Effect of the Manurial Conditions on the Nutritive and
             Vitamin Values of Millet and Wheat, *Ind. Journal of Medicine,* 1924.
          5. Rowlands, M. and B. Wilkenson, The Vitamin B Content of Grass Seeds
             in Relationship to Manure, *Biochemistry Journal,* 24:199, 1930.
          6. Ressel, E., *Soil Conditions and Crop Growth*, Russian, 1933.
          7. Leong, F., Effect of Soil Treatment on the Vitamin B-1 Content of Wheat
             and Barley, *Biochemistry Journal,* 33: 1397, 1939.
          8. Lebedev, S. I., The Physiological Role of Carotene in Plants, *Trans. Crop.
             Section, Kiev,* 1933.
          9. Krasilnikov, N. A., *Soil Microorganisms and Higher Plants.* Translated from
             Russian by Dr. Y. Halparin, *Israel Program Scientific Trans.*, Jerusalem,
             1961.
164   Facts About Their Magnitude, *Let's Live*, February and March 1964.
          1. Dittmer, H., A Quantitative Study of the Roots and Root Hairs of Winter
             Rye Plant, *American Journal of Botany*, 24:417, 1937; 25: number 90 , 1938.
165   2. Previously cited.
165   3. Lyon, T. L. and Wilson, J., Liberation of Organic Matter by Roots of Living
             Plants, *Cornell Agricultural Experiment Station Mem.*, 40, 1921.
          4. Starkey, R., Some Influences of the Higher Plants on the Microorganisms
             of the Soil, *Soil Science,* 27:319, 335, 433, 1929; *Soil Science*, 32:367, 395,
             1931.
167   Revelations of Species, *Let's Live*, April 1964.
          1. Hood, S. C., Survey of Root-Inhabiting Fungi on North Carolina and
             Florida Plants, *Bul. Hood Laboratory*, number 7, 1963.
168   2. Nelson-Jones, R. and Kinder, M., *Role of Mycorrhiza in Tree Nutrition,* 1949.
          3. Weinding, R., Trichoderma Lignorium as a Parasite on Other Fungi,
             Phytopathology 22: 837-845, 1932.
          4. Brian, P. W., Production of Gliotoxin by Trichoderma Viride, *Nature* 154:
             667, 1944.

5. Brian, P. W., and Curtis, Hemming and McGowan, The Production of Viridin by Pigment-Forming Strains of Trichoderma Viride, *Annals of Applied Biology* 33:190-200, 1946.

6. Previously cited.

169   Parasite or Symbiont According to Soil Nutrition, *Let's Live*, Jun 1964.

170
1. Hedges, C. S., Fungi Isolated From Southern Forestry Nurseries Soil, *Mycologie*, 54:221, 1962.

2. Miller, J. J., Giddens, J. E., and Foster, A. A., A Survey of the Fungi of Forest and Cultivated Soils of Georgia, *Mycologie,* XLIX, November and December 1957.

3. Jackson, C. R., Soil Fungi of Chrysanthemum Plantings in Florida, *Quarterly Journal of the Academy of Science,* 22: 147, 1949.

4. Durrell, L. W., and Shields, Lara, Fungi Isolated from Soils of Nevada Test Site, *Mycologie* 52:636, 1960.

5. Yousef-Al-Doory et al, On the Fungus Flora of Iraq Soils, *Mycologie* 51:429, 1959.

170   Some Field Observations, *Let's Live*, July and August 1964.

172   Proteins, Amino Acids and Benzene Rings, *Let's Live,* September and October 1964.
1. Polczar, M. J., Jr. and Reid, R. D., *Microbiology,* McGraw-Hill Company, New York, 1958.

173
2. Albrecht, W. A., *Soil Fertility and Animal Health,* Angus Journal, 1957.

3. Sheldon, V. L., Blue, W. G., and Albrecht, W. A., Biosynthesis of Amino Acids According to Soil Fertility, *I Tryptophan in Forage Crops and Soil,* 3:33-40, 1951.

4. Cochrane, *Physiology of Fungi,* Wiley and Sons, 1958.

174
5. Wright, J., Production of Antibiotics in Soil, *Annals of Applied Biology,* 43:288, 1955.

6. Jeffries, E., The Stability of Antibiotics in Soil, *Journal of General Microbiology,* 7:295, 1952.

175   Early Beliefs Lately Confirmed, *Let's Live*, November 1964.
1. Dr. Ludwig Jost, *Lectures on Plant Physiology* (1903), Translated by R. J. Harvey Gibson (1907), Clarendon Press, Oxford (p. 241).

2. Jahrb. f. wiss. Botany. 34-539, 1900.

3. F. Bryan Clark, Endotrophic Mycorrhiza Influence Yellow Poplar Seedling Growth, *Science* 140:1220-1221, June 14, 1963

CHAPTER 6. THE CALCIUM CONNECTION

178   Limestone — The Foremost of Natural Fertilizers, *Pit and Quarry,* May 1947.

185   Limestone — A Fertilizer, *Capper's Farmer,* June 1941.

186   Lime the Soil to Correct Its Major Fertility Deficiencies, *Rock Products,* April 1954.

191   Blast Furnace Slag — A Soil Builder, *Let's Live,* November 1956.

192   Drilling Powdered Agricultural Limestone, *Agricultural Engineering,* volume 14, number 4, April 1933. This was originally a contribution from the Departments of Soils and Agricultural Engineering, Missouri Agricultural Experiment Station, Journal Series Number 353. It was signed by William A. Albrecht and M. M. Jones, a professor of agricultural engineering, University of Missouri.

196   Drilling Fine Limestone for Legumes, University of Missouri Agricultural Experiment Station, Columbia, Missouri, *Bulletin 367,* August 1936.

206   Lime for Backbone! *Business of Farming,* September and October 1942.

207   It's the Calcium . . . Not the Alkalinity, *Soybean Digest,* September 1941.

211   Purpose of Liming Soil an Enigma, *Let's Live,* June 1962.

214   Calcium as a Factor in Seed Germination, *Journal of the American Society of Agronomy,* volume 33, number 2, February 1941. This was a contribution from the Department of Soils, Missouri Agricultural Experiment Station, Columbia, Missouri, Journal Series Number 706.

216   Now We Know Lime is a Plant Food — Not Merely a Treament for Acidity, *Missouri Ruralist,* January 1953.

218   Soil Acidity is Beneficial, *Let's Live,* October 1952.

219	Soil Alters Calcium Digestibility in Leafy Greens, *Let's Live*, July 1956.
221	We Can Grow Legumes on Acid Soils, *Hoard's Dairyman*, 1947. Also in the *Farmer's Digest*, 1947.
226	Dangerous Grass, *Capper's Farmer*, December 1939.
230	Should Farmers Receive Tax Allowance for Soil-Building? *Missouri Farm News Service*, August 24, 1955.
232	Calcium-Bearing Versus Neutral Fertilizers, *Commercial Fertilizer Yearbook*, 1941
236	1. Albrecht, William A., Nitrogen Fixation as Influenced by Calcium, *Proceedings of the Second International Congress of Soil Science* 3 (1930) 29-39.
234	2. Albrecht, William A., Inoculation of Legumes as Related to Soil Acidity, Journal for the American Society of Agronomy 25 (1933) 512-522.
235	3. Albrecht, William A., Some Soil Factors in Nitrogen Fixation by Legumes, *Trans. Third Com. International Society of Soil Science*, New Brunswick, New Jersey, U. S. A. (1939) 71-84.
235	4. Albrecht, William A., Calcium as a Factor in Seed Germination, *Journal of the American Society of Agronomy* 33 (1941) 153-155.
236	5. Albrecht, William A., Plants and the Exchangeable Calcium of the Soil, *American Journal of Botany* 28 (1931). In press.
235	6. Albrecht, William A., and Hans Jenny, Available Soil Calcium in Relation to "Damping Off" of Soybean Seedlings, *Botanical Gazette* 92 (1931) 263-278.
236	7. Albrecht, William A., and A. W. Klemme, Limestone Mobilizes Phosphates into Korean Lespedeza, *Journal of the American Society of Agronomy* 31 (1939) 284-286.
240	8. Albrecht, William A., and N. C. Smith, Kalzium und Phosphor in ihrem Einflusz auf die Manganaufnahme durch die Futterpflanze, *Bodenkunde und Pflanzenernahrung* 21-22 (1940) 757-767.
232	9. Bunzell, Herbert H., On Vitamins in Wheat Germ, *Science*, 93 (1940) 238.
238	10. Davis, Franklin L., Effect of Different Nitrogenous Fertilizers on the pH and Available Phosphorus of Soils and Their Relation to the Yield of Cotton, *American Fertilizer*, May 14, 1938.
237	11. Fox, Robert E., and Hubert E. Hudgings. Unpublished data.
234	12. Horner, Glenn M., Relation of the Degree of Base Saturation of a Colloidal Clay by Calcium to the Growth, Nodulation and Composition of Soybeans, *Missouri Agriculture Experiment Station Res. Bulletin 232* (1935).
238	13. Louisiana Agriculture Experiment Station Report, 1940, mimeographed sheets.
239	14. Paden, W.R., Responses from Various Sources of Nitrogen Fertilizer, *South Carolina Agriculture Experiment Station Bulletin 309* (1937).
240	15. Schroeder, Raymond A., *Proceedings of the American Society for Horticultural Science* 38, (1940). In press.
239	16. Tidmore, J.W., and C.F. Simmons. The Use of Limestone in Mixed Fertilizers. *Alabama Agriculture Experiment Station Circular 67* (1934).
	17. Tidmore, J.W., and J.T. Williamson. Experiments with Commercial Nitrogenous Fertilizers. *Alabama Agriculture Experiment Station Bulletin 238* (1932).
236	18. True, Rodney H., The Function of Calcium in the Nutrition of Seedlings., *Journal of American Society of Agronomy 13* (1921) 91-107.
239	19. Willis, L.G., The Value of Gypsum as a Supplement to a Concentrated Fertilizer, *North Carolina Agriculture Experiment Station Bulletin 299* (1934).
242	Bugaboo of Soil Acidity Dispelled, *Buda (Illinois) Plain Dealer*, 1943.
243	Lime Soil to Feed Crops — Not to Remove Soil Acidity, *Missouri Farm News Service*, May 5, 1954.
245	Lime-Rich Soils Give Size and Vigor to French Stock, *National Livestock Producer*, June 1946.
249	Lime Your Soils For Better Crops, Agricultural Extension Service, University of Missouri, College of Agriculture, *Circular 566*, November 1948.

CHAPTER 7. MAGNESIUM

273	1. B. R. Fudge, Relation of Magnesium Deficiency in Grapefruit Leaves to Yield and Chemical Composition of Fruit, *Florida Agricultural Experiment Station Bulletin 331*. January 1939.
274	2. Frank M. Eaton, Formulas for Estimating Leaching and Gypsum Requirements for Irrigation Waters, *Texas Agricultural Experiment Station*, Miscellaneous Publication, 1954.
275	Rhododendrons . . . A Problem of Soil Fertility, Not Acidity, *Let's Live*, January 1957.
277	*Land Bulletin*, number 85, Ontario, Canada, 1964. Published by Crosby Lockwood and Son, Ltd., 26 Old Brompton Road, London SW 7, 1963.

CHAPTER 8. DIFFERENT SOILS, DIFFERENT PLANTS

279	Soil Fertility: Its Climatic Pattern, *The Journal of Osteopathy*, December 1950. Also *Let's Live*, January 1955.
284	Too Much Nitrogen or Not Enough Else? *Let's Live*, June 1959.
286	"Grow" Foods or Only "Go" Foods According to the Soil, *School Science and Mathematics*, January 1944. This paper was delivered at the Central Association of Science and Mathematics Teachers assembly, Chicago, November 26, 1943.
287	Both Soil and Plants are Responsible, *Let's Live*, July and August 1959.
290	Phosphorus in Crop Varies with Nitrogen Applied, *Let's Live*, September 1959.
292	Importance of Phosphorus in Soil is Shown in College Experiment, unidentified newspaper clipping, no date.
294	Soil Nitrogen and Vitamin C in Plants, *Let's Live*, October 1959.
295	Varied Soil Potassium Means Varied Organic Values, *Let's Live*, November 1959.
299	Balanced Soil Fertility Requires High Phosphorus, *Let's Live*, December 1959.
300	Bacteria Help Legume Roots Mobilize Fertility, *Let's Live*, January 1960.
302	Microbes Give Legumes Their Protein Power, *Let's Live*, February 1960.
304	Fertility Effects Show Early in Plants, *Let's Live*, March 1960.
306	Big Yields of Bulk—Low Phosphorus Concentration, *Let's Live*, April 1960.
	1. Thirty Years of Soil Fertility Investigations in South Dakota, *South Dakota Agricultural Experiment Station Bulletin 325*, 1938.
308	Boron Interrelated with Potassium, *Let's Live*, May 1960.
309	Boron Improves Alfalfa Quality, *Missouri Farm News Service*, May 19, 1954.
310	Boron Helps Maintain Potassium Balance, *Let's Live*, June 1960.
312	Soil Exhaustion, *Let's Live*, July 1960.
	1. Food Facts vs. Food Fallacies, *World Health Day Kit*, April 7, 1957, Food and Drug Administration, Washington 25, D. C.
315	The Feeding Power of Their Roots, *Let's Live*, October 1960.
316	Vegetable Quality Reveals Its Connection with Soil Organic Matter, *Let's Live*, November 1960.
318	Chelation, *Let's Live*, December 1960.
320	Natural Laws Regarding Soils and Plant Compositions, *Let's Live*, January 1961.
321	Depleted Soils–Species Extinction, *Let's Live*, February 1961.
323	Soil Organic Matter Mobilizes the Phosphorus for Plants, *Let's Live*, March and April 1961.
324	1. Chelation Phenomena—Annals, *New York Academy of Sciences*, 88: art. 2, pages 281-532, August 1960. Report on conference of December 7 and 8, 1959. Franklin N. Furness, Managing Editor.
325	2. P. C. deKock, Influence of Humic Acids on Plant Growth, *Science* 121:474, 1955.
326	3. A. W. Blair, The Agricultural Value of Greensand Marl, *Circular 61*, page 3, New Jersey Experiment Station, May 15, 1916.
	4. C. G. Hopkins, *Soil Fertility and Permanent Agriculture*, 1910, Ginn and Company, Boston & New York.
326	Depleted Soils Change Sugar, Starch, Proteins and Yields of Crop, *Let's Live*, May 1961.
328	"Deep Rooting", *Flying Plowman*, November-December 1950.

CHAPTER 9. THE PROTEIN STRUGGLE

INDEX

The Albrecht Papers from Acres U.S.A.

William A. Albrecht, Ph.D. was undoubtedly the preeminent soil scientist of his time. During his long and distinguished career, Dr. Albrecht made the case for an agronomy based on healthy, balanced soil ecosystems rather than simplistic chemical inputs, even as this latter approach was being introduced as the "scientific" agriculture of the future. Time has shown the destructiveness of chemical agriculture, as more and more farmers and agronomists are turning to the genuine science of Dr. Albrecht, whose observations and precepts are as applicable today as when they were first written.

ALBRECHT'S FOUNDATION CONCEPTS
THE ALBRECHT PAPERS, VOL. I

William A. Albrecht, Ph.D. Nature gave up her rare secrets to Dr. Albrecht simply because he was a curious farm boy who liked logic and adventure. Through his extensive experiments with growing plants, soils and their effect on animals, he showed that a declining soil fertility, due to a lack of organic material, major elements, and trace minerals — or a marked imbalance in these nutrients — was responsible for poor crops and in turn for pathological conditions in animals fed deficient feeds from soils. *Softcover, 515 pages.*

SOIL FERTILITY & ANIMAL HEALTH
THE ALBRECHT PAPERS, VOL. II

William A. Albrecht, Ph.D. Albrecht was dismayed by the rapid chemicalization of farming that followed WWII. This book is a well-organized explanation of the relationship between soil fertility and animal and human health. This is a great book for those just familiarizing themselves with these concepts. *Softcover, 192 pages.*

ALBRECHT'S ENDURING VISION
THE ALBRECHT PAPERS, VOL. IV

William A. Albrecht, Ph.D. This collection presents more of Professor Albrecht's brilliant, classic essays providing essential insights into the health of our soil. Albrecht explains how the soil-crop system works, and provides his substantiated theory and observation that the lack of major elements and trace minerals is responsible for depleted crops, weeds, and poor animal health. *Softcover, 325 pages.*

ALBRECHT ON CALCIUM
THE ALBRECHT PAPERS, VOL. V

William A. Albrecht, Ph.D. Readers will find an organized and convincing explanation of the relationship between calcium and soil fertility. It is not possible to discuss calcium, which Albrecht proclaims as the "King of Nutrients" without being led into the entire mosaic that Albrecht considers biologically correct farming. *Softcover, 320 pages.*